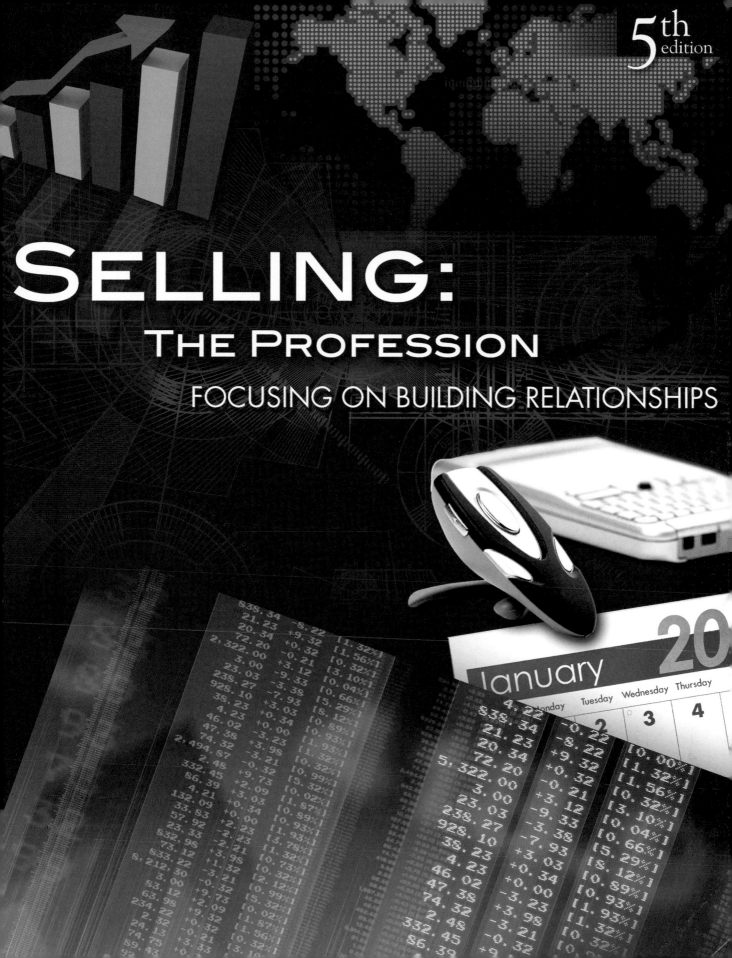

SELLING:
THE PROFESSION
FOCUSING ON BUILDING RELATIONSHIPS

5th edition

Creative Directors: Brian Hamblen, Jennifer Lill

Project Manager: Martha Lill

Design Manager: Jay Arnold

Cover Design: Brian Hamblen

Graphic Design: iDesign Inc.

Technical Consultants: Don Evans, Barb Evans

Editorial Assistance: Anthony Davis, Bryce Damuth, Mary Yost

Feel free to contact the authors if you want specific information on how to access all aspects of the Web site developed exclusively to assist you in the preparation of lecture material, tests, case studies, and other sales-related classroom activities.

Web site: www.sellingtheprofession.com

This book may be purchased for educational, business, or sales promotional use. For information or to order, please contact:

DM Bass Publications
6635 Broken Bow Drive
Antioch, TN 37013
615.941.2747 (work)
615.476.5035 (mobile)
615.941.2458 (fax)
dlill48@comcast.net

ISBN-13:   978-0-9800406-0-9
ISBN-10:   0-9800406-0-4

Copyright © 2008, 2005, 2002, 1999, 1996 by DM Bass Publications
FIFTH EDITON
The Library of Congress Cataloging-in-Publication data
Lill, David J. and Jennifer K. Lill

Selling: The Profession / Focusing on Building Relationships / Dr. David J. Lill and Jennifer K. Lill

5th ed. ISBN 978-0-9800406-0-9 (paper)

1. Business 2. Sales Training 3. Career Development 4. Self Help

Printed in China

Dedication

To Martha - A loving wife and mother.
We love you so much!

BRIEF CONTENTS

TABLE OF CONTENTS

PART **1**

Relationship Building and the Sales Cycle Framework

1 A Career in Professional Selling   5

2 Relationship Selling   23

PART 2

Cultivating an Ethics Climate and Developing Communication Skills

PART **3**

Gaining Knowledge, Preparing, and Planning for the Presentation

PART 4

The Face-to-Face Relationship Model of Selling

12 Handling Objections 253

13 Closing the Sale 275

PART **5**

Management Aspects: Personal and Organizational

14 Service After the Sale 299

15   Personal, Time, and Territory Management   317

16   Sales Force Management   339

PREFACE

Approach and Purpose

The ideas, concepts, and style of this text are the result of years spent teaching professional selling to college students, conducting seminars for sales professionals, and professional business consulting, combined with over thirty years of personal experience in various phases of the business of selling. As professionals and seasoned salespeople who love the sales environment and desire to see an improvement in the ethical business climate, we wanted a text that would: 1) Show that selling can be an honest, respected profession; 2) convince motivated, creative students that selling is a profession to consider—not just something you do until something better comes along; and 3) demonstrate that, if practiced as explained in this text, a sales career will be a source of financial and personal satisfaction.

Selling: The Profession focuses on building relationships. It is this relationship-building style that spells success for salespeople operating in a highly competitive business environment and dealing with today's sophisticated buyers who demand correct answers to complex problems. The book's style and organization makes it fun to read, easy to comprehend, and highly practical as a training tool for anyone really interested in developing their skills as a salesperson. The sales process is broken down into its most basic components, in an attempt to simplify the complex buyer-seller interaction that takes place in an actual selling situation, with the result being an *eight-step sales cycle model* that we explore in depth in over one-half of the book.

Because attitude is so important for achieving success in selling, verbal and nonverbal communication and social style technology chapters are included as foundation stones. An understanding of these concepts allows you to more readily appreciate the complex, dynamic behavioral relationships that take place in selling. You will be introduced to the availability and usefulness of sales force automation and the numerous technology products available. Global competition has enlarged the playing field. As global competition brings new challenges, technology brings new tools that help sales professionals sell more effectively and efficiently.

Throughout the text, you see the "real world" of selling through review of the current sales literature, personal experience, and, most importantly, interviews with successful active sales professionals who put the theory contained in the book into everyday practice. As one top salesperson said, *"Practice without theory is blind and theory without practice is sterile."*

Selling: The Profession is your guide for success in today's selling environment. Becoming a great salesperson involves no less a commitment to your profession than does becoming a great student, physician, lawyer, or teacher. Success begins by taking a single step. It begins by learning the correct principles and gaining the proper knowledge to lead you down the right path to success.

Your ability to develop and maintain long-term relationships is the key to your success as a person, a student, and a business professional. For customers, a buying decision means a decision to enter into a relationship with a salesperson and their company. It is very much like a "business marriage." *Selling: The Profession* shows you how to bring about that union.

Relationships can be more important than the actual product being sold. Customers don't always know the ingredients or components of a product, how a company functions, or how they will be treated after money changes hands, but they can make an assessment about a salesperson and about the relationship that has occurred over the course of the selling process. Ultimately, customers' decisions are based on the fact that they trust and believe in what a salesperson says. Therefore, the quality of the relationship with a customer is the competitive advantage that enables salespeople to succeed over rivals who may have similar products and services.

Just as optometrists help improve their patients' vision, this textbook serves as a "prescription" for the study of professional selling. No one would expect to enhance their eyesight without the right corrective lenses. So why would anyone expect their understanding of relationship selling to improve without having the right tools for success? Consider this book as the solution for acquiring the selling focus.

Read the following five part descriptions so that you can see the logic of the chapter sequence and how you can get the most out of the organization of the book. Remember, this is *your* textbook, your personal prescription for sharpened focus and success in relationship selling.

PART 1 Relationship Building and the Sales Cycle Framework

Chapter 1 discusses the consultative nature and problem-solving approach to professional selling and details the characteristics that successful salespeople possess. Relationship selling is interactive, involves two-way communication, encourages prospect participation, employs empathy, and promotes a win-win environment. Today's style of selling favors building close and trusting long-term relationships. Positioning yourself as a consultant creates a partnership with customers. You are peers working to solve problems together.

You gain a better understanding of the complete selling situation and the problems it generates by breaking the sale into its basic tasks. There are several steps to achieving a successful sale. An eight-step sales cycle is introduced in **chapter 2** and explained in detail in chapters 7 to 14. It just makes sense that if you understand what the steps are in the *Sales Cycle Framework for Relationship Selling*, and what is required to make each step a successful endeavor, you will become a professional in selling much quicker than those who are simply stumbling through the process trying to figure it out. The chapters included in this section are:

1. A Career in Professional Selling
2. Relationship Selling

PART 2 Cultivating an Ethical Climate and Developing Communication Skills

Few professions give you more opportunities for rejection on a daily basis than does the field of sales. **Chapter 3** discusses the need for a strong ethical and moral character to sustain a sales career. Honest and caring service brings customers back and assures success.

Success in professional selling also depends upon your ability to have a productive exchange of information with prospects and customers. As detailed in **chapter 4**, the more you understand about prospects and their decision-making process, the more readily you can discover what they need and want. Because success in relationship selling depends on accurately getting your message across to prospects, chapter 4 also describes how to break through communication barriers.

An especially useful tool for gaining insight into how the prospect is thinking is knowledge of the social styles model, presented in **chapter 5**. A social style is the way a person sends and receives information. It is a method for finding the best way to approach a prospect and to set up a working relationship with that person. The chapters included in this section are:

3. Ethical and Legal Issues in Selling
4. Purchase Behavior and Communication
5. Finding Your Selling Style

PART **3** Gaining Knowledge, Preparing, and Planning for the Presentation

The information in **chapter 6** prepares you for success in a sales career by focusing on gaining product knowledge, developing a plan for self-motivation and goal setting, and introducing the use of sales force automation.

Chapters 7 and 8 discuss the procedures for locating and qualifying prospects and identifying the information needed to prepare for an effective presentation. **Chapter 7** is a thorough look at prospecting. As the saying goes, "I'd rather be a master prospector than a wizard of speech and have no one to tell my story to." **Chapter 8** discusses the process of gathering preapproach information and presents a *six-step telephone track* for making appointments for that all-important personal interview. The chapters in this section are:

6. Preparation For Success in Selling
7. Becoming a Master Prospector
8. Preapproach and Telephone Techniques

PART **4** The Face-to-Face Relationship Model of Selling

Chapters 9 to 13 are the very heart of professional selling. This is considered the "how to" portion of the textbook. This is referred to as the face-to-face portion of the sales cycle. It is the valuable time spent in the actual sales interview—the time when a commitment is obtained and kept.

What happens in the opening minutes is crucial to the overall success of the sales interview, so **chapter 9** focuses on the approach. **Chapter 10** is devoted to the art of asking questions and listening effectively. Questioning and listening guidelines are presented to carry you through the entire sales interview. The *SPIN® Selling* technique is explained and dramatized using a very practical example. **Chapter 11** details the techniques to use in the actual presentation. Units of conviction are the building blocks for creating and making a meaningful sales presentation. The five elements that comprise a complete unit of conviction are explained and illustrated.

Chapters 12 and 13 present the psychology behind handling objections and closing the sale. A plan to handle objections is introduced, and a separate section in **chapter 12** explains several ways of dealing with the difficult price objection. **Chapter 13** stresses that closing the sale is the natural conclusion to a successful sales interview. The chapters in this section are:

9. Approaching the Prospect
10. Identifying Needs by Questioning and Listening
11. Making the Presentation
12. Handling Objections
13. Closing the Sale

PART **5** Management Aspect: Personal and Organizational

The service you give the customer after the sale has been completed can be as important, or even more important, than the sale itself. Keeping current customers happy and regaining lost clients is the focus of **chapter 14**. The customer absolutely defines quality in every transaction. Great salespeople don't talk customer service—*they live perfect service.*

Chapter 15 shows you how to get better control of your time and your activities. The chapter really is all about personal organization and self-management. You cannot manage time, but you can manage yourself and your personal activities. Administrative ability on the part of the salesperson is fundamental to success. Statistics indicate that only about 20 percent of a salesperson's time during a typical day is spent in face-to-face interviews with prospects. **Chapter 16** details the job responsibilities of the sales manager, and provides a useful introduction for classes in sales management. The chapters in this section are:

14. Service After the Sale
15. Personal, Time, and Territory Management
16. Sales Force Management

CHAPTER STRUCTURE

This seven-part structure is a guide for you to follow as you study and learn the material in the various chapters:

1. **Learning Objectives**. These bullet points at the beginning of each chapter acquaint you with the important concepts. They appear on the first page and serve as guidelines to follow as you read through the chapter.

2. **Main Chapter Body**. Chapters are organized in outline form to make it readily available for study and review. Each chapter is complemented by examples of actual "sales situations" that take the theory and put it into practice. The material in all 16 chapters is well documented with exhibits, tables, and figures, most taken from actual sales experience.

3. **Developing Partnerships Using Technology**. Technology boxes in various chapters illustrate how sales force automation tools will impact the "road warriors" of the twenty-first century. They demonstrate how to increase sales efficiency in three functional areas: 1) Personal Productivity; 2) Improved Communications; and 3) Transactional Processing.

4. **Summary**. This section outlines the main points of the chapter to reinforce learning. Reading the various summaries in bullet point format gives you a feel for the content of the chapter, the key points to remember, and provides you with a tremendous resource to use when attempting to pull together concepts from several chapters.

5. **Review Questions**. Each chapter ends with a series of questions to challenge the student's understanding of the material. These questions are useful when studying for quizzes or exams.

6. **Role-Play Exercises**. These practical exercises are designed to have you do things inside and outside the classroom. Role playing exercises get you involved in active learning. The best way to learn new skills is through action— actually doing things. Research shows that students who just sit and listen to a teacher retain only 20 percent of what they hear. However, participants involved in active learning and doing retain 90 percent of the information.

7. **Case Studies**. The case studies require you to apply the critical skills discussed in the chapter and give you training through simulation, role-playing, and practical learning situations.

ABOUT THE AUTHORS

David J. Lill has a combined 30 years of professional sales, sales training, and teaching experience. He taught selling and marketing classes at Baylor University, Belmont University and New Mexico State University. He earned his Ph.D. degree in Marketing from the University of Alabama. Dr. Lill is also a business consultant specializing in sales, advertising, and communications skills development. He currently conducts seminars and training courses on sales and marketing related topics. His relationship selling model is being successfully used by companies throughout the country in a wide variety of industries including insurance, telecommunications, real estate, publishing, banking, hospitality, chemical, and automotive.

Dr. Lill is the founder and president of DM Bass Publications through which he wrote, published, marketed, and sold his highly acclaimed textbook, *Selling: The Profession*, now in its 5th edition. He owned and operated an advertising firm in Louisiana where he developed and implemented advertising and marketing campaigns for a number of companies, including a local bank and department store.

Dr. Lill is the co-author of *The Handbook for Relationship Selling: Acquire Your Selling Focus* as well as *The Official Handbook for Health Club Sales: Strengthen Membership Sales in 30 Days*. In addition, Dr. Lill has published over 85 articles in various academic, trade, and professional publications. These include*: Selling Power, Journal of Advertising, Journal of the Academy of Marketing Science, Sales & Marketing Management, Business Topics, Nashville Business Journal*, and the *Journal of Pharmaceutical Marketing & Management*.

Dr. Lill has sold successfully for two large telecommunications companies, specializing in marketing information technology. In addition, Dr. Lill was the number one salesperson in Gold Unlimited, Inc and was a Shaklee distributor for over 25 years. He also worked for the *Milwaukee Journal* in their Milwaukee Advertising Laboratory Division. While there, he brought in prestigious clients such as General Mills, General Foods, and Nabisco and conducted marketing studies using Milwaukee as a test market for new product launches.

David lives in Nashville, TN with his wife, Martha. A housewife turned commercial real estate agent, she is one of the company's top producers. They are blessed to have two exceptional children, David, Jr. and Jennifer. David is an engineer with TVA in New Johnsonville, TN and Jennifer is a published author, entrepreneur, and marketing consultant.

Jennifer K. Lill comes from a background of sales, authorship, and entrepreneurship. She has co-authored two books on professional selling, *The Official Handbook for Health Club Sales: Strengthen Membership Sales in 30 Days* and *The Handbook for Relationship Selling: Acquire Your Selling Focus*. In addition, she was the president and co-founder, along with business partner and mentor Tom Black, of the Tom Black Center for Selling Inc., located in Nashville, TN. While working with Tom, she edited and produced his widely acclaimed sales book, *The Boxcar Millionaire: Tom Black's Proven System of Sales Success*. The company was formed as a conduit for national sales training and publisher of business training products. Jennifer marketed and promoted Tom Black as a business leader, keynote speaker, and sales trainer through a personal branding strategy that she formulated. In addition, she spearheaded production of a professional Web site equipped with eCommerce, designed press kits for a national marketing campaign, conducted negotiations for all strategic partnerships, and oversaw advertising efforts.

While obtaining her degree from the University of Alabama, Jennifer had the opportunity to sell for one of the most respected sales organizations in the country, the Southwestern Company. She sold educational products door-to-door by relocating and fully running the business from concept to sales, delivery, and customer service. She was the awarded "Top

First Year Dealer Award" and facilitated the recruitment and sales training of new recruits, as well as formulating and developing a system of lead finding and a unique delivery method.

Today Jennifer resides in Nashville as a free-lance author and business consultant, having worked with such leading publishers as Thomas Nelson. She is pursuing her Ph.D. with the eventual goal of following in her father's footsteps to become a college professor and mentor to countless aspiring salespeople as well as the most seasoned professionals.

ACKNOWLEDGMENTS

Since one of our primary goals was to produce a text with "real world" concepts and applications, we could not have been successful without the assistance of all those in sales who took time to share their thoughts, as well as a team of supportive friends and family. The insightful comments made by the sales professionals highlighted throughout the book add an important dimension to student learning. The success they have achieved in all areas of their lives through hard work and dedication, while upholding high standards of business ethics, should serve as a model for young, aspiring business professionals.

David Lill's Acknowledgements

Special thanks goes to four friends and business colleagues who have been true blessings to me: Deryl Bass, Tanis Cornell, Tom Hoek, and Emil Wanke—all consummate professionals, who each in their own way have had a profound effect on the way I think and the actions I take.

I want to thank Donald Silberstein, former Director of Business Development for the Bureau of Business Practice, Inc., for his efforts in providing the 150 cases that he made available for my use. Twenty-four of these cases were used as end-of-chapter cases in this book. Each of these cases is based on an *actual* sales situation and provides the student with an excellent learning opportunity.

My thanks and appreciation to the following professors, business associates, friends and colleagues. Their insightful suggestions, organizational ideas, and encouragement added significantly to the content of this textbook: Deborah Adams, Kingwood College (TX); Carol Anderson, United Tribes Technical College (ND); Carol Arnone, Frostburg State University; Erin Baca, University of Texas, El Paso; Dennis Bechtol, Northwood University (FL); Vicki Befort, Arapahoe Community College (CO); Gary Benson, Benedictine College (KS); Harry Bernstein, Essex County College (NJ); L. Dean Bittick, East Central College; Dr. Kenneth Blanchard, founder of Blanchard Training & Development; Laurie Breakey, Pennsylvania State University; Frank Bingham, Bryant University; Bob Bricker, Pikes Peak Community College; David Braun, L.A. Pierce College; Miriam Burgos, Azusa Pacific University (CA); Laura Cailloux, Skagit Valley College; Cindy Claycomb, Wichita State University; Jack Chism, Greenville College (IL); Dave Colby, Mid-State Technical College (WI); Gary Corona, Florida Community College; Kristi Cranwell, NCTA (NE); Dale Davis, Eastern New Mexico University; Patricia DeCorte, Delta College (MI); Sandy Denero, Athens Technical College (GA); Bruce Dickinson, Southeast Technical Institute; Claude Dotson, Northwest College; Donna Duffy, Johnson County Community College; Terri Dwyer, Montana State University; Cinda Echard, Glenville State College (WV); Kevin Ellis, University of Georgia; Pat Ellsburg, Lower Columbia College (WA); Richard English, San Diego State University; Ken Erby, Northeastern Technical College (SC); David Fee, Utah Valley State College; Sandra Fields, University of Delaware; Bert Fisher, COO, Our Community Credit Union (WA); Olene Fuller, San Jacinto College (Pasadena, TX); Wil Goodheer, president of International University (Vienna, Austria); Shawn Green, Aurora University (IL); Carl

Grunander, Weber State University (UT); Donna Gutschmidt, Lake Region State College; Starla Haislip, Boise State University; Dan Hall, East Central College; Michael Harstine, Grace College & Seminary; Bob Hausladen, University of Louisville (KY); Donna Heilig, Phoenix College; Tom Hoek, former president of Insurance Systems of Tennessee; Norm Humble, Kirkwood Community College; Denise Hunt, Allegany College of Maryland; Marie Johnson, Skagit Valley College; George Johnson, Marshalltown Community College; Carolyn Keck, San Jacinto College; David Kimball, Elms College (MA); Gary Kritz, Coastal Carolina University; Nancy Krumland, Southeast Community College (NE); Carsha Lapp, Northwest Technical College (MN); Desiree Larsen, Weber State University (UT); John Lavin, WCTC (WI); James Lollar, Radford University (VA); Ruth Lumb, Concordia College at Moorhead; Shawna MaHaffey, Delta College (MI); Cathy Marsh, Southeast Technical Institute (SD); Cyndy Mascola, Trumbull Business College (OH); Luis Martinez, Manager, Five Star Program, Chrysler Corporation; Dr. Morris L. Mayer, University of Alabama; Claudine McIntyre, Mt. San Antonio College (CA); Cheryl McCarthy, executive vice president, Surado Solutions; Roxanna McKenna, Southeast Technical Institute (SD); Becky Miles, Delaware Tech; Duane Miller, SUNY College at Cobleskill (NY); Linda Mohr, Northwood University (FL); David Miller, Panhandle State University (TX); Dan Moore, vice president of marketing, The Southwestern Company; Elizabeth Murata, Edmonds Community College (WA); Gary Mucica, University of Massachusetts, Lowell; Judith Nickel, WCTC (WI); Philip Nitse, Idaho State University; Darren Olson, Bemidji State University (MN); Barbara Ollhoff, WCTC (WI); Dr. Norman Vincent Peale, author of *The Power of Positive Thinking*; Phillip M. Pfeffer, former president of Random House Inc.; Robin Peterson, New Mexico State University; Chris Plouffe, Washington State University; Bob Quade, Centenary College (NJ); Lyn Richardson, Ball State University; John Robbins, Winthrop University; Michael Powell, North Georgia College & State University; Tim Reese, Eastern Idaho Technical College; Nita Robbins, San Sacinto College; Les Rubenstein, St. Mary College; Allen Schemmel, WSM-AM/FM Radio (Nashville); Holly Schrank, Purdue University; Kent Sickmeyer, Kaskaskia College (IL); Judy Signaw, Cornell University; Mary Lee Short, Santa Fe Community College; Robert Skalla, Blackhawk Technical College; Pat Swarthout, Central Lakes College (MN); Bob Tangsrud, University of North Dakota; Sandra Taylor, Athens Area Technical Institute (GA); Harry Taute, Utah Valley State College; Ray Thomas, Edith Cowan University, Perth, Australia; Kevin Ward, Augusta Tech College (GA); Patricia Watson, Mid-State Technical College (WI); Carolyn Waits, Cincinnati State Community College; Emma Watson, Arizona State University; Amy Wojciechowski, West Shore Community College; Curtis Youngman, Salt Lake Community College.

These people warrant a special thank you: Gladys Hudson, former vice-president of Success Motivation in Waco, TX. She was my original mentor, editor and creative inspiration for many ideas in this textbook.

To my wonderful wife, Martha – the love of my life! And my two remarkable children: David Jr., you have made me so proud—what a phenomenal man you have become. And Jennifer—what a daughter! My co-author and editor-in-chief of the 4th and 5th editions! There is no way this book could have been completed without their love and support.

Jennifer Lill's Acknowledgements

Gratitude goes first and foremost to my family.

To my father, Dr. Lill – Dad, thanks for giving me the opportunity to work on the various book projects with you and hone my writing and editing skills. And my deepest gratitude for your love, unconditional support, and belief in me!

To my mother, Martha – Mom you are my best friend and sounding board for all things large and small. I love you more than you could ever know.

To my brother, David – You are a voice of reason when I need sound advice, and more importantly, you are the best brother a girl could ever hope for.

To the team at iDesign Inc, in Nashville, TN – Your creativity and hard work made this edition possible. We couldn't have done it without you. Jay Arnold, thanks for the long days and many revisions. Brian Hamblen, Anthony Davis, and Bryce Damuth, you guys are the best—as both business partners and true friends.

To Ken Abraham – Your mentorship means the world to me. Because of you, I now have opportunities in publishing that I never thought possible. Thanks for believing in me and recognizing my talent.

To Tom Black – *The Boxcar Millionaire*, you are the quintessential salesman. No one can sell like you can. You believed in my abilities and saw potential in me that extended far beyond a résumé. You trusted me to represent your name and reputation and allowed me to spread my creative wings and create something new and exciting. I will always be grateful to you for the opportunity you gave me, and I thank you for your guidance.

Appreciation also goes to Dean Barry Mason, Dean of the School of Commerce and Business Administration at the University of Alabama, and to Dr. David Heggem, Dr. Lew Silver, and Dr. Kim Campbell of the University of Alabama. And special thanks goes to Bandit Lill.

"Knowing is not enough; we must apply.
Willing is not enough; we must do."

-Johann Wolfgang von Goethe

Relationship Building and the Sales Cycle Framework

CHAPTER 2

CHAPTER 1

Chapter 1 discusses the consultative nature and problem-solving approach to professional selling and details the characteristics that successful salespeople possess. Relationship selling is interactive, involves two-way communication, encourages prospect participation, employs empathy, and promotes a win-win environment. Today's style of selling favors building close and trusting long-term relationships. Positioning yourself as a consultant creates a partnership with customers. You are peers working to solve problems together.

You gain a better understanding of the complete selling situation and the problems it generates by breaking the sale into its basic tasks. There are several steps to achieving a successful sale. An eight-step sales cycle is introduced in chapter 2 and explained in detail in chapters 7 to 14. It makes sense that if you understand what the steps are in the Sales Cycle Framework for Relationship Selling, and what is required to make each step a successful endeavor, then you will become a professional in selling much quicker than those who are simply stumbling through the process trying to figure it out. The chapters included in this section are:

1. A Career in Professional Selling
2. Relationship Selling

CREATE
THE SALES EDGE

Get Focused, and you can...

C HANGE is often desirable, frequently necessary, and always inevitable.

R EMEMBER...only you can give yourself permission to approve of you. Free your mind from negative thinking.

E NVISION yourself as a success. What you think about, you become.

A TTITUDE does determine your altitude. It is what's inside that makes you rise.

T HE right angle to solve a problem is the try-angle.

E LIMINATE failure as an option, and progress naturally occurs.

T HE best is yet to come. Yesterday's impossibilities are today's possibilities.

H AVE your dreams. They are the stuff great people are made of. Reach for the stars, but keep your feet on the ground.

E XTRAORDINARY desire and persistence drive ordinary people to achieve great things. Achievers are not extraordinary people.

S EVEN days without laughter makes one weak.

A smile is the shortest distance between two people.

L ISTEN twice as much as you talk. You have two ears and one tongue.

E NCOURAGING feedback is a process for learning about your impact on those around you.

S UCCESS is the progressive realization of worthwhile, predetermined, personal goals.

E XCUSES are for losers. Winners have ways. May we all find the way.

D ETERMINE never to give up. It's when things seem worse that you must not quit.

G OALS are dreams with a due date.

E XPECT the best of yourself. Be somebody special. The best never consider success optional.

CHAPTER 1

A Career in Professional Selling

LEARNING OBJECTIVES

- Appreciate the role of selling in our economy.

- Understand the purpose of personal selling.

- Recognize the different types of sales jobs and the requirements for success in each.

- Identify the personal characteristics that are needed for success in a selling career.

- Examine professional selling as a viable career opportunity.

Countless daily interactions between people involve the act of selling. Some of them are universally recognized as selling: Retail salespeople sell you clothes, furniture, or cameras; a salesperson sells you a car; and your insurance agent sells you a policy. In fact, a company is not in business until somebody makes a sale.

However, many other common transactions not typically recognized as selling involve the same skills, goals, and behavior patterns that professional salespeople use: Waiters may sell you on trying a new entrée or getting dessert; politicians try to convince constituents to vote for them or persuade other politicians to join them in promoting certain projects; trial lawyers sell themselves, their clients, and their interpretation of the law to judges and juries; and family members influence decisions such as where to live, who will use the family car on Friday night, whether to borrow money for a vacation, and even what to fix for dinner.

In other words, *you are already selling*. You are selling yourself, your ideas, and your desire for cooperation and companionship to almost everyone you engage in anything more than the most casual conversation.

Partnerships, maintaining customer relationships, team selling, strategic alliances, and global strategies are more than mere words to sales organizations today. They are the tools with which winning strategies are fashioned. There is a growing competitiveness among the world's major corporations, and using yesterday's sales strategies is dangerous and increasingly ineffective as global competitors battle each other. The latest and best marketing and sales practices are essential in gaining new markets and defending those you currently serve. The sales profession must rise to the challenge because, as Will Rogers said, "Even if you're on the right track, you'll get run over if you just sit there."[1]

It is crucial to understand the business world today and know what challenges customers face, so you can truly become a *solutions provider*. Sales professionals demonstrate their value to customers by providing productive information and helping solve problems.

Understanding global strategies is essential in today's competitive marketplace.

The Value of Salespeople

New and innovative products and services are never accepted automatically. Neither individual nor business consumers can keep up with all the innovations that become available. So how do businesses expect to keep up with significant developments just in their own fields? They rely on salespeople!

A salesperson's job is to identify customer needs, determine ways those needs could be met by the products or services offered, and then provide that information to the customer. They also work in the other direction, by identifying customer needs that cannot be satisfied by their current product line and communicating those needs to their company for consideration in the development of new products. Salespeople who consistently bring an implicit sales approach to their work build trust and loyalty with customers and become an invaluable resource to their company.[2] Therefore, they are facilitators of information that keeps them and their customers competitive. Sales is the most important job in any organization.

Compensation Potential

Because of their vital role in business, salespeople are among the best-paid employees of a company. More salespeople earn above $100,000 annually than persons in any other profession.[3] According to an annual survey of inside sales compensation, top performing telemarketers and lead generation managers are earning from $80,000 to $120,000 a year.[4] And according to a survey conducted by *Sales and Marketing Management* Magazine, top performers (those who call on clients in person) are walking away with the fattest wallets by far, averaging $139,826 in total compensation. Some are even doing better than their bosses. The survey also found that an entry level salesperson who is a mid-level performer makes close to $83,000, and even average salespeople can bring in salaries close to $60,000.[5]

These are just averages—some salespeople make less, while some make considerably more. Salespeople are the catalysts of the economy. They are responsible for keeping goods, services, and ideas flowing.

Importance of Sales Training

In today's exceedingly competitive environment, all kinds of companies provide continuing sales training on a regular basis—and many of these companies spend considerable amounts of money for training. For example, Kodak spends more than $20 million a year sending people through its courses at its Marketing Education Center. The reason is simple: Kodak sees sales training as the basis for winning all future battles.

"It is absolutely imperative that you make sure that your people are properly trained to take advantage of your equipment investments," says Scott Voris, president and owner of Kelmscott Press in Aurora, Illinois. "Employee education fosters work force pride, and helps a company produce a better product." Voris says that Kelmscott Press employees attend both vendor and industry-sponsored seminars and trade shows, and are offered tuition reimbursement for approved education courses. The company invests 3 percent of its gross income on employee training and development. According to Voris, 80 percent of his company's employees are cross-trained for more than one assignment.[6]

In the past, some companies viewed extensive training as an *expense*, which if not properly planned and budgeted for, may be true. However, today's corporations properly view sales training as an *investment*, and adequate training generates a desired return in the form of increased gross and net profits as well as improved cash flow.[7] Companies know that it is essential to spend money on training productive salespeople who will be long-term assets to the organization. In a survey of 250 sales organizations, conducted by the Krannert School of Management at Purdue University, the cost of replacing a single sales representative (including recruitment, training, and lost-opportunity costs) ranges from $50,000 to $75,000.

In a recent survey by the *American Banker* of twenty-five private-client groups to estimate the cost of replacing a relationship sales consultant, they concluded that the costs can range from $305,000 to $515,000 for a top producer.[8] A similar report by Bill Ruch, president of Aptitude Testing for Industry, revealed a survey of 125 manufacturing companies showing that every unsuccessful salesperson hired costs a company between $150,000 and $300,000.[9] As you can see, a well-trained salesperson is indispensable!

After spending large amounts of money and devoting months to training, companies have made a significant investment in each salesperson. Productive salespeople are eager to receive this training because they know that learning never stops, and their companies are equally interested in their continued growth. Sales training should not be seen as an insult. We are all simply most comfortable selling what we understand. By providing intensive hands-on training programs, companies build confidence in their sales force, enabling them to make superior product presentations. This ability also shows customers that they are dealing with a product expert who knows how to solve their problems by providing educated solutions.[10]

The Positive Nature of Selling

The difficulty with recruiting talented new salespeople is made more challenging, particularly for those firms who seek college graduates, because many college students have historically held less than positive perceptions and attitudes toward selling as a career. Surveys indicate that a majority of college students see sales jobs as nothing more than excessive travel, obtrusive to home and leisure time, frustrating, and open only to extroverted personality styles.

Why do these negative perceptions exist and persist? It may be due to the fact that many of us have had little opportunity to observe career salespeople at work. Our primary contact with salespeople has been with grocery store checkers, retail salespeople (many of whom have been put on the floor with too little sales training), and the telemarketing reps who call you in the middle of dinner. Unfortunately, these are the models we see when we think of sales, and consequently many tend to view sales as a job to accept if nothing better is available rather than an exciting career option.

More accurate information and education today is helping to improve attitudes toward sales as a career. Students responding to recent surveys now support the view that selling is more challenging and prestigious, requires creativity, offers career opportunities, fosters increasing integrity, and provides better financial incentives than did students in earlier studies.[11]

An increasing number of sales managers who recruit at colleges and universities are pleased with the caliber of young men and women they find. They recognize that recruiting students from college can uncover outstanding sales talent. "Get 'em while they're young" is the motto of today's college recruiters.[12] Students may not be as streetwise as someone with years of experience, but they tend to be highly technologically proficient. They also have an abundance of energy and enthusiasm, and can be hired before they develop bad habits.

An understanding of the personal attributes that a career in professional selling actually requires quickly dispels any outdated myths an individual may still possess. Four areas of your personality are involved:

Personal Integrity. Continued success in sales requires the highest possible ethical standards for dealing with prospects, established customers, and your own company. A salesperson who lies or deceives customers to complete a sale is soon out of a job, because customers do not place repeat orders and prospects soon get the word that this person is not to be trusted. An outstanding salesperson has high values and always operates in the most ethical manner.

Personality Structure. Sales is a demanding career, which is why you must have a confident personality, a positive self-image, and a sense of self-worth. A person who is unable to accept the reality that not every prospect becomes a client will be devastated by failures and feel an overwhelming sense of personal rejection. The persistent myth that salespeople are arrogant, overbearing, and excessively aggressive contradicts reality. Successful salespeople are, instead, highly interested in other people and their needs and eager to be of real service to prospects and clients.

Personal Relationships. Salespeople are in an excellent position to attain status and recognition in the community. They are recognized as productive, capable professionals. You are not required to pretend, to subjugate your own personality or needs, or to become a doormat for customers. Success in professional selling does not call for assuming an inferior position socially, psychologically, or financially. The most successful salespeople find that their customers become friends with whom they form lasting personal relationships. Companies can spend millions on customer relationship management systems to monitor customer retention and defection. But a vigilant salesperson can just as effectively use the personal touch to solve a problem and keep customers from leaving.[13]

Personal Abilities. Success in sales requires high levels of intellect and developed skills. You must be able to understand—sometimes quickly and almost intuitively— a customer's business needs and problems. Salespeople must interpret those needs and suggest viable solutions even if customers themselves do not have a clear picture of their own needs or cannot verbalize those needs clearly. You need a broad knowledge of the field in which you operate, and must understand people and how to relate to them positively. The development of these skills requires not only intelligence but also continuous training.

The Basics of Personal Selling

A comprehensive definition of personal selling which forms the basis around which this book is developed is the following:

> **Personal Selling** is the process of *seeking* out people who have a particular need, *assisting* them to recognize and define that need, *demonstrating* to them how a particular service or product fills that need, and *persuading* them to make a decision to use that service or product.

This definition is broad enough to include any type of selling in which you may engage. It describes the commercial aspect of selling a product or service, as well as the process used to solicit funds for charitable organizations or enlist leaders for youth organizations. It also includes the activities of athletic coaches, political parties, clergy, and personnel officers in all kinds of organizations.

Because every sales situation is unique, your career in sales is an exciting and demanding one in which every day brings opportunities to develop new skills and sales strategies and ways to refine existing ones. The potential for personal and professional growth never ends. Because different prospects have varying needs, interests, ability to pay, and authority to make decisions, selling is different in every situation—and this constant change creates new possibilities and increased income potential.

Salespeople are Made, not Born

Too many people involved in selling have not attempted to learn the basic skills needed for success in the profession. They are quick to throw in the towel, claiming that they weren't born to be salespeople. They can be called "90-day wonders" because after 90 days they wonder why they ever got into the sales business. On the other hand, professional salespeople read books, take courses, ask questions, study the techniques of successful salespeople, work for their customers, and continually strive to outperform themselves.

Selling requires a working knowledge of psychology, sociology, communication, and persuasion. It is not a natural process to close a sale. It is a skill to be learned, just like anything else. Even experienced salespeople can fail if they get to the point where they think they know it all. Success in selling is a constant learning process. You must always be a student of your profession. Successful salespeople are made, not born, and they are made with concentrated attention, repeated practice, and goal-directed action.[14]

Exhibit 1.1 illustrates the ongoing debate—*Can selling be taught?* We are all like computers; in that we are only as good as we have programmed ourselves to be philosophically, emotionally, and intellectually. Becoming a master salesperson takes time and effort. Even the best salespeople continually adapt and refine their professional skills throughout their careers.

Salespeople: Can selling be taught?

Absolutely! Josh Hinds, founder of BusinessNetworkingAdvice.com, says that while it is true that getting out of your shell and calling on prospects comes easier to some people, that doesn't mean that anyone who's willing to learn and model what other effective salespeople do can't also get similar or better results. There are countless introverted personalities that have learned to become highly effective sales professionals.[15]

Selling is definitely an art for many successful salespeople, but it is also a skill that must be honed and practiced. Someone who may not be a natural at selling can be successful with diligent and persistent study and training.[16] As the old saying goes, "you get out what you put in." The same is true for honing your sales skills. Everything for the most part can be learned. The question is if you are willing to put in the time and effort necessary to make sales a successful career.

Advantages of a Sales Career

The once-popular "Wide World of Sports" television program promised the viewer "the thrill of victory, the agony of defeat." This thrill of victory makes sales an exciting and satisfying career, but the thrill comes not just from earning the monetary rewards or beating out the competition. Those are actually minor parts of the satisfaction of successful selling.[17]

The true victory you will enjoy as a successful salesperson consists of satisfying higher personal needs.[18] Maslow's Hierarchy of Needs—as shown in Exhibit 1.2—has special significance for you as a professional salesperson.

In the beginning, salespeople concentrate on supplying their lower-order needs: earning a living, providing security for themselves and their families, and being accepted socially by their peers. As they satisfy these basic needs, salespeople can concentrate on the higher-level needs: self-acceptance (a positive self-image), making a contribution to community life, and self-actualization (becoming all one can be; knowledge and achievement for their own sake).

Δ **Exhibit 1.2**

Hierarchy of Personal Needs ·

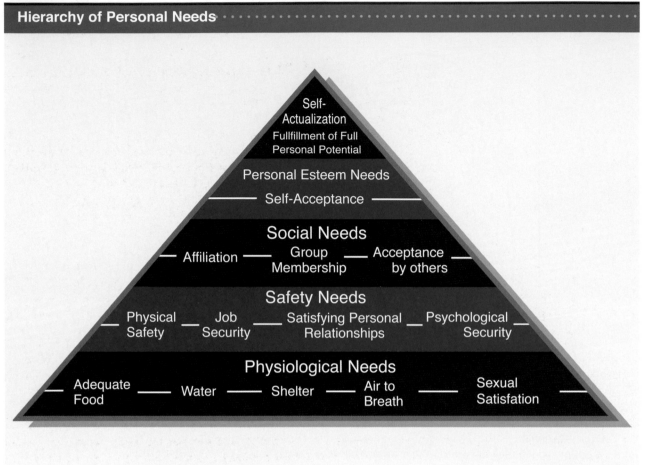

A Sense of Independence and Variety

A sales career frees you from a mundane daily routine. Salespeople are likely to work in a variety of places and deal with prospects who have widely different personalities. What works with one prospect may antagonize another. Consequently, they must always be aware of every element of the environment and adjust quickly. *Selling is never boring.*

Salespeople can exercise a greater measure of control over their time and activities than many other professionals. Sales is not a nine-to-five job. The hours are usually flexible, long one day and short another. Because their jobs are not usually structured, they must also be self-starters and stay motivated.

Opportunities for Advancement

Effective salespeople are not forced into one career path. Almost any option for career advancement is open to those who are motivated to be successful and seek advancement. Exhibit 1.3 illustrates a potential career path for a highly motivated salesperson. As you move up the corporate hierarchy, the various options require a different blending of personal skills and characteristics. As a result, there is no guarantee that a successful salesperson will also make a successful manager. In fact, many talented salespeople actually refuse promotion to higher managerial positions. They simply love what they do, and can often earn more money selling than they could by moving into a middle-management position.

A Potential Career Path For Professionals in Selling

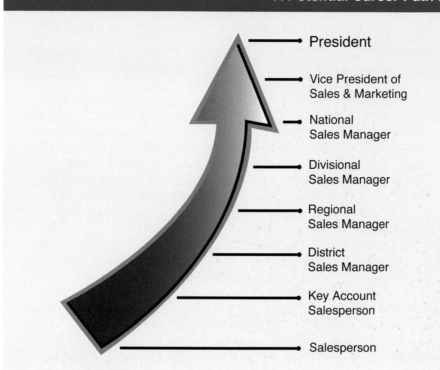

- President
- Vice President of Sales & Marketing
- National Sales Manager
- Divisional Sales Manager
- Regional Sales Manager
- District Sales Manager
- Key Account Salesperson
- Salesperson

Entrepreneurship. Sales is an ideal career for those who plan to one day own and run their own businesses. No business can survive without a viable marketing organization. An owner or chief executive who has been involved in sales truly understands this part of the business and is in an excellent position to launch and manage a new enterprise successfully. An entrepreneur can find people who understand manufacturing and finance, but the sales and marketing staff must share the founder's dream if the concept is to reach fruition.

Promotion to Sales Management. A sales manager may have either limited or extremely broad duties. The first step into sales management often consists of supervising two or three other salespeople—monitoring their activities, providing field training through joint sales calls, and recruiting additional sales representatives while continuing personal sales activities. More comprehensive sales management positions involve managing an entire local, regional, or nationwide sales division. Such a position might include budgeting, planning for sales training, sales promotion, and recruiting, in addition to executive duties and status in the company.

Top Management Positions. Sales experience makes an executive a valuable member of the management team. Although chief executive officers (CEOs) have traditionally come from the financial and legal ranks, companies are increasingly tapping into the sales and marketing departments to find their leaders. Organizations are looking for CEOs who are good leaders of people and have good strategic minds.[19] Many skills used in selling closely resemble those needed in top management. Both jobs require great people skills. It is important in both positions to maintain control under stress, to recognize opportunities and threats, and to locate, and analyze vast amounts of information. Exhibit 1.4 explains the increasing awareness of just how critical sales experience has become for the leader of a corporation.

The head of a forward thinking company simply must have intimate knowledge of specific sales methodologies to understand how to make improvements, and ultimately, increase the company's bottom line.

Δ **Exhibit 1.4**

The CEO—A Company's Best Salesperson ·

As CEOs become more removed from the daily operations of their companies, they also become disconnected from the source of their companies' livelihood—sales and the processes used to generate them. "A CEO in a fast-growing company might not be able to disappear, if the CEO wants to keep the company on a high growth curve," says James L. Horton in his essay, "CEO Visibility in a Post-Bubble World."

A CEO can never stop being a salesperson—the best one in the company, in fact—in order to sustain profitability and secure future profits. However, it is also the CEO who sets the example for the rest of the company by focusing on what is most important.

If profitability is most important, then selling must be the CEO's focus. Since selling is the key to generating profits, the CEO must be actively engaged in the process. The CEO is the person who leads everyone by selling them—from employees to clients to stockholders.

While many CEOs have used their selling skills to build their companies into successful businesses, not every CEO is or has been a salesperson. As difficult as it is for a person in this position of power to admit, choosing to acknowledge what he or she does not know opens the door to acquiring the knowledge to become an effective salesperson. Just like anyone new to the company's sales department, the CEO may need training in the company's sales process as well.

How can a CEO be tuned in to the company without being intimately acquainted with how its most important objective—achieving, sustaining and increasing profitability—is accomplished? By learning and utilizing an effective sales process, CEOs can lead by example, directly affect revenue growth, and ensure a secure financial future for the company, its employees, and its shareholders.[20]

Security

Companies will always need salespeople. In fact, the demand appears to be steadily increasing rather than decreasing. Ambitious salespeople are eagerly sought, and most organizations provide excellent rewards and special treatment for their top sales performers. They know that quality salespeople who become dissatisfied can easily go to work for a competitor and possibly take their established customers with them.

Because salespeople are usually paid according to performance, you can directly affect your own income by deciding how much time and effort to invest in the job. Thus, your security comes from your own personal decisions about how hard and how efficiently you want to work. *Work, in many ways, is like money; if you are willing to expend enough of it, you can have almost anything you want.*[21]

Disadvantages of a Sales Career

Like any other profession, selling has some drawbacks and reasons why it is not right for everybody. The same qualities that some may see as advantages to a career in selling are in fact distinct disadvantages to others. Some people view a fixed salary as more secure than an income dependent entirely upon their direct performance in a given time period. Others dislike the irregular hours or the traveling around to meet clients that salespeople see as the variety that gives spice to their lives.

Probably the greatest problem faced by every salesperson is handling rejection. Not every sales presentation produces a sale. Not every prospect needs the service or product, and an ethical salesperson never presses for an order from a prospect whose needs will not be met by that product. No salesperson can ever be 100 percent successful in closing sales, even when the prospect truly needs the product or service. The best salespeople learn quickly that rejection is not directed toward them personally. Prospects who do not buy are rejecting the product or service—not the salesperson.

Salespeople must realize that not every presentation will lead to a sale.

The decision seldom has anything to do with the salesperson's worth as a human being. Even the occasional prospect who reacts negatively to a salesperson does so as a result of the prospect's personal opinion—an opinion that may be colored by prejudice or completely unfounded. Rejection is not proof that the salesperson is in some way unworthy or inadequate. Salespeople who cannot separate their own personal worth from the product they sell may become too paralyzed by fear to approach another prospect because they face a renewal of rejection.

Classification of Sales Jobs

Sales jobs are so diverse that they fit a wide variety of personal needs and interests. Variety exists from industry to industry. The responsibilities of a salesperson who calls on large manufacturing companies to create awareness of computer systems for production-control are vastly different from those of the real estate salesperson who sells homes to families. Sales careers vary within industries as well. For example, the residential real estate salesperson is in a different world from that of the real estate developer who puts together multimillion-dollar projects for shopping centers, office complexes, and industrial parks.

As different as sales jobs may be, they all share some basic similarities:

- The need to understand the prospect's problem.
- The need for appropriate technical and/or product knowledge.
- The need for self-discipline to relentlessly execute a sales plan.
- The ability to translate product features into benefits that resolve the prospect's problem.

Derek Newton developed a classification format for sales jobs that has become a standard model. Because it has been empirically researched, his format is presented here. Newton studied responses from over 1,000 sales executives from manufacturing, wholesaling, retail, and service firms. He identifies four types of selling found across this variety of industries.[22]

1. Trade Selling

The trade seller's primary responsibility is to increase business from present and potential customers through merchandising and promotional assistance. They usually deal with buyers who are resellers (wholesalers and retailers). Long-term relationships are important for success. In addition to delivering orders and replenishing inventory, this salesperson's tasks involve persuading the customer to provide additional shelf space, setting up product displays in the store, rotating stock as inventory is replenished, and perhaps conducting in-store demonstrations or distributing samples to customers. Companies usually do not encourage their trade sellers to conduct vigorous sales efforts. They are expected to generate increased sales by assisting the customer move a larger volume of inventory.

2. Missionary Selling

The missionary salesperson's task is largely one of educating those who ultimately decide what product the consumer will use. The most familiar example of the missionary salesperson is the drug detail salesperson who calls on physicians to introduce and describe the pharmaceutical company's products and persuade them to prescribe their medications for patients who could benefit from them. In addition to pharmaceutical firms, food and beverage manufacturers, transportation firms, and public utility companies employ missionary salespeople.

3. Technical Selling

A fast-growing class of salespeople is the technical specialist group, the engineers, scientists, and others with the technical expertise to explain the advantages of the company's product. These salespeople sell directly to the firms that use their products. They are very important in such industries as chemicals and machinery. They act like management consultants in that they identify, analyze, and solve their customers' problems. In the past, technical specialists have been more concerned with explaining the product than with securing the order, but many decision-makers are now more knowledgeable about technology and more likely to respond favorably to the technical specialist. Consequently, many companies are teaching these salespeople basic selling skills to help them be persuasive in making presentations and closing sales.

4. New Business Selling

This type of salesperson seeks out and persuades new customers to buy for the very first time. They are extremely vital to firms putting their focus on sales growth. New business selling includes selling new products to existing customers or existing products to new customers. The characteristics discussed later in this chapter—perseverance, empathy, ability to ask questions, initiative, and resourcefulness—are vital to sales success for this category of salesperson.

Selling for a Manufacturer. Manufacturers' sales reps sell the products produced by the company that employs them. They might sell to other manufacturers, various marketing middlemen, or directly to consumers. Exhibit 1.5 list five specific categories of salespeople and describes the content of their jobs.

Δ **Exhibit 1.5**

Five Types of Salespeople ●

1   **Account Representative**—A salesperson who calls on a large number of already established customers in, for example, the food, textiles, apparel, or wholesaling industries. Much of this selling is low key and there is minimal pressure to develop new business.

2   **Detail Salesperson**—A salesperson who, instead of directly soliciting an order, concentrates on performing promotional activities and introducing products. The medical detail salesperson, for example, seeks to persuade doctors, the indirect customers, to specify the pharmaceutical company's trade name product for prescriptions. The company's actual sales are ultimately made through a wholesaler or direct to pharmacists who fill prescriptions.

3   **Sales Engineer**—A salesperson who sells products for which technical know-how and the ability to discuss technical aspects of the product are extremely important. The salesperson's expertise in identifying, analyzing, and solving customer problems is another critical factor. This type of selling is common in the chemical, machinery, and heavy-equipment industries.

4   **Industrial Products Salesperson, Non-technical**—This salesperson sells a tangible product to industrial or commercial purchasers; no high degree of technical knowledge is required. Industries such as packaging materials or standard office equipment use this type.

5   **Service Salesperson**—A salesperson who sells intangibles, such as insurance and advertising. Unlike the four preceding types, those who sell services must be able to sell the benefits of intangibles.

Selling at Retail. The largest number of salespeople are employed in the various aspects of retail selling. A retail salesperson sells products or services to customers for their own personal use. They may be residential real estate brokers, retail store clerks, insurance agents, telephone salespeople, or direct-to-consumer salespeople who hold group meetings or sell door-to-door.

Several million direct-to-consumer salespeople represent hundreds of direct-selling companies such as Amway and Mary Kay.[23] The Pampered Chef is a direct sales company launched in 1980 with a $3,000 bank loan by stay-at-home mom Doris Christopher in her suburban Chicago basement. Today, the Pampered Chef has 73,000 consultants worldwide, nearly 1,000 company employees, $700 million in sales, 12 million customers, and over a million home parties a year.[24]

The Order Taker Versus the Order Getter. The *order taker* simply responds to requests and the *order getter* is a creative problem solver. The salesperson whose work is described as order taking reacts to customers' expressed desires. Responsive selling jobs may be either inside or outside. Inside sales jobs include retail clerks in department stores and other retail establishments. By being helpful and pleasant, retail clerks may create a few sales, but they generally just assist customers in completing the purchase of goods they have already chosen. Outside order takers are route salespeople who mainly service retail clients to deliver orders or replenish inventory.

The order taker may engage in *suggestive selling*—that is, ask you to purchase an additional item. The next time you stop at a McDonald's drive-thru and the person asks in a barely discernible voice, "Would you like an apple pie with your Big Mac and fries?" You are observing suggestive selling in action. And it works!

Order getting, or creative selling, requires ingenuity and the ability to generate demand for a product or service among potential buyers. The product may be tangible such as automobiles or real estate, or the product may be intangible such as investment services or advertising. Creative personal selling generally offers the greatest opportunity for high income because it demands the highest level of personal skill, dedication, and effort.

Attributes of Successful Salespeople

No one list of traits accurately describes every successful salesperson. They are as diverse as members of any other profession. They include both extroverts and introverts—and all the degrees in between: Shy and outspoken, talkative and quiet. However, certain core characteristics seem to be present to some degree in most successful salespeople, despite the numerous ways individuals express those characteristics and adapt them to their own styles and purposes.[25]

Enthusiasm

Ralph Waldo Emerson said, "Nothing great was ever achieved without enthusiasm."[26] One of the most important characteristics in new salespeople is enthusiasm—but a distinction must be made between people who are enthusiastic about their product and those who are merely eager to take the prospect's money.[27] Enthusiasm in salespeople is based on a genuine belief in the product and a conviction that it will serve the needs of the prospect.[28] Such enthusiasm is communicated both verbally and nonverbally to the prospect in terms of your own personality. Enthusiasm may be expressed as calm, quiet confidence or as excited activity. However it is demonstrated, real enthusiasm is highly attractive and reassuring to prospects.

*"**Nothing can stop the man** with the right mental attitude from achieving his goal; nothing on earth can help the man with the wrong mental attitude."*

- Thomas Jefferson

Empathy

Empathy, the ability to understand another person's concerns, opinions, and needs, whether sharing them or not, provides salespeople with the sales edge of being able to think and understand "with" the prospect during a sales call. Empathy is the ability to pick up on the subtle clues and cues provided by others in order to accurately assess what they are feeling. Empathy is not "sympathy." Intrinsic in sympathy is loyalty, which results in a loss of objectivity. Empathic salespeople recognize how others feel while at the same time viewing them in a dispassionate and objective manner. This critical quality helps you understand a prospect while maintaining your own identity, purpose and objectives.[29]

Empathy is most useful in the sales process for handling objections and midcourse changes by the prospect. Empathic salespeople can sense changes in prospects and adjust their presentations accordingly. By careful listening, effective salespeople absorb prospects' reactions, generate an upbeat environment, and sell themselves to prospects. The combination of sincerity and empathy enables them to tailor the presentation to mesh precisely with the prospect's stated problems.

Goal Direction

Stay focused on your goals and daily activities. A handful of critical factors make 80 percent of the difference between success and failure. Ask yourself what things contribute the most to your success.[30] Goal-directed salespeople often respond positively to incentives such as money, prestige, recognition, and pride of accomplishment, which they see as tools they can use to reach their overall goals. When these incentives fit into their overall plan for achieving the goals that represent self-actualization for them, salespeople go all-out to win them.

Ability to Ask Questions

Good salespeople ask questions; poor ones just keep talking. You need to remain in control of the sales interview, and the person who is asking questions is the one in control. When you learn to ask the right kinds of questions, you will gain new prospects, discover valuable qualifying information, uncover the prospects' buying motives, and be able to anticipate most objections. Questioning is your best tool for keeping the interview on track and moving toward a successful close, while also giving the prospect the feeling of remaining in control of the situation.

Resourcefulness

Top salespeople are the ones who are most resourceful. On the spur of the moment, they can think of new ways to make an old point, new applications and creative uses for products, and unique reasons for a particular prospect to make a buying decision. They can think on their feet under pressure. For these people, resourcefulness is an automatic response, like a reflex. Resourcefulness comes from an agile and analytical mind and allows you to stay on the right side of the fine line between being just right and very wrong. In the sales situation, the right word or phrase clears away the fog and reveals the solutions. The wrong word or phrase is like putting a drop of ink into a glass full of water: It obscures everything.

Resourceful salespeople always seem to have at hand a barrelful of ideas, tactics, and strategies. Exhibit 1.6 highlights the thoughts of Tanis Cornell, AT&T Global Enterprise Manager at Network Appliance, in Addison, Texas. Tanis recognizes the importance of resourcefulness and creativity in a salesperson.[31]

Remain focused on your journey to successful selling.

Δ Exhibit 1.6

The Power of Resourcefulness

Is professional selling a viable career choice for an ambitious person who wants to maximize earning capacity, use unique skills and talents, and enjoy the satisfaction of being personally productive? Tanis Cornell's answer is a resounding "yes."

"In today's competitive market," Cornell says, "many products, companies, and even salespeople start to look alike to the prospect. I look for men and women with the creativity to differentiate themselves from their competition. Much more emphasis is directed at keeping current customers happy and providing long-term solutions." Salespeople must not only excel at prospecting and finding that new customer, but excel at building long-term relationships with existing customers.

"In my years as a salesperson and as a manager, I noticed one very interesting thing," states Cornell. "There are certain individuals, regardless of gender, that excel each and every year. You can change their compensation plan; you can move them to another job or another location; you can throw any number of challenges at them that would disturb the average salesperson; but for top performers, it doesn't matter."

Administrative Ability

Efficient self-management, especially the management of time, is essential to success in selling. Your most productive time is spent face-to-face with prospects. But you are also required to attend meetings, travel, wait, prepare for interviews, read, study, attend to paperwork, and conduct after-sale follow-up and service.

Salespeople must engage in a number of non-selling and administrative tasks. This means that only a small portion of their precious time can be spent in direct contact with prospects and clients. Efficient time management can make the difference between success and failure. Time and territory management is one of the most critical issues for salespeople today. According to a recent survey of 1,500 salespeople from 13 industries, conducted by Proudfoot Consulting, they found that on average, salespeople spend 60 percent of their time on administrative duties or travel. Add on downtime and other non-sales duties, and the remaining 40 percent of the workday amounts to limited time with customers. "Many reps spent as little as 15 percent of their time with clients," says Linas Kaknevicius, director of marketing for Proudfoot.

Too many sales professionals spend time analyzing data rather than talking to clients. "It's surprising how often you have a sales rep who has a meeting in Atlanta one day and Miami the next, and it doesn't occur to him to think, if he's in Miami, he can drop by another client there." Kaknevicius says that successful salespeople must take their own initiative to spend more time with or gain new clients rather than look for direction from their managers.[32]

Initiative

All great salespeople have a powerful, unrelenting, internal drive to excel. This intrinsic motivation can be shaped and molded, but it cannot be taught.[33] Successful salespeople are self-motivated. They are self-starters who exercise initiative. They do not wait to be told to prospect, to be assigned calls to make, or to be urged to end the presentation with a close. They see the work that needs to be done and take personal responsibility for doing it. Creative ideas that surface during a presentation must be implemented then and there—without time to ask the sales manager for advice. Salespeople who have self-confidence supported by solid product knowledge and belief in their own ability to succeed feel free to exercise initiative.

Perseverance

Setbacks often outnumber triumphs, and salespeople must have reserves of strength and resilience to fall back on when this happens. Depending upon the type of sales activity and the product or service being marketed, the number of sales closed compared to the number of presentations made usually ranges from 5 percent to 50 percent or more. Salespeople need perseverance in several areas:

- The ability to keep going to another prospect no matter how many have refused to buy.
- The ability to make repeated presentations to the same prospect over a period of time.
- The ability to continue asking for an appointment to make a presentation until one is finally granted.

Consider the story of Richard Sutton, who as a young boy met Herbert Hoover while living in Hawaii. Hoover took a liking to him and advised him to become a lawyer, and Sutton followed his advice. Hoover later urged Sutton to run for state office as a representative of the Republican party, even though Hawaii was strongly Democratic. Richard ran and lost. Disheartened, Richard wrote Hoover asking for advice. Hoover offered him sound words of wisdom: Keep running until you win. Richard followed his mentor's advice, running a staggering twelve campaigns before he finally won. The lesson from the story is this: Tell yourself you will be patient, persistent and persevere until there is tangible progress. [34]

Pleasant Personality

The way to make a friend is to be one. The salesperson with a pleasant, outgoing disposition is remembered and favored. A key to forming a pleasant personality is to like people and genuinely enjoy knowing as many different kinds of people as possible. People respond to those who like them.

Department store entrepreneur J.C. Penney said, "All great business is built on friendship."[35] How do you build friendships in today's tough competitive sales climate? Find out what the buyer needs, then make every effort to deliver it. Ask yourself: "What would I do if I really wanted to be friends with this person?" The answer will tell you how to build a long-term relationship.

SUMMARY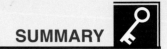

- Selling is a basic component of all human interaction. It involves discovering needs and providing products or services that satisfy those needs.

- Salespeople are among the highest-paid professionals and make the greatest impact on profitability and success for an organization.

- Partnerships, customer relationship management, strategic alliances, empowerment, team selling, and global alliances are more than mere words to a growing number of sales organizations today. They are the tools with which winning strategies are fashioned.

- Professional selling offers opportunities that involve a number of different skill levels and a wide diversity of activities.

- All personality types can be successful in sales, but certain characteristics enhance the likelihood of success: Enthusiasm, empathy, goal direction, ability to ask questions, resourcefulness, administrative ability, initiative, perseverance, and a pleasant personality.

- Selling is a demanding career that offers substantial rewards and outstanding opportunities for personal achievement.

REVIEW QUESTIONS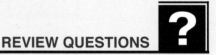

1. In the sense that all persuasion is a form of "selling," name the types of situations in which you most frequently "sell." In which of these are you most often successful? If persuasion is an important part of selling, is selling also a form of leadership? Explain your answer.

2. What career limits are imposed on one who chooses sales? Illustrate.

3. Are salespeople born or made? Justify your answer.

4. Why is a feeling of rejection a problem for salespeople? Is this feeling an inevitable part of a sales career?

5. Describe the four broad classes of sales jobs and give examples of each.

6. In addition to securing orders for products, in what ways do companies depend upon salespeople?

7. What responsibilities belong to the salesperson after the order is signed? How does the discharge of these responsibilities affect the entire sales process?

8. Salespeople are interdependent with other individuals in their company. Why is this true in respect to the following factors: product changes, pricing, shipping, and competition?

9. Name some qualities that seem to be shared by most successful salespeople. How do these traits contribute to success? Can they be developed, or are they innate? Does this mean that a single type of personality style is required for success in sales?

ROLE-PLAY EXERCISES

The following role-play exercises help build teams, improve communication, and emphasize the "real-world" side of selling. They are meant to be challenging, to learn how to deal with problems that have no single "right" answer and to use a variety of skills beyond those employed in a typical review question. Read and complete each activity. Then in the next class, discuss and compare answers with other classmates. Have some students take the role of the salesperson, and see how they would react. Remember, "*You learn more about a person in an hour of play than in a lifetime of conversation.*"–Plato

1. Interview sales managers in a variety of companies and ask what qualities that manager looks for when hiring salespeople. Also ask what personal qualities are evident in most of the top salespeople in that organization.

CASE STUDY

CASE 1.1—A Critical Choice To Make

Mary Landown will soon graduate from college with a degree in marketing. Mary entered college as a biology major but felt she might not be able to get a job in that field without going to graduate school. She has enjoyed her marketing classes, has been active in student government, and is eager to start earning some money, especially since she has been on a strict budget throughout college and has college loans to repay.

Concerned about what kind of job she should seek, Mary has recently taken a career interest survey that showed high scores in public speaking, sales, marketing, medical science and service, teaching, and writing; she made average scores in home management, agriculture, engineering, music, and drama; low scores were reported in nature, athletics, social science, mathematics, and clerical.

Mary has been offered the following three jobs:

1. SALES REPRESENTATIVE FOR A CABINETRY COMPANY

After a month's training at the home office, Mary would call on contractors, kitchen designers, and commercial interior designers. This offer includes a moderate salary plus commissions and an automobile allowance. Advancement to senior sales representative is possible after two years and to branch manager after six to eight years.

2. DETAIL SALESPERSON FOR PHARMACEUTICALS

Mary would, after three months' training, begin calling on doctors and pharmacists to explain the details and qualities of new drugs. She would also be expected to open new accounts. The job provides an automobile and travel allowance, and two or three nights per week of travel are standard. This company offers the highest total pay of any of the job possibilities, but the salary alone is relatively low if bonuses are not earned.

3. SALES REPRESENTATIVE FOR A MAJOR BUSINESS MACHINES COMPANY

Mary would start out selling computer software to small businesses. If successful, she would move into selling small computer systems, primarily with financial applications. She would be on a straight base salary the first year and move to a base plus commissions thereafter.

1. Which job should Mary take? Why?
2. Which job would you take? Why?

Relationship Selling

LEARNING OBJECTIVES

- Understand the role of relationship selling in today's market and how it differs from past stereotypes of selling.

- Learn the steps in relationship selling and the purpose of each step.

- Compare and contrast relationship selling and the traditional sales model.

- Examine the usefulness of continuous quality improvement in a sales organization.

- Recognize how to build relationships through team selling.

The profound effects of the Internet and technology on professional selling are impossible to deny. Recent reports predict that online sales will increase by 22 percent to $172.4 billion this year, and yet the e-commerce revolution is not the most important change in sales trends.[1] There is a second revolution occurring—it is in the relationship selling process where the buyer requires advice and advanced expertise. It is here that face-to-face selling has been the most effective channel to the customer. Unless you sell a product that has only a local appeal, searching for leads in the phone book or advertising in the newspaper are becoming things of the past.[2] Even Internet sales companies, such as Charles Schwab and Dell Computer, have created face-to-face sales forces to reach the segments of their markets requiring complex customized products and services. Their "clicks-and-mortar" strategies rely on sales professionals who can create significant customer value by helping clients define their problems and design unique solutions. This new selling is all about value creation: How the selling process itself can be used to create value for the customer.

> ***Your professionalism*** is defined not by the business you are in, but by the way you are in business. —Dr. Tony Alessandra

Relationship selling, in which sales professionals demonstrate not just a product's technical features, but how it can solve a business problem and save money, isn't a novel idea. Yet it is estimated that only 20 percent of companies have adopted this style of selling.[3] Positioning yourself as consultant and partner creates a more equal relationship with prospects and customers. The willingness and ability to meet each client's needs is the cornerstone of building partnerships. Prospects and customers want *business partners*, not *tennis partners*.

Build or Break a Relationship

Partnership is a positive word that makes customers feel that you are looking out for their best interests. The partnership formed between the buyer and seller is not a *legal* partnership. Rather it is a part of the continuous quality improvement process companies are implementing. Today's sales forces take time to get to know the customer's business situation, needs, cash flow problems, decision-making process, and the competitive environment. For customers, a buying decision usually means a decision to enter into a long-term relationship with salespeople and their companies. It is much like a "business marriage." They have a variety of options and choices open to them, including not buying anything at all. But when customers make a decision to buy from a salesperson, they become dependent on that sales rep. And since they have probably had unpleasant buying experiences in the past, they are very uneasy and uncertain about getting into this kind of dependency relationship.[4]

Exhibit 2.1 illustrates the key elements that can build or break this trust-bond relationship between buyer and seller. Relationship selling allows you to grasp a company's needs by putting yourself on the customer's side of the desk. *You are first a diagnostician.*

△ Exhibit 2.1

How to Build or Break a Relationship

Relationship Builders

1. Treat customers like lifelong partners.
2. Become a solutions provider.
3. Deliver more service than you promise.
4. Schedule regular service calls.
5. Develop open and honest communication.
6. Use the "we can" approach.
7. Take responsibility for mistakes made.
8. Be an ally for the customer's business.

Relationship Breakers

1. Focus only on making the sale.
2. Simply wait for a problem to develop.
3. Over-promise and under-deliver.
4. Wait for customers to call you.
5. Lie or make exaggerated claims.
6. Use the "us versus them" approach.
7. Blame somebody else. Knock a competitor.
8. Focus on your own personal gain.

Relationship salespeople create an information transfer, a support for client goals, and enthusiasm for their success. The top salespeople have escaped the *selling mentality* and let the customer tell them their needs. In the face of increased competition in the home improvement market, Sears recently recognized the need to more fully address and cater to customers' specific needs. Mark Good, executive vice president and general manager of Sears' home services division, states, "We provide the end-to-end solution that we don't think the others provide. What we are focused on is continually getting better, and getting better on our customers' terms."[5] And that is the precise mentality that will insure a company's survival. It isn't always about who has the better product or best price, but who can best *provide solutions* to the customer on a consistent basis, and on their terms.

> To be a consultant rather than just a salesperson you have to be a creative resource, a value provider, and a friend to clients. The relationship salesperson works hard helping others succeed—not just helping them purchase. Unless you are willing to commit to excellence, consultation will not occur. Here are some key characteristics of relationship selling:
>
> • Discover and understand the customers' problems and needs.
>
> • Partner with your customers and become a valuable resource for information.
>
> • Demonstrate to customers how they can achieve their goals with your product or service.
>
> • Have a true conviction that your company, product, and services are the best for your customers.
>
> • Believe in yourself because a positive attitude makes it all work.

Relationship Selling Versus Traditional Selling

If you understand what the steps are in the *Relationship Cycle of Selling*, and what it takes to make each step a successful endeavor, then you will become a professional in selling much more quickly than those individuals who are simply stumbling through the process trying to figure it out. The sales cycle model in the actual face-to-face meeting between the salesperson and the prospect includes these four steps:

1. **The Approach**

2. **Identifying Needs**

3. **Making the Presentation**

4. **Handling Objections and Gaining Commitment**

Exhibit 2.2 contrasts the amount of time the relationship salesperson and the traditional salesperson spend in each step. You can see from the figure that the old pyramid model of selling has been turned upside down.[6] The 40 percent of the equation for the traditional model that used to be closing is now *building trust* in the relationship model. Meanwhile *reassuring the customer and closing* has shrunk to just 10 percent in the new model.

The relationship salesperson spends the vast majority of time in the first two steps, whereas the traditional salesperson exerts most of the effort and the majority of time on presenting features and trying to close. The goal is to learn how to communicate with your business partners and establish an alliance that is extensive in scope and relevant to the customer's own vision.[7]

Δ Exhibit 2.2
Relationship Selling Versus Traditional Selling

Phases	Relationship Model of Selling	time spent in each phase	Traditional Sales Model	time spent in each phase
Approach	Building Trust (Rapport)	40%	Telling	10%
Identifying Needs	Probe, Ask Questions, and Listen	30%	Qualifying	20%
Making the Presentation	Sell Benefits	20%	Presenting Features	30%
Resistance and Gaining Commitment	Reassure and Close	10%	Closing Long and Hard	40%

Customers Buy Solutions

Technology helps open new markets, speeds communications between sellers and their prospects and customers, and frankly, creates a whole new set of problems that you can help clients solve. Customers can now conduct many of their transactions online and have little need for a salesperson that doesn't add value to the transaction. This requires a much more sophisticated and complex set of skills than those possessed by the traditional salesperson.

Low-end selling—which is essentially transaction processing and order taking—continues to shift away from traditional sales forces into the more efficient, cost-effective, and faster setting provided by online sales. But this doesn't mean that the Internet will replace the professional salesperson; selling is simply becoming more strategic. It's moving up the food chain, and the need for relationship selling is increasing. Your company may sell accounting services, office equipment, or design Websites. However, that's really not what customers are buying—customers are trying to increase sales and improve efficiency. By demonstrating how you can help customers achieve the goals of their

You are a solutions provider.

organization, you distinguish yourself from competitors. Selling is still about relationships, and people buy from people they like.[8] Order-takers will vanish, but creative salespeople who know that selling is about building long-term partnerships will flourish.

The Relationship Selling Cycle

A better understanding of the complete selling situation and the problems it generates may be gained by breaking the sale into its basic tasks. These steps are presented in a logical sequence, but *they are not necessarily chronological* and the order of the steps will vary. The ebb and flow of a sales interview defies attempts to package it into nice, neat compartments.

Regardless of account size or potential, certain predictable tasks must be performed. These tasks, such as identifying prospects and determining needs, may be called the steps in a sale or the *selling cycle*. When organized into a prescribed sequence they comprise an overall structure rather than a lock-step approach to selling. The eight basics of successful selling described in Exhibit 2.3 are the focus of chapters 7 through 14, and they represent your guide to a successful sales career.

Δ **Exhibit 2.3**

A Sales Cycle Framework for Relationship Selling ·

Phase One

Identifying Qualified Prospects. Prospecting is the process of searching for someone with a need for the product or service, the ability to pay for it, and the authority to make a buying decision. One of the first steps in the process of finding these qualified prospects is to review your current accounts to see who needs service, who might want to increase the quantity purchased, or who may buy new products for the first time. At the same time, survey your territory to identify new leads and find out information on the businesses in your area that might be interested in your product. The reason for this step is simple: sales professionals must study the people they want to approach.

Planning Preapproach Activities. After you identify qualified prospects, establish a definite purpose for each sales call. To accomplish this, you must make an evaluation of your potential customers' needs and determine also who the decision-makers are in the companies you have studied. These activities equip you to interact with the customer and then develop an action plan and call schedule to set appointments.

Phase Two

Approaching the Prospect. Treat prospects as individuals and not as carbon copies of everyone else. What happens during the opening minutes of the face-to-face encounter affects the success of the whole presentation. Some people simply do not thaw out immediately, and you must find icebreakers that help the prospect feel at ease with you. This is why you should spend time finding the prospect's comfort level. Most first-time meetings between salesperson and prospect produce an *egocentric predicament* arising from your fear of being rejected and the prospect's fear of being sold something that is not really wanted or needed. By redesigning your approach to selling, you can calm the prospect's fear of buying and reduce your own fear of selling.

Discovering Needs. During this step of the sales encounter, you and your client discover whether the client needs or wants something that you can provide. Because the success of the whole process rests on this basic discovery, the relationship salesperson spends whatever time is necessary and asks questions to get to know the prospect's needs and problems. For this reason, one of your primary goals in every sales situation should be to create an atmosphere within which an act of trust can occur—to make a friend rather than a sale, a customer who has confidence in the integrity and ability of the salesperson, and confidence in the company and its product or service. You don't talk prospects into a sale; you listen them into a sale.

Listen and take notes to discover needs.

Making the Presentation. Your evaluation of the prospect's situation should lead you naturally into the presentation of product benefits that fit the needs your client expressed. Every product or service has both features and benefits. A *feature* is any fact about the product or service, tangible or intangible. For example, a feature of a particular automobile is front-wheel drive. However, prospects want to know about benefits rather than features. The front-wheel drive feature is meaningless unless it satisfies some need, solves some problem, or provides some benefit to the prospective customer. The benefits of front-wheel drive might be explained in terms of ease of handling, safety, or some other performance quality that promises to satisfy the prospect's need.

Even better than showcasing the value of the product is to allow prospects to assess that value by discovering for themselves the benefits of owning it. The relationship salesperson is customer-oriented. A prospect does not buy without being certain that what you are saying is true. That is why you do not create sales; rather, people buy based on their own expectations. *No one likes to be sold*. They like to see the value of what is being presented, and then they make their own buying decisions based on their own assessment of whether or not your product satisfies their needs.

> **"In professional selling, as in medicine, prescription before diagnosis is malpractice."**

Exhibit 2.4 illustrates how the power of expectation works. The salesperson who holds confident, positive expectations closes far more sales than the one who expects rejection.

Δ Exhibit 2.4

The Power of Expectation

Expectation is powerful. Three mess hall sergeants received large shipments of dried apricots. At first, they were all dismayed because they didn't see how they could ever use that many apricots. They each dealt with the problem differently. The first one "knew" no one in his outfit wanted apricots; so he cooked a large pot of stewed apricots, stuck a ladle in the pot, and set it at the end of the serving line. Sure enough, at the end of three days, his negative expectations were fulfilled; he still had most of the apricots. The second one adopted a more positive approach. He also cooked a large pot of stewed apricots; but he stood in the serving line with a big smile and a ladle in hand. "Let me serve you some apricots," he offered, as people came through the serving line. He disposed of more apricots than the first sergeant. The third sergeant decided to create a demand. He put up signs at the beginning and end of the serving line: *"Coming Tuesday: Apricots just like your Mother served. Your choice."* On Tuesday at breakfast time, a big sign on the door announced: *"It's Tuesday! Mother's apricots are here!"* He had prepared stewed apricots and a mix of chopped dried apricots, raisins, and nuts to sprinkle on cereal. For lunch and dinner, he offered apricot fried pies, baked apricot pies, and apricot bread. His shipment of apricots disappeared quickly.

Handling Objections and Gaining Commitment. Now is the time to verbally clarify and confirm what both you and the client will do to make the solution work. This part of the overall process helps to avoid misunderstandings by bringing any that exist out into the open so they can be handled. Each clarification and confirmation adds weight to the case in favor of a positive decision. As shown in Exhibit 2.5, when the scale of decision tips far enough toward the positive side, the prospect can, and does, say yes. When that happens, everyone wins—the client, you, and your company. Relationship selling is a matter of presenting positive benefits that respond to a need, use, and value. Selling in this manner reduces your need to deal with resistance, answer objections, or haggle over price. Since the client has been an active participant throughout, the commitment and close should be the natural conclusion to a successful sales interview.

Δ Exhibit 2.5

The Scale of Decision

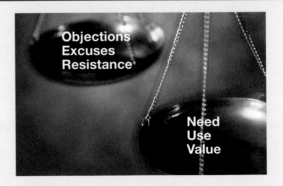

Selling positive benefits tips the scale of decision...

Objections
Excuses
Resistance

Need
Use
Value

Phase Three

Service After the Sale. The final phase of relationship selling is service after the sale. After all, one of the purposes of a business is to create and keep a customer.[9] Service, service, and more service is what counts and gives you a competitive edge. Plenty of satisfied customers do not come back unless you create some kind of trust-bond relationship. Ultimately, you should look at customer satisfaction as an economic asset just like any other asset of the company. Service after the sale must be viewed as another essential step within the sales cycle.[10] Creating customer satisfaction is an income-producing endeavor. Too many salespeople perform service mechanically, without thinking of the impact their actions have on customers. Clients must sense that you truly care about them. Service after the sale is your way of expressing appreciation for their business. Service makes the difference and is as important as the quality of the product.

Continuous Quality Improvement

There has been so much written on Total Quality Management that some have dismissed it as merely a theory that is discussed because it sounds good. But to ignore the underlying principles of TQM would not be sensible. The scope of a typical TQM program covers three main areas: 1. The quality system, 2. The process of continuous improvement, and 3. The development of the staff involved.[11] TQM is an essential building block for relationship selling, and the principles have practical implications for salespeople.[12]

How does TQM fit into relationship selling? Most organizations have a strong strategic plan in place to achieve excellence and make sales. Where they struggle is in the *execution*. Organizations get the outcomes they seek only when they successfully hardwire excellence across all operational areas, and one way to achieve this is through implementation of Total Quality Management.[13] TQM has a customer orientation, and it is an outside-in approach to business. The center of all discussions is the customer; every one inside and outside the company is a customer. Continuous quality improvement is a philosophy, an overall style of management that focuses on customer satisfaction. Federal Express CEO Fred Smith states that, "We aim for 100 percent customer satisfaction and all FedEx employees must have an 'above and beyond' attitude when doing their jobs. The attitude of doing whatever it takes to serve the customers is reflected from top to bottom in the organization's structure; this kind of spirit is integral to the FedEx work culture."[14] But even before the customers can be serviced, Smith states that, "Employee satisfaction is a prerequisite to customer satisfaction."[15] Therefore, TQM not only focuses on fostering healthy relationships with customers, but also on building connections within organizations.

The list below highlights the main points of TQM that deal directly with fostering relationships and building lasting associations. While there are variations in the language and scope of TQM programs, it is possible to target these five principles that are especially relevant in the practice of relationship selling:

1. *Listen and learn* from your customers and your employees.
2. *Continuously improve* the partnership.
3. *Build teamwork* by establishing trust and mutual respect.
4. *Do it right the first time* to ensure customer satisfaction.
5. *Improve communication* in your own company to broaden the utilization of your company's resources. Everybody is involved in the relationship.

Service Quality

What does an organization have to do to provide exceptional service quality and how does the salesperson fit into the process? First, everyone in your company must think in terms of the whole process rather than their own tasks. The goal is to develop a customer, and that's a process in which the salesperson is only one player. The process includes production people, finance and marketing people, as well as customer service reps. So it's not left to you to solve a customer's problem; the whole organization gets behind the effort. Building customer relationships is everybody's responsibility.

It is important to focus on how you relate to plant and office employees, because this can make a difference in the way they treat your customers. It pays to be liked and appreciated by staff people, especially those in sales support, credit, billing, and shipping. Take a lesson from Mark Twain, who said, "I can live for two months on a good compliment." Take a moment from time to time to compliment and thank the support people in your company for the great job they are doing.

TQM is established today thanks to the pioneering work of W. Edwards Deming. One of Deming's most important lessons is his "85-15" rule.[16] When things go wrong in the field, there is an 85 percent chance the system is at fault. Only about 15 percent of the time can the individual salesperson be blamed. TQM means the organization's culture is defined by and supports the constant attainment of customer satisfaction, through an integrated system of tools, techniques, and training. Prospects and customers notice and think about everyone they come in contact with during the sales encounter. The relationship between perceived effort and customer service is a powerful one. When you and the customer interact, the quality of the interaction itself is an important part of the relationship.[17] Exhibit 2.6 shows the dynamics of this interaction. Service quality has two dimensions: 1.The process of delivering the service, and 2. The actual outcome.

Δ **Exhibit 2.6**

The Service Quality Interaction ·

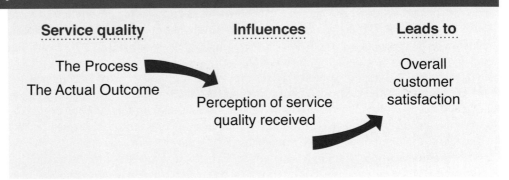

Most business success stories involve taking an old idea or product and doing a better job with it than the next company. Wal-Mart didn't invent discount selling; Sam Walton just did it better. And the executives who now run Wal-Mart are improving the way they buy and stock merchandise to drive their costs and prices even lower. Then there is Starbucks! Coffee shops have been around for a long time, but no one before Starbucks had figured out how to organize and run several thousand of them. The overall point is this: You can get a lot out of a current product or service if you change the processes around it, or change the process by which it is delivered. The objective is to change those processes enough that you are delivering more value to your customers or, at the very least, hold on to those customers by offering a fair price.

The $332,000 Customer

Tom Peters, author of *A Passion for Excellence*, says, "A customer is not a transaction; a customer is a relationship."[18] The missing link in service often is intense awareness of the customer's point of view. The process of handling the problem is as important to customers as the solution of the problem itself. The logical inference is that every company better organize its service delivery system to answer every customer's implied question: "What are you going to do for me today?"

Peters uses the example of Dallas car dealer Carl Sewell, who has written a book called *The $332,000 Customer* because a loyal lifetime Cadillac customer buys that much from him. Peters goes on to suggest that happy lifetime customers generate four or five happy lifetime customers for you. So in fact, one Cadillac customer is roughly a $1,500,000 customer. Two investments Sewell has made illustrate his understanding of the value he places on customer satisfaction. Number one, he bought a street sweeper to keep the front of his dealership extra clean. First impressions count for everything, and people judge his dealership by the cleanliness of everything including the road in front of it. Secondly, he convinced an upscale local restaurant to open a branch in his service bay. When it's a simple repair, a lot of his customers come in and enjoy a hot meal while the work is being done.

Exhibit 2.7 illustrates the kind of behavior wanted in a quality-driven sales organization and the kind that exists in the typical organization.[19] To move from left to right, use the twelve essential elements of TQM and your commitment to customer satisfaction to guide you. Some salespeople will read this and say, "This is nothing new; it is simply common sense." They are right, of course, but it has taken many years for men such as W. Edwards Deming, Joseph Juran, and Genichi Taguchi to refine and teach this philosophy.[20]

Customers for Life

Δ **Exhibit 2.7**

Culture Changes in a Sales Organization

Traditional Management Model	Total Quality Management Model
Focus on product	Focus on service
Company knows best	Customer knows best
Transactions	Relationships
Individual performance	Team performance
Firefighting management	Continuous improvement
Blame/punishment	Support/reward
Short-term (year or less)	Long-term (years)
Intolerant of errors	Allows mistakes
Autocratic leadership	Participative leadership
Bureaucratic	Entrepreneurial
Top-down decisions	Consensus decisions
Inward-focused	Outward (customer)-focused

Team Selling

Companies facing the dual problem of increasingly fierce competition and the need to increase the efficiency of sales functions are learning from the example of industries like telecommunications and pharmaceuticals. These industries have mastered the art of "bundled sales." Bundled selling is a strategy wherein companies sell a number of their products or services "bundled" together. By successfully reconfiguring their sales organizations to allow representatives to sell across many sectors, they've increased their market share and, as a result, their profitability.[21] But with this bundling of products comes a need for a larger sales team who can efficiently handle the growing packages of goods and services; and that is where team selling comes in as an indispensable force in today's aggressive market.

Team Selling is a cooperative action by two or more professionals directed to selling a product or service. The sales team often consists of at least one salesperson, supported by technical specialists, a combination that utilizes the relationship expertise of the salesperson as well as the technical competency of other personnel throughout the organization.[22] Team selling involves not only several people from the seller's company but also a purchasing team from the prospect's company. The concept of team selling balances perfectly with the principles behind TQM because team sales builds lasting relationships, breaks down walls, and opens communication through teamwork. That's why two heads really are better than one.

The team approach gains an advantage over one-on-one selling, because it utilizes the strengths of each individual on the team. Some professional salespeople may lack the patience and attention to detail that is required to eventually guide the prospect to commit. Yet, technical support people involved on the team may possess these very characteristics, as they tend to be detail-oriented by nature. Similarly, a personality that appears too abrupt in the eyes of a client may be offset by a conservative personality who can energize the client with a sense of confidence. Team selling greatly increases the chances for chemistry with the decision makers of the purchasing company.[23]

Benefits of Team Selling

A healthy team attitude begins with a solid commitment to help team members win. There is no room for prima donnas within the team. The only person who is allowed to be the prima donna is the customer.[24] One of the primary benefits of team selling is that it enables a company to improve its relationship with customers, by allowing direct communication between the buyer and product specialists before the sale is made. Thus, the seller can more accurately define the customer's needs, and the buyer can have questions answered by an individual who has an intimate knowledge of the product. This creates an aura of authority and trustworthiness for the company and the salesperson.

Imagine the technical expertise required to sell satellite time to the telecommunications industry, a service of Satellite Corporation. The needs of each client are unique, and once the sale is made, the relationship has just begun. Buyers not only want to know what the service can do for their company, but also who will be working with them after the sale is made. For these reasons, Satellite Corporation requires that all employees act as informal partners of the sales department and are expected to contribute their expertise in making all sales. Technical people, for instance, frequently accompany salespeople on calls, and the salespeople work closely with their marketing colleagues to produce the brochures, technical guides, and other materials used in setting up and closing a sale.

Team Member Roles

The sales manager should appoint the account's salesperson as the team leader, and the technical and creative experts assume supportive roles. The leader may begin, coordinate, and close the presentation, calling on specific personnel to use their expertise in amplifying certain points. Appoint a strong leader to enhance team development. The leader must have the authority to ensure that all members of the team participate and perform their assigned team duties.[25] During the presentation, technical experts must know when to contribute and when to remain silent. Team members should reinforce the leader's presentation with body language and affirmation.

Teamwork Closed a $575,000 Sale

Bill King, sales manager of Laerdal Medical Corporation in Illinois, has seen first hand the value of a well-built sales team. King had been pursuing a client, a local community college, for over a year. Rather than give up on the school and return home after a sales trip to Chicago, King made one more stop. An administrator at the college called him and said the school was still interested in looking at Laerdal's mannequins, on which the school's nursing students could practice medical procedures. During King's last contact with the prospect, he was unable to work through the college's budget limitations. So for over a year, King had his inside sales team maintain a relationship with the client via e-mail and phone calls. For months, salespeople called to persuade college officials that buying the mannequins, who start at $50,000, would place the college in the ranks of the University of Chicago for medical training. To appear sharp for each call, the sales team maintained precise conversation notes through an electronic sales tracking system. The payoff was remarkable. King returned to the school for one final demonstration—and then closed the $575,000 deal. "The most important thing was that everyone on the team worked together," he says.[26]

Guidelines for Effective Team Selling

Nalco Chemical Company is accomplished at the art of team selling. Nalco is the world's largest supplier of specialty chemicals for water treatment. They service customers in the refining, steel, and metalworking industries, as well as paper manufacturers, hospitals, universities, and food producers. Jim Scott, vice-president for corporate sales, says, "Our customers are buying applied technologies along with our chemicals, so we must also sell ourselves as experts on their businesses and manufacturing methods. Our reps have to be on-site consultants to the customers."[27]

Generally, the companies Nalco calls on have a purchasing team that usually includes the vice-president of operations, the purchasing director, and engineering reps from individual plants. Nalco counters with a team consisting of an account executive to facilitate negotiations, sales managers, general managers, marketing managers, and district sales representatives. Nalco is able to exclude technical support staff on its selling teams because its field reps are themselves engineers or technical consultants specializing in the customer's

business. Thus, they have mastered the skill of assembling knowledgeable members who are also competent team players. Exhibit 2.8 presents a number of guidelines gleaned from Nalco's approach to team selling.

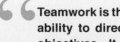 **Teamwork is the ability to work together toward a common vision. The ability to direct individual accomplishments toward organizational objectives. It is the fuel that allows common people to attain uncommon results.** 99

-Andrew Carnegie

Δ **Exhibit 2.8**

Team Selling at the Nalco Chemical Company ·

Nalco's customers have a team-like decision-making process that involves multiple stages of approval. So it is critical that Nalco needs to have a team on its side as well. At Nalco, these guidelines are essential for effective team selling:

1. Know who needs to be part of the team by studying your customer's needs.

2. Provide the customer with the necessary details.

3. Make sure you have the right mix on the team to meet needs.

4. Look for a second opinion to help you assemble the team, especially if you are new to this process.

5. Develop good relationships with team members and keep up-to-date on what each one can offer to the process.

6. The lead salesperson should be on hand for the installation to represent the team.

7. Know your own limits and call for help when it is needed.

Find a Combination That Works For You

While some companies like Nalco do have extensive teams, one very common sort of teamwork is the two-person sales call team, often made up of a sales rep and a sales manager or a sales rep and a technical expert. It is so common that many companies don't think of this as team selling.[28] There is much to gain by pairing salespeople. Such partnerships can be productive both for the individual sales reps and their companies. To illustrate how this partnering could prove beneficial, consider this illustration:

Openers and Closers. For some salespeople, their greatest skill is the ability to capture the attention and interest of prospects. This is analogous to the carnival barker whose job it is to get you inside the circus tent. We know that making a good first impression is critical to future sales success. The problem is, some salespeople lack substance and depth in subsequent meetings with a prospect, and hence can benefit by being teamed with a detail-oriented sales rep who knows how to close. Together, the opener and closer produce a winning performance.

Major-league baseball managers have a similar situation to the one just described. A manager has starting pitchers (openers) and relief pitchers (closers) on his ball club. Many of baseball's best starting pitchers average six or seven strong innings each time out. The relief pitcher then comes in and shuts down the opposing team and saves the game for the starter. Neither player is complete on his own. Together, however, they produce a winning performance.

SUMMARY

- The traditional role of selling has evolved from the art of persuasion to the psychology of relationship selling.

- The relationship cycle of selling begins with approaching the prospect, discovering needs, presenting your product or service as the solution, overcoming objections, and gaining commitment. Service after the sale completes the cycle.

- The purpose of the relationship approach to selling is to discover the needs or problems of the prospect. You become a solutions provider! It is customer-oriented and requires extensive knowledge of the prospect.

- Build relationships through customer-oriented continuous quality improvement. This is an outside-in approach, encouraging the mindset that every one inside and outside the company is a customer.

- Team selling fosters relationships by encouraging a sharing of ideas, resources, capabilities, and responsibilities.

REVIEW QUESTIONS

1. Compare and contrast the stereotype of traditional selling and professional relationship selling.

2. What questions must a salesperson answer 'yes' to before it is possible to make a recommendation to buy?

3. What is the difference between the features of the product and its benefits? Which is most useful in the selling situation? Why? Should the other, then, be mentioned at all? How?

4. Name at least three reasons why a prospect may resist making a buying decision. For each reason, tell how the salesperson could have prevented this particular type of resistance.

5. If sales resistance is encountered, how can the salesperson close the sale in spite of the resistance? Is this always synonymous with what is regarded as "hard sell"?

6. What is the purpose of service after the sale? What does it include? Whose responsibility is such service?

7. Who needs to be conversant with the organization's basic philosophy of business? If that philosophy is not understood by all members of the organization, what types of problems might result? Why?

8. To what extent must a sales rep agree with the company's commitment to continuous quality improvement?

9. What are the key principles of the Total Quality Management philosophy?

10. What is Team Selling? Is it a relatively new concept? Describe the benefits and specific guidelines for successful team selling.

ROLE-PLAY EXERCISES

The following role-play exercises help build teams, improve communication, and emphasize the "real-world" side of selling. They are meant to be challenging, to learn how to deal with problems that have no single "right" answer and to use a variety of skills beyond those employed in a typical review question. Read and complete each activity. Then in the next class, discuss and compare answers with other classmates. Have some students take the role of the salesperson, and see how they would react. Remember, *"You learn more about a person in an hour of play than in a lifetime of conversation."* – Plato

1. Think of an experience with a traditional, "hard-sell" salesperson with the class. Likewise, if you have had an experience with a relationship building salesperson, share that with the class. Discuss what you would have done differently if you had been the "hard- sell" salesperson, and then talk about the positive qualities of the relationship salesperson. Have half the class act out the role of the relationship salesperson, and then the other half pretends they are "hard-sell" salespeople. Compare and contrast both types.

2. You are in the market for a new car. Go to a local car dealer and shop for a car of your choice. Take note of whether the salesperson tries to discover your needs. Did the salesperson use an effective approach, attempt to discover your needs, or did he/she move directly to a presentation of benefits? What was your reaction to the salesperson's approach with you? Back in the class, act out the scenario, with one student playing the part of the salesperson, and discuss what the salesperson did right, and what he could have done better.

3. It's graduation time and you are looking for your first post- graduation job. Examine advertisements in magazines, newspapers, or the Internet. Choose three ads for which you believe there are follow-up salespeople and determine what features and benefits that salesperson would likely present. Then hold class interviews for a few of the positions to see if you have what it takes!

CASE STUDY

Case 2.1—Riding Out the Storm

Hargis Corporation showed 100% growth in sales its first two years in business. It was a dream come true for Bob Hargis and his partner Dan Gillette, also his son-in-law. After attending a few new seminars in relationship selling, improving their production and purchasing processes, and creating a strategic plan they were ready to "turn the world on its ear." Bob managed production and purchasing, while Dan sold the consumer products and took charge of orders and shipping for their six-person enterprise. Dan possessed basic selling skills and always believed that the relationship selling approach was the best all-around way to work with customers. Now they faced a new dilemma—the beginning of a market shift and a recession.

After losing a number of accounts during the past three months, Dan realized that he must spend more time with his most important customers and generate at least one new account each week. Both partners sensed they must make the change from relationship selling to consultative selling in order to keep their customer base and succeed. It may not be possible to grow sales 100 percent this third year; however, it was reasonable to increase business by 25 percent.

Dan's relationship sales approach included the following:

- Discover the customer's problems and needs
- Believe in himself and make a positive attitude work for him
- Hold a true conviction that his business and products are the best
- Treat people in a friendly, courteous manner at all times
- Finds things the customer and he had in common and build on this

The shift in the market, increased competition, and recession trends began taking their toll on Hargis Corporation. Regional competitors began imitating some of the best selling products and these were becoming commonplace. One competitor operated at a lower cost structure that it passed on to its customers in the form of a lower price. Dan discovered that another firm acted as a strong consultant and not merely a product presenter. The sales rep was penetrating far into his customer base and was providing better solutions to customer problems.

He could see that his sales training was inferior and he was spending too much time with the details of processing and shipping orders. Bob Hargis and Dan Gillette knew they must act quickly to survive. Two years of hard work and personal investments could not be lost. Too many people were counting on them.

1. Do you think a good salesperson should be able to change selling approaches?
2. Would you recommend using a consultative approach as an extension of relationship selling?
3. What could the company do to make the transition as soon as possible with in-house and outside training?

Case 2.2 - Recipe for Sales

The Supreme Cookware Company has been in business for more than forty years. After a slow start, it became a leader in its field, but its record in recent years has been one of steady decline. The number of its accounts has been shrinking, and the sales volume of the average account has been declining as well. An outside consulting firm was brought in to study the firm's situation and to determine, if possible, the reasons for its difficulties. After careful research, this firm reported that Supreme had fallen behind in styling. Consequently, dealers were reluctant to carry its line. In implementing the suggestions of the consulting firm, Supreme made a careful market study to discover how best to correct its deficiencies. As a result, a completely new and modern line of cookware was developed. They also decided to begin a strong marketing campaign to introduce the new line and to reestablish the reputation of the company. One executive was unhappy with the study. He raised the question of revitalizing the sales force and pointed out that most of the salespeople had been with the firm for two decades or more. Perhaps some or much of the firm's trouble stemmed from the fact that the sales staff had aged perceptibly and no longer had the energy or drive to go out and sell. He suggested that the firm release many of its older salespeople and bring in new blood.

This suggestion precipitated a near-violent argument, as the sales manager defended his staff. He emphasized that his salespeople had proved their ability in earlier years and that they would be successful with the new line if given a chance to show what they could do. How could they have been productive selling a line with admitted deficiencies? The first executive argued that good salespeople should be able to sell anything. He said further that if the salespeople had really been communicating with their customers, they would have realized the problems the customers had with the cookware line and reported it to the company.

1. Do you think a good salesperson should be able to sell anything?
2. Do you think the sales manager was right in defending his staff so courageously?
3. What could the company do to aid salespeople in achieving success in selling the new cookware line?

Cultivating an Ethics Climate
and Developing Communication Skills

CHAPTER
4

CHAPTER
3

CHAPTER
5

Few professions give you more opportunities for rejection on a daily basis than does the field of sales. Because of the often-cutthroat nature of selling, some salespeople do whatever it takes to stay ahead and edge out the competition. Chapter 3 discusses the need for a strong ethical and moral character to sustain a sales career. Honest and caring service brings customers back and assures success. Success in professional selling also depends upon your ability to have a productive exchange of information with prospects and customers.

The more you understand about prospects and their decision-making process, the more readily you can discover what they need and want, and this is covered in more detail in chapter 4. Because success in relationship selling depends on accurately getting your message across to prospects, chapter 4 also describes how to break through communication barriers.

An especially useful tool for gaining insight into how the prospect is thinking is knowledge of the social styles model, which is discussed in chapter 5. A social style is the way a person sends and receives information. It is a method for finding the best way to approach a prospect and to set up a working relationship with that person. The chapters included in this section are:

3. Ethical and Legal Issues in Selling
4. Purchase Behavior and Communication
5. Finding Your Selling Style

"It's OK, Kid, Everybody Does It"
by Jack Griffin

When Johnny was 6 years old, he was with his father when they were caught speeding. His father handed the officer a twenty-dollar bill with his driver's license. "It's OK, son," his father said as they drove off. "Everybody does it."

When he was 8, he was present at a family council presided over by Uncle George, on the surest means to shave points off the income tax return. "It's OK, kid," his uncle said. "Everybody does it."

When he was 9, his mother took him to his first theater production. The box office man couldn't find any seats until his mother discovered an extra $5 in her purse. "It's OK, son," she said. "Everybody does it."

When he was 12, he broke his glasses on the way to school. His Aunt Francine persuaded the insurance company that they had been stolen and they collected $75. "It's OK, son," she said. "Everybody does it."

When he was 15, he made right guard on the high school football team. His coach showed him how to block and at the same time grab the opposing end by the shirt so the official couldn't see it. "It's OK, son," the coach said. "Everybody does it."

When he was 16, he took his first summer job at the supermarket. His assignment was to put the overripe strawberries in the bottom of the boxes and the good ones on top where they would show. "It's OK, son," the manager said. "Everybody does it."

When he was 18, Johnny and a neighbor applied for a college scholarship. Johnny was a marginal student. His neighbor was in the top 3 percent of his class, but couldn't play right guard. Johnny got the scholarship. "It's OK, son," his parents said. "Everybody does it."

When he was 19, he was approached by an upperclassman who offered the test answers for $50. "It's OK, kid," he said. "Everybody does it."

Johnny was caught and sent home in disgrace."How could you do this to your mother and me?" his father said. "You never learned anything like this at home." His aunt and uncle were also shocked.

If there's one thing the adult world can't stand, it's a kid who cheats.

Ethical and Legal Issues in Selling

LEARNING OBJECTIVES

- Develop principles upon which to base ethical behavior.

- Identify the sources of influence on ethics and ethical behavior.

- Understand your role in maintaining the ethical position of the organization and simultaneously behaving in an ethical manner toward customers.

- Discover what loyalty to the company requires in the event that your employers may be involved in questionable ethical behavior.

- Recognize the implications of federal and local laws regarding ethical standards.

One of most the significant books published in the area of business ethics is *The Power of Ethical Management*. Written by Dr. Kenneth Blanchard and Dr. Norman Vincent Peale, this book is of special significance for salespeople who are on the firing line between their customers and clients.

Few individuals have had as great an impact on successful company management as has Kenneth Blanchard, co-author of *The One Minute Manager* and *The One Minute Manager Library*. Dr. Blanchard is the founder of a management consulting firm, Blanchard Training and Development Inc., in Escondido, California.

Dr. Norman Vincent Peale was the author of thirty-four books. *The Power of Positive Thinking* is one of the most widely circulated books ever published. It has been translated into forty languages and has enjoyed sales of over twenty million copies. He was also the founder of the monthly magazine *Guideposts*, which has a circulation of sixteen million.

The basic message of *The Power of Ethical Management* is simple: You don't have to cheat to win! Blanchard and Peale tell us that many people demand immediate tangible evidence that ethical conduct works, but such evidence is often not available. In fact, you may actually get farther in the short run by cheating. But in the long run, where it really counts, you never gain by unethical conduct. They remind us that "nice guys may appear to finish last, but usually they're running in a different race." Unethical behavior occurs in sales because people forget the real purpose of professional selling—to fill the needs of others.

Salespeople sometimes say near the end of the day, "I ought to make one more sales call before I go home. I wonder who I might be able to see this late?" Blanchard and Peale suggest that the better question might be, "I wonder if there is someone else I can help before I go home?" When salespeople focus on their purpose—solving the problems of clients and helping customers be more successful and more profitable—they understand the need for ethical behavior. Cheating, lying, and short-changing the customer on service may bring a satisfactory profit today, but is a sure way to court failure for the future.

A Question of Ethics

Erin Hood feels as though she is being torn apart. The pharmaceutical company she works for is pressuring her to meet a sales quota twenty percent higher than last year's. She is a single parent with two children to support, and she sees an opportunity to meet her sales quota if she can beat out a competitor for a large order from a drugstore chain. She is tempted to plant some carefully worded negative comments about the competitor in the ear of the store chain's purchasing agent. What should she do? What would you do?

Erin is facing a situation that falls in the category of ethical considerations. Because salespeople are relatively free and independent operators, they may encounter more ethical dilemmas than many other business people. For this reason, you must be clear on your own ethical standards before getting caught up in something that escalates beyond your control.

Ethics is an old subject, but it is certainly not worn out. The Greek philosophers, for example, suggested that, "A merchant does better to take a loss than to make a dishonest profit." And as Rob Roy once said, "Honor is a gift man gives himself."[1] A loss may be momentarily painful, but dishonesty does irreparable damage. America is reeling from the shocking, unethical, and immoral activities of a variety of business and government leaders and other public figures. It is not companies, institutions and political organizations, however, that are unethical; individual people are unethical. Ethics is a personal matter. The ethics of a business, government, or other organizations is merely a reflection of the combined value systems of its members.

Business ethics is an aspect of societal ethics. Traditional values seem to have given way to a widespread sense of "anything goes," and "sell at any cost," seemed the mantra the early salesperson in the U.S. learned.[2] Look at what we parade in front of people, implying approval, in the media and society: sexual allure, constant violence, conspicuous consumption, the soft life, "reach for all the gusto you can," and enjoy life now. As a result, many Americans want immediate personal gratification and will act in whatever manner seems to promise it. Business ethics in selling has been under attack—and for good reason. Almost every day seems to bring new revelations of corporate malfeasance, accounting fraud, and business conflicts of interest.[3]

Some say that business ethics is an *oxymoron*, a contradiction in terms. They suggest that business has no ethics or that ethics is something that people worry about on Sunday and not when they are out selling in the real world.[4] This thinking is ludicrous! The notion that honest salespeople finish last is poisonous, and it is untrue. Unethical behavior is self-destructive; it generates more unethical conduct until a person hits rock bottom financially, spiritually, and morally.

"THE GOVERNMENT AND I DISAGREED ON WHAT ETHICS ARE EXACTLY."

Used with permission from The Boxcar Millionaire.[5]

The Origin of Ethics

A *legal* standard is enforced by laws and statutes, but an *ethical standard* is an outgrowth of the customs and attitudes of a society. Most of us have a shared idea of what we mean by ethics, but defining it in a way that everyone would accept is hard. Essentially, ethics is a systematic effort to judge human behavior as right or wrong in terms of two major criteria: Truth and Justice.

The root of the word ethics derives from the Greek word *ethos*, which means the character or sentiment of the community. A society cannot exist unless people agree fundamentally on what is right and wrong, just and unjust. Without shared norms of behavior, we would have anarchy in our political system and chaos in our daily lives. If we consider the United States to be our larger community, our ethical standards have been influenced philosophically by "Greco-Roman thought, by the Judaic and Christian religions, by Enlightenment philosophy, and by the Scientific Revolution."[6] The three most important value-forming institutions in America are family, church, and school. Many people believe that the decreasing strength and changing roles of these three institutions have produced a society with lower ethical standards than those of its earlier history.

The Bases for Ethical Systems

Philosophers and ethicists point to two systems to describe ethical thinking. The first of these is the *deontological* base, the use of specifically stated rules, for example, the Ten Commandments or the Golden Rule. Some believe these rules come from a higher power, some think the rules are intuitive, and still others hold that the rules are discovered by using reason.

The second system of describing ethical systems is the *teleological* approach. This system defines right and wrong in terms of end results. A study reported by Dr. Thomas Wotruba found that marketing executives' response to ethical problems is predominantly utilitarian.[7] The utilitarian model falls under this category and is illustrated by the idea proposed in the nineteenth century by Jeremy Benthem that society's goal is to produce "the greatest good for the greatest number." This approach says that in trying to determine a course of action in an ethical dilemma, the individual should assess what good or harm would come to the parties involved and follow the course of action that would have the most positive results for the most people.

Above all, "to thine own self be true." – Shakespeare

With these two bases consciously or unconsciously affecting us, we can expect to experience ambivalent attitudes when faced with making ethical decisions. In the best seller, *The Closing of the American Mind*, Allan Bloom theorized that much of our moral and ethical ambivalence comes from family and educational system teachings in which almost everything is relative, in which there are no moral absolutes. He says that, "the family's moral training comes down to inculcating the bare minimum of social behavior, not lying or stealing, and produces university students who can say nothing more about the ground of their moral actions than 'If I did that to him, he could do it to me,' an explanation that does not even satisfy those who utter it."[8]

Guidelines for Ethical Behavior

Today, no matter which specific method of ethical decision-making is followed, most Americans embrace three basic guidelines: Universal nature, truth telling, and responsibility for one's actions. Without them, the free enterprise system itself would be threatened and any kind of business exchange would be difficult. Our society would disintegrate into a "dog-eat-dog" environment.

Universal Nature. The universal nature guideline is a derivation of the Golden Rule. We want others to play by the same basic rules by which we would play in a similar situation. This guideline sets up a basic level of trust between people and makes life predictable.

Truth Telling. A salesperson needs to believe that what others say is true. The idea of honesty may originate in a set of rules we have been taught, but truth telling makes sense on purely logical grounds as well. Trust facilitates cooperation, buyer commitment, and the development and maintenance of long-term, client-salesperson relationships.[9]

It's not always simple to be truthful with prospects. At times, it is easier to tell a little white lie if it means setting up the all-important face-to-face interview or getting a commitment over the phone. For that reason, some salespeople's "techniques" when cold calling have become entrenched in lies. Have you ever received a call from a telemarketer who told you he was calling to take a survey, only to discover moments later that this was his way of keeping you on the phone long enough to explain why he was really calling and what he was selling?[10] Some might say this technique is acceptable; but the truth is, that salesperson lied to you. Would you trust someone who lies in his or her first conversation with you? Of course not—and neither will your prospects.

Responsibility for Your Actions. President Harry S. Truman kept a sign on his desk stating, "The buck stops here." He reminded himself that he had no one to blame when things went wrong. Individuals may choose to live by this attitude and accept personal responsibility for their actions, or they may attempt to follow the impulse of the moment and blame someone else for the consequences. If we and society demonstrated a higher level of trust and credibility based on a willingness to accept responsibility for personal actions, our system would work more efficiently and in a less suspicious atmosphere.

Influences on a Salesperson's Ethics

Although individual salespeople each have a basic value system and may know what is right and wrong, they encounter many new influences and experience many new pressures on the job. Nothing creates more direction for employee's decision-making, or a better balance for judgment than ethical guidelines.[11] Knowing in advance what can be expected and having a feel for how to balance and integrate them into a personal code of ethics make handling ethical decisions easier.

Company Code of Ethics

Many companies have codes of ethics; some companies adhere strictly to the code as part of corporate culture and may have ethics training for new employees and an ethics committee to rule on ethical dilemmas. A recent study examined the relationships among ethics code awareness, perceived corporate ethical values, and organizational commitment. Two key findings emerged. First, those aware of the existence of an ethics code in their organizations viewed their organizations as having more ethical values than those not aware of an ethics code. Second, respondents showed higher levels of commitment when they were aware of an ethics code in their companies. The results suggest that ethics codes may lead to higher levels of commitment by increasing the belief that their organizations have strong ethical values, as long as the existence of these codes are adequately communicated.[12]

Exhibit 3.1 is a brief overview of the United Professional Sales Association's Ethical Code of Conduct.[13] The UPSA is an organization of member-based sales professionals whose overall mission is "advancing the profession of sales." They have designed an entire Ethics Selling Framework upon which its members must abide; it reflects best practices and points out what is not permissible in today's business climate. The fundamental principles of the Framework are of a general nature and provide excellent guidelines for the buying-selling experience. Members agree to uphold the intent of the Code of Conduct, Ethical Code, and a Professional Buyer's Bill of Rights. These types of ethical practices and codes are becoming more commonplace as organizations with large sales forces see the need to improve and build on mutual trust between their prospects and their salespeople.

△ **Exhibit 3.1**

The USPA Ethical Code of Conduct

- **I will maintain high standards of integrity and professional conduct.**

- **I will accept responsibility for my actions.**

- **I will continually seek to enhance my professional capabilities.**

- **I will practice with fairness and honesty.**

- **I will encourage others in the profession to act in an ethical and professional manner.**

Federal sentencing guidelines have been established that reduce punitive damages based in part on what a company has done to prevent ethical problems.[14] Driven by these government actions and fear of retribution, companies are paying more attention than ever to the behavior of their employees. Ethics is a monetary issue as well! A survey conducted by the Center for Business Ethics at Bentley College reports that of two hundred seventy nine top U.S. companies responding to the questionnaire, 208 had written codes of conduct and 99 had formal training programs in ethics for their employees. Seventeen had telephone "hot lines" to assist employees with ethical problems. Typical issues covered in these ethics programs for salespeople include:

1. The use of expense accounts.

2. The appropriateness of gift giving.

3. Dealing with a prospect's unethical demands.

4. Promises made to clients about product performance or delivery.

Some companies are as thorough and exacting in implementing a code of ethics, but others keep their codes buried in filing cabinets; still others have no formal code of any kind. Implementing a code of conduct statement communicates to salespeople—and their customers—that companies have high moral standards. In addition, organizations can gain several benefits when they adhere to a core set of ethical values embodied in a code of conduct, such as:[15]

Greater Motivation Among Co-Workers. Although many employers have yet to fully recognize the significance of staff morale, in a recent U.S. survey, 94 percent of responding employees declared company ethics to be an important, if not critical, aspect to their working lives.

A Demonstrated Respect for the Law. When top management makes a formal commitment to endorse an ethical company culture, the subject becomes of greater significance and, consequently, the company's personnel pay more attention to compliance with the laws and regulations affecting the organization.

Protection of the Company's Reputation. In the eyes of the consumer and the general public, companies are responsible for the activities undertaken by all of the partners with whom they deal, including customers and suppliers. A company culture based on solid ethical standards contributes to preserving and improving the company's reputation.

Improved Business Relationships. Due to recent pressures exerted by investors, consumers, and human rights groups, advertising campaigns have been launched to boycott the products of certain companies that were accused of not adopting ethical standards. From this perspective, a clearly defined ethical culture is a useful way to choose business partners with which long-term ties are desired.

The findings of a recent survey by the Ethics Resource Center and the Society for Human Resources Management show widespread usage of ethics statements: 84 percent of surveyed companies have codes of conduct, and 45 percent have ethics offices. These guidelines can only be effective if sales managers are reinforcing them on a daily basis-traveling with reps, guiding them through the sales process, and engaging them in open, honest dialogue.[16] As a salesperson, you need to know where the company stands and whether its stand is consistent with your own. And the time to do this is before you're hired, not after.

Perhaps in response to growing ethical problems, some leading companies have openly profiled themselves as socially responsible. The new term that is being widely used is "corporate social responsibility" (CSR). The framework of CSR focuses on the actions undertaken to display conformity to principled standards for both management and salespeople. CSR focuses on the managerial processes needed to monitor, meet, and even exceed, ethical norms. Reportedly, the proper use of CSR can generate increased stakeholder support for companies.[17]

Executives as Role Models

The likelihood that unacceptable selling practices will occur has more to do with how executives behave. If a sales manager gives the impression that you must do anything possible to make more sales, salespeople infer that dealing unethically is acceptable in order to succeed. More than anything an organization's culture influences sales reps behavior with clients. Dr. Eli Jones, co-director of the *Program for Excellence in Selling* at the University of Houston, says, "Sales managers must emphasize ethical selling behavior in words and actions."[18]

The company's top executives must keep in check the pressure the managers put on their salespeople. If the CEO comes around once a year with a pep talk on moral behavior but proceeds the rest of the year to use underhanded methods of doing business, salespeople get a mixed message. When individuals are confronted with ethical dilemmas, they draw on some various sources for guidance in making decisions. Salespeople's decisions are guided by organizational policies, codes, rules and norms, as well as interactions with other people in the organization.

> **"As a manager the important thing is not what happens when you are there, but what happens when you are not there."**
> **-Dr. Kenneth Blanchard**

Ethical conflict may arise when salespeople's ethical values differ from those perceived to be held by their immediate supervisor or top management. Here are some ideas to consider that may foster ethical behavior within an organization:[19]

- Codes of ethics that are effectively communicated are likely to result in greater ethical behavior.

- The presence and enforcement of codes of ethics have been found to be associated with higher levels of ethical behavior.

- Corporate goals and stated policies strongly influence managers' decisions on whether to act ethically or unethically.

- When a climate is created where ethical values and behaviors are fostered, supported, and rewarded, more ethical behavior will exist.

Examples Set by Colleagues and Competitors

A salesperson sometimes discovers that colleagues and/or competitors are acting unethically. Imagine that you are riding in a cab one day, and a colleague asks the driver to provide a receipt for expense account purposes and to indicate a figure higher than the actual fare. As an observer, do you join in the activity, rebuke the colleague, report the colleague (commonly called blowing the whistle), or ignore it? A customer reports that a competitor has said you have an alcohol problem and are therefore undependable. Do you simply deny the charge, or do you retaliate by making detrimental remarks about your competitor?

Often, a whistleblower who quits or is fired can find another good job. Some employers are happy to hire workers who demonstrate such a strong commitment to high ethical standards. Nevertheless, there is no guarantee of employment, especially in a slow market. The whistleblower may lose seniority and retirement benefits, and must often move to another city. The needs of family members must be considered. Moreover, the whistleblower frequently lacks the team spirit that many employers prize, but instead comes across as a complainer or fanatic.[20]

The Bottom Line

One of the most powerful influences on salespeople is profits—their own and those of the company. Saul Gellerman, in explaining why good people can make poor ethical choices, says that "contrary to popular mythology, maximizing profits is a company's second priority—not its first. The first is ensuring its survival."[21] Its survival will surely be compromised if salespeople take casual views of the legal and ethical implications of their behavior. The company's short-term profits may be maximized by unethical behavior, but the company's very existence could be threatened if it were hit with huge fines or an unwanted exposure in the media. Although short-term profits are important for both the company and its salespeople, the long-term success and good name of the company must always be the first priority.

Do what is right regardless.

Groupthink and Gamesmanship

Groupthink refers to the pressure exerted on salespeople to be part of the group and not to buck the system—to be team players, no matter what. Being a team player is good if the team has ethical goals and plays by ethical rules, but if the group's thinking runs afoul of your own personal code of ethics, you must weigh your options carefully. Psychologist Irving L. Janis warns against "groupthink," which he suggests can cause flawed judgment.[22]

Unfortunately there are examples of groupthink in every profession, and the pharmaceutical industry has not been spared its share of such activity. Two salespeople and three pharmacists pleaded guilty to their roles in a scheme involving the illegal sales of drug samples to pharmacies in New Jersey and New York. The operation generated more than a $1 million in illicit profits for all the parties involved. The salespeople, former Procter & Gamble reps, stole samples from doctors' offices and sold them to the pharmacists.[23] They also paid doctors and office personnel to obtain supplies. Here a number of people conspired to cheat others and somehow convinced themselves that what they were doing was all right. After all, if others in the industry were engaging in similar activity, making money at it, and not getting caught, then why shouldn't they? Groupthink is the same force that is called peer pressure when applied to teenagers.[24]

Gamesmanship is becoming totally caught up in winning simply for the sheer joy of victory and a dislike of losing. Much of our culture nurtures this type of competitive spirit—from winning the high school football game to beating a friend at chess or golf. The typical gamesman in selling looks for shortcuts and is willing to use any technique to sell a product or service. To the gamesman, winning means doing whatever is necessary to make the sale.

One case study demonstrated that, in numerous circumstances, salespeople and staff in a hostile workplace full of a gamesmanship mentality simply used their feelings in order to survive. The study showed irrational emotions being used as strategic tools of defense against a vindictive, aggressive, and hostile work place.[25] The dangers of gamesmanship are quite clear—the temptation to cross over the line into unethical or illegal behavior.

Developing a Personal Code of Ethics

Clearly many competing forces that influence a salesperson's decisions have an ethical dimension. Situations often arise in which a clear right or wrong is not easily apparent and discretion in behavior is up to the individual. Because the influences that come to bear upon a salesperson do not always agree and because conflicting demands are numerous, each salesperson must develop a personal code of ethics that supersedes all other claims.

Responsibility to Self

In the final analysis, the still, small voice of conscience is the arbiter of conflicting ethical claims. It provides the ability to say that you have made the best decision under the circumstances and take full responsibility for it. If you have personal integrity, then you cannot be dishonest with others—company, competitors, or customers.

Responsibility to the Company

Salespeople sometimes rationalize that cheating here or there in dealing with the company would not hurt. After all, the company makes lots of money and what you do would never be noticed. Several areas particularly lend themselves to temptations to be less than ethical.

Accuracy in Expense Accounts. Often padding expense accounts is relatively easy. A salesperson can add extra mileage, submit charges for a meal that was actually eaten at a friend's house, or take friends out to dinner and report the charge as entertaining customers. Tennessee Valley Authority officials discovered that about fifty TVA nuclear power employees conspired with hotel and motel representatives to bilk rate payers through travel expenses over several years to the tune of over $189,000.[26] Falsification of expense accounts is unethical and can lead to dismissal if detected. As a practical matter, it unnecessarily increases the costs of the company and may put it at a competitive disadvantage.

Honesty in Using Time and Resources. The temptation to do some shopping between sales calls, to linger over a third cup of coffee in a restaurant, and to sleep late in a hotel room are examples of ways a salesperson may misuse time. No time card is punched, and slipping in personal time may be relatively easy. This ultimately hurts both the salesperson and the company because fewer sales calls are made. It is estimated that losses of goods and cash to worker theft have reached an estimated $120 billion a year.[27] Misusing resources such as automobiles and selling samples for one's own profit hurt the company.

Accuracy in Filling Out Order Forms. Certain kinds of compensation plans, particularly contests, may cause salespeople to withhold or delay orders or to oversell some items. This practice ultimately hurts the company because it results in unhappy customers. It also takes unfair advantage of co-workers who compete fairly to win contests.

Representing the Company. The salesperson is the spokesperson for the company and for that reason must accurately represent products and services and deliver the kind of follow-up service that the company promises. Exaggerating the capabilities of a product or failing to point out any problems that might be associated with its use is unethical and can be disastrous to a long-term relationship with a customer. In some instances, it is also illegal, with the potential for causing both the salesperson and the company serious legal consequences. In addition, a company that prides itself on service to customers will be sorely disappointed with a salesperson who makes a sale and neglects to check with the customer about any additional service needs.

Responsibility to Competitors

Being honest and refraining from taking unfair advantage are the basic guidelines when dealing with competitors. Making untrue, derogatory comments about competitors or their products is poor business. At the very least, the legal implications of this behavior simply make the risks too great. In the same sense, pumping a competitor's salesperson for information at a trade show in order to steal their customers is not ethical. Some salespeople go so far as to use sabotage, espionage, and dirty tricks to gain unfair advantage over a competitor. These tactics include hiding the competitor's products on a display shelf and planting "spies" in a business to hear their sales presentation. Persuading a customer to put out a fake request for bids to see what bids competitors would submit is another unfair tactic sometimes practiced. The basic theme in this area is to gain customers fairly and squarely by providing quality products and superior service.

Responsibility to Customers

Behaving honestly and providing quality information and services are the primary ingredients for establishing mutually satisfying relationships with customers. Fortunately, the stereotype of the silver-tongued, flattering, deceptive, door-to-door salesperson of the past is disappearing. Still, many opportunities for unethical tactics exist.

Overselling or Misrepresenting Products or Services. Some salespeople persuade customers to buy more than they need because the salesperson needs to meet a quota or wants to win a trip to the Caribbean. Overselling eventually catches up with the salesperson because customers realize that they have more than they need. In addition, repeat sales probably won't be possible for a very long time.

Lying about the capabilities of a product, the date the company can make delivery, or the nature of the warranty are all unethical ways to win a quick sale while running the risk of legal action or a permanent loss of the customer in the long run.

Keeping Confidences. Because of the relationship between the salesperson and the customer, the salesperson may be privy to valuable information. That information could be very useful to some other customer, and providing it might ingratiate the salesperson with the new customer. Failing to keep confidences is, of course, unethical, and eventually it results in a reputation for the salesperson as an untrustworthy gossip. The word "salesperson" has, for a lot of people, come to suggest a less-than-honest person, and many consumers have been burned by the unethical behavior of a salesperson. To break through this stigma and have an open, honest dialogue requires that salespeople pass two tests shortly after they walk in the door. First, they must make the prospect comfortable. Second, salespeople must pass the "credibility" test. One of the best tools for creating credibility is a story—an example of how the salesperson helped someone like the prospect solve a similar problem.[28]

Gift Giving. Although giving a customer a token gift as a thank-you or as a reminder of the salesperson and the company is customary, the intent with which a gift is given usually reveals its ethical or unethical nature. If a gift is a way to get business or a bribe, then it is unethical and may well be illegal. Sometimes a salesperson may even give an "under-the-table" gift in order to secure an order.[29] The value of the gift in comparison to the sale is also something to consider. According to *Business & Incentives* magazine, approximately $3.5 billion is spent on business gifts yearly. Most companies usually spend around $25 on gifts, because it can be tax deductible as business expenses.[30]

Entertaining Clients. Policies regarding entertainment are similar to those that cover gift giving. In some industries entertaining a client with a meal, an excursion, or tickets to the theater or a football game is customary. If the intent is as a means of saying thank-you to a customer or of developing a more personal relationship, entertainment may be acceptable and even expected. Finding out the rules of behavior in a particular industry and within an individual company is important. For instance, the United States government has a code of conduct letting executive-branch officials know precisely what is ethical regarding free lunches-corruption begins with the fifth lunch out. A bureaucrat can dine at the expense of a lobbyist or journalist provided the meal does not exceed $25. One official can only eat four times a year on any one organization's tab. The fifth one is unethical.[31]

Operating in a Global Environment

Salespeople today may operate not only in the United States but also in a foreign country where norms of behavior may be different. Which morality should salespeople follow, their own or that of the country in which they find themselves? In the General Dynamics twenty-page code of ethics, the company instructs its sales force what to do in this event: "In countries where common practice might indicate acceptance of conduct lower than that to which we aspire, salespeople will follow the company's standards."[32] In some countries, "grease" or "speed" money makes the wheels of a government agency or a company move faster. In Japan, there is much gift giving in business relationships, and it is viewed as a time-honored tradition rather than a bribe. A company usually has guidelines for an employee to follow in a foreign country, but bribery is universally condemned and is in fact illegal whether it is practiced at home or abroad.

Americans selling overseas must abide by both United States law and the laws of the countries in which they sell. Patronage or payments to people in exchange for favors that would be considered bribes in America are the accepted way of doing business in many countries. Operating as a free and independent agent in a foreign country can be extremely difficult. To ease operations in countries with customs much different from the United States, most companies align themselves with a local company or agent who can deal with ethical and cultural issues and cut a path through foreign laws and bureaucracy.

Ethics and Job Tenure

When is it time to look for a new job? Of course, you want to be affiliated with a company of which you as a salesperson can be proud. Disagreements or issues of unethical behavior on the part of the company may, however, emerge during your employment. Deciding how to handle conflicts involving ethics can be stressful because your decision may mean either your termination or resignation. Weigh the options carefully and determine who is being helped and who is being hurt. Are there any alternative, creative options that minimize risk and allow career and conscience to be reconciled?

Whistle-Blowing

According to Nancy R. Hauserman, "In the pursuit of the goals of productivity and consumption, we have failed to preserve individual and community values. The individual has been reduced to a cog in the corporate wheel, a capital investment, a corporate property."[33] This attitude can make salespeople feel unimportant and fear that their ideas, suggestions, or revelations are not valid. This reaction is particularly true if they attempt to pass on valuable information to superiors and are rebuffed.

Consider the following scenario:

Six months ago Jim Duerr started a job with an industrial supplier selling valves for acid lines. A safety engineer at a chemical company has noticed that the secondary lining on the valve is not strong enough to keep acid from splattering in the event that the internal seal fails.

Jim informed the appropriate people at his company that a major safety problem has been revealed to him, but they told him to keep selling the valves with no modifications.

What should someone like Jim Duerr do?

In Jim's situation, a number of options could be considered:

- Negotiate and build consensus for a change in management's views.
- File away a memo that explains that he was outranked when he brought up the problem.
- Blow the whistle on the company.
- Ignore the whole situation and continue selling.
- Look for another job.

As careful as a salesperson may be when joining a company, an ethical dilemma such as this may arise eventually. In the best of all possible worlds, the violation should be exposed and those responsible punished, but what if pointing a finger at someone would cause the whistle-blower to be fired and put self and family in financial difficulties?

On the surface, the wiser course appears to be to keep quiet and let the problem resolve itself. Sometimes the best policy is to keep quiet until solid evidence can be accumulated or until the co-conspirators are identified, but silence as a long-term strategy is indefensible. The violation is likely to be exposed at some point, and being part of a cover-up is not a desirable position. Inaction can even be grounds for legal action.

We all naturally desire a positive work environment, and most people do not like to have disagreements with their bosses or co-workers. Nor do people want to be branded as a "rat" or somehow disloyal to the company by revealing unethical practices. So, when should you blow the whistle, and when should you "keep quiet?" Here are some basic guidelines to use when deciding if a situation merits whistleblowing.[34] These guidelines may not be applicable to every situation you encounter, but they are a good place to start:

Probability of Effect. The probability that the action will actually take place and will cause harm to many people must be considered. An employee should be sure that the action in question will actually happen. The employee must then have absolute proof that the event will occur and that harm will be done.

Temporal Immediacy. An employee must consider the length of time between the present and the possibly harmful event. An employee must also consider the urgency of the problem in question. The more immediate the consequences of the potentially unethical practice, the stronger the case for whistleblowing.

Concentration of Effort. A person must determine the intensity of the unethical practice or behavior. The question is how much intensity does the specific infraction carry. For example, according to this principle, stealing $1,000 from one person is more unethical than stealing $1 from 1,000 people.

How the Company Treats the Salesperson

The company may treat its salespeople as partners joined with it in a common mission or simply regard them as cannon fodder out in the field. Salespeople are an extremely valuable resource to a company and deserve to be treated fairly, informed of decisions affecting them, and protected from situations in which they might be under pressure to make unethical decisions.

Glenn Wilson discusses what companies can do to prevent unethical behavior among salespeople.[35]

- Avoid setting up management-incentive systems in a way that makes fudging the data tempting.

- Be accessible to salespeople in order to get early warnings on troublesome developments.

- Set up appropriate controls not only on financial accounts but also in customer complaints, salesperson dissatisfaction, and expense accounts.

- Set sales goals that are motivating but not impossible to achieve.

If salespeople know that their ideas are important and their judgment valued, they feel ownership in the organization and want to do a better job overall. Companies like Southwest Airlines and Levi Strauss have adapted to this new reality that workers need to feel valuable, so they are treating their employees not as forces to be controlled but as individuals to be empowered, in order to unshackle their skills, talents and potential.

At Levi Strauss, for example, the predominant vision is that customer value comes from the values of its employees. That's why one-third of a manager's raise can depend on how well he or she lives up to the company's value-based philosophy.[36]

Managing the Sales Territory

One of the most excruciating decisions that salespeople face is that concerning territories. A salesperson may have spent years cultivating customers in a territory and then have it divided by management or even taken away. A key account that is the salesperson's bread and butter may be made a house account so that the salesperson no longer gets those commissions. One of the common e-commerce blunders is that companies do not consider the impact of their Web strategies on sales force compensation.

The most important thing is to involve your sales reps in the decision and treat them in a straightforward manner. That's exactly what Tupperware Corporation did when it began selling its household products on its Web site. According to Christine Hanneman, "our salespeople are involved in all of our channels, including our Web site."[37] Customers who purchase the Tupperware products on the company's Web site are asked who referred them, and the referring salesperson gets the normal commission.

Other aspects of fair treatment are involved in firing, demotion, and payment. When salespeople must be fired or demoted, they should be told the real reason. Decisions concerning compensation for salespeople should be handled with kid gloves, especially if reductions are forthcoming. In addition, decreasing compensation calls for careful, ethical decision making; such action is, moreover, extremely demoralizing and may lead to losing salespeople who will cost the company money to replace and retrain.

Sexual Harassment

A number of prominent sexual harassment cases have made the news in recent years. Perhaps the most famous was the case involving Anita Hill and Supreme Court Justice Clarence Thomas. In today's legal environment, any institution's failure to recognize the consequences of workplace sexual harassment can be a capital blunder. For employees in organizations lacking sound policy practices, the negative impact from sexual harassment—including liability, embarrassment and lost productivity—can be extensive. Title VII of The Civil Rights Act of 1964 strictly prohibits sexual harassment.[38] The Equal Employment Opportunity Commission (EEOC) defines sexual harassment this way:

"Unwelcome sexual advances, requests for sexual favors, and other verbal or physical conduct of a sexual nature constitutes sexual harassment when submission to or rejection of the conduct explicitly or implicitly affects an individual's employment, unreasonably interferes with an individual's work performance or creates an intimidating, hostile or offensive work environment."

Sexual Harassment in Action

Read the following true-life situation and imagine what you would do if you were in Sue's position.

"Yes sir, I'll schedule that with our driver for a Tuesday delivery," Sue said to the customer on the line, making a note of the request on her pad. "You're welcome," she responded to the customer's appreciative "Thank you." But before she could put the phone down, another line began flashing. "Customer service, Sue speaking," her voice sang out into the receiver. "How can I help you?"

While Sue was busy listening to the customer's request, Mike, her boss, came up behind her. He dropped a piece of paper on her desk and quickly left. He was bending over with laughter. Sue recognized the paper as the company's standard performance appraisal. The scale ran from one to five, with one representing "unacceptable" and five saying "exceeds expectations." In the section where Mike was to fill in the key duties of her job and rank them, he had written the following:

Face = 3; Breasts = 1; Butt = 5; and Legs = 3

Sue's face turned red and her teeth clenched in anger as she tried to maintain her composure. When the customer came back on the line, she strained to keep a smile in her voice.

The situation just described is one of 36 authentic workplace incidents on sexual harassment documented by Dr. N. Elizabeth Fried in her book, *Sex, Laws, and Stereotypes*. How would you handle such a situation if it were reported to you? What would you expect Sue to do? Would it make any difference if Sue had been a male receptionist and Mike harassed him in a similar way? Should the company itself be held liable for Mike's odious behavior (even though they had no prior knowledge of it)?

On the surface, sexual harassment in the workplace appears to be on the decline. Complaints made to the Equal Employment Opportunity Commission dipped below 13,000 last year for the first time in 14 years, falling for the sixth straight year. That's likely because companies are being more aggressive in encouraging people to report problems and then investigating them, thereby catching complaints before they reach the levels that prompt lawsuits. "By the time a lawsuit has been filed, it's too late," said Daniel A. Rizzi, deputy practice group leader of Nixon Peabody's national labor and employment law group in Jericho, New York. "An employer and HR professional should be looking to engage in preventative measures. An ounce of prevention is worth a pound of cure."[39]

National surveys of more than 1,000 organizations found that sexual harassment had become one of the hottest topics in formal training programs.[40] In the past several years, sexual harassment consultant Maria Gottlieb says she has seen training requests on the issue rise by 75 percent, particularly in sales.[41] When considering employment with a particular company, make sure that there is a clearly defined sexual harassment policy firmly in place.

Ethics As Good Business

The key to making repeat sales is building trusting relationships.

Ethical behavior may sometimes appear to be an unattractive alternative. After all, for every inside trader, fraudulent salesperson, or immoral politician who gets caught, perhaps hundreds get away with unethical behaviors. However, the recent bumper crop of ethical scandals in corporate America has brought with it a renewed concern for ethics. Some of the newfound conscience in corporations has filtered down to business people and individuals in every walk of life.

Gary Edwards of the nonprofit Ethics Resource Center in Washington, D.C., says that ethics is receiving more attention partially because of awareness on the part of businesses of "the enormous costs of unethical activity, in fines and penalties, in increased government regulation, and in damage to their public image."[42] In short, companies are paying attention to ethics because it happens to be good business strategy.

Professional salespeople who are honest and aboveboard in relationships with employers, customers, and competitors alike become trusted and valued individuals. The key to making repeat sales is to build up these kinds of relationships and maintain them. A well-defined personal code of ethics as part of one's character and as a basis for behavior is an invaluable asset.

Checkpoints in Ethical Decision Making

When faced with an ethical conflict, a standard set of questions to ask yourself is helpful. Use the five questions suggested below to guide your thinking.

A Five-Question Ethics Checklist ·

1. **Is it legal? Look at the law and other standards.**

2. **Is it fair to all concerned?**

3. **Would I want someone else to act this way toward me?**

4. **How would I explain my actions to someone else?**

5. **How will it make me feel about myself?**

These questions first require careful evaluation regarding existing standards and personal liability. Next, the questions are designed to activate your sense of fairness and rationality. Last, realize that your personal feelings are important because negative feelings adversely affect positive performance. Ultimately, if your truthful answer to any one of these questions damages your self-image or causes you to be troubled by your conscience, then you should probably avoid the action in question.[43]

These questions can also be applied to the actions of a salesperson's company. An issue many sales professionals face today is how to sell products and services for a company that condones unethical practices. Salespeople who conduct business properly despite other ethical breaches within their companies aren't safe from trouble. Salespeople would be wise to report the problems through multiple channels within the organization to ensure that their concerns are heard.[44]

Legal Issues Facing the Salesperson

A serious problem faced by company sales forces today is a combination of antitrust law complexity and inadequate preventive legal guidance. Selling can sometimes be a mine field for salespeople who lack the legal expertise required to avoid violating various antitrust laws.[45] Often without realizing it, sales representatives violate legal regulations through various actions every day, and they can be held personally liable. Fines can be imposed up to $100,000 for individuals and $1 million for companies; criminal sanctions may also be imposed. Exhibit 3.2 illustrates some of the legal traps for unwary salespeople.[46]

Δ **Exhibit 3.2**

Legal Traps for the Unwary Salesperson

Product quality below standard specified at time of sale

Violation of contractual delivery date

Pricing concessions given to favored customers

Instructions wrong or incomplete

Price fixing, collusion with supplier or competitor

Selling one brand, delivering another

Misrepresenting manufacturer's specified use

Slandering or lying about competitor

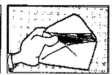

Kickbacks to buyers

Charges added without notifying the buyer

Unauthorized use of proprietary data.

Signing agreements without the proper authority

Companies must properly train salespeople about required legal compliance to keep violations to a minimum. Actually, we would have practically no need for laws if all businesses played by the same ethical rules of the game. However, too many firms and individuals find the temptation to violate rules irresistible. Their violations, basically, fall into two broad categories:

1. Monopolistic actions, such as price-fixing or the acquisition of competitors.
2. Deceptive actions, such as false claims about products or services; or disparaging remarks about competitors.

A number of laws have been passed to preserve fair competition. You might consider these government regulations to be your rules of the game. They serve to protect two groups: The consumer by preventing monopolies and eliminating practices that tend to be deceptive, and business competitors by establishing rules that prevent powerful rivals from depriving smaller firms free access to the market and by protecting competitors from those who would engage in deceptive practices.

Exhibit 3.3 outlines the antitrust legislation that most profoundly affect salespeople. Whenever you aggressively pursue an account, you can face temptations. In the heat of the battle, you may exaggerate or perhaps actually think you have said something clearly to the prospect. For example, the sales representative must completely, and in the clearest language possible, warn the prospect of any potential hazard connected with use of the product. Saying, "Use of this equipment at improper voltage levels will result in damage to the product and concomitant operator hazard" may not be good enough.

A better statement would be: "It must be plugged into 115 volts only. If used at a higher voltage, it can fly apart and injure or kill you."[47] The courts may rule that the vague wording in the first statement is analogous to a sign in your yard that reads *"Please keep off the grass,"* which is an insufficient warning if you know that the grass conceals rattlesnakes.

Δ **Exhibit 3.3**

Key Antitrust Legislation Affecting Salespeople ·

Sherman Antitrust Act (1890). Section 1 deals with competition. It prohibits contracts, combinations, or conspiracies in restraint of trade. Section 2 deals with market control. It prohibits monopolies or attempts to monopolize.

Federal Trade Commission Act (1914). Established the Federal Trade Commission, a 5-member board of specialists with broad powers to investigate and to issue cease-and-desist orders. Section 5 of the act declares that "unfair methods of competition in commerce are unlawful" along with "unfair or deceptive acts or practices." (this latter phrase was added by the Wheeler Lea Act of 1938, which amended the FTC Act.)

Clayton Act (1914). Supplements the vagueness of the Sherman Act of 1890 by prohibiting certain practices. For instance, Section 2 of the act deals with price discrimination; Section 3 deals with tying clauses and exclusive dealings; Section 7 with intercorporate stockholdings; and Section 8 with interlocking directories. The key phrase stated in the law is, "where the effect may be to substantially lessen competition or tend to create a monopoly in any line of commerce." It provides that company personnel who violate the act can be held individually responsible.

Robinson-Patman Act (1936). Specifically amends Section 2 of the Clayton Act. It adds the phrase "to injure, destroy, or prevent competition." The law: (1) defines price discrimination as illegal (subject to certain defenses), (2) provides the Federal Trade Commission with the right to establish limits on quantity discounts, (3) prohibits promotional allowances except where made available to all "on proportionately equal terms," and (4) forbids brokerage allowances except to independent brokers.

The pharmaceutical industry has had some recent struggles over anti-trust legislation. A case filed on behalf of 14 independent California pharmacists targets not only the price differences between the United States and other countries, but also recent efforts by some American drug makers to prevent cheaper drugs from coming into the U.S. "Some American drug makers are selfishly protecting the domestic market, where they have high fixed prices," says attorney Joseph Alioto, who has spent much of his career pursuing antitrust cases.[48]

In view of all the laws affecting business, obviously sales representatives can say or do many things to get themselves, as well as their companies, into quite a bit of trouble. According to Robert Posch, the jail time for those who break antitrust laws has doubled, and they face much higher fines. He says, "In sum, crime simply does not pay; it's corporate suicide to commit antitrust crimes today."[49] Exhibit 3.4 points out six tactics for salespeople to consider following as protection for themselves and for their companies when out in the field selling.[50]

△ Exhibit 3.4

. . . . **How Salespeople Can Protect Against Violating Antitrust Laws**

1. Know the difference between "sales puffery" and specific statements of fact made during the sales presentation and avoid using unwarranted exaggeration to make your story sound good.

2. Thoroughly educate each customer on all aspects of the product before completing the sale.

3. Know the technical specifications, capabilities, design peculiarities, and special characteristics of the products you sell.

4. Read carefully any and all promotional literature published by your company on the products being sold. Challenge what you consider to be untrue or exaggerated claims.

5. Study the company's terms of sale policies. Overstating your authority to establish prices can legally bind the company.

6. Stay current on all federal as well as state laws which affect warranties and guarantees.

The Uniform Commercial Code (UCC)

In addition to the federal antitrust laws, many other laws in all fifty states deal directly or indirectly with personal selling. Because of the diversity of these state laws, an attempt to cover them here is impractical. However, one set of regulations is consistent among the forty-nine states that have adopted it (Louisiana is the lone exception). The Uniform Commercial Code is a set of guidelines that spell out in some detail the conditions under which a sale may be consummated. It is a law that covers virtually all business transactions.[51] The following aspects are governed by the UCC:

1. An offer to sell may be legally binding if it is made in writing or simply stated orally by the salesperson. A distinction is made between a legitimate offer to sell and an invitation to negotiate or deal.

2. The financing of the product or service must be explained clearly and completely. Salespeople must know the legal ramifications of any credit arrangements made with customers. Truth in lending also requires full disclosure of finance charges prior to closing the sale.

3. The salesperson must know the legal responsibilities if either party fails to live up to respective contractual obligations. For example, if the buyer is not able to pay the monthly finance charge, when can the seller take back the merchandise? If the goods are damaged or destroyed in transit, who is responsible for them?

4. Warranties and guarantees offered by the seller are basically the same and are governed by the UCC. The code defines both express warranties and implied warranties. *Express warranties* are statements and promises found in the advertising, sales literature, and labeling and in oral statements made by the salesperson. *Implied warranties* are a result of state law and the assumption that the product complies with those laws. Implied warranties are also in effect unless a disclaimer is made.[52] To be on the safe side, the salesperson should state what is promised as well as what is not promised. The warranty statement should also set time or use limits and clearly specify who is providing the warranty. For example, if you are a distributor representing a manufacturer's product, make certain the customer knows that the manufacturer, not you, is providing the warranty.

Cooling-Off Law

In addition to the regulations provided by the UCC, nearly all states have additional laws regulating door-to-door selling. Much in-home selling has been characterized as high-pressure selling. The cooling-off law gives buyers three days to think over their decision without a salesperson present. If buyers feel the decision is really not in their best interest, they may void the contract. This law applies to purchases for $25 or more. Firms selling door-to-door must typically provide potential buyers with information concerning these factors:

1. The number of days before the contract is binding.

2. How to cancel the agreement legally.

3. Any penalties involved in cancellation.

Despite any short terms gains you may make by behaving unethically in dealing with companies or individuals, doing the right thing is the only way to conduct yourself in the long run. Unethical behavior is selfish behavior, but when you abide by honest practices, you can rest easy knowing that you have other's best interests at heart and not simply your own.

There is no pillow as soft as *a clear conscience*.

SUMMARY

- It is essential that you develop your own personal code of ethics, but you should also be aware of the ethical obligations your company sets forth.

- Salespeople who find themselves in situations in which company violations are evident must make difficult choices about whether to blow the whistle on the company or settle on another strategy that could include finding another job.

- Ethics is a smart business decision because salespeople who are honest in relationships with employers, customers, and competitors become trusted and respected business professionals.

- When faced with an ethical conflict, use a standard checklist of principled questions to guide your thinking.

- A series of federal laws was passed beginning in 1890 with the Sherman Antitrust Act, followed by the Federal Trade Commission Act, the Clayton Act, and the Robinson-Patman Act. These make engaging in practices that inhibit fair competition or deceive the customer illegal.

- Forty-nine states have adopted the Uniform Commercial Code, which defines in some detail the conditions under which a sale may be consummated. It defines exactly what is meant by a sale, sets out required information for financing and truth in lending, and states a salesperson's legal responsibilities.

- Because door-to-door selling has had the reputation of being high-pressure, special cooling-off laws have been passed in most states. These laws give the buyer a three-day period to break a sales agreement.

REVIEW QUESTIONS

1. We have heard much about questionable corporate activities, insider trading scandals, defense contract fraud, health risk cover-ups, and so on. Does this mean that corporations are not interested in ethics—that the bottom line is that corporate greed takes precedence over moral responsibility?

2. What kinds of management tactics make salespeople more likely to exhibit unethical behavior?

3. Should there be any focus on morality in institutions? After all, you cannot have institutional integrity without first having individual integrity, and isn't that the domain of home, church, and school?

4. Does having a corporate code of ethics for salespeople really do any good? Out in the real world where salespeople compete for sales, is a code of ethics practical? Do salespeople need channels of communication and support structures along with an ethics code?

5. Some years ago a Fordham University priest attended the Friday luncheon meeting of the Sales Executives Club of New York where he talked much about honesty in day-to-day business dealings. Asked why he did this, he replied, "What sales executives have to do puts them, among all business people, at the greatest risk of losing their souls." Do you agree with his statement?

6. Forty years ago the medical department at Johns Manville Corporation began to receive information implicating asbestos inhalation as a cause of asbestosis. Manville's managers suppressed the research and concealed the information from employees. The entire company was eventually brought to its knees by questions of corporate ethics. How can we explain this behavior? Were more than forty years' worth of Manville executives immoral?

7. Name the major pieces of legislation and their basic requirements that govern the ethical behavior of companies and salespeople.

8. Explain the operation of the cooling-off law.

9. When some specific safety precautions are needed in connection with using a product, what are the responsibilities of the salesperson in giving this information to the customer?

10. For your personal reflection: Do you believe you would ever be at risk of succumbing to groupthink or gamesmanship and participating in unethical or illegal activities? Have you ever been persuaded by peer pressure to do something for which you were later sorry? What can you do to lessen the possibility of compromising your own personal ethics?

ROLE-PLAY EXERCISES

The following role-play exercises help build teams, improve communication, and emphasize the "real-world" side of selling. They are meant to be challenging, to learn how to deal with problems that have no single "right" answer and to use a variety of skills beyond those employed in a typical review question. Read and complete each activity. Then in the next class, discuss and compare answers with other classmates. Have some students take the role of the salesperson, and see how they would react. Remember, *"You learn more about a person in an hour of play than in a lifetime of conversation."* – Plato

1. Invite to class an attorney that works with sales contracts and a sales representative he or she is acquainted with. Ask the attorney and sales rep to present several real-life mini scenarios of borderline sales activities from their personal experiences. Let the students decide (in writing and orally) if those involved acted ethically and legally and explain why.

2. Interview a sales manager in a local company. Ask about the company's code of ethics: Does the company have a formal written code? Does it have an unwritten but specific set of ethical guidelines? How is the code communicated to salespeople? What penalties are exacted if a salesperson violates the code? Formulate your estimate of the sales manager's and the company's approach to the question of ethics. After your interview, would you feel comfortable and safe doing business with this company?

3. Interview a salesperson. Ask about their company's code of ethics. Does the salesperson feel that the ethics policy of the company is strong enough? Too strong? How was the ethics policy of the company presented to the salesperson? Is the salesperson not sure what the company policy is in any area? Does the company actually enforce the policy?

CASE 3.1 - *Muscle for Clients*

Have you ever faced a conflict of interest? Mike Townsend reached this point in his business and questioned what he should do about it. He had worked hard to build up a clientele and now faced the possibility of losing them. He wanted to do the right thing.

Mike worked out at the local YMCA where he was a member and worked part-time there as a lifeguard to supplement his income from a growing clientele. Mike ran ads in the local newspapers and put up flyers advertising his services as a personal trainer in area gyms and schools. What started out as a part-time fun endeavor was becoming a full-time job.

Mike was qualified in his position. He played football for two years and was on the track team for two years while in high school. He left both of these sports for bodybuilding. At age 17 he won the Kentucky high school teenage bodybuilding competition. At 19 he placed tenth in the National teen bodybuilding championship in his weight class in Pittsburg. He is nationally certified in these areas: personal trainer, aerobics trainer, health nutritionist, lifeguard, swim instructor, and CPR. He studied in his spare time and passed the certification exams with a national fitness training firm located in Nashville.

Most of Townsend's clients are trained at their workout gyms, in their home gyms, and in the local schools and colleges. To build a client base faster and quit the lifeguard job (he only made half the hourly rate as a lifeguard), he began recruiting members of the local YMCA while working out in the gym and life guarding with the sales pitch, "Let me take you to the next level." None of the members seemed to mind his sales efforts and the director ignored what Mike was doing because he was a good lifeguard. Dependable lifeguards are hard to find in the market area.

Everyone was surprised when the director decided to transfer to a YMCA near his home town and extended family. Shelia, the new director, played by a different set of rules. She felt Mike's selling efforts were definitely a conflict of interest and did not want to be held liable for accidents, injuries, or complaints. She could not accept the idea that Mike was getting paid for personal training in their facility without being an employee in this area.

1. Was Mike Townsend participating in a conflict of interest? If so, why?

2. Does Mike seem to have adopted a personal code of ethics?

3. Would you say Townsend's position was legal and ethical, legal and unethical, or illegal? and unethical?

4. What other issues do both Shelia and Mike face?

CASE 3.2 - *Dinner Date with Disaster*

Dr. Donald Barnwell is a college professor teaching personal selling. One of his former students, Alicia Ramirez, called to ask his advice regarding what she considers to be an unethical situation. The company she works for gives each salesperson a $1,000 monthly expense allowance for entertainment of clients. After her first month on the job, she attempted to return the unused portion. The sales manager said, "Don't ever do that again. You must spend it all even it if means treating your friends, family, or former professors to free dinners. If top management discovers that we don't need that large an allowance, they will reduce it. We don't want that to happen, now, do we?"

Alicia felt confused. She asked Dr. Barnwell to go to dinner with her to discuss what she should do about this situation.

1. Do you think he should go to dinner with her?

2. In attempting to understand the entire situation, what questions would you ask Alicia if you were in Dr. Barnwell's position?

Case 3.3 - The Value of Self-Control

Ray Morrison is a regional manager for a company that has just gone nationwide in the distribution of a non-contact system to detect the presence or absence of moving objects. Low-intensity gamma radiation is the detecting agent. This system is designed for applications where severe environmental conditions prevent the use of conventional devices such as infrared detectors, limit switches, and photoelectric and sonic sensors.

Morrison has one major competitor in his region, a company that has had a virtual monopoly as a supplier of motion detection units in areas where severe environmental conditions existed. In addition, this company, Saferay Inc., was backed up by a complete service department that guaranteed that no system would ever be out of operation for more than six hours. When Saferay's competition established nationwide distribution, Morrison, who at the time was security chief for a large chemical company, was made a regional manager. Instead of being one of Saferay's best customers, he was now a competitor. The Saferay representative could not get used to the idea that a person he had considered to be a friend was selling in direct competition in the same territory.

One reaction of the Saferay salesman, Will Gager, has been to run down Morrison's products and services to every buyer he meets. Today's call at a new plant of a worldwide chemical company was no exception. Morrison was greeted by the chief of security with: "What do you think of the Saferay product?"

Morrison gave his standard answer to this often-asked question: "I think it's a fine system. And I know because I used it when I was a security chief myself.''

"Well, they don't think much of yours," the prospect said.

"Oh, in what respect?" Morrison asked.

"Do you know Will Gager?"

"Sure, he's a good friend of mine. He used to call on me before I started selling,"

Morrison said. "That's interesting. He tells me that the Security Council Lab almost refused to issue an approval label to your motion detectors because they just barely met minimum standards in a couple of environmental conditions," the security chief said.

1. If you were Ray Morrison, what would you do?

2. What are the ethical issues involved?

Purchase Behavior and Communication

LEARNING OBJECTIVES

- Determine the differences between individual and organizational buyers.

- Learn environmental influences on the purchase decision process.

- Find out what goes into the successful sending and receiving of a message.

- Examine methods for overcoming communication barriers.

- Understand the importance of using the voice as a communication tool.

- Explore the effects of body language and proxemics in selling.

△ **Exhibit 4.1**

Lincoln's Gettysburg Address

"Four score and seven years ago our fathers brought forth on this continent, a new nation, conceived in Liberty, and dedicated to the proposition that all men are created equal.

Now we are engaged in a great civil war, testing whether that nation, or any nation so conceived and so dedicated, can long endure. We are met on a great battlefield of that war. We have come to dedicate a portion of that field, as a final resting place for those who here gave their lives that that nation might live. It is altogether fitting and proper that we should do this.

But, in a larger sense, we cannot dedicate—we cannot consecrate—we cannot hallow—this ground. The brave men, living and dead, who struggled here, have consecrated it, far above our poor power to add or detract. The world will little note, nor long remember what we say here, but it can never forget what they did here. It is for us the living, rather, to be dedicated here to the unfinished work which they who fought here have thus far so nobly advanced. It is rather for us to be here dedicated to the great task remaining before us -- that from these honored dead we take increased devotion to that cause for which they gave the last full measure of devotion—that we here highly resolve that these dead shall not have died in vain—that this nation, under God, shall have a new birth of freedom -- and that government of the people, by the people, for the people, shall not perish from the earth."

The famous speech delivered by President Abraham Lincoln at the dedication of the Gettysburg National Cemetery on November 19, 1863

Exhibit 4.1 is the famous Gettysburg Address given by President Abraham Lincoln. The entire speech lasted about two minutes for a total of 268 words: 198 are one-syllable words, 50 are two-syllable words, and only 20 are words of more than two syllables. Despite the lack of eloquent or complicated verbiage, the Gettysburg Address is recognized as a classic model of the noblest kind of oratory.

When asked to explain Britain's wartime policy to Parliament, Prime Minister Winston Churchill said, "It is to wage war, by sea, land and air, with all our might and with all the strength that God can give us." As Neil Armstrong first set foot on the moon he said simply, "That's one small step for man, one giant leap for mankind." These leaders demonstrate that you don't have to use big words to make a *big* impact.

Not only are small words more understandable and exact than large words, they also add elegance to your speaking and writing. Realize and appreciate the persuasive power of a well-written sales proposal. Just think how much more you could sell if you could talk and write equally well. If you must choose between a large word and a small word, pick the small word every time. Take a lesson from your local highway department. Place a sign at the boundaries of your speech that reads: *Caution—Small Words at Work.*

CONSUMER BEHAVIOR: WHY PEOPLE BUY

- A retail salesperson working at a Hickory Farms store in Denver convinces a young couple to purchase three pounds of Scandinavian butter cheese. They take it home and serve it to their guests at a reception honoring a group of foreign exchange students from Norway.

- An alumnus of a small private college in Prescott, Arizona, receives a personal call from the school's president, who tells him of a $20 million campaign now under way to underwrite expansion into the twenty-first century. The president convinces him to participate in the Leadership Campaign with a five-year pledge of $300 per year.

- The Mars Candy Company in McLean, Virginia, has decided to make and market a new candy bar with a peanut butter center coated in a creamy milk chocolate of a specific viscosity. Three competing salespeople offering a machine to make this product begin calling on Mars. This major capital investment requires consideration by top executives, tax specialists, production personnel, and marketing personnel. The three salespeople will have direct, frequent contact with all of these Mars personnel and will call in technical experts to assist. The purchase decision will take many months to complete.

These three situations involve consumer behavior and illustrate some diverse aspects of the purchase decision process. *Consumer behavior* is the set of actions that make up an individual's consideration, purchase, and use of products and services.[1] The term consumer behavior includes both the purchase and the consumption of products or services. Your role is vital in this process of matching the company's product offerings to the needs of the prospective buyer.

Countless factors determine whether or not a prospect will purchase any given product. One major determinant of a brand's competitiveness is how a product's package is perceived. The difficulty lies in measuring or projecting the marketplace impact of a particular design system for your product or service. For years, it has been accepted that consumer research should take place to test potential packaging changes for well-established brands. Certainly, fundamental changes to the appearance of Cheerios, Tide, or Kraft products would not happen without consumer research to assess new design systems. However, relatively few companies take a disciplined approach to evaluating the performance of their current packaging. As a result, major decisions to change a brand's appearance are often made on the basis of intuition or in response to competitive activity. As a result, many packaging changes come years too late, after the brand has gone into decline. In other cases, unnecessary redesigns may waste resources and risk confusing or alienating its users. Brand usage and familiarity are powerful forces, and it is vital that your product appeal to the senses of your prospect, especially for higher priced items.[2]

However, the process does not end with the sale of a product or service neatly presented in a well-designed package. Salespeople must be equally concerned with consumer satisfaction after the sale. This chapter introduces a model of the consumer's decision-making process, considers a number of environmental factors that influence this process, and then examines both the verbal and nonverbal elements of the communication process, with special emphasis on body *language* and *proxemics* (the use of space).

The Purchase Decision Process

Consumers make multiple product decisions every day, and each decision-making process depends on how they process information.[3] The model shown in Exhibit 4.2 provides a useful tool for examining the buying process. It presents a view of the buyer as someone observed not in a single act, but in a complex problem-solving process. Obviously, this model cannot provide all the answers for salespeople, but it does provide knowledge that can be used in individual sales situations as a guide for understanding what the prospect faces and deciding how you can best assist in the decision-making process.[4]

△ Exhibit 4.2

Compare P21(

Model of the Purchase Decision Process

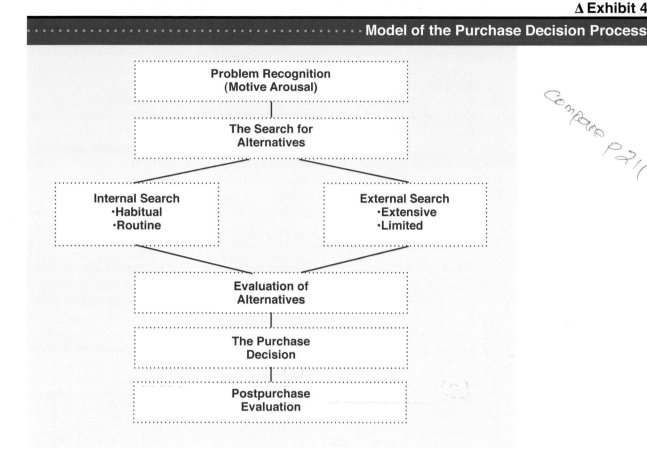

Problem Recognition
(Motive Arousal)

The Search for
Alternatives

Internal Search
·Habitual
·Routine

External Search
·Extensive
·Limited

Evaluation of
Alternatives

The Purchase
Decision

Postpurchase
Evaluation

To understand why an individual makes a certain purchase decision, you must look at events leading up to and then following the purchase act itself. A buyer passes through five stages:

1. Problem recognition
2. Search for alternatives
3. Evaluation of alternatives
4. The purchase decision
5. Post-purchase evaluation

Problem Recognition. The purchase process begins with conscious recognition that a problem or need exists and must be satisfied. A need may be something regarded as necessary, or something that the individual wants or desires and therefore perceives as a need. No one takes action until motivated to do so, and this motivation arises from the awareness of a need. Therefore, salespeople must recognize needs that are already active or to find a way to create or stimulate recognition of a need of which the prospective buyer has not yet become aware. *All kinds of needs affect buying decisions.* Abraham Maslow defined the five levels of needs as physiological, safety, social, esteem, and self-actualization. Regardless of the kind of need, some buyers will not be aware of the nature of their needs until a salesperson brings them out into the open.

Search for Alternatives. After recognizing an unsatisfied need, the buyer begins to search for information concerning the available alternatives. The search may involve both internal and external sources. The internal search makes use of the buyer's previous experiences, learning, and attitudes, and often occurs without conscious effort. Even in the organizational markets, much purchasing is routine. A great deal of it can be done through catalogs or simply a phone call to a regular supplier. However, the external search process adds dynamics. It may require an extensive information search or a more limited search for alternatives.

The Internet provides consumers with faster, more advanced ways to search for alternatives. Companies that want to survive in this information-rich marketplace must demonstrate that they can effectively communicate with customers and prospects through the latest methods of technology.[5] Paul O'Brian, manager of Interactive Marketing at Hewlitt Packard, says that "online shopping is the mall of the new millennium." The percentage of people purchasing HP products online grows exponentially each year as consumers continue to do more and more of their shopping online.[6] Online buying provides more options because customers can research and compare competing products. In fact, the popularity of *comparison shopping Web sites* such as SmartShopper.com and NexTag.com have seen substantial growth in the last several years because they allow purchasers to read reviews and compare products side-by-side in every area, from appearance to performance.

Evaluation of Alternatives. The search process provides the buyer with knowledge of several alternative products. All individual consumers have specific criteria they use for making a decision—personal mental rules for matching alternatives with motives. These criteria are learned by actual experience with the product or derived from information obtained from commercial or social sources.

If you can determine the buyer's *choice criteria*, you can tailor the presentation to focus on specific product or service benefits that differentiate your product from those of the competition. Once you have matched the prospect's buying motives with what you have to offer, the determinant attributes come into play: Price, reputation, service capabilities, and design components. Identifying the dominant buying motives that determine a particular buyer's behavior in the actual decision-making process is vital to closing the sale.

Purchase Decision. After evaluating all the alternatives discovered during the search process, the buyer is ready to make the purchase decision—actually, a whole set of decisions. Buyers want to minimize their risk and simplify the decision-making process as much as possible. The professional salesperson knows this and assists the buyer in making decisions. The salesperson finds out how the product or service fits into the buyer's system by asking questions: *Who else will use it? How is it to be used? Where? When? With what other products will it be used?* Your role in assisting prospects to reach a satisfactory purchasing decision is what makes relationship selling such a rewarding and fulfilling career.

Post-purchase Evaluation. The purchase decision process continues after the product or service choice has been made. The buyer evaluates the purchase in terms of pre-purchase expectations and decides whether it has been satisfactory. Sometimes the buyer experiences post-purchase anxiety or *cognitive dissonance*, also commonly known as buyer's remorse. The magnitude of the anxiety or tension depends on the importance of the decision and the attractiveness of the rejected alternatives. You can help lessen this feeling by providing exceptional customer service and follow-up after the sale (as discussed in Chapter 14).

Influences on the Purchase Decision Process

Buying motives cannot be observed directly, but can be inferred from observed behavior. Exhibit 4.3 illustrates some of the many *psychological* and *sociocultural* factors that influence a buyer's purchase decision process. You must understand the significance and impact of these factors at the various stages of the decision-making process:

1. Behavioral concepts, such as perception and self-image, affect problem recognition.

2. Sociocultural factors, such as culture, physical environment, and social class, all influence the nature and scope of the information search.
3. Psychological factors, such as the mood of the moment, attitudes, and perception of oneself, combine with sociocultural factors to influence purchase decisions.

You can make positive use of these factors by becoming proficient in the art of communication—the sending and receiving of messages in a manner that results in understanding, productive discussion, and fulfillment of a need or needs.

Δ Exhibit 4.3

Influences on the Buyer's Purchase Decision Process

Psychological Influences
- Perception
- Mood of the Moment
- Attitudes
- Self-image

Sociocultural Influences
- Culture
- Global customs
- Physical environment
- Social class

Buyer
(psyche)

Psychological Influences: It's All in Your Head

Several psychological factors affect a prospect's buying decision. You must be aware of these factors and understand the role they play in the process. Once you learn how these factors influence the sales process, you can use them to your advantage in future selling situations as they enable you to more accurately read the prospect's overall disposition.

Perception. Individual behavior is an organized and meaningful response to the world as that particular person sees it. We perceive situations according to our own personal needs, values, expectations, past experience, and training. Exhibit 4.4 illustrates the difference in individual perceptions. How many squares do you see? Can you find them? Check the answer given in the chapter endnotes.[7] If you didn't see that many, you may be exercising selective perception. What prospects perceive as important to themselves is often not what you think is most important. It's not good enough to just say "hello" when you call on someone. While recognition is a good thing, it doesn't take the place of meeting the customer's expectations. Clients, as well as prospective customers, now have significantly higher service expectations today than ever before.

Δ Exhibit 4.4

How Many Squares Do You See?

The sophisticated market and high levels of competition have educated the business world and the individual consumer to expect more.[8] You must work to build the right perception in the minds of your customers and prospects.

Mood of the Moment. Perception is also influenced by an individual's psychological state or the mood of the moment. On some days a minor mishap may be laughed off, but if nothing has gone right all day, the same situation may completely infuriate you.

Attitude. Attitudes are merely habits of thought and habitual patterns of response to stimuli and experiences. Because they have been used so often, they have become automatic and are used to save the time that would be required to think about a situation and make a decision. For example, some prospects operate from the concept that what has been done in the past is the best way to do things in the future. In other words, their attitude is that change is bad. Any attitude that makes the purchase decision more difficult creates a barrier that must be overcome before a sale can be made.

Negative attitudes are a problem because they are often unconscious. Because they are often habitual responses based on past experience, the individual involved no longer thinks about them and is unaware that they exist. In contrast, prospects who adopt attitudes of open-mindedness, enthusiasm, innovativeness, and willingness to explore new ideas are a joy for the relationship salesperson to find.

Self-Image. Self-image is an individual's unique and personal self-appraisal at a given moment in time. It affects what is perceived as reality and, as a result, how communication proceeds. In choosing how to communicate, even more important than what is true is what the person believes is true.[9] Self-image often has a great deal of influence on a prospect's tendency to be a conspicuous consumer. *Conspicuous consumption* is a relatively new trend in which consumers spend money on unnecessary and unproductive leisure expenditures and

Self-image affects how we see and react to circumstances.

big-ticket items that are considered more "flashy" than practical. Perhaps it is a way purchasers can compensate for a less than positive self-image, or perhaps they practice conspicuous consumption for other reasons. Regardless of the motive, be aware of the power of this buying motive.[10]

Most psychologists suggest that by age seven or eight we have decided what kind of person we are, the kind of person we will become, how our world will respond or react to us, with what kind of people we want to deal, and what our environment will be like.[11] The self-image includes dimensions that are not technically "self," but they are so closely identified with the self that they operate as though they are real. For example, people routinely talk about "my" company or "my" school, and some parents see their children as extensions of themselves. We as humans have a tendency to attach ownership to anything we can.

Every behavior can be explained if the individual's self-image is understood. In one sense we are all self-centered, and we act in keeping with what we consider best for us at the moment. If you wish to communicate effectively, you must learn to recognize these important dimensions of the prospect's self-image:

1. **Physical**. People picture themselves as tall or short, weak or strong, attractive or unattractive, lean or overweight. They buy products that fit their self-image or promise to change it to fit a desired goal.
2. **Social**. Individuals see themselves as liked or disliked, accepted or rejected, loved or unwanted, successful or failing.
3. **Moral**. Internalized values give people a picture of themselves as loyal or disloyal, honest or dishonest, straightforward or devious.

Sociocultural Influences

In addition to psychological influences, it is essential to understand how sociocultural influences operate to determine people's communication.

Culture. Culture is a way of looking at life that is handed down from one generation to another. Arguably, it is almost completely learned. The effects of culture can be observed in what people do, see, and use, and in how they reach judgments about people, events, and experiences. Individuals' values develop as a result of their reactions to the environment in which they live. Our cultural environment exerts a powerful influence on how messages are both sent and received. A large percentage of Americans attach a positive connotation to concepts such as success, competition, efficiency, freedom, and material wealth. However, the positive reception to these words is not universal. Even within the United States, subcultures of many kinds exist, each with its own set of values, priorities, and concepts. Even more pronounced are cultural differences that affect communication among people from different parts of the world, a fact that has broad implications for salespeople in the global marketplace of today.[12] Exhibit 4.5 illustrates that selling to and dealing with prospects from overseas demands cultural sensitivity. For example, in Japan that means showing a business card the same respect you would show a person.[13]

Δ Exhibit 4.5

Treat a Business Card with Respect

Steve Waterhouse had the moment he had been waiting for. His firm had been courting a Tokyo meeting planning company for the past six months. At a National Speakers Association convention in San Antonio, Texas, Waterhouse had the good fortune (or so it seemed) to meet with the firm's representative to discuss services his company might buy. "He handed his business card to me in the traditional Japanese way," Waterhouse recalls—extending the card while holding onto both corners. "I took the card and scribbled a note on the back of it." Much to his dismay, Waterhouse looked up to find the man appalled at what he had just done. "I quickly put it away and then apologized profusely, but the damage was already done." Steve Waterhouse lost a sale worth $100,000 to his company!

A Global Perspective. Foreign cultures adhere to business customs, protocols, and body language used in basic communication that differ greatly from those used in America. If you want to sell to international customers, whether here or overseas, you must first establish rapport. Insensitivity to other people's customs and ways of communicating may derail your best selling efforts. With major companies moving large portions of their operations overseas, American business people, and specifically those in sales, must be aware of the differences they will encounter when dealing with others outside the U.S. and learn how to best use those differences to their advantage.[14]

Those who sell to international customers may get by with a wink and a "see ya later," but only if they know how their language and gestures will be interpreted; body talk does not have a universal language. According to Diane Ackerman's book, *A Natural History of the Senses*, "Members of a tribe in New Guinea say good-bye by putting a hand in each other's armpit, withdrawing it, and stroking it over themselves, thus becoming coated with the friend's scent." Thank goodness that when we say goodbye to a client, we can just shake hands—or can we?

In France, the traditional American handshake is considered much too rough; a quick handshake with slight pressure is preferred. Throughout Latin America, however, the greeting is often more exuberant. A hearty embrace is common among both men and women. They often follow it with a slap on the back. In Ecuador, greeting a person without shaking hands is a sign of special respect. Throughout India, it is considered rude to touch women, so never offer to shake their hands. Exhibit 4.6 illustrates several cross-cultural considerations when conducting business globally.

△ Exhibit 4.6

Cultural Differences From a Global Perspective ·

1. Avoid slang or sports metaphors such as, "That proposal is way out in left field!" or "Are we in the ballpark on price?" They may mean nothing to other cultures.

2. Always use your last name when answering the telephone in Germany such as, "Bond speaking." When you call a customer say your last name first: "This is Bond, James Bond."

3. Americans and Canadians typically take a business card and pocket it without reviewing the information. In France, Italy, Switzerland, and Japan, the business card is an extension of the person who gives it so cards need to be treated with much respect.

4. After introductions, Americans and Canadians will tend to move quickly into business. However, in Latin America and China business can only proceed after a relationship has been built.

5. In Japan, you can never be too polite, too humble, or too apologetic. Make apologizing routine. This is one of the greatest areas of cultural difference between our two countries.

6. Always appear to be less informed and less skilled in the negotiation process than you really are. To the Japanese there is no such thing as a quick deal.

7. The British and Russians are masters at using the pressure of silence. Don't speak until your prospect has responded to your last comment.

Physical Environment. Americans usually keep their houses and offices at a cozy 72 to 78 degrees; the British prefer an indoor setting of 60 to 65 degrees. Other elements of the environment, such as sound level, are also important. Most people of middle age and older enjoy a quiet, restful environment; younger people tend to be stimulated by loud music and object less strenuously to machine noise. Don't attempt to make a presentation to a 60-year-old prospect over dinner in a restaurant that features live rock music, unless of course that prospect is Mick Jagger. The physical environment must be conducive to communication.

Social Class. From the beginning of civilization, social classes have existed to some degree. In the United States, social structure is less rigid than in some other nations, in which it may be tied to religion, kinship, or inherited ownership of land. Americans often climb into new social classes by earning higher educations and filling prestigious jobs. Social class groupings are based largely on source of wealth, occupation, education, type of housing, and location. It is important to be aware that people tend to adopt buying behaviors, tastes, and ways of communicating that are in keeping with the social class to which they consider themselves members.

Organizational Versus Consumer Buying

Business-to-business buyers include all organizations—both profit and nonprofit—that buy products or services for their own use, resell to other organizations, or sell to the ultimate consumer. Individual consumers, with a comparatively small number of transactions, are not considered in this category. The five-stage purchase decision process fits the ultimate consumer buyer adequately, and the two processes are generally similar, but the organizational buyer follows a more complex purchase decision process. The following are the four main areas where fundamental differences exist between consumer purchasing and organizational buying:

Decision Maker. The ultimate consumer is the decision maker in a purchase. In an organizational setting, decisions are often made by a team, commonly referred to as a buying center. The *buying center* is an ad hoc, cross-departmental, decision-making unit consisting of all individuals who play a role in formulating the purchasing recommendation.

Buying Criteria. Individual consumers have a limited set of factors to weigh in making a buying decision, whereas business markets often require products that are complex, expensive, and purchased in larger quantities.

Length of Relationship. Organizational buyers desire to stay with suppliers longer, to reduce the need for frequent negotiation. This interdependence underlies the need to build a long-term relationship. As a result, many business buyers and sellers have formed what are referred to as strategic business alliances.

Buying Motives. Every buying decision made—consumer or organizational—is based on a dominant motive. Buying motives may be either rational or emotional. Your selling skills are not nearly as important as the customer's reasons for buying. In fact, your reasons for selling are useless if they don't match the customer's reasons for buying.[15] Individual consumers often buy based on emotion and later attempt to rationalize their decisions. For organizational buyers, however, rational motives are usually dominant, though they must take emotional motives into account as well. Exhibit 4.7 lists the basic motives that lead to both consumer and organizational purchases.

Δ **Exhibit 4.7**

Consumer and Organizational Buying Motives

Consumer Buying Motives	Organizational Buying Motives
• Alleviate fear	• Economy
• Secure social approval	• Flexibility
• Satisfy bodily needs	• Uniformity of output
• Experience happiness or pleasure	• Salability
• Gain an advantage	• Protection
• Imitate	• Utility
• Dominate others	• Guarantees
• Enjoy recreation	• Delivery
• Improve health	• Quality

Multiple Buying Influences

The responsibility for organizational buying decisions may lie with more than a single individual. Organizations often set dollar limits beyond which purchase decisions must involve additional executives, more red tape, and more paperwork. Buying committees or teams drawn from the various departments become involved in decision making. The members of this team, called a buying center, share common goals and knowledge relevant to the purchase decision. A major reason for working with the buying center is to discover the key person or persons who actually make or strongly influence the final decision. Researchers have identified five specific roles played by the people who constitute a buying center: [16]

1. **Users**. These individuals are those who will actually use the product or service purchased; for example, a telemarketing sales force whose members will be the primary users of a proposed new telephone system.
2. **Buyers**. Buyers have formal authority to make the purchase, such as the purchasing agent.
3. **Influencers**. Influencers are the individuals who provide information, directly or indirectly, throughout the buying process to members of the buying center. For example, the supervisor for the telemarketing division may suggest certain features needed in a telephone system to make the calling process more efficient.
4. **Deciders**. This role is played by those who have the power and authority to choose from among the various suppliers. They make the final decision.
5. **Gatekeepers**. Within any typical organization, the information needed in the decision-making process is influenced by the gatekeepers—those who control the flow of information into the buying center.[17] Gatekeepers are invaluable to the group's decision-making process.

The Communication Agenda

Relationship selling thrives on good communication. Communication can be viewed as the verbal and nonverbal passing of information between you, the *sender*, and your prospect, the *receiver*. However, for effective communication to take place, each person must understand the intended message. Thus, the goal of communication is a *mutual understanding*.[18]

Exhibit 4.8 shows the channel through which communication must flow in a selling situation. At each intersection the potential exists for both roadblocks and opportunities. Although the model considers communication from the salesperson's perspective, in any successful relationship both parties participate meaningfully in an active two-way process.[19]

Δ Exhibit 4.8

The Communication Model for Verbal and Nonverbal Messages · · · · · · · · · · · · · · ·

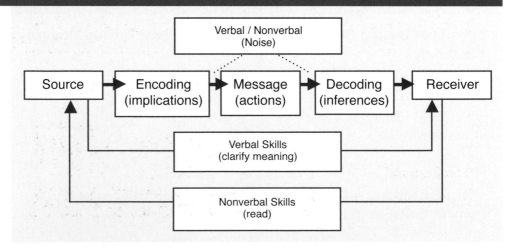

Encoding the Message

Encoding is the process in which the salesperson converts an idea or concept into *symbols* the buyer can clearly understand. You know what you are trying to say; the real challenge is getting your point across.[20] This requires the proper mix of symbols to express your meaning correctly. The most common symbols used in delivering a message are words, pictures, numbers, sounds, physical touch, smell, body movement, and taste. You must encode the message, organize it, and put it into a presentation format the prospect will understand, accept, and believe. Effective encoding of your message is based on a thorough knowledge, or at least awareness, of the prospect's needs.

Communication is successful if the symbols chosen make it possible for the prospect to understand. The ultimate challenge in communication is to transfer your thoughts, ideas, and intentions without distortion or omission. Because communication is affected by the assumptions and needs of both parties—as well as by outside factors such as time constraints, interruptions, and the environment—communication is often far from perfect.

There are three basic purposes for encoding your message:

1. To influence the attitudes and behavior of the prospect.

2. To move the buyer through a sequence of mind changes until a buying decision is made.

3. To obtain affirmative action upon the five fundamental buying decisions: need, product, source, price, and time.

The Message Itself: More Than Words

The actual message is a blend of symbols that are used to influence a change in a prospect's attitude or behavior, and it involves both verbal and nonverbal elements. In his book, *Silent Messages*, Albert Mehrabian points out that words convey only 7 percent of feelings and emotions, tone of voice conveys 38 percent, and visual communication conveys the remaining 55 percent.[21] Nonverbal elements in the presentation make up the majority of the total impact. In essence, *it's not what you say, but how you say it.*

If verbal and nonverbal messages conflict, the listener generally relies on the nonverbal message. Exhibit 4.9 illustrates the contribution of various factors to the messages we deliver to others and the amount of control we maintain over each one. The factors most easily controlled are those that have the least effect, and those with the biggest impact are the most difficult to control because they happen automatically.

Δ **Exhibit 4.9**

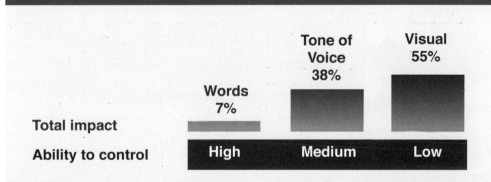

The Ability to Manage Communication Dimensions

Words 7% — Tone of Voice 38% — Visual 55%

Total impact

Ability to control — High — Medium — Low

The process of delivering the message begins with visual impressions because they happen first. If a salesperson walks hesitantly into a prospect's office wearing a listless or worried expression, the prospect is immediately wary. That provides an instantly unappealing visual message. If the salesperson then extends a clammy palm with a "dead-fish" handshake, an unpleasant touch is added; and if an unenthusiastic message is delivered in a monotone, the sound itself drowns out the words. In this scenario, the cluster of negative nonverbal cues completely masks the real message.

Research suggests that if the first thirty seconds of a communication result in a negative impression, you must spend the next four minutes just to overcome that impression before any communication can truly begin.[22] Unfortunately, the prospect may decide not to buy before the situation can be reversed.

Decoding is the mental process by which prospects figure out the meaning of a message. It is the way in which your prospect attempts to translate the symbols used in your presentation into something that relates to their needs. If the message was obviously both understood as intended and also accepted, there is no problem. At this step in the process, either real communication or misunderstanding will occur. Your prospects listen to your message, and then make their own conclusions. If the prospect fails to understand the message, the result is called *noise*, which means that a breakdown in communication has occurred. This happens when there are barriers to effective communication, as discussed in the following section.

Overcoming Communication Barriers

Seldom does the buyer interpret exactly the same meaning that you perhaps intended, and when the result of decoding is different from what you encoded, noise exists. Anything that interferes with or distorts understanding of the intended message is called *noise*, and it can take many forms that may affect any or all parts of the communication process. There are logical reasons why your sales message may not be understood or accepted. Here are some common reasons for such miscommunication:

Words. All language is a code. Even if you and your prospect use the same words, you are likely putting out different meanings.[23] Words only represent ideas. Noise is created when words are inappropriate. For example, casual profanity that may offend the listener, language implying that the listener is poorly informed, language that assumes too much knowledge on the listener's part, or language that obscures the real meaning.

Distractions. Any element that may focus the prospect's attention on something other than the message is a distraction. Some typical distractions are inappropriate dress, uncomfortable room temperature, loud noise that makes concentration difficult, or a nagging personal problem occupying the prospect's mind.

Timing. If a prospect has some reason for not wanting to listen, no amount of communication skill on your part is enough. The prospect may be feeling under the weather, may be preoccupied with an unpleasant disciplinary task, or may be facing a pressing deadline. Some prospects need time to warm up before getting down to business; others want to get right to your proposal and skip the small talk.

Interruptions. Phone calls, people walking in to ask questions, and emergencies represent the kinds of interruptions that reduce or distort the impact of the message.

Technical Erudition. Information overload often complicates a message. An unconscious desire to appear personally knowledgeable often results in the salesperson talking too much, poorly organizing the presentation of features and benefits, or wrongly assuming that the prospect has adequate knowledge.

As a result, the prospect fails to see a need for the product or service. Avoid using technical terms or jargon without clarification.[24]

Listening Habits. If the prospect is a poor listener, the salesperson is faced with a monumental challenge in designing a message and delivering it in an effective and successful manner. The other end of the spectrum is the salesperson who is a poor listener, who never picks up the prospect's cues that are the keys to molding the message for quick acceptance.[25]

The buyer will draw conclusions from the messages received and react accordingly. Recognizing this feedback is crucial to a salesperson's success. During face-to-face communication, verbal and nonverbal feedback is immediate and quite revealing. Become skilled in receiving feedback so that you can adapt your sales presentation to fit each individual buyer's requirements. Use the feedback loop from the prospect to you to bring you closer to an exact understanding of what is being said by each participant. This filters out the noise and results in clear communication.[26]

Using Your Voice As a Sales Tool

The first impression you make is often based on your voice. When you call for an appointment, your voice is all you have for communicating. A voice that is pleasing and confident is a great asset. Your voice and how you use it play an important part in your success in selling. Several basic components of verbal communication deserve your attention.[27]

Articulation. Do you recall the device Professor Higgins used in *My Fair Lady* to help Eliza Doolittle improve her speech? He had her talk with marbles in her mouth. To be understood at all, she was forced to form her words with extreme care. As a result, her articulation improved. When you speak, do people hear separate words and syllables, or *doyourwordsallruntogether*? A salesperson with poor articulation leaves prospects confused and bewildered.

Volume. The normal volume of the speaking voice varies during conversation. The same is true of a sales presentation. Stressing a benefit may call for increased volume. Lowering your voice, sometimes almost to a whisper, may produce quite a dramatic effect; it causes the prospect to lean forward (a body position that signals agreement or approval) to avoid missing your words. Variation in volume enhances the message if it is not overdone.

Silence. Silence is a powerful selling tool. Use it to give the prospect time to absorb the full impact of what you have said. Slight pauses between major points in the presentation suggest that you are thoughtful, intelligent, and analytical. Pauses also give the prospect an opportunity to comment, ask a question, or think about how the idea you have presented can be applied to an existing need or problem. Avoid becoming so enamored with the sound of your own voice that you talk all the time.

Rhythm. The rhythmic pattern of your speech comes from your basic personality style and your emotions of the moment. Some voices seem to flow in long, continuous sentences, whereas others come in short, choppy chunks. Just as the rhythm in music changes to indicate that something new is happening, the same thing happens in speech patterns. Be alert to any changes in your own or the prospect's speech patterns. Changes are even more revealing than initial patterns. If the prospect suddenly shifts to a more drawn-out rhythm, for example, the message may be "Let me think more about that" or "I don't believe what you're saying."

Rate. The tempo of your delivery should be comfortable for you as a speaker and for your listener. Speaking too rapidly may cause you to lose a prospect who customarily speaks more slowly and feels that your fast pace is pushing for a decision without allowing time for thought. Speaking too slowly may make the prospect want to push your fast-forward button. A moderate pace allows you to enunciate clearly, establish natural rhythmic patterns, and speed up or slow down for proper emphasis of some point.

Selling Without Words

Although people have the option not to speak, they can never not communicate. Nonverbal signals are a rich source of information, and one's own nonverbal behavior can be useful in responding to others, making stronger connections with clients and colleagues, and conveying certain impressions about oneself.[28] Different people have different levels of competence in nonverbal communication skills, and some professions require more skill than others. The success of a professional gambler depends on the ability to exercise strict control over nonverbal messages to disguise a bluff. A mime depends exclusively on nonverbal skills to deliver a message. However, to achieve excellence in the sales profession, you must be skilled in both verbal and nonverbal communication. Two particularly important components of nonverbal communication are *body language* and *proxemics*.

Body Language

Body language can be conceived of as messages sent without using words. The essential elements of body language include shifts in posture or stance (body angle), facial expressions, eye movements, and arm, hand, and leg movements. It includes every movement and gesture, from the subtle raising of an eyebrow to the obvious leaning forward of an interested listener. Through body language, prospects express their emotions, desires, and attitudes. As a result, body language is a valuable tool for discovering what the prospect is really saying. When you can read the prospect's body language and, in addition, control your own body signals to add impact to your words, you are likely to be understood.

The Language of Gestures. Important signals involve body angle; position of hands, arms, legs, and the face—especially the eyes and lips.[29] All of these should be observed as a cluster of gestures that together state a message. A prospect sitting with arms crossed may be communicating doubt or rejection or may simply be sitting comfortably. In this case, you must also observe whether the legs are crossed, the body withdrawn, the eyes glancing sideways, and an eyebrow raised. All these signs, taken together, surely suggest doubt or rejection, but one of them in isolation is inconclusive.

Body Signals. A hunched figure, rigid posture, restless stance, or nervous pacing may contradict what a person says verbally. Prospects allow you to sit closer if they feel comfortable and lean toward you if they like what you are saying and are intent on listening. John Molloy used videotape to study the behavior of successful and unsuccessful salespeople. One mannerism difference noted was the relative calmness of professional salespeople in comparison to those who were less successful. Their body movements were smooth and unhurried; there were no jerky motions, particularly when handing a contract or a pen across the table. Every movement was gradual. Less successful salespeople exhibited jumpy, nervous movements that were picked up—perhaps unconsciously—by prospects.

Look for changes in the prospect's body posture and gestures. For example, one who is ready to buy shows signs of relaxation: Nodding in agreement, mirroring your movements, moving to the front of the chair, extending the palm of the hand outward toward you, and uncrossing legs. Your posture and gestures also communicate your feelings to the prospect. If you sit in an open, relaxed position, you are likely to be more persuasive and better accepted than if you sit in a tight, closed posture.

Hand Movements. Rubbing the back of the neck may indicate frustration, but it can also indicate that the prospect has a sore or stiff neck from painting the bathroom ceiling over the weekend. Next time you are speaking with a client, notice his hand movements and read his hands as indicators of what he is really feeling. People can say so much with simple, unthinking hand motions. If you begin to notice that you are also making involuntary hand gestures during a meeting, focus your hand gestures toward your presentation or notes rather than letting them give away what you are feeling!

Evaluate the following hand gestures in the context of other nonverbal clues.

1. **Hand and head gestures**. Tugging at the ear suggests the desire to interrupt. Pinching the bridge of the nose and closing the eyes says that a matter is being given serious thought.
2. **Posture**. Leaning back in the chair with both hands behind the head communicates a sense of superiority.
3. **Involuntary gestures**. Involuntary hand gestures that contradict a facial expression are likely to reveal the true feelings. Tightly clasped hands or fists indicate tenseness.
4. **Steepling of the hands**. Fingertips together, forming what looks like a church steeple, often indicate smugness, self-confidence, or feelings of superiority.

Facial Expressions. Eyebrows, eyelids, eyes, lips, jaw, mouth, and facial muscles all work together to communicate feelings and emotions. Research attributes as much as 70 percent of nonverbal message sending to the muscles of the face.[30]

The face is a highly reliable indicator of attitude. A person may avoid eye contact when trying to cover up true feelings. Increased eye contact signals honesty and interest. Be sure to maintain eye contact at critical moments of the presentation. For example, when describing technical characteristics of the product, direct the prospect's eyes to the product itself, the brochure, or the specification sheet. In contrast, when stressing the benefits of using the product, maintain direct eye contact. Lack of eye contact sends a negative message that neutralizes the impact of the intended benefit. Proper eye contact makes a positive statement that words alone cannot.[31] In a survey by Incomm Research, 80 percent of trade show attendees said they were more likely to perceive a company or product positively if its sales reps were smiling.

Barry Maher, author of *No Lie: Truth Is the Ultimate Sales Tool*, offers workshops that demonstrate how factors like voice tone, proximity, or eye contact affect customers.[32]

Suspicion and anger are shown by tightness around the cheeks or along the jaw line. Muscle movement at the back of the jaw line just below the ears indicates an angry gritting of the teeth. A sudden flush of facial redness may warn that the situation has taken a bad turn; embarrassment or hostility may be radiating under an apparently calm exterior.

An isolated gesture or posture is seldom a reliable indicator of attitude or feelings. Obviously, you have to take a look at the buyer in the context of the whole situation. The buyer may fold her arms just to be more comfortable. Generally, if there is an objection, the whole body will become more rigid. You will see other signals as well: Skin texture will tighten up; voice tone will change. The prospect may even have a frustrated look on her face. When a cluster of gestures is consistent with the verbal messages, it is relatively safe to accept their validity.[33]

The Science of Proxemics

Proxemics is the distance individuals prefer to maintain between themselves and others. Most people seem to consider the observation of desired distance a matter of courtesy. Violations of distance comfort risk closing down the communication process. Highly successful salespeople tend to move closer to clients when closing a sale. Their skill in reading the individual prospect allows them to move as close as possible without causing discomfort for the prospect. The difference between how successful and unsuccessful salespeople use physical closeness can be observed in the prospect's reaction. Carefully test for the existence of comfort barriers; then place yourself just outside those barriers.

Exhibit 4.10 shows the four basic zones or ranges that apply in the typical sales situation. Generally speaking, the intimate zone is about two feet (hence the expression, "Keeping someone at arm's length"). Enter this range only if invited. Moving inside the intimate zone, except for a handshake, is not a good idea. Beyond that, we all have a personal zone, which is an envelope around us extending from two to four feet. Move into the buyer's personal zone only after invitation, which typically occurs after you establish a satisfying professional relationship. The outer shell is the social zone, which extends up to 12 feet.[34]

Δ Exhibit 4.10

How to Use Space ·

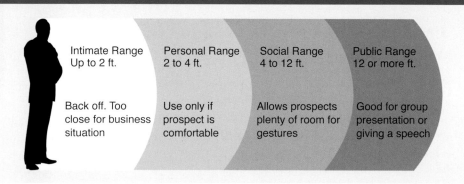

Intimate Range Up to 2 ft.	Personal Range 2 to 4 ft.	Social Range 4 to 12 ft.	Public Range 12 or more ft.
Back off. Too close for business situation	Use only if prospect is comfortable	Allows prospects plenty of room for gestures	Good for group presentation or giving a speech

A number of factors enter into the amount of space various individuals need. Cultural differences, age, gender, and personality are important, as is the type of relationship that exists between salesperson and client. Peers tolerate a closer range of contact than people with a wide gap in age or status. Conversations between two women occur at closer range that those between two men or between a man and a woman. People with outgoing, open personalities are willing to be closer than those who are shy or withdrawn. Salespeople can move closer to long-term clients than to new prospects.

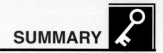

SUMMARY

- The consumer's purchase decision process involves five stages:
    1. Problem recognition
    2. Search for alternatives
    3. Evaluation of alternatives
    4. The purchase decision
    5. Post-purchase evaluation

- Organizational buyers must abide by specific restrictions and buying procedures, often consult with other executives, and must deal with budget constraints. Purchases of this nature often involve a purchasing team, sometimes referred to as a buying center.

- Salespeople are successful in closing sales when they discover the buying motives of the prospect, present benefits of the product that relate to those motives, and are sensitive to both psychological and sociocultural influences.

- Communication is the vehicle for delivering your message in a manner that the buyer comprehends, accepts, and believes.

- Understanding body language and how prospects use their space adds to your ability to communicate with the prospect.

- We send the majority of our messages in daily communication through nonverbal means. We cannot *not* communicate!

REVIEW QUESTIONS

1. Formulate a brief definition of consumer behavior.

2. Why must salespeople understand consumer behavior?

3. What are the five stages of the buying-decision process? What is a salesperson's function in each of these stages?

4. What is cognitive dissonance? How can a salesperson prevent it?

5. What differences exist between individual and organizational buyers?

6. What is a buying center?

7. What are the four purposes a salesperson may have in encoding a message to be presented to a prospect?

8. How can you be sure someone has received, understood, and accepted your message?

9. What is the role of perception in the buying-decision process?

10. What are some of the psychological influences on the purchase decision process?

ROLE-PLAY EXERCISES

The following role-play exercises help build teams, improve communication, and emphasize the "real-world" side of selling. They are meant to be challenging, to learn how to deal with problems that have no single "right" answer and to use a variety of skills beyond those employed in a typical review question. Read and complete each activity. Then in the next class, discuss and compare answers with other classmates. Have some students take the role of the salesperson, and see how they would react. Remember, *"You learn more about a person in an hour of play than in a lifetime of conversation."* — Plato

1. Appoint 3 students to participate in an active role-play in front of the class. Divide the class into teams and give each group a brief selling situation. Give each group fifteen minutes to prepare a presentation and invite the 3 students in the role play to present their situation to the class. Allow each team to critique the presentation in terms of their own ideas and the following:
   * The model of the purchase decision process
   * The ultimate consumer or organizational buying motives
   * Any psychological or sociocultural influences present
   * The communication process in general
   * Barriers to effective communication

2. One student acts as a salesperson and another as a prospect. For two minutes, the salesperson chooses a product and describes the benefits of owning it. The prospect listens but says nothing. From watching the prospect's body language, the class determines whether the salesperson is likely to close the sale.

3. Does word choice affect understanding? What common saying has been reworded in each of the statements below?
   * A single in-and-out movement of a small cylindrical object with an oblong opening in one end through which an elongated fiber is passed produces the fortuitous circumstance of precluding the necessity of performing nine such procedures at some future date.

   * A wildly gyrating fragment of consolidated solid mineral matter is never encapsulated in a cutaneous layer of bryophytic living organisms that do not possess locomotive qualities in themselves.

   * You may succeed in conducting a large, solid hoofed herbivorous mammal of the family Equidae to the brink of a reservoir of liquid oxide of hydrogen, but there is no surety that you will succeed in coercing said mammal to imbibe a potation.

   * Members of the populace who sojourn in habitations of an amorphous inorganic transparent material made largely of silicates are well advised to eschew propelling concretions of earthy or mineral matter.

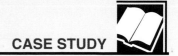

CASE STUDY

Case 4.1—Never Judge a Book by its Cover

Maria Zambli was a very productive real estate agent for a national realty company. She became confused with the Brownell's attitude toward a new house they obviously liked very much, but were resisting to buy. In her mind she is asking, "What is going on? This is simple."

Joseph and Katie Brownell are a young couple each twenty two years old who have been married for two years. This is their first home purchase and they are excited. They lived with his parents for a year and rented an apartment for the past year. Joseph and Katie recognized the problem they faced - high rent and "nothing to show for it" when they moved out. Both of them saw a need to build equity in a home and property and be in more control of their own circumstances.

The couple chose the home because of a combination of location, features, and price. They did not know the agent beforehand and had no experience with such an involved purchase transaction or such an enthusiastic sales person. Maria could see that the young couple had minimal education, came from a low income situation, and seemed to have trouble with all of the technical aspects of a home purchase. She just took it for granted that everyone understood the basics of home buying. Maria must communicate well or take a chance of losing the sale.

Maria, the Brownells, and the seller agreed on a selling price—so far, so good. Neither of the buyers had ever paid real estate property taxes before and could not understand the dramatic increase in taxes over the current property valuation. In their area property is reevaluated every three years. Last year the empty lot was valued at $18,000 and taxed accordingly. Now that the new house was built, the lot and house together are valued at $95,000 and the taxes are five times the lot rate. The assessor will not value the property for two more years and the Brownells could not understand that taxes for now would have to be based on the market price.

Homeowners insurance was new to Joseph and Katie. They did not need this type of coverage when they lived with his parents and were not even aware that renter's insurance was available. When they saw the estimate for the house payment, property taxes, and insurance they began to complain that it would be impossible to come up with this much money on their incomes. Maria explained that taxes and insurance did not have to be paid annually in lump sums and that they could escrow these payments. Escrow? What a strange sounding word to them. The agent explained they could put aside money each month to pay these costs and this would help their cash flow.

So many technical terms were confusing to Katie and Joseph. A sale that normally took Maria about 30 to 45 minutes to complete took two and one half hours. She was happy for the Brownells but was glad it was all over. How did communication become so difficult?

1. Identify the areas in the purchase decision process where the major problems occurred.

2. Were there any psychological influences at play in this scenario? If yes, what are they?

3. What areas in the communication model should be strengthened?

4. Did Maria assume too much? Explain how she could have communicated better.

Case 4.2—Easy Does It

Margie Barnes, sales representative for Easy-System Business Forms, has been assigned a sales territory that includes Kentucky, Tennessee, Alabama, and Georgia. Easy-System is a newcomer in the business forms field, and Barnes is its newest sales representative. Easy-System does little advertising and instead relies on its sales force to inform prospective customers about its products. The company as yet has no formal training program for sales personnel. It depends on the individual to be familiar with product features and company services.

Barnes's first selling effort was to a manufacturer of microchips. Future Chip is presently revamping its accounting and bookkeeping system; unfortunately, Barnes was unaware of this. In fact, she has taken very little time to acquaint herself with Future Chip's operations or with the microchip industry as a whole.

Barnes entered the office of Future Chip and asked to see the chief accountant. Although he usually saw salespeople by appointment only, Byron Glover consented to see her. They met briefly, and Glover called Ken Campbell, a systems analyst, and asked him to join them. Barnes emphasized the low price of the products, their convenient size, practicality, color coding to help the accountant, ease of ordering, prompt delivery, and easy credit terms. The meeting was interrupted by several telephone calls for Glover and Campbell and by a visitor looking for Campbell. Barnes tried to point out the merits of each form but failed to present them as an integrated system. Glover and Campbell asked several questions, but Barnes sensed that their interest was artificial. When she was ready to leave, she offered some sample forms that Glover and Campbell could examine and use. They declined the offer and told Barnes they would call her after they had better determined their needs.

1. Identify some of the barriers to effective communication in this case and suggest ways in which they might have been eliminated or reduced.

2. Did anything take place that should have given Barnes an idea that this prospective client was interested in a total system?

Case 4.3 - Getting "Teed" Off

Bob Andrews was five minutes early for his 2:00 p.m. appointment with the purchasing agent for Belton County Consolidated School District. The purchasing agent, Dan Lane, arrived at the office at 2:30, nodded toward Andrews, and began discussing afternoon appointments and a golf game scheduled later that day with his receptionist.

At 2:45, the receptionist ushered Andrews into Lane's office. Lane said, "What's up?" and began sorting a stack of mail on the desk. Soon after Andrews started his presentation, Lane's golf partner called and chatted for ten minutes.

At that point, Lane instructed the receptionist to hold all calls and briefly turned his attention to Bob before he began to clip his fingernails. When the receptionist entered to remind Lane of an important meeting with the superintendent of schools, he apologized to Andrews for not having much time, rose, and thanked him for his call. Andrews quickly got up, said, "You're welcome," and stomped out.

1. What verbal and nonverbal communication cues were available for Andrews to evaluate when he called on Lane?

2. If you had been in Andrew's place, how would you have handled the situation?

Finding Your Selling Style

LEARNING OBJECTIVES

- Recognize the different behavioral styles.

- Identify your own dominant social style.

- Learn how to deal with people who operate from each of the various styles.

- Understand the concept of versatility and how it affects your ability to relate to all social styles.

- Become familiar with gender issues in selling.

- Discover how neurolinguistic programming can be useful to salespeople.

Six weeks into his job as a sales and marketing executive in a technology manufacturing company, Don Evans realized that something was very wrong. Not the work itself—Evans loved digging for the facts, arranging timetables, charting the development of new products. The job was fine. It was the boss he couldn't stand. Recently, Evans approached his boss with a brand new product development plan. Everything was detailed to precision: Target dates, costs, sales approaches, and presentation data—the works. Halfway through the presentation, the boss leaped to her feet and began tossing out ideas right and left. Some were impractical; all would throw the carefully thought-out plan completely out of whack. When Evans pointed this out, his boss got miffed and charged out of the room, ordering over her shoulder, "Now you've got the concept. Go to it." "Go to what?" Evans pondered. "All I've got to work with is a blast of hot air."

Some call such an incident a personality conflict. Others would say they are simply not on the same wavelength, or perhaps they're not seeing eye-to-eye. Let's call it what it really is—a difference in social styles. Conflict or miscommunication will exist not simply because of work pressures, but because of social style differences. Don, as you will learn in this chapter, has an *analytical* social style, while his boss has an *expressive* style. Unknowingly, they communicate disrespect to one another. This lack of understanding and knowledge concerning behavioral styles can cause lost sales, frustration, resentment, or resignation.

Proper communication ceased in the situation because Don did not recognize that his ideas got his boss thinking, and she did not stick around to clarify her suggestions. Don stopped listening and took her brainstorming personally, seeing it as criticism rather than as development of his original thoughts. They were like the two old-timers who sat on the front porch in their rocking chairs reminiscing about days gone by. Both were so hard of hearing that neither ever knew for sure what the other was saying. They just took turns talking, each lost in his own memories, but content that there was someone nearby. If you want to close more sales, however, "being nearby" isn't enough.

Success and Behavioral Styles

Because of the importance of communication in the selling process, successful salespeople constantly search for new ways to make their communication more effective. They are eager to learn how they may better anticipate and avoid conflict situations. Gauging your client's personality will help you close the sale and succeed in business.[1] A selling transaction, whether it involves products, services, or ideas, is a communication exchange in which two individuals develop a mutually desirable solution to a problem about which both are concerned. The best sales relationships are long-term ones based on mutual trust and credibility. The pertinent question then becomes, "How can I sell so that I demonstrate respect for the customer, build credibility for myself and my product, and set up a win-win situation for both of us?"

The concept of behavioral styles is of tremendous importance for salespeople; and it is an idea formally developed by the Swiss psychologist Carl Jung.[2] Jung built upon and extended the knowledge of the adult ego state developed by Sigmund Freud, who first introduced the idea. Jung's work on behavioral functions resulted in a theory of personality that included four functions: *Intuition, thinking, feeling,* and *sensing.* Since his death in 1961, his work has become increasingly popular through the publication of his writings and the work of others who interpret and continue to apply his principles.

Several behavioral style models of special interest to salespeople have been developed and introduced by various authors. David Merrill and Roger Reid began the development of their

Social Styles Model in the early 1960s. Dr. Paul Mok, working independently of Merrill and Reid, developed what he referred to as the Communicating Styles Technology Model. More recently the Wilson Learning Corporation and Dr. Tony Alessandra and Associates Inc. have expanded and added their own research to these original models. The material presented in this chapter has been gleaned from these four related approaches.[3]

The Social Styles Model

Everyone learns as a child that family members and friends have different personalities. Perhaps you could always elicit sympathy from your mother but found that your father considered each situation and evaluated the circumstances prior to sympathizing or reprimanding you. You may have had a sibling who had a totally different personality from everyone else in the household. In your family, you had time to learn the ways you can best persuade or get along with various relatives. In a business or social situation, you have less time to evaluate and adjust your persuasive skills. The prospect's manner and social style are often deceptive and you may miss what is happening. The most common mistake is not understanding how prospects think and make decisions.[4] The social styles model provides a useful tool for making such an evaluation in the shortest possible time. The better you understand personality types, the more successful you will be in communicating with the various people you meet.

Each person has a primary communicating style that is blended or fine-tuned by a secondary style. These primary and secondary styles shape others' perceptions of you and filter your perceptions of other people. A second dimension to this model comes into play when you are under stress. At such times, you may shift to a different style of behavior. You may be aware of the shift yet feel unable to prevent it. People use four basic styles to deal with the world. Each is based upon one of four basic functions of human personality:

1. The driver or sensing function of taking in here-and-now sensory information and reacting to it.

2. The expressive or intuitive function of imagination and abstract thought.

3. The amiable or feeling function of personal and emotional reactions to experience.

4. The analytical or thinking function of organizing and analyzing information in a logical fashion.

The Four Communicating Styles:

Driver   Expressive   Amiable   Analytical

Everyone uses each of the four functions, but the frequency of use differs among individuals.[5] These styles can even be observed in young children. Behavioral patterns, Jung claimed, are genetically determined and are seen in infants during their first days of life. Like adults, young children process experience according to their own individual styles. It is important to recognize that on occasion, people will have the tendency to switch from one pattern to another as their mood, nature or purpose of the purchase changes.[6]

Basic Communication Concepts

Four basic concepts underlie the behavioral styles communication model presented in this chapter:

1. A style is an overall approach used to receive and send messages. It consists of verbal, nonverbal, and behavioral elements. Everyone uses a blend of the driver, expressive, amiable, and analytical styles, although each person has a favorite style that is used more often than others.

2. Every person operates the majority of the time from a favorite style. This is the primary style. Everyone also has a secondary or backup style that may replace or modify the primary style.

3. Because style is reflected in behavior, you can identify someone else's primary style by observing behavioral clues. These clues include use of time, manner of speech, typical reaction to others, and approach to job performance.

4. People respond favorably to a style that is similar or complementary to their own primary and backup styles. When a salesperson's style is too different from that of the prospect, the resulting style conflict can be disastrous to the outcome of the transaction. What is said is often much less important than how it is said.[7]

Behavioral Styles in Selling

In selling, most of us tend to use one or two predominant styles, and your choice of style affects what you do and say. It also affects what prospects hear and believe during your presentation. Understanding the strengths and liabilities of your primary communicating style and learning to be versatile in your style can help you sell to more prospects more often.[8] The objective of this chapter then is to help you learn how to manage your daily interactions with customers and prospects more productively.

Exhibit 5.1 illustrates that your most damaging weaknesses (-) are merely exaggerations or over-extensions of your strengths (+). Your behavior responds to circumstances like the volume dial of a radio. When the volume is just right, the music is pleasing.

Δ **Exhibit 5.1**

Social Style Strengths and Weaknesses

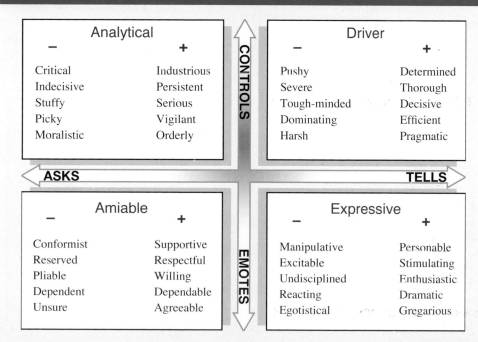

Analytical			Driver	
−	+	CONTROLS	−	+
Critical	Industrious		Pushy	Determined
Indecisive	Persistent		Severe	Thorough
Stuffy	Serious		Tough-minded	Decisive
Picky	Vigilant		Dominating	Efficient
Moralistic	Orderly		Harsh	Pragmatic

ASKS ← → TELLS

Amiable			Expressive	
−	+	EMOTES	−	+
Conformist	Supportive		Manipulative	Personable
Reserved	Respectful		Excitable	Stimulating
Pliable	Willing		Undisciplined	Enthusiastic
Dependent	Dependable		Reacting	Dramatic
Unsure	Agreeable		Egotistical	Gregarious

Similarly, when a behavioral style is used in moderation it is seen as a strength; when overused (that is, when the volume is too high), it becomes a weakness and leads to ineffective communication. Professional selling is all about managing relationships. Remember that a customer is not a transaction—a customer is a relationship! Most people don't even think about working on relationships in their daily lives. On the other hand, relationship salespeople take time to think about and understand the people around them. The relationship selling approach will strengthen and enhance your selling style by turning you into a relationship-oriented helper. The relationship style of selling is the 21st-century approach to helping clients and prospects buy.

When you go for your next job interview, you will likely be asked to take a personality test. The use of personality inventories in personnel selection has grown in popularity over the past decade. A recent study that summarized the results of fifteen prior studies that investigated the relationship between personality traits and job performance has found convincing evidence of the effectiveness of the use of personality inventories in applicant selection.[9] Although your personality style is not a true predictor of overall work performance, it can predict success in specific occupations or relate to specific criteria, which is why is it vital that you determine where you fall in the behavioral styles model and the descriptions found in this chapter.

Remember that the emphasis in studying behavioral style characteristics is on surface behavior, not on an in-depth personality analysis. Human behavior is predictable because ninety percent of our actions are controlled by habits and attitudes. The social styles model does not describe a person's complete personality because it omits reference to the individual's beliefs, ethics, abilities, and intelligence. What it does is describe the basic attributes or characteristics of behavior: *assertiveness* and *responsiveness*.

Attributes of Behavior

When you meet someone for the first time, your mind subconsciously reacts to two main characteristics: assertiveness and responsiveness. *Assertiveness* represents the effort a person makes to influence or control the thoughts and actions of others. *Responsiveness* is the willingness with which a person outwardly shares feelings or emotions and develops relationships.[10]

Assertiveness and responsiveness levels vary from one individual to another, and anyone may be high or low in either dimension or in both dimensions or anywhere in between. Several basic terms provide a thumbnail sketch of the characteristics of each dimension:

Low in Responsiveness	**High in Responsiveness**
• formal and proper	• relaxed and warm
• fact-oriented	• open and approachable
• guarded, cool, and aloof	• dramatic and animated
• disciplined about time	• flexible about time
• seldom makes gestures	• oriented toward relationships
• controlled body language	and feelings

Low in Assertiveness	**High in Assertiveness**
• introverted	• risk-taker
• supportive, a team player	• swift in decision-making
• easygoing	• willing to confront others
• avoids taking risks	• very competitive
• good listener	• take-charge attitude
• reserved in their opinions	• expresses opinions

Recognizing Social Styles

Combining the assertiveness and responsiveness characteristics makes it possible to develop a map of what others are doing or saying. Exhibit 5.2 shows the relationships among the four social styles. The horizontal axis is the range from the least to most assertive. Assertive people take a stand and make their position clear to others. Because they are ambitious, competitive, and quick to take action and express strong opinions, they are located on the telling end of the social style axis. Nonassertive individuals are seen as cooperative, silent, and slow to act, and they are located at the asking end of the axis. The least assertive individuals are in quartile D, and the most assertive in quartile A, with quartiles B and C representing intermediate levels of assertiveness.

The vertical axis indicates the range from least to most responsive. Non-responsive individuals, those in quartile 1, are largely indifferent to the feelings of others, reserved, and no-nonsense in attitude. The responsive individuals found in quartile 4 are strongly people-oriented, concerned about relationships, and subjective. Those in quartiles 2 and 3 display intermediate levels of responsiveness.

Δ Exhibit 5.2

The Social Styles Profile

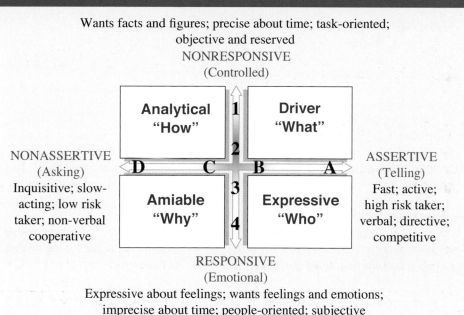

Wants facts and figures; precise about time; task-oriented; objective and reserved

NONRESPONSIVE
(Controlled)

| Analytical "How" | 1 | Driver "What" |

NONASSERTIVE (Asking)
Inquisitive; slow-acting; low risk taker; non-verbal cooperative

D   C   B   A

ASSERTIVE (Telling)
Fast; active; high risk taker; verbal; directive; competitive

2

| Amiable "Why" | 3 | Expressive "Who" |
| | 4 | |

RESPONSIVE
(Emotional)

Expressive about feelings; wants feelings and emotions; imprecise about time; people-oriented; subjective

Identifying the Four Behavioral Styles

Identifying the levels of assertiveness and responsiveness a person demonstrates is not a precise method of complete personality evaluation. With study and practice, however, Dr. Mok suggests that you can become 70 to 80 percent effective in using your observations to predict habitual behavioral patterns and be prepared to use your knowledge to improve the communication environment. Each possible combination of the two traits suggests one of the basic social styles. The four styles are linked to distinctive and unique habits of interactive behavior. The name given to each style reflects general characteristics rather than full, specific details. Keep in mind that no one style is preferred over another. Each has its own strengths and weaknesses, and successful people as well as failures are found in each style group, as are people of both sexes and all ethnic groups, ages, and other segments of the population.[11]

Drivers tell and control, are high in assertiveness, and low in responsiveness. They control others by telling them what to do and control themselves by remaining objective. They are task-oriented and combine personal power and emotional control in relationships with others. They are *control specialists*.

Expressives tell and emote. Like drivers, they are highly assertive, but they are also high in emotional responsiveness. They attempt to tell people what to do, but place more emphasis on their relationships with people than they do on the task itself. They are *social specialists*.

Amiables ask and emote, are low in assertiveness, and high in responsiveness. They rely on a personal feeling approach to get things done. They are *support specialists*, combining personal reserve and emotional expression.

Analyticals ask and control, and they are low in both assertiveness and responsiveness. They are highly task-oriented but soften that style with low assertiveness. They ask rather than direct. They are *technical specialists*, combining personal reserve and emotional control.

The Professor of Human Behavior

Tom Hoek has earned what could be called a Ph.B—he is a *Professor of Human Behavior*. He says that we are all in the people business. As salespeople we observe and verify behavior and have a constant need to become expert at interpreting what we see. Tom is the president of Insurance Systems of Tennessee, Inc., a training firm specializing in insurance and investment training courses.

In any personal relationship that you have, Tom suggests everybody has their own particular point of view. Ultimately, in every situation, the most persuasive person wins. When you understand behavioral styles technology and what motivates each of the styles you can adapt your own style to meet the needs of others. Just exercise a bit of applied psychology. All of us have a way we like to be treated.

Tom uses the phrase *Psychological Reciprocity* to describe what should happen in a sales situation. You make the initial attempt to adapt to the prospect's social style. The prospect is then motivated to move toward you—to reciprocate. Real communication and understanding occur much quicker than if each person stays firmly entrenched in their own particular style.

Behavioral styles technology helps you present the right product in the right way. Tom suggests that styles are fixed early in life—it's what you do with your style that makes a difference. Tom uses style flexing to complement the other person's style. He says this is truly win-win selling. Tom's motto is: "He who trims himself to suit everybody will soon whittle himself away."

Versatility as a Communication Tool

When people of different styles meet and behave strictly according to the characteristics of their own personal styles, conflict often results. A salesperson who is an amiable and a prospect who is a driver can quickly arrive at cross-purposes. A driver client wants to get facts and to accomplish the task at hand; the amiable salesperson wants to cultivate a personal relationship.

When such a situation occurs, the only way to avoid an escalation in miscommunication or a conflict is for one of the two people involved to engage in some style flexibility. In an ideal situation, both are willing to move part way, but the salesperson must be capable of making most of any necessary temporary adjustments. This willingness to try behaviors not necessarily characteristic of your style is called behavioral flexibility or versatility.[12]

Versatility or behavioral flexibility is a person's willingness to control personal behavior patterns and adapt to other people as a means of reducing the possibility of ineffective communication. The salesperson's own personal style does not change, but rather techniques are applied that work in that particular situation.[13] For example, when meeting with an analytical, the expressive salesperson can incorporate versatility by talking less, listening more, and focusing on facts. Versatility should never be equated with either insincerity or mere imitation of the prospect's style. Versatile salespeople seek a reasonable compromise. They do not become so highly changeable that their pace and priority needs are constantly set aside for those of clients.

Be versatile with prospects and you'll find you make more sales more often.

Some salespeople are far more successful than others. Why do these people always seem to be able to close the sale? The truth is that certain natural-born salespeople have learned how to adapt their sales presentation to each unique client while serving everyone equally. They are at ease with both the demanding and the easygoing client. Sometimes their communication is loud and forceful. Other times, it's quiet and reassuring. What these successful salespeople know is that selling is personal. Gauging each client's personality helps them predict and influence behavior.[14]

The prospect's preferences in pace and priorities must be recognized and given the importance that seems right to the prospect. Strive for *Psychological Reciprocity*. That is, as the salesperson, you make the initial attempt to get into the client's world. The person is then challenged to move toward you; to reciprocate. *And you connect!* Rapport is established with the client much quicker than if each of you had stayed firmly entrenched in your own particular social style.[15]

Be aware of the multitude of areas in a sales situation that make versatility one of the greatest tools you have to get a *yes* from your prospects. The following aspects of a face-to-face interview often illicit the need for you to stay versatile, responsive, and ultimately, willing to adapt and change to fit each situation:[16]

Comfort. Does the prospect seem nervous or edgy?

Tension. Is there an air of tension or general discomfort?

Prospect assertiveness in asking questions. Does the prospect provide you with more sales ammo by asking questions that may reveal a way to sell them?

Prospect responsiveness to your presentation. Is the prospect with you, or do they seem to be preoccupied.

Level of openness. Is the prospect sharing pertinent information that will help you better discover how to serve his needs?

The Interaction of Styles

The dimensions of assertiveness and responsiveness operate in people's pace and their priorities. *Pace* is the speed at which a person prefers to move. Those who are low in assertiveness (analyticals and amiables) prefer a slow pace; those high in assertiveness (drivers and expressives) prefer a fast pace in conversation, deliberation, and problem solving.[17]

Priorities concern what a person considers important and tend to be related to the dimension of responsiveness. Those who are low in responsiveness put tasks at the top of their priority list, and those who are high in responsiveness put relationships in first place. These conflicts may be summarized as follows:

Styles Shared	Dimension	Source of Conflict	Area of Agreement
Analytical/Amiable	Low assertiveness	Priorities	Pace
Driver/Expressive	High assertiveness	Priorities	Pace
Analytical/Driver	Low responsiveness	Pace	Priorities
Amiable/Expressive	High responsiveness	Pace	Priorities
Analytical/Expressive	None	Both	None
Amiable/Driver	None	Both	None

Conflicts that involve only priorities or only pace can be handled with relative ease; real trouble results when the styles of two people conflict in both pace and priorities.

Fortunately, few people are locked into a single style. Between the extremes of each dimension are many degrees of responsiveness and assertiveness. The descriptions of the four styles, then, do not represent absolutes. If you deal with every customer in the same way, you will close a small percentage of all your contacts, because you will only close one personality style. But if you learn how to effectively work with all four personality styles, you can significantly increase your closing ratio.[18]

Salespeople who do not adjust their behavior to meet the style needs of clients face deteriorating situations. For example, an expressive salesperson's questions may be interpreted as a personal challenge or attack by an analytical prospect. If the analytical prospect responds to the questions merely to save face, the expressive salesperson then tends to talk more, move faster, and push the analytical into still greater conflict.

In any situation, conflict is finally relieved in a manner typical of the individual style. The expressive usually attacks verbally. The driver tends to become overbearing, pushy, and dictatorial. The amiable generally submits in order to avoid conflict at all costs but experiences resentment and distrust. The analytical withdraws—flight rather than fight. In a conflict situation, most people tend to move to the extreme dimensions of their favorite style.

To avoid distrust and ultimately a breakdown in communication, you must meet the needs of your prospects, especially their behavioral style needs. Treat them as they want to be treated, and move according to the pace and priority they desire. The most successful salespeople are be able to help customers verbalize problems, and to create a solution that customers would not have developed alone by letting them set the pace.[19]

Identifying Pace and Priority

How do you go about determining someone's pace and priorities? Ask yourself these three questions and observe the answers:

1. How *fast* does the person make decisions and get things done?

2. How *competitive* is the person? Not primarily in sports, but
   • Is the person competitive in a conversation?
   • Does the person fight for air time in a meeting?

3. How much *feeling* is displayed in a verbal and nonverbal communication?

• How often does the person smile?
• Do they gesture broadly?

Your goal is to identify pace and priorities accurately and respond in an appropriate manner. How can you find out your prospect's information preferences? Use one of these statements to assist you:[20]

1. "Ordinarily I have an organized presentation and get right to it, but today maybe I should get to know you better. What would you like me to do?"

2. "I am prepared to get right into my presentation or if you prefer we can chat a bit so that I can learn about you and your organization. Which do you prefer?"

3. "There are a lot of ways I can start explaining exactly how this process would work based on the concerns you were kind enough to share with me at our meeting last week. Would you prefer I start with the end in mind and then work backwards, or would you like to hear the step-by-step details first?"

The expressive and amiable styles would respond to these statements indicating a desire to chat and get to know one another. The driver and analytical styles would want you to begin your presentation.

Gender Style Differences

While it is essential to recognize and adjust to different social styles, it is also necessary to recognize the contribution that gender makes to our communication in the business world. The issue of proxemics, the distance that individuals prefer to keep between themselves and others, also becomes more recognizable when speaking to someone of the opposite sex.[21] That is why we must be sensitive to gender issues and adjust to them just as we do for social style differences. If not handled correctly, these seemingly insignificant differences can break down communication lines and damage relationships, and this ultimately hurts your company and your income!

Use the strengths unique to your gender and style.

One way to ensure effective cross-gender communication is to emphasize and encourage male and female distinctions in management processes and interpersonal relationships. By emphasizing the differences in a positive manner, the different viewpoints can be highly productive. Both men and women bring to the selling table different perspectives, experiences, and communication skills, and they interpret language in very distinct ways. Ultimately, however, they use these distinctly different styles and patterns of speech to deliver roughly the same message.

There is no proven significant differences between men and women in how smart they work, in how hard they work or in how well they perform.[22] Although there have been numerous studies conducted over the past several years regarding sex-related differences, the results are often contradictory. The plethora of research does, however, provide some new perspectives to consider concerning the growing role of women in corporate America. In various studies, women demonstrated higher levels of contingent reward, or behaviors in which a leader rewards followers for the completion of tasks. Contingent reward behavior has been identified as a predictor of effectiveness which would suggest that women may actually possess a leadership advantage in some cases.[23]

Relating to the Opposite Sex

Whether or not you have experienced how gender differences hinder relationships in selling when handled improperly, it is clear that the unequal treatment of employees by management hinders the success of any business. A research study by Russ & McNeilly concluded that managers who treat male and female sales reps the same miss the potential benefits that different gender styles provide.[24]

A key question to ask is whether or not gender differences, in and of themselves, create diverse ways of thinking or different behavioral relationships. If so, what are some things to be aware of when you're selling to someone of the opposite sex? Research by Siguaw & Honeycutt found that women were engaged more frequently in customer-oriented selling than were their male counterparts.[25]

Despite significant advances in gender relations, inequalities still exist in the business world that sometimes make it difficult for men and women to fully relate to each other. Vicki Donlan, publisher of *Women's Business Boston*, explains that despite a law that was instated over forty years ago requiring equal pay for equal work, a large number of women still get paid less for the same job than do their male counterparts. She cites two reasons for this: discrimination is a still a force in the social and economic structure, and more significantly, the stereotypes of past generation (i.e. women stay home and raise families) are still with us.[26] As salespeople, we must work to overcome ingrained stereotypical ideas of gender roles and recognize the importance of both sexes at the negotiation table.

When men and women find themselves sitting across from one another at the bargaining table, they must learn to adjust their styles. During the sales interview they should use the strengths unique to their gender.

Our society is changing, and one of the key ways it is changing, at least in the business world, is that men and women are becoming more alike in their dealings with clients and customers. Just because something is written about the differences between men and women, it does not mean that it has value in every selling encounter between men and women. For example, when a woman nods her head, that doesn't necessarily mean she agrees with what a man is saying. When a woman crosses her arms, she is not automatically indicating she is closed to the idea being presented. She just may be tired or cold. Likewise, if a man doesn't look you in the eye when he is speaking, that does not necessarily mean he's hiding something—it may be his style. Acting on generalities, regardless of gender, can kill a sale more quickly than anything else.[27]

Exhibit 5.3 provides some suggestions for dealing with gender differences. You must be prepared to communicate effectively with your male and female sales managers, fellow sales reps, as well as the men and women decision-makers you call on. No one can make a sweeping statement about how all women or all men like to sell or be sold. In any selling situation it's vital to communicate in a way that substantiates what's meaningful to that individual, and gender may help determine what a client feels is important. Subtle, gender-based changes may give you the edge you're looking for to boost sales.[28]

Salesmen:

- *Report talk vs. rapport talk.* Male bonding through storytelling and anecdotes is fine; however, women are more interested in your product than your latest fishing trip.

- *Stop interrupting.* Men interrupt women more often than other men. This is a good way to lose a sale. Learn to listen.

- *Feel the sale.* There is more to selling than numbers. Women are interested in emotional satisfaction as well as the bottom line.

- *Control your language.* Never again in a professional situation use the words "honey," "dear," or "sweetie." This is simply intolerable and might be offensive to some people.

Saleswomen:

- *Speak confidently and clearly.* It has been established that men will interrupt women, especially if they sound tentative or unsure.

- *Feed them data.* Men love facts and the illusion of being cool and rational. Let them know you have also done your homework. Remain enthusiastic; just rein it in a bit.

- *Practice your humor.* Women tend to use humor less than men. Being funny at the right moment is very important.

- *Watch your language.* Avoid "girl talk" when presenting to men. Words like "lovely," "charming," or "adorable" should be excluded from your sales vocabulary.

Reading the Prospect's Environment

Important clues to a client's style are in the environment as well as in verbal and nonverbal actions. Observe how the office is decorated and arranged, how objects are displayed, and what seating arrangements are available. Suppose that upon entering a prospect's office, you notice family pictures on the desk, nature posters, a round desk, and a separate seating area with four comfortable chairs. What would be your first impression of that client's behavioral style? Did you say *amiable*? If so, you are right. Next, you can confirm or adjust your initial impression by observing the prospect's actions and speech. If the prospect rises to greet you personally and sits in an easy chair your impression of amiable would tend to be confirmed.

Let's try another example. You enter the prospect's office and notice a diploma, an achievement plaque, and a poster on the wall that says "Why not?" The desk presents several jumbled stacks of paper and a generally chaotic appearance. Two overstuffed chairs by the open side of the desk provide seating. A bookcase with stacks of books and folders intermixed and a plant on the file cabinet, complete the furnishings. The disorganization, the wall decorations emphasizing achievement, and the comfortable and accessible seating suggest that this office houses an *expressive*.

However, a word of caution is needed. Roger Reid tells of a Texas company that mandated that all of its top executives display pictures of their families on top of their desks. He also notes that in some companies the top executives do not select or arrange anything in their offices. The pictures on the wall, chairs and desks, and office layout are selected and done for the executives by staff or consultants. Thus, you must confirm any initial environmental impression by noting the prospect's actions, tone of voice, speech patterns, and interpersonal behavior.[29]

Verbal, Nonverbal, and Behavioral Characteristics

You can use knowledge of these styles to characterize the observable behavior of most prospects. Although we all possess traits from each of the styles, one style ordinarily dominates. Of course, identifying a social style does not provide a crystal ball that unerringly predicts a person's future actions and decisions, but it does provide a basis for forming reasonably accurate expectations about recurring behavior and for being prepared to respond appropriately. Both verbal and nonverbal clues are useful in identifying social style. Exhibit 5.4 summarizes the behavior typical of each of the four styles.[30]

Δ **Exhibit 5.4**

Typical Behavior Associated With Each of the Four Social Styles ·

Analytical	Driver
• Cautious in decisions and action	• Decisive in action and decision making
• Likes organization and structure	• Likes control; dislikes inaction
• Asks specific questions	• Prefers maximum freedom to manage self and others
• Prefers objective, task-oriented, intellectual work	• Cool, independent, and competitive with others
• Wants to be right, so collects much data	• Low tolerance for feelings, attitudes, and advice of others
• Works slowly, precisely, and alone	• Works quickly and impressively alone
• Has good problem-solving skills	• Has good administrative skills

Amiable	Expressive
• Slow in making decisions or taking actions	• Spontaneous actions and decisions
• Likes close, personal relationships	• Exaggerates and generalizes
• Dislikes interpersonal conflict	• Tends to dream and get others caught up in those dreams
• Supports and actively listens to others	• Jumps from one activity to another
• Weak in goal setting and self-direction	• Works quickly and excitedly with others
• Seeks security and identification with a group	• Seeks esteem and group identification
• Has good counseling and listening skills	• Has good persuasive skills

Drivers

Drivers exhibit minimum concern for the feelings of others. A vice-president of marketing for a major theme park in Ohio was heard to say, "My secretary used to drive me to distraction. I'd ask her how her weekend went and she'd actually tell me. In detail! All I wanted to hear was fine or not so hot." Now those are the words of a true driver. If you say something harsh, they don't even seem to notice. They consider yes-people to be weak. Stand up to drivers. Sell to them by showing them what your product can do. Drivers' feelings are not easily hurt because they do not take things personally.

Drivers tend to be intense, competitive, fast-paced, and goal-oriented. They pride themselves on the ability to get things done. They like to make things happen. Convince them that your proposed action works and that it will provide all the benefits you promise. They are more impressed by what they see and hear than by what others say about you or your offering.

At their best, drivers are human dynamos. Resourceful, organized, and pragmatic, they impose high standards on themselves and others. As a result, they may be seen as impatient or tireless. They push to perfect their own skills but also invest time and effort in coaching other people in skill development. At their worst, they appear to give inadequate consideration to the long-range consequences of their actions. They draw criticism for seeking to impose on others their expectations for drive, speed and zeal. Under stress, drivers can seem anti-intellectual and may defensively overreact to any opinions differing from their own, especially to those that seem to resist action. Drivers are likely to feel that any failure is evidence that others were not loyal enough or willing to work hard enough to make the project a success.

Customize Your Selling Style to Hit A Hole In One With The Driver

Drivers do not care about developing a personal relationship with you. They are impatient and need to be in control. Therefore:

1. Spend little time attempting to relate to them on a personal level.

2. Move fast and isolate the most dollar-related product benefits that can be verified by producing concrete evidence.

3. Do not make a lengthy presentation citing all the benefits. Be brief and stress the bottom line.

4. The fewer visual aids you use, the better. Any visuals you choose to show must be absolutely relevant to the major points.

5. Ask questions to involve them, get them to talk, and allow them to lead. Depend on your choice of subject matter in asking questions to maintain control of the interview.

6. They will test you to see what you are made of; so be willing to joust with them. If you challenge them, challenge the concepts rather than the person.

7. Answer objections immediately, and never try to bluff.

8. Present several alternatives from which they may select their own solution. Avoid telling them what is best.

9. An action close stressing an immediate opportunity works well.

Expressives

Expressives temper assertiveness with concern for the feelings of others. You must compliment them. They desire success, but are recognition motivated. Show them how to win. Let them talk and they often sell themselves. Tell them who else uses your product. Testimonials from well-known people or people they respect are important.

Expressives pride themselves on originality, foresight, and the ability to see the big picture. Reinforce their self-image as visionaries and idea people, and they will be receptive to your ideas. At their best, expressives often see new possibilities and present fresh ideas and approaches to problems. At their worst, they seem to base decisions on opinions, hunches, or intuition rather than on facts. They want to delegate the details to someone who has time for it while they are free to dream. They may be impatient when others demand some documentation before accepting the vision or ideas they offer. Under stress, expressives run the risk of seeming detached. They appear indifferent to problems and seem to be living in an ivory tower. They may spend time defending their ideas instead of trying to make them work in practical manner.

The expressive's love of risk-taking makes it easier for them to take a chance on your product. Refer to the product as a "sure bet" or guarantee that you will "make this risk pay off big." Emphasize the importance of risk-taking to making progress and meeting goals, and show the expressive your product's payoff potential by sharing exactly what it can do and what that means to them. When you have a qualified expressive whose needs match your product's benefits, you should not have to do much persuading. Remember, expressives are intuition-driven.[31]

A Presentation Strategy For The Expressive

Expressives are visionaries and dreamers. Therefore:

1. Plan to show them how they can personally win and how their company can benefit.

2. Open with innovative ideas for them to grow and win with through your offering.

3. Ask open-end questions that allow them to talk at length about "their" plans for growth. Then relate your product's benefits to their plans.

4. Present proposals and seek feedback, using them as sounding boards. Convey respect for their intelligence, foresight, and prominence. Be careful, however, to avoid patronizing them.

5. Use some showmanship. They like to see the yellow binder, but are not necessarily interested in the details of what it contains.

6. Never argue or back them into a corner.

7. Ask if they want you to respond to their stated concerns. Often they respond, "No, I just wanted you to know how I am thinking."

8. Use testimonials, especially from well-known people because they identify with who else uses the product.

9. Allow them to carry out their own game plan, not yours.

Amiables

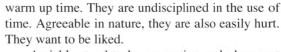

Amiables are submissive and willing to go along with the crowd. They need time to get to know you personally, so allow plenty of warm up time. They are undisciplined in the use of time. Agreeable in nature, they are also easily hurt. They want to be liked.

Amiables tend to be perceptive and observant individuals who are concerned with whether they like you, trust you, and can picture a positive long-term relationship with you. They are highly people-oriented in their management style and resent doing business with anyone who makes them uncomfortable or is unresponsive to their feelings. Their business decisions are markedly influenced by how their various options might impact the people in the organization. Before they accept your proposal or idea, they must be convinced that you personally believe in it. They must also know what risks are involved—especially risks to personal relationships.

Amiables at their best are truly perceptive and aware, skilled in communication, and empathetic listeners. Their insight enables them to assess organizational politics accurately. At their worst, they seem more concerned with the process of interaction than with the content of the matter at hand. They appear to be flying by the seat of their pants instead of relying in any measure on logic and thought. They seem to regard their own emotions as facts and act on the basis of their feelings. They may be criticized for being defensive, over-reactive, and too subjective.

To sell effectively to amiables, you have to show them you're a team player. Position yourself as their newest team member by first building rapport, then work side-by-side with them to accomplish the goals they've set. To minimize the amiable's insecurities, talk about the problems your product can solve and how solving them will help improve control and performance in the workplace, which will enhance management's image of them. It is the amiable's job to nurture the team, so don't forget to outline what your product will do for the people in the company.

A Presentation Strategy For The Amiable

Amiables must be convinced that you are authentic and have their best interests at heart. They have a difficult time saying yes. Therefore:

1. Plan to approach with as much personal information as possible.

2. Avoid a rigid or canned approach and presentation.

3. Make an informal presentation with visuals and testimonial information integrated.

4. Use empathy and show that you understand and accept their feelings.

5. Spend some time relating. Move to a first-name basis quickly.

6. Be open and candid. Develop a personal relationship with them.

7. Offer them money-back guarantees and personal assurances.

8. Avoid asking directly for their business. Instead, assume that they are favorably disposed to your proposition and suggest an easy next step.

9. Be prepared to use third-party references and case histories that link them to others.

Analyticals

Analyticals need time to assess and assimilate what they hear and see. They want to know just how things work and often say they want time to think things over. Product information is crucial. Know everything possible about your product, and don't expect to hear them say much.

Analyticals are highly logical, organized, and unsentimental. They tend to be fact-oriented. Their contribution to the management team is their ability to solve difficult problems and make sound, rational business decisions based on evidence and intelligent inferences rather than on imagination or gut feelings. They take a logical approach to responsibilities. The more supporting data you can provide for your ideas, the more likely you are to sell to them. They have little interest in your opinions and more in your ability to assemble and organize supportive data for use in weighing options and arriving at a systematic, well-thought-out solution to problems.

At their best, analyticals appear to be a consistent force for progress. They are top-flight planners and doers. They can cut through untested ideas and emotional fervor to find the core truth. They are effective organizers for research and planning. They are valuable in executing logical, painstaking, and profitable projects. At their worst, they are overly cautious and conservative.

They emphasize deliberation over action. They may become so involved in evaluating all the various details of a situation that others may regard them as indecisive stumbling blocks to innovative action. Under stress, analyticals can become rigid and insecure. They may fear taking risks. They seem more concerned with being right than with seizing opportunities.

In sales interviews with analyticals, be well prepared and equipped to answer all questions. Be cordial, but move quickly to the task. Study their needs logically. Ask lots of questions that show a clear direction and pay close attention to their answers. Support your logical proposal with full documentation.

Customize Your Sales Presentation For The Analytical

Analyticals are data-oriented and slow to make decisions. They are naturally suspicious and extremely cautious. They read and study everything. Therefore:

1. Know their business thoroughly. Go in with facts and the evidence to back them up.

2. Use a logic-based, low-key style of relating.

3. Be sure prospects understand the structure of how you will present the information and solicit feedback.

4. Emphasize tested, proven, well-documented aspects of your product's benefits.

5. Make use of visual aids—charts, graphs, written "leave-behind" documents— in the presentation.

6. Present information in a controlled, professional, highly organized fashion.

7. Point out the pros and cons of your offering. They will be thinking about them.

8. Present a detailed summary of major points and use the summary as a close.

9. Avoid saying, "Well, in my opinion. . ." They don't care about your opinions, just facts that you can document.

Neurolinguistic Programming

An entirely different approach to communicating effectively and understanding more about prospects is offered by neurolinguistic programming (NLP). It looks at how people create the results they want. In your career, this understanding can be the difference between success and a lost sale.[32] The primary focus of NLP is to pinpoint styles by eye-movement exercises designed to ascertain whether one is visual, auditory, or kinesthetic.[33] When it first began to attract attention, many people considered NLP to be just another pop-psychology craze similar to the various communication approaches that have been offered as the ultimate answer for managers who wanted increased personal power and influence, for lawyers who wanted to sway judges and juries, and for salespeople who wanted to sell anything to anyone. Instead, however, NLP offers one more way to observe people and understand their needs. It is entirely different from the behavioral styles theory, but in no way contradicts it. Neurolinguistic programming is the brainchild of linguist John Grinder and psychotherapist Richard Bandler.[34]

Identifying Modes of Perception

NLP is based on recognizing and then appealing to the dominant modes of perception used by another person. We all use these modes to map reality and build a model of what the world is like that can guide us through our environment. NLP is the science of how the brain learns. All of us have a basic learning mode: visual, auditory or kinesthetic. Each is used in various situations, yet most of us will favor one mode.[35]

Auditory. Some people perceive the world largely by hearing. They learn more quickly by listening than by reading or seeing. Experiences presented through other senses are mentally translated into an auditory mode. These are the people who test ideas by how they sound. They often use responses like, "I hear what you're saying," "It sounds good to me," and "I'm hearing a lot of complaints about that situation."

Visual. Other people perceive the world largely through sight. They learn and form opinions from what they see. They are the ones who originated the saying, "Seeing is believing." They form mental pictures of their experiences as a means of interpretation. They frequently use sentences like, "I see what you mean," "I'm in a fog about the whole concept," and "Do you get the picture?"

Kinesthetic. A smaller number of people perceive the world through the sense of touch. They feel life. Everything has a texture that either attracts or repels them. Subsets of the kinesthetic mode are the gustatory (taste) and the olfactory (smell) modes that sometimes come into play for kinesthetic people. Those operating in the kinesthetic mode say things like, "This deal just feels right (or wrong)," "That was a smooth presentation," "That transaction left a bad taste in my mouth," and "I smell something rotten about this deal."

Bandler and Grinder first used this information to teach therapists how to recognize these representational modes and use them to build rapport with their patients, to establish a climate of trust, and to improve communication. They soon realized that this powerful communication tool would work for people other than therapists. They began to train a number of people to teach these techniques.

NLP has been used by people who have turned it into a powerful manipulative tool for their own benefit to the detriment of others. When used ethically, however, it is a helpful method for cutting down the time needed to build trust and rapport—a necessary process in relationship selling.[36] Its misuse does not discount its effectiveness; many kinds of knowledge can be twisted into tools for satisfying personal greed by those whose value systems allow such unethical action. If you look at NLP as an additional tool for interpreting the behavior, needs, and motivation of people, you can use it just as ethically and helpfully as you can use the information about behavioral styles and body language.

Some salespeople seem to have a natural or intuitive ability to identify a prospect's behavior and personality traits and to adapt to them. They seem to possess an automatic radar system that instantly and unobtrusively sends out test signals, interprets the feedback, and then chooses the best tactics for establishing rapport. Developing such skills is one of the most difficult parts of sales training. NLP is one technique you can use to develop this ability.

Learning Eye Cues

Our eyes are seldom still. The direction they move during a conversation reveals the system of perception that is active at the moment. Exhibit 5.5 illustrates the various eye cues that help to identify the operative system. Eye movements in most people are similar and can usually be expected to show these processes:[37]

Δ **Exhibit 5.5**

Eye Cues Indicating Thought Processes ·

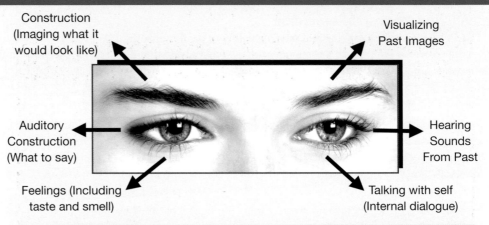

Construction (Imaging what it would look like)

Visualizing Past Images

Auditory Construction (What to say)

Hearing Sounds From Past

Feelings (Including taste and smell)

Talking with self (Internal dialogue)

Visual Perception	
Looking up and left	Visualizing (remembering) from the past; picturing the past mentally
Looking up and right	Visually constructing an image to see what it would look like

Kinesthetic Perception	
Looking down and right	Remembering past feelings

Auditory Perception	
Looking sideways to left	Hearing sounds or voices from the past (remembering)
Looking sideways to right	Constructing a future conversation; thinking of the right words to use
Looking down to left	Holding an internal dialogue with oneself; how something sounds

Some left-handed people reverse the normal right and left eye cues; therefore, eye cues can be used only as clues to be confirmed by further observation.

Interpreting Predicate Words

Most people are fairly consistent in eye movements, body language, behavior style, and all the other ways anyone has devised to help salespeople tune in on their prospects. NLP teaches us to look at eye cues and test them against predicate words, that is, how people talk. Exhibit 5.6 provides a list of predicate words that provide important information to confirm what is observed from eye cues. These words tell you how the other person is processing information. When these words match eye cues, you are on fairly safe ground in deciding which mode of perception is operating for the prospect at that moment.[38]

Δ Exhibit 5.6

Predicate Words: A Guide to the Modes of Perception

Visual		Auditory		Kinesthetic	
analyze	look	announce	noise	active	intuition
angle	notice	articulate	proclaim	affected	lukewarm
appear	obscure	audible	pronounce	bearable	motion
cognizant	observe	discuss	remark	concrete	panicky
conspicuous	perception	dissonant	report	emotional	pressure
dream	perspective	divulge	roar	feel	sensitive
examine	picture	earshot	rumor	firm	shallow
focus	scene	enunciate	shrill	flow	softly
foresee	sight	gossip	silence	foundation	solid
glance	sketchy	hear	sound	grasp	structured
hindsight	survey	hush	squeal	grip	tension
horizon	vague	inquire	talk	hanging	tied
idea	view	interview	tell	hassle	touch

Salespeople who are good builders of rapport use a few initial questions to get the prospect to talk so they can discover which type of system is in use. Salespeople do not have to memorize a long list of specific questions to evoke the crucial responses needed to determine a prospect's system. The usual opening dialogue a salesperson uses to get acquainted and put the prospect at ease serves admirably. For example, compare the two responses given to the question below and determine which system the answers seem to indicate:

QUESTION: That's an impressive trophy. Do you play a lot of golf?

ANSWER A: I play in a club foursome almost every Saturday. I enjoy keeping active. It wards off some of the pressure. Sometimes when things get into an unbearable hassle, golf relieves some of the tension. Gripping the club, feeling the impact as I hit the ball, and getting into the swing of the physical motion seems to put me back on a concrete foundation and makes me ready to get back in touch with reality instead of lapsing into panicky emotions.

ANSWER B: I play on Wednesday afternoons and see it as an opportunity to get away from the work scene when the picture gets too crowded or blurred. On the golf course I have time to lose myself in a new perspective. I look down the fairway all the way to the horizon and dream of seeing my ball fly all the way to the hole in one shot. Of course, I've actually done that only once, but the dream lets me focus on what is most important, observe the obstacles, and picture a way to avoid them. Then when I get back to work, the whole view seems to have more clarity and the path around the obstacles becomes conspicuous where before it had been obscured because I was too close to the trees to see the forest.

How did you identify the systems used by these two different people? The first was *kinesthetic*. Did you note some of the key words such as:

active	feeling	panicky	pressure	motion	emotions
hassle	foundation	concrete	tension	touch	

The second answer was *visual*. Note the key words in this response:

see	look	picture	scene	horizon	view
picture	conspicuous	dream	clarity	blurred	focus

Be sure to take into account the eye cues, body language, and any other information you have about the prospect as you attempt to decide which system the prospect is using. Remember that we all use the different perceptual fields, often in quick succession, but most of us have one we use more often than the others. When eye cues fit the predicate words used, the salesperson has a fairly sound basis for deciding what is going on in the prospect's mind. Once you know the prospect's favorite system, you know how that person usually maps out the environment and plans a route to the solution of a problem or to the reaching of a goal. Then you can speak a language the auditory prospect can *hear*, draw a picture the visual prospect can *see*, or structure something concrete the kinesthetic prospect can *grasp*.

The following chart summarizes some of the key features of the four social styles. Salespeople are only as good as their reflex actions allow them to be. Rather than a Ph.D., perhaps a salesperson should have a Ph.B.—Professor of Human Behavior. Study the chart below; learn how to read behavioral styles. There's an old saying—if you want to get better at something, learn more about it.

Social Styles Summary

	Driver	Expressive	Amiable	Analytical
Backup Style	Autocratic	Attacker	Acquiescer	Avoider
Measures personal value by	Results	Applause or approval	Security	Accuracy, "being right"
For growth needs to	Listen	Check	Initiate	Decide
Needs climate that	Allows to build own structure	Inspires to reach goals	Suggests	Provides details
Takes time to be	Efficient	Stimulating	Agreeable	Accurate
Support their	Conclusions and actions	Dreams and Intuitions	Relationships and feelings	Principles and thinking
Present benefits that tell	What	Who	Why	How
For decisions, give them	Options and probabilities	Testimonials and incentives	Guarantees and assurances	Evidence and service
Their specialty is	Controlling	Socializing	Supporting	Technical

SUMMARY

- Knowledge of behavioral styles is a useful tool for gaining insight into the thinking of buyers. The model uses the assertiveness and responsiveness dimensions of behavior to assess an individual's social style.

- Versatility is your ability to adjust your own personal pace and priorities to facilitate interaction with a person of another style.

- Recognizing typical behavioral cues makes it possible to classify people quickly into one of four basic personality styles: Driver, expressive, amiable, or analytical.

- Gender differences require diverse ways of thinking and using our behavioral relationships. Adjust to different gender styles to enhance communication.

- A related tool for communication is neurolinguistic programming (NLP), which uses observation of eye cues and typical predicate words to discover the particular perceptual field a person is using at a given time.

- Never attempt to adopt a style that is an insincere imitation of the prospect. Take the lead in finding common ground with the prospect. Practice and use psychological reciprocity.

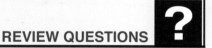

REVIEW QUESTIONS

1. What is meant by assertiveness and responsiveness as dimensions of behavioral style?

2. Which style is characterized by each of these pairs of dimensions?

   Low assertiveness and high responsiveness
   Low assertiveness and low responsiveness
   High assertiveness and high responsiveness
   High assertiveness and low responsiveness

3. What is a backup style and what is its importance to the salesperson?

4. Explain this statement: The strengths of a particular behavioral style are the source of that style's typical weaknesses.

5. Point out some strengths of each of the four behavioral styles and show how they can be used as assets in selling. Identify some of the weaknesses of each and tell how they can damage sales effectiveness.

6. What is a perceptual field? How is it observed in a person's behavior?

7. Read the statements below and determine what perceptual field the speaker is probably using:
   a. There is so much noise in here, I can't hear myself think.

   b. The atmosphere was heavy and damp; there was an oppressive stillness, thick with apprehension.

   c. I am watching developments in that particular stock; before I buy, I want to see the progress it makes this quarter and get a picture of what to expect in the future.

    d. The rookie quarterback was calling the first play of his career. He repeated the coach's instructions in his head, and the murmur of the crowd filled his ears. He could hear his heart pounding with excitement.

    e. The rookie quarterback was calling the first play of his career. He could still see the coach's face in his mind, imposed on the vision of the great sea of faces in the stands, with all eyes focused on him—a tiny speck on the playing field.

8. What kind of sales aids would you use in making a presentation to a person with a visual perceptual field? What changes would you make when talking to a prospect with an auditory field? How would you deal with a prospect with a kinesthetic field?

9. Is it ethical for a salesperson, by employing behavioral flexibility or versatility, to alter personal behavioral style or to match perceptual fields with a prospect? Are there limits to which such adaptation should adhere? Explain.

ROLE-PLAY EXERCISES

The following role-play exercises help build teams, improve communication, and emphasize the "real-world" side of selling. They are meant to be challenging, to learn how to deal with problems that have no single "right" answer and to use a variety of skills beyond those employed in a typical review question. Read and complete each activity. Then in the next class, discuss and compare answers with other classmates. Have some students take the role of the salesperson, and see how they would react. Remember, *"You learn more about a person in an hour of play than in a lifetime of conversation."*–Plato

1. You are a celebrity social style analyst. What styles do you see in the individuals below? Consider assertiveness and responsiveness dimensions and the behavioral characteristics of each style to determine your answer.

    • Jay Leno, star of the "Tonight Show"
    • Brian Williams, anchorman for CBS News
    • Sandra Bullock, movie star
    • Bill Clinton, former president of the United States

2. In this chapter, two examples were given of prospects' answers to the question, "That's an impressive trophy; do you play a lot of golf?" One answer revealed a kinesthetic perceptual field at work, and the other a visual perceptual field. Construct a similar answer that might be made by a prospect using an auditory field, and then in groups of two or three, compare your answer with other students. Review Exhibit 5.6 for the appropriate types of predicate words that you might use.

CASE STUDY

Case 5.1 - To Chit-Chat or Not to Chit-Chat

    Karen Bradfield, a financial planner, is calling on Sue Johnson, self-made president of an employment agency. As Bradfield enters Johnson's office, she notices good-quality furnishings, a large backlog of work on Johnson's desk, and stacks of files on the credenza. Johnson is dressed casually in a skirt and sweater. The conversation begins like this:

BRADFIELD: Good morning, Ms. Johnson. I am Karen Bradfield, and as I told you on the phone, I have my own financial planning firm.

JOHNSON: Sit down, Karen. I've been making more money lately and want to do something with it besides investing in CDs. I'd like to see what kind of plan you could suggest for me.

BRADFIELD: Yes, I will. I couldn't help noticing that you've acquired more office space. This company has really been growing, hasn't it?

JOHNSON: Yes. Now I have fifty thousand to invest, and I was thinking about some municipal bonds or some mutual funds.

BRADFIELD: Oh, there are many to choose from, and I'm sure we will find something suitable. Oh, I see from your diploma on the wall that you went to my alma mater. When did you graduate?

1. What two communication styles are operating here?

2. Do you think Bradfield will make the sale if she continues as she is now?

3. What change, if any, does Bradfield need to make in her procedure to be successful in selling to Johnson?

Case 5.2 - *Fish Stories*

John Long is a sales representative for a commercial office furniture supplier. He has already called once on Larry Lavine, president of Evergreen Savings and Loan Association. At that first meeting, Lavine appeared to be running behind schedule. He had multiple projects going on simultaneously and had taken phone calls while telling Long to continue with his presentation. During the middle of the interview, he seemed to become more relaxed when Long asked him about his golf game and his fly fishing. At the time, Lavine offered to play golf with Long but said he would beat him and take all of his money.

Lavine's office was full of his ego—pictures of himself shaking hands with the mayor, receiving awards, fly fishing, and playing golf. During that first interview, he regales Long with stories about his community involvement and the positive changes he had masterminded at Evergreen. Long had found it difficult to get a word in.

1. Long is now preparing to call on Lavine a second time. What is Lavine's social style?

2. What kinds of strategies should Long employ in this second interview?

Gaining Knowledge, Preparing, and Planning for the Presentation

CHAPTER 6

CHAPTER 7

CHAPTER 8

Part three is comprised of the all-important processes that must occur before the first sales call is ever made. Chapter 6 prepares you for success in a sales career by focusing on gaining product knowledge, developing a specific plan for self-motivation and goal setting, and introducing the use of sales force automation.

Chapters 7 and 8 discuss the procedures for locating and qualifying prospects and identifying the information needed to prepare for an effective presentation. Chapter 7 is a thorough look at prospecting. As the saying goes, "I'd rather be a master prospector than a wizard of speech and have no one to tell my story to." Chapter 8 discusses the process of gathering preapproach information and presents a six-step telephone track for scheduling that critical first appointment with a prospect. The chapters in this section are:

Goal Setting

is the strongest

human force

for self-motivation.

Preparation For Success In Selling

LEARNING OBJECTIVES

- Study what type of information makes up the product knowledge needed for success in selling.

- See how sales technology tools impact salespeople and how to use them to your advantage.

- Understand the concept of product positioning.

- Identify the three types of motivation and how they operate in affecting human behavior.

- Learn how to accept personal responsibility for maintaining self-motivation and exercising initiative in selling.

- Recognize the importance of setting and achieving goals for personal success.

Success in sales involves more than simply getting a person to say yes. If it were, every salesperson would be successful. Rather, a lucrative, long term selling career involves a combination of the training provided by your company with your own active preparation in learning as well as personal commitment. Because the company's bottom line ultimately depends upon your efforts, your preparation is a significant mutual concern; and the more help your company gives, the easier your job becomes. Adequate preparation for success in selling involves at least three areas that are discussed in this chapter.

- Product knowledge

- Sales force automation

- Motivation and goal setting

Certain elements in each of these three areas are the primary responsibility of the company; some are primarily your responsibility. No matter who bears the responsibility, both you and your company are active participants. Too much is at stake for either party to take a passive approach to preparation.

Product Knowledge

Newly hired salespeople may have some general knowledge of the company's field or industry and may even have some knowledge of the specific product they will be marketing. However, salespeople are often hired with little or no knowledge of the company and its products, or even of the industry. Obtaining product knowledge is one of the first prerequisites to success. "Preparing for sales calls is time well spent," says Adrian Miller, owner of Port Washington-based Adrian Miller Sales Training. "And buyers are not very receptive to those who skip this step. If buyers perceive you as unprepared, you won't get that chance to call on them again."[1] Ultimately two things must take place: first, your company must provide you with adequate product information to make you feel comfortable representing the product, and more importantly, it is up to you to study and learn about your product.

What do you need to know about the product? One answer to that question is everything! Nevertheless, you cannot delay beginning sales activity until you have learned everything. In fact, in most cases it is impossible to learn everything due to changes in product lines and advances in technology. And once you do begin making calls and closing sales, you can never cease to learn about the product or service. Gaining product knowledge is an ongoing process.

The Product Itself

Product knowledge begins with the product itself: its specific features, its benefits, and its acceptance in the marketplace. Product knowledge includes knowing all available options—how it can be adapted to the particular customer's needs, and how it performs under varying conditions. Detailed product knowledge prepares you to answer any question a customer might have and to offer whatever reassurance is necessary in the process that helps the customer reach a decision.

When you are thoroughly educated on the product, you can answer detailed, technical questions from expert buyers or explain it in simple terms to someone who is considering such a purchase for the first time. You seldom tell a prospect all the information you have, but having all the information gives you an entire library from which you can choose the best items for the current situation. Exhibit 6.1 shows how two salespeople used specific product knowledge with varying results.

∆ **Exhibit 6.1**

Using Product Knowledge To Close The Sale ·

A computer salesman called on the owner of a small business who was looking for a solution to the mountain of paperwork that was burying his accounting department in red tape and slowing up shipping of orders. The salesman had been well trained in product knowledge and was eager to demonstrate his expertise. He overwhelmed the prospect with computer jargon—bits and bytes and megabytes, wireless cards, and firewalls—and he peppered his sales talk with terms like GHz, RAM, and GPS. He left without an order.

Later, another technical salesperson called. She told the prospect how quickly the equipment she represented would process orders so they could be shipped, and how time and paper handling could be reduced in preparing and mailing invoices. She then explained that daily reports could be produced to summarize orders received and shipped, cash received, and other transactions that would provide solid information upon which good business decisions could be made in a timely manner. She got the order!

Product Performance

Performance information is another vital area of product knowledge. How long will your product last? What kind of wear and stress does it tolerate? How fast does it run? What is its output? How much training is necessary for an employee to operate or use this product? How much fuel or power is needed to run it? Can it be repaired? How much maintenance is required? Who performs needed maintenance? Are spare parts readily available? These are all questions relating to specific performance issues, and if your customer doesn't voice them, rest assured that he is thinking them.

In the more technical industries, salespeople have access to company engineers and advisors who furnish engineering and technical information when it is required; sales knowledge in this case means knowing who to call on and when to ask for back up. If a product is too technical for a person to understand, be sure you can explain the benefits in a way that your customer will understand.

Manufacturing

Product knowledge also includes knowledge of the manufacturing methods and processes that affect the performance or durability of the product; and these vital ingredients of quality affect buying decisions. An understanding of the manufacturing process may help enable you to explain why a price that seems high to the prospect is actually quite reasonable, or why delivery takes longer than the buyer had expected.

Distribution Channels

The company's distribution methods are another important area of product knowledge. What delivery channels are used? Why? Are exclusive dealerships granted in certain areas? Is selective distribution used? Do discount houses and chains sell the product in competition with other types of retail outlets? Another important element of distribution concerns pricing policies. Such policies include dealers' costs, availability of quantity discounts, applicable credit terms, and whether the company will consider negotiating special deals.[2] Not every customer will be interested in such details and merely want to know they will receive the product as promised. However, for your more thorough prospects, these particulars must not be omitted.

Company Information

Product knowledge also involves gaining as much information as possible about the company you represent. You need to know something about the history of the company: who founded it and when, how the present product line evolved, the company's position in the marketplace, its past and present performance and growth, its primary customers or clients, and any other information that may be of interest to prospects are a few examples of the types of facts that help you sell more effectively.[3] It is important to be aware that your prospects may be almost as knowledgeable about your company and its products and performance and as you are.

In the world of investment sales, customers now perceive themselves as more sophisticated and knowledgeable about various companies and their investments than ever before. A recent survey showed that 79 percent of prospective investors are either somewhat or very confident about making their own investment decisions. When asked where they turn for information and advice, a significant majority of these prospects said they are using the cable news channels. Whether they watch MSNBC, Fox News, or CNN, these individuals believe they're becoming increasingly aware of differences in investment companies, types of investments, and financial products.[4] With the amount of up-to-the-minute news and sources of information available to today's consumer, it is essential that you stay current on your company, your product, and the market.

Service Available

Once the product is sold, your responsibilities have just begun. It is outstanding service after the sale that will cement the client-salesperson relationship and ensure repeat orders for years to come—and repeat commissions! You must know the company's service policy in regard to repairs, updates, and replacements. Which of these is the company's responsibility, if any? What charges are made for service? Who performs the service? On what kind of time schedule? What kind of consulting service is available to adapt or adjust the product to the customer's needs? Your customers will inevitably ask some or all of these questions, so it is imperative that you know the answers.

Product Knowledge Application

Product knowledge is ineffective unless you can apply it to the specific problems or needs of a particular client. When you know the exact materials and specifications used in manufacturing, you can successfully advise a prospect to order your product and expect it to perform as desired. This knowledge also helps you suggest what custom changes might be made in the product to fit the specific needs of a client.

It is likely that the products or services you sell are readily available commodities. However, exemplary service is not a readily available commodity. Therefore, if you have outstanding product knowledge and deliver it through an exceptional service model, you can differentiate yourself, attract clients, and build long-lasting professional relationships.[5]

Product knowledge can either be a help or a hindrance, depending on how it is used. Exhibit 6.2 illustrates how salespeople can use their special knowledge to close—or lose—a sale.

∆ Exhibit 6.2

Using Product Knowledge To Fit The Need ·

An automobile salesman was showing a new car to a husband and wife. They informed him that the wife would be primarily driving the car for neighborhood errands. The salesman spent a lot of time explaining that the car had front-wheel drive and that the motor was mounted at a ninety-degree angle to the traditional position. He loaded his sales talk with terms like engine ratios, rpm's, and torque; and he bragged about the car's ability to accelerate from zero to sixty faster than any of the competition. The woman's questions about what purpose those features served for her needs produced even more complicated explanations that did not interest her or her husband. Ultimately, the couple bought a car demonstrated by a salesperson from another dealer. He stressed styling, leather upholstery, the comfort of adjustable seats, and the added visibility provided by the rear-window defroster; and then he invited the wife to test-drive the car. You may know the intricate details of your product, but unless you first listen to the prospect, you may as well know nothing.

Knowledge of the Competition

Another overlooked area of product knowledge is information about the competition. Learn about your major competitors' product lines; know their credit terms, their prices, their delivery schedules, and their reputations for service. Most buyers—either personal consumers or company purchasing agents—are not weighing the advantages of buying a product against those of not buying; rather, they are trying to decide which product to buy, yours or the competition's. The following story is an example of how one salesperson used his knowledge of the competition's product to make the sale:

Ken Andrews was involved in a highly competitive bidding situation for his company, a manufacturer of GPS systems for automobiles. He was facing a representative of a Japanese competitor who Ken knew had a lesser-quality product but offered it at a lower price. Ken's product had superior attributes and was easier to use, therefore giving him the edge in technology and quality. The selling opportunity presented for him was to show how the prospect's company could save money by buying a more expensive, but higher-quality product. The end result of his sale was that he won at a higher price through a better product offering.[6]

One of the advantages of studying your competition is that you are reminded of the good points of your own product and what makes it unique. This will help refresh your presentations, especially if you have been selling the same product or service for a long period of time. Once you are reminded of what makes your product different from the competition, you can stress those areas where your product excels and effectively gain a lasting advantage over your competition. Exhibit 6.3 provides an overview of the four areas of competitive advantage.

Δ **Exhibit 6.3**

Differential Competitive Advantage

Product Superiority		Service Superiority	
Versatility	Apperance	Delivery	Installation
Efficiency	Design	Inventory	Maintenance
Storage	Mobility	Credit	
Handling Time	Packaging	Training	
Safety	Life Expectancy	Merchandising	
Adaptability			
Source Superiority		**People Superiority**	
Time Established		Personal Knowledge and Skill	
Competitive Standing		Knowledge and Skill of Support Personnel	
Community Image		Integrity and Character	
Location		Standing in Community	
Size		Flexibility of Call Schedule	
Financial Soundness		Interpersonal Skills	
Policies and Practices		Mutual Friends	
		Cooperation	

Sales Force Automation

Paper calendars and Rolodexes are on the endangered species list. The electronic information age has arrived! Today's professional salespeople are not simply computer-savvy; they use every outlet available to them to do their jobs. Email, the Web, integrated marketing, and database marketing are just a few of the tools that salespeople use every day to communicate with their customers and companies. The computer has become an instrumental and indispensable tool to foster and build relationships with customers, and to manage information and key accounts with greater efficiency.

Today the sales industry is experiencing an explosive trend toward automation.[7] Salespeople can have clear direction and the right incentives, but if they don't have the right tools, their numbers will suffer despite their best intentions. Sales force and sales task automation is inevitable, but there is one danger to such mechanization. It goes back to the old adage of "garbage in, garbage out." Mark Engelberg, president of TimeLinx Software said this: "Companies always want to put in the latest technology, thinking it is the answer to their problems. But if you automate a mess, you just have an automated mess."[8] The fact is that many companies simply don't take the time to understand the underlying processes before adding the technology. For example, your company could add an expense reporting system for salespeople to submit to accounting, but then forget to buy a license for the accounting department to allow them to use the system. For this reason, proper steps must be taken to ensure that you and your company are ready to automate!

To keep up with the increasing demands of the continually changing, increasingly competitive marketplace, salespeople are expected to become more productive at everything they do. They must see more prospects, provide more value, and do a better job with each customer on which they call. The good news is that computers relieve salespeople of many administrative duties that would normally rob them of time that could be spent planning and selling. Through the use of technology, salespeople can quickly analyze facts and figures and transmit information efficiently to both their customers and companies. Exhibit 6.4 illustrates the impact technology has on product training.[9]

Δ **Exhibit 6.4**

Aflac: Embracing The Way Of The Future In Sales Training ·

When it comes to sales training, the top priority for Aflac, the $14 billion insurance powerhouse, is to match the type of training to the salesperson and the content. "We look at what format worked best in the past, as well as the learner's individual preference," says Dena Wilson, talent manager for Aflac in Columbus, Georgia. Aflac takes advantage of all training formats, including webcasts, instructor-led classroom training, internally developed courses, Web-based courses, and anything else that might work and fit the content, Wilson says.

Until recently, when a company like Aflac brought in a trainer to teach its sales force, business as usual would grind to a halt as the company's entire sales team sat trapped in a room for often days at a time. But the Internet has changed the old way of doing things. Today, through the use of webcasts and online training, salespeople can receive real-time or delayed training from experts from all over the world, and the company can choose when they want to participate. Ultimately, a blend of webcasts, books, and classroom training may be the best option.

Web-Based Sales Training

Gone are the days when the only method of sales training was to either rotate people through a long and arduous program or close down once a year for an annual sales seminar. Web-based technology makes training easier and more affordable by maximizing flexibility and effectiveness for both the sales force and sales managers. Web-based training can range from simple text-based product information to intricate simulations that mirror a real-life sales interview.[10] The benefits of Web-based training include:

- 24-hour access to training programs—allows for fast and convenient training.
- Easier management of large and spread out sales teams.
- Instant access to new product information and current product updates—keeps sales force up to date on a daily or even hourly basis.
- Direct performance measurements with immediate feedback.
- Reduces costs of airfare, hotel stays, and convention expenses.
- Sales reps can focus their attention on the specific training they need.

One such Internet-based training system is called WebEx. The WebEx Training Center allows companies to utilize the value and reach of all three major forms of training: online, in-person and self-paced training. WebEx supports real-time application sharing, on-demand presentation delivery, breakout sessions, virtual hands-on labs, automated assessments, and even e-commerce capabilities. It is one of the most comprehensive training platforms on the market today. WebEx Training Center is an open service platform, which means it allows partners and users to have access to content management, training management, and self-paced training so that the users and their company have an integral say in the content and pace of learning.[11]

Another online training system, ePath Learning, is one of the newest providers of affordable online eLearning solutions. The company's strategy is to deliver the "technology platform of convergence" resulting in a solution that delivers the best of both technologies via its browser-based, easy-to-use delivery model. Dudley Molina, President and CEO of ePath Learning states that, "Considering our extensive product portfolio and continuing development of new products and services, ePath Learning provides sales managers with the capability to dynamically train and certify their sales team to meet the changing needs of the market while ensuring consistency in the message being communicated. This indeed is a strategic competitive advantage."[12]

Thanks to eLearning, sales training is at your fingertips.

E-learning is not where it needs to be when it comes to interpersonal sales training. Even the best Internet training cannot replace live sales training, role plays, and simulation exercises. The industry is ultimately headed toward blended training. It is not wise to totally eradicate face-to-face training, but when combined with online training, they form a mutually beneficial relationship.[13]

The Impact of Sales Technology Tools

The companies that find ways to respond quickly to customer needs and make information readily available to their business partners will gain the all important competitive edge. The implementation of an effective sales force automation program provides numerous company benefits which relate directly to improving the bottom-line—your company's profit.[14] Sales force automation can help increase your sales efficiency in three functional areas:

I. Personal Productivity

Laptop Computers and Handhelds. Laptops provide you with desktop power wherever you go and are quickly gaining in popularity over the desktop despite their slightly higher prices. Handheld computers and PDAs—such as the Sony Treo™ and the Blackberry™— give you instant access to important contact information, sales scripts, and documents all in your pocket. Most handhelds come with such built-in core applications as a calendar, contact book, memo pad, calculator, and even an expense report program. Many versions have Internet access, which means you will never miss an important email again while on a sales call or at lunch.

Contact Management Software. When it comes to your prospect list, there will be no more paper mess and scribbled notes that are easily lost.[15] Contact Managers are programs that enable salespeople to keep track of their leads, appointments, and tasks. They are related to calendars, but integrate email and personal file information such as phone numbers and addresses with task lists and histories of interactions. In addition to providing the functionality of an electronic listing all your customer contacts, contact management software offers you powerful tools for tracking detailed customer information; scheduling appointments, activities, and to-dos; and integrating a number of Web resources into a single sales force automation solution.[16] Some of the better-known software programs available today include Goldmine™, Telemagic™, ACT!™, Entourage™, and Smart Contact Manager™. There are quite a few quality programs available. The key is to find one with which you feel comfortable working and can easily understand.

Customer Relationship Management (CRM) Software. CRM technology is a popular trend in the world of professional selling. Customer relationship management (CRM) is a broad term that covers concepts used by companies to manage their relationships with customers, including the capture, storage and analysis of customer information. CRM software is designed to help firms remember what they promised, whom they talked to, and the specific details of each of their relationships. CRM is more than just contact management software; it is a tool that can move companies to a higher level with customers. Well-integrated CRM systems are used daily as the central point of customer contact.[17] Read below how Microsoft's latest CRM software helps give salespeople more ways to access information and increase their sales.

> Microsoft Dynamics™ CRM (the "Titan" release) offers users the choice of on-premise, partner-hosted, and Microsoft-hosted models, whichever is more conducive to the operations of the company and its salespeople. The "Titan" upgrade from its previous version also allows for multiple customer accounts on a single server, making Dynamics more competitive with the current leading CRM software, salesforce.com. Users can also access CRM capabilities within Microsoft Office Outlook™ through their web browsers, as well as from various mobile devices such as the Blackberry™ or Apple iPhone™. It reinforces Microsoft's long-term strategy to provide customers with the power of choice.[18]

Mapping Programs and GPS Technology. With the level of sophisticated mapping technology available today, no salesperson will ever be lost or late to an appointment. Real-time location finders and interactive mapping systems are widely available on PDAs, handhelds, and come standard in many new car models. With the information clearly plotted on a map and a friendly voice guiding you, effectively navigating your territory has become immeasurably more accurate.

II. Improved Communication

Smart Phones. Smart phones have it all. They are a computer, the Web, your email, phone, PDA, address book, notepad, road map, and entertainment all in one. One of the newer phones on the market today is Apple's iPhone™, but several other phones exist with similar capabilities such as the Motorola Q™, BlackBerry™, and Sony Treo™. With these phones, you will be doing more than just calling.

Internet and Videoconferencing. Face-to-face interaction with clients globally without the travel costs is a way of life for business today. Live-feed videoconferencing is also great for proposals and presentations. This may well be the personal selling medium of the future.

Telecommuting. No more fighting rush-hour traffic! Not only can you check email, but you can update databases, product information, and appointments from the comfort of your home. Many companies encourage their salespeople to conduct business from the office, but for the more disciplined salespeople, this is an excellent option.

III. Transactional Processing

Electronic Data Interchange (EDI) Technology. With EDI technology, your entire company has up-to-date order, processing, and fulfillment information. When customers place an order they have instant access to product information, sent to them in an email or a link to an informational Web site. The selling chain is automated to include customers, distributors, and suppliers.

Corporate Contact Management and Custom Reporting Programs. These programs and software provide shared contact information that is modified and updated by everyone in the sales office. You can customize reports to the specific needs for each of your individual customers and prospects.

Internet Database Development Technologies. These provide online order and product information and order entry for salespeople or their customers. Utilizing Web sites is an effective method of advancing information between a company, its sales channel members, and its customers.

Developing Partnerships Using Technology describes how contact management systems can enhance a salesperson's time management skills. Your entire sales plan for the day can be scheduled, studied, and prioritized while you are having your morning coffee. Because of advances in hand-held devices, all of this information can be taken along and updated on the road. Time has become an ally of the salesperson rather than an adversary.

Developing Partnerships Using Technology

CONTACT MANAGERS
TAKE CONTROL OF YOUR DAY!

Here is what a professional salesperson's scheduling program might include:

Customizable Calendar. The calendar program gives you a range of dates by day, week, or month. They can be further broken down by hour or appointment. It enables you to look ahead and modify or change appointments according to circumstances.

Appointment Reminders. These clever programs remind you of appointments with sounds or messages. You can choose for these reminders to come days, hours, or minutes before the meeting is actually scheduled.

Task Lists. Instead of losing track of what activities need to be accomplished, you can make "to do" lists directly onto the device. Now your daily and weekly goals are always available to examine or update whenever necessary.

Smart Card Reader. Transfer business card information directly into a database with programs that have a business card reader. Users can search for contacts based on these notes. It saves you the time of having to type or write in contact information for new prospects and customers and protects against data entry error.

Check out these Web sites for additional information:

www.goldmine.com

www.maximizer.com

www.telemagic.com

www.apple.com/entourage

www.smartcontactmanager.com

www.palmpilot.com

Product Positioning

The level of competition today is astounding. There are so many brands, and for every brand there are salespeople trying to get the sale before the next guy. It's a fast-paced, cutthroat race, and the competition is coming from all over the world. That makes positioning—the marketing strategy of differentiating a product or company in the mind of a prospect—more important than ever. Once a business identifies what makes it unique in the eyes of the consumer, that element should become the focus of its entire marketing and sales strategy. What makes your company and your product line different? Exhibit 6.5 gives sales professionals five points that will enable them to go into an organization and say, "Allow me to explain to you how and why my company and its products are different."

Δ Exhibit 6.5

Key Points for Developing a Powerful Market Position ·

FIND OUT what qualities of your products and services are most important to your customers. Use that information to custom-design a unique niche for yourself.

PUT TOGETHER a marketing strategy built around several features that are important to your customers and will set you apart from the competition. And then develop an integrated marketing communication message that reinforces those attributes in the customer's mind.

REMEMBER the way you service your customers or sell to them can be a powerful difference. For example, if you are in an industry where the prevailing culture stresses face-to-face selling, the ability to buy directly online can be very attractive.

RECOGNIZE that focusing on the few attributes that really set you apart means you can't be all things to all people. When you shout, "Hey, everybody," you end up satisfying nobody. Focus on those customers that are a part of your specific target market.

KEEP an eye on how your competitors are positioning themselves. Be ready to respond to their claims and make sure you maintain a differential competitive advantage.

Positioning refers to developing a specific marketing mix to influence potential customers' overall perception of a brand, product line, or organization. The term was popularized by Jack Trout and Al Ries in their book, *Positioning: The Battle for Your Mind*. Positioning is the place a product occupies in potential customers' minds relative to competing offerings. Once a position is selected, product, price, place, and promotion strategies and tactics are designed to reinforce the sought-after position. These marketing mix components represent a bundle of individual dimensions that are designed to work together to create a competitive advantage.

For years, the Otis Elevator Company has consistently positioned itself as an innovator that offers unique benefits for its customers. For instance, their Remote Elevator Monitoring system (REM) allows Otis to monitor the performance of its elevators in their clients' buildings, allowing mechanics to easily identify and fix minor problems before they cause a major shutdown. Otis has created an e-commerce plan that gives prospects and customers the opportunity to research and buy its elevators on the Web, and moved the REM system online, enabling existing customers to monitor the service of their elevators as well. These innovations have helped Otis expand its relationships with customers. Mark Granato, Otis' vice-president of communications, says, "In a competitive industry that is exceedingly price-conscious, having the reputation of a leader is increasingly important—and takes constant planning. You get a head start on them—that's the key."[19]

Integrated Marketing Communication

Setting in motion all the pieces in a sales and marketing program takes coordination. Integrated marketing communication uses computerized databases to orchestrate the conception, timing, and execution of all the marketing elements. Each of the seven modules shown in Exhibit 6.6 has a specific function, and they should be designed to work together as a company-wide, interactive, closed-loop communication system. Integrated marketing provides management with the ability to quantitatively measure the impact a specific action has on sales and customer perceptions and determine the optimal level of sales stimuli—price, advertising, sales promotion, direct mail, and personal selling—needed to bring a specific reaction in the market. The logical solution is to create a marketing database accessible to all parties. The salespeople who go through this process will know more about their prospect and customers than anyone else in the company.

Δ **Exhibit 6.6**

A Closed Loop, Integrated Marketing Communication System

The goal is to deliver marketing communications tailored to the unique needs of a target audience. In the consumer goods market, for example, Avon delivers a series of coordinated messages by using a combination of communication vehicles: sales promotion, telemarketing, mass media advertising, cable TV, and response-specific direct mail. As a result of this multi-pronged approach, Avon is able to have daily interaction with the millions of people in its database.[20] This is a truly integrated approach to sales and marketing.

Integrated marketing is a communication campaign in which all the elements come together to form one comprehensive and consistent positioning strategy. Depending on the situation, an organization selects what kinds of communication should be used and when. This may include direct mail, telephone selling, customer service, public relations, trade shows, or face-to-face selling. Schuster Electronics—a regional distributor of amplifiers, relays, and similar gear in Cincinnati, Ohio—designed an Integrated Marketing Communication system to keep up with and service the 6,000 customers in its database, with both in-house telemarketers and field salespeople working off the same database.

Schuster is able to target not just a company, but individuals who may have radically different responsibilities within that company. When a field salesperson pays a personal visit, he doesn't try to see everyone but comes away with names of influencers in, say, production, quality control, or engineering. These names go into a database for follow-up by mail or by telephone. Integrated marketing enables Schuster to view the actual sales call as just one among many marketing tools at their disposal. Similarly, in its business-to-business markets, Kodak positions itself by using a blend of marketing, trade shows and exhibitions, displays, and personal selling to reach prospects for its copiers and desktop publishing business.[21]

The most obvious effect of the Internet and technology on the economy is that the business world now operates on a completely global level. Because of this, most companies have had to rethink their global branding and positioning. Harvard Business School professor Theodore Levitt once argued that corporations should grow by selling standardized products all over the world. So global strategies now rule marketing. Global branding has lost more luster recently because international companies have been under siege. The reaction of most international companies has been to try to fly below the radar, but global brands can't escape notice. Rather than ignore the global characteristics of their brands, it is critical for firms to manage those characteristics, because future growth for most companies will likely come from foreign markets. The trend for consumers is to base their preferences on three dimensions of global brands: 1. quality, 2. the cultural myths behind a brand or company, and 3. a company's efforts to address social problems.[22]

Motivation And Goal Setting

Salespeople often find that they have the needed product knowledge and sales and computer skills but have trouble getting around to using them, or else they work hard and long but find that what they accomplish fails to bring them lasting satisfaction. The missing ingredient is motivation.

Numerous definitions have been given for motivation. Perhaps the simplest is that *motivation is the reason for taking action*. This definition can be expanded slightly to say that motivation is the *impetus* to begin a task, the *incentive* to expend an amount of effort in accomplishing the task, and the *willingness* to sustain the effort until the task is completed.

The question most asked of business consultants is, "How can we motivate our sales force?" The answer most given by consultants is, "You can't." The reason for this answer is that the question typically implies that somewhere there are strategies, techniques, or gimmicks that, once discovered and implemented, will double or triple sales motivation and productivity. Consultants realize that genuine and lasting motivation is not something management does, but rather a process that management fosters and allows to happen.[23]

The primary responsibility for developing and sustaining motivation rests with you; the company's role is to provide a supportive climate in which the development and sustaining of motivation is encouraged. Bob Nelson, author of *1001 Ways to Reward Employees*, says, "What motivates people the most takes just a little time and thoughtfulness." Recognize them as individuals and you're giving them what they most crave. Read *The Lighthouse Story* for an inspirational idea that cost just a few dollars but paid enormous dividends.[24]

The Lighthouse Story

Jonathan Berger, director of strategic accounts for Square D/Schneider Electric, had a salesperson on his team close a very important account that put a fairly large bonus in the sales rep's pocket. So Berger decided to take the extra step that made this sale a truly memorable triumph. He knew the sales rep's wife had a passion for photographing lighthouses, so he sent her a small crystal lighthouse with a note that recognized her husband's achievements and thanked her for her support and the time she had invested. The wife wrote Berger back and said, "Never has anyone in any company ever acknowledged my existence or the contribution I make to my husband's career." This story is good enough to pass on.

Practical Motivation for Salespeople

All motivation theories agree that motivation arises as a response to either an external or internal stimulus. Recognizing those stimuli that operate in your own experience can help you discover ways to control either the stimuli or your responses to them in a way that produces a positive, sustained motivational power and the success you desire. Motivation may arise in fear—the fear of punishment or withholding of acceptance if behavior does not conform to expectations. It may come from incentive— the promise of reward for desired behavior. But the most effective type of motivation is that arising in attitude—behavior chosen because it fits the values and standards chosen by the individual as guiding principles for living and performing.[25]

Fear Motivation. Fear as a motivating force has some value. Fear is a natural emotion designed as protection from danger. Fear motivation has some advantages.

- It protects the individual from self-destruction or harm.
- It protects society from undesirable behavior.
- It is sometimes the quickest way to accomplish a desired reaction.

In spite of these advantages, fear motivation has serious disadvantages that more than offset its benefits.

- *Fear is external.* It is effective only as long as the enforcing power is stable. When the parent, teacher, or sales manager is out of sight, fear motivation is materially weakened.

- *Fear is temporary.* Threats or punishment may control behavior for a time, but people tune out warnings if they discover that threats are not always carried out.

- *Fear is negative.* It is directed largely toward not doing something or toward doing something unpleasant merely because it is an imposed duty rather than a chosen activity. A warning not to do something creates a void that may be filled by another equally undesirable behavior.

Incentive Motivation. The use of incentives for motivation is generally considered more enlightened than the use of fear. An incentive is the promise of a benefit or reward to be earned in return for certain behaviors. The attempt to produce motivated activity by offering incentives is common in sales organizations. Some common incentives used include the appeal to work harder to earn increased commissions; contests, certificates, and plaques for quotas reached; bonuses; the promise of an enlarged or better sales territory; and perks such as a reserved parking place, a private office, a personal secretary, or a company car. You have to understand what motivates each individual on your team and use that information.[26] Like fear motivation, incentive motivation has advantages.

- *Incentive motivation calls for extra effort.* When a promised reward is highly desirable, salespeople put forth almost superhuman effort to win it.
- *Incentive motivation is positive* and promises something desirable. Salespeople are not frozen into inaction by fear of being punished or deprived.

It's All a Matter of Perspective

Two salesmen fell on hard times and ended up broke in a small town in Montana. They needed money to move on and learned that the town paid $20 each for wolf pelts. They sensed the opportunity. That night they set out with a couple of clubs and some borrowed supplies and made camp in the distant hills. They were no sooner asleep than one was startled by an eerie howl. He crawled outside the tent to find himself surrounded by hundreds of snarling wolves. Back into the tent he crawled and shook his buddy. "Wake up!" he cried. "Wake up! We're rich! " It's really all a matter of perspective!

Like fear motivation, however, incentive motivation carries built-in disadvantages.

- *Incentive motivation is external.* Behavior depends upon the initiative of the person who offers the reward rather than upon the salesperson who will earn it.
- *Incentive motivation is temporary.* A salesperson may put forth a great deal of effort to win a sales contest or to earn some desired reward but not continue that level of activity or effort once the contest is over.
- A promised reward that is *not perceived as desirable* provides no motivation for action.
- Incentives once earned often come to be *regarded as rights* instead of a special privilege for outstanding performance. For example, salespeople who qualify for a company car by high productivity and enjoy this reward for several years feel incensed if the requirements for having a company car are raised and they fail to meet the new quota, even though they improve their sales for the year.

Attitude Motivation. Attitude motivation operates on the concept that the only lasting and uniformly effective motivation is the personal motivation that comes from the internal structure of the individual. It is based on a strong self-image and a belief in the possibility of success. Attitude motivation is self-motivation. All great salespeople inherently possess this powerful, internal drive. Self-motivation can be shaped and molded, but it cannot be taught.[27]

Self-motivation is the result of the choices made by individuals in response to conditioning influences. Fear and self-doubt are the habitual attitudes of some people, but others choose, instead, to respond to life positively. For example, some salespeople who are told they're too inexperienced decide that they are and always will be. Then they wait for someone to tell them what to do. However, others respond to the statement by choosing to believe that their condition is temporary. As a result, they are willing and eager to try different activities, stretch their imaginations, and attempt new goals.

They do not wait for someone else to motivate them; they are always reaching out for new experiences. These salespeople are self-motivated. What you are, then, is not entirely a result of what happens to you. What you are is a result of how you react to what happens to you, and your reactions are a matter of choice.[28]

The advantages of attitude motivation are the opposites of the disadvantages of fear and incentive motivation:

- *Attitude motivation is internal.* Because attitudes come from within, you do not need to wait for an outside stimulus to make appropriate choices and take action.
- *Attitude motivation is permanent.* An attitude, once thoroughly established, continues to operate on an automatic basis until you do something to alter it. Self-motivation is the only kind of motivation that can be sustained over a long period of time.

Attitude Motivation Through Goal Setting

The single most important tool for developing self-motivation is a program of personal goals. A personal goals program creates desire—one of the most powerful emotions operating in human experience. If you want to be able to choose where you will go with your sales effort, and how you will get there, you need clear goals and strategies. Only then will you have the power to direct your efforts.[29]

Exhibit 6.7 on the following page is the Million Dollar Personal Success Plan that Paul J. Meyer, founder and chairman of the board of SMI International, developed for his own use at the age of nineteen. It provides a workable plan for achieving success in selling.

Crystallized Thinking. You must know what you want to achieve. If your goals are hazy and poorly defined, you cannot plan concrete action steps for their achievement. You must write down and date your goals. Monitoring your status keeps you focused.[30] Without specific action plans, much of your time and effort is wasted. Chapter 15 will address action plans and effective time management techniques in much greater detail.

A Plan of Action with Deadlines. A written plan of action keeps you on track and headed toward the achievement of your goals. You know exactly what to do next. A written plan also reveals conflicts between various goals so that you can plan ahead and make a reasonable schedule for the time and resources needed to reach all your goals. Deadlines provide you with the needed time frame for achieving your goals. They give you something to aim for.[31] Because most of us now use such a small percentage of our real potential, target dates serve the purpose of drawing out more potential and using it to bring desired goals into being. Deadlines help you maintain a positive attitude of expectancy toward goals achievement. They eliminate distractions and help you to think creatively.

Sincere Desire. A burning desire to achieve the goals you want often makes the difference between a wish and a goal. A *wish* is something you would like to have but are not willing to invest enough time or effort in order to achieve it; a *goal* is something you want so intensely that you will exert whatever effort is needed to reach it. The more goals you achieve, the more desire you develop. The greater your desire, the more you can achieve. Desire is an ascending spiral of success.

Supreme Confidence. Success demands supreme confidence in yourself and your ability. Self-confidence enables you to undertake challenging goals and believe you can succeed. Self-confidence lets you see problems as opportunities and obstacles as stepping-stones to success. Self-confidence builds your credibility so that the buyer is open to considering the solutions suggested. Self-confidence makes it easy to ask for the order– not once, but again and again until the sale is closed successfully.

The secret to developing this kind of confidence is a growing list of goals accomplished. Each time you succeed in reaching a goal you have set and worked toward, you gain added belief in your own capability to achieve. Confidence in your own personal ability is the greatest source of security you can possess.

Δ **Exhibit 6.7**

The Million Dollar Personal Success Plan

THE MILLION DOLLAR PERSONAL SUCCESS PLAN

by *Paul J. Meyer*

FOUNDER & CHAIRMAN OF THE BOARD
SMI INTERNATIONAL, INC.
WACO, TEXAS

I - Crystallize Your Thinking

Determine what specific goal you want to achieve. Then dedicate yourself to its attainment with unswerving singleness of purpose, the trenchant zeal of a crusader.

II - Develop a Plan for Achieving Your Goal, and a Deadline for Its Attainment

Plan your progress carefully: hour-by-hour, day-by-day, month-by-month. Organized activity and maintained enthusiasm are the well-springs of your power.

III - Develop a Sincere Desire for the Things You Want in Life

A burning desire is the greatest motivator of every human action. The desire for success implants "success consciousness" which; in turn, creates a vigorous and ever-increasing "habit of success."

IV - Develop Supreme Confidence in Yourself and Your Own Abilities

Enter every activity without giving mental recognition to the possibility of defeat. Concentrate on your strengths, instead of your weaknesses ... on your powers, instead of your problems.

V - Develop a Dogged Determination to Follow Through on Your Plan, Regardless of Obstacles, Criticism or Circumstances or What Other People Say, Think or Do

Construct your Determination with Sustained Effort, Controlled Attention, and Concentrated Energy.
OPPORTUNITIES never come to those who wait ... they are captured by those who dare to ATTACK.

Dogged Determination. Determination to stick to your plan of action until your goal is achieved is an outgrowth of desire and confidence. When you have a burning desire to achieve your goals, you are not easily swayed by others' thoughtless comments, by the disapproval of someone who does not understand your goals, or the active opposition of those who fear to be compared with you in either effort or results. Determination is the quality that enables you to continue calling on a difficult prospect until you close the sale. Determination gives you the creative freedom to discover new tactics for achieving your goal when your first effort fails and to think up more ideas until you discover a way that works.

It takes more than money to make a person rich.

All of these success elements are interdependent. Use of each increases your power to use the others. Success in any one intensifies your belief in the others. Self-motivation is the only real and lasting motivation. Its development is your responsibility. The company and sales manager can provide a climate in which self-motivation is easier, but even the most negative climate cannot de-motivate you without your permission.

Success and the Total Person

Organizations emphasize that sales forces are essential to corporate success. However, organizations seldom pay much attention to what constitutes success for an individual. Too often success for salespeople is measured only in terms of the amount of sales generated. This narrow view of success has been responsible for destroying the self-confidence of untold numbers of salespeople. An understanding of what success really means frees you to become all that your potential allows.

One of the most comprehensive definitions of success is this: "Success is the progressive realization of worthwhile, predetermined, personal goals."[32] This definition is especially applicable to salespeople, who can begin their careers with relatively little training compared to that required of other professionals. Because success is progressive, you can be successful immediately just by choosing to pursue goals that are personally fulfilling and then beginning to work toward them. Obviously, such a beginning is not made at the level expected of a master salesperson with long experience but at a level consistent with present reality. When you learn this truth, you have the patience to study, learn the art of selling, and practice your skills.

Too many people fall into the same erroneous thinking that organizations often follow in measuring success. Those "worthwhile, predetermined goals" must involve more than money and position or the success that is achieved is likely to be hollow. Mike Singletary, former all-pro middle linebacker for the Chicago Bears, is a much sought after speaker by Christian youth groups all over the country. In his motivational and inspirational talks, Singletary encourages his young audiences to develop their potential in all areas of life, not just their athletic skills. Likewise, salespeople who concentrate only on career success and neglect other areas of life find their lives less than happy.

Money and position are fairly low on the hierarchy of needs that all people experience. For this reason, goals must be set in every area of life: physical and health, mental and educational, family and home, spiritual and ethical, social and cultural, financial and career. Total personal growth in these areas is effectively pictured in Exhibit 6.8 as spokes on a wheel. If some spokes are uneven, the wheel that represents total life achievement is not round. The ride is very bumpy, and the passenger feels dissatisfaction and a vague sense of uneasiness or unhappiness. Unmet needs prevent the enjoyment of achievements in other areas. Monetary success means little to the salesperson whose family life is shattered, health ruined, or the respect of friends lost. All areas of life must be included in a plan for becoming a "total person."

Δ **Exhibit 6.8**

The Wheel of Life

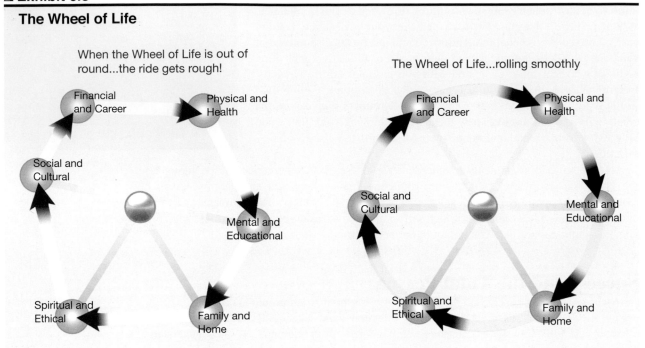

When the Wheel of Life is out of round...the ride gets rough!

The Wheel of Life...rolling smoothly

This definition of success also implies that success has different meanings for different people and that not every salesperson belongs in a particular organization selling a specific product or service. To succeed, salespeople must market a product or service in which they personally believe. Once salespeople know what they want from a selling career and dedicate themselves to achieving those goals, the responsibility for reaching success is largely in their own hands. *Too many people confuse action with progress and effort with results.* Trying hard does not guarantee success. Success comes as a result of determining the desired goals, finding out what activity is required to reach those goals, and then completing those actions based on a personal commitment to oneself. Real success never comes by accident.

SUMMARY

Key Points to Remember

- Preparing for success in a sales career includes three areas of special importance: Product knowledge, sales force automation, and motivation and goal setting.

- Product knowledge includes knowledge of the entire industry or field and specific knowledge about your product or service.

- Sales force automation and computer technology help increase your personal productivity, communications capabilities, and transaction-processing efficiency.

- Positioning refers to the place a product occupies in customers' minds relative to competing offerings. Once you select a position, design product, price, and promotion strategies to reinforce the desired position.

- All motivation comes primarily from one of three sources: Fear, incentive, and attitude. Fear and incentives used as motivating forces are limited in effectiveness because they depend on someone else as the source. Attitude motivation is internal and permanent.

- Successful goal setting begins with crystallized thinking about what is important to you, then developing a plan of action with deadlines for achievement.

REVIEW QUESTIONS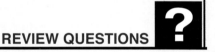

1. What contribution can business school courses make to success in selling? How much academic work in sales or marketing is necessary to guarantee success in professional selling?

2. Does the company that hires you have any responsibility for preparing you for sales success? If so, what specific types of knowledge, information, or other input is the company's responsibility?

3. Name at least four areas of product knowledge that are important for salespeople.

4. What advantage does knowledge of the competition's offerings provide for the salesperson?

5. What would you do about product knowledge if you were hired to sell a highly technical product for which you have little background or understanding?

6. Sales force automation can help increase a salesperson's effectiveness in at least three distinct ways. Discuss each one and give an example to illustrate.

7. Explain how fear and incentives are used as sources of motivation. Can you give an example from your own experience of how both of these were used by someone else in an attempt to motivate you?

8. What limits the effectiveness of fear and incentives as motivating forces?

9. What are the advantages of using attitude as a basis of motivation?

10. Explain how goal setting affects self-motivation.

11. How does a personal goals program produce self-confidence? What is the value of self-confidence to salespeople?

ROLE-PLAY EXERCISES

The following role-play exercises help build teams, improve communication, and emphasize the "real-world" side of selling. They are meant to be challenging, to learn how to deal with problems that have no single "right" answer and to use a variety of skills beyond those employed in a typical review question. Read and complete each activity. Then in the next class, discuss and compare answers with other classmates. Have some students take the role of the salesperson, and see how they would react. Remember, *"You learn more about a person in an hour of play than in a lifetime of conversation."* – Plato

1. There are now a number of sites that offer online Customer Relationship Management (CRM) functions. You can literally have CRM access from almost anywhere. These sites virtually eliminate the need for software. These services also offer the ability to access your data from a Palm Pilot or with Microsoft Outlook. Check out any one of these Web sites, then in class discussion, use the information you found on the Web sites to discuss how you would use CRM technology to drive immediate results in a company. This would make a great term paper topic as well.

   • www.siebel.com
   • www.salesforce.com
   • www.salesnet.com

2. You are writing an article about the importance of product knowledge for *Selling Power* magazine. Interview a successful salesperson and ask how that person acquired product knowledge initially, how much help the company gave, and how much time was required to become familiar enough with the product to feel fully prepared to answer prospects' questions. Inquire also about how that salesperson keeps product knowledge current. Write a brief report of your interview and discuss your results with the class.

CASE STUDY

Case 6.1–Who Goofed?

Ted Ransom has been one of the top salespeople for the industrial division of Islander Paint and Varnish Companies for the past ten years. His territory covers the New England industrial area. He is respected by his clients as an authority on finishes of all kinds. He likes prospecting and making cold calls, and his obvious product knowledge pays handsome dividends in the form of a growing customer list.

When he read in the financial section of the newspaper about the opening of a new firm, ElecMotor, in the Boston area, Ted was right on the job with a call on the company. When he told the purchasing agent that he sold industrial paints, he had a pleasant surprise. "Talk about good timing," the purchasing agent said. "I was talking to our production manager about a line of mini-motors that is going into production in a few weeks, and he said we needed to talk to some paint salespeople pretty soon. Let me see if he is available."

When Ted met the production manager, Dan Miller, he was glad to learn that they wanted a soft green paint for the motor housing, a color that would complement the company trademark. Ted's all-purpose paint came in the exact shade they desired, and his knowledgeable presentation brought him a nice order. The order went through promptly and delivery was made in five days. Ted planned to follow up with Dan the next time he was in Boston, but Dan called in less than two weeks with a disturbing report. They had applied the paint, but during testing, Dan reported, as soon as the motors began to heat up, the paint peeled off every one.

"Every one?" Ted asked incredulously.

"Yes, every one." Then Dan added, "I guess my decision to buy was too quick. I'd better talk to some other paint companies. And I'm returning the full shipment to you for a refund."

1. Is there a possibility that Ted's product knowledge is less complete than it should be? Remember his good reputation in this area.

2. Is it possible that a prompt follow-up service call could have saved the account? How?

CASE 6.2 - They're Just Cosmetics. Aren't They?

Debbie Adamek had just taken a job as a manufacturer's representative for a new line of cosmetics being introduced by Grayson's Laboratories. The new line, called Capture, was designed to appeal especially to teenagers. Debbie's job was to call on wholesale distributors and chains to obtain orders for distribution to their retail outlets. Grayson's had conducted an extensive media advertising campaign and anticipated considerable demand for the new products.

Debbie, along with other salespeople who were to introduce the new line, was given a week's intensive training on the new products. Frankly, Debbie was bored. She had taken this job because she wanted to get away from the classroom scene, the load of reading she had hated in college, and people telling her what to do. She thought selling cosmetics would be easy because she considered herself an expert makeup artist; she knew exactly how to use every kind of aid imaginable to take advantage of her best points. Customers should know just by looking at her that any cosmetics she had to offer would obviously be the top of the line.

Before she made her first sales call, Debbie experimented with every item in the new line. She became familiar with the color-matching scheme and learned the best way to apply each item. Imagine her shock when her first prospect began asking questions: Is it necessary to observe any precautions about temperature where the products are stored? What percentage of customers are likely to experience adverse skin reactions to the products? What kind of customer response was received when the products were field-tested? Will users experience any special difficulties in extreme hot weather or extreme cold weather? What cooperative advertising plan is available? How much advertising is planned for this state, in what media, and when?

It took only two or three days for Debbie to come to the sobering realization that she didn't know enough about her product to sell it to wholesalers.

1. What are Debbie Adamek's options at this point?

2. Would Debbie's type of product knowledge be adequate for another selling situation?

3. Can someone who begins a sales career on such a naive basis achieve success? What would success require?

"**Sales are contingent upon the attitude of the salesman, not the attitude of the prospect.**"

-W. Clement Stone

CHAPTER 7

Becoming a Master Prospector

LEARNING OBJECTIVES

- Understand the importance of prospecting.

- Find out who your prospects are.

- Learn the characteristics of a qualified prospect.

- Become familiar with a variety of prospecting methods.

- Understand how to manage prospect information accurately and consistently.

- See the value of technology in the management of prospect information.

A salesperson without prospects is as useful as a doctor without patients. Great salespeople ask smart questions, know how to close a deal, and have excellent follow-up techniques; and the one trait they demonstrate more consistently than any other is constant prospecting, enhanced by creative approaches that build value and lasting relationships. They see opportunities everywhere and they know it's not just the numbers—but the numbers are what count.[1] After all, you have to see more to sell more.

If your closing ratio is lower than you'd like, the problem may be that you don't have enough qualified prospects, and not that you are a poor closer. If you see enough people, sooner or later you will sell to someone. Confucius said, "Dig the well before you thirst." To succeed in selling, locate qualified prospects in advance—before you need them. Develop multiple sources from which names of prospects flow constantly.

As competition in many fields grows, it is increasingly difficult to turn prospects into customers. To further complicate issues, recent surveys find that as many as 70 percent of sales leads never receive proper follow-up. In other words, salespeople aren't handling the leads they do get correctly, thus throwing away potential customers—and commission! Paul Peterson, Senior Director for FrontRange Solutions' CRM Business Unit, said, "That is a startling statistic, and I think a lot of executives don't even know they have this problem in their company. Leads that fall by the wayside are off the radar and it can be an invisible problem." The bottom line is that both the marketing and sales departments need access to a central storehouse of all prospects and customers—a "corporate memory"—where employees can track responses to marketing campaigns and look at the history of sales efforts. As the company interacts with that prospect or customer, every piece of communication and history needs to be in one spot. Call it a CRM system or a sales force automation (SFA) system, but the key is to get marketing, sales and, if possible, other departments to work from the same contact record.[2] Here are three other basic principles to help you hold onto leads in a highly competitive market:

1. **Qualify Leads**. Pay attention to lead qualification. Have a process in place and the resources and skills to qualify those leads. Generating leads is akin to building the Alaskan pipeline. Figure out how to build the pipeline and get the oil flowing.[3]

2. **Nurture Leads**. There will likely be some leads that aren't ready for sales. A nurturing process that includes phone calls, e-mail, and postal mail is necessary to keep in touch with those prospects until they're ready to see a salesperson.

3. **Add Value**. The worst thing you can say is, "I'm just calling to find out if you've gotten that budget yet." Send case studies, newsletters, or e-magazines with editorial content. That way, you are not only checking in, you are contributing to their productivity.

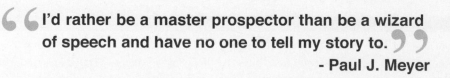

66 **I'd rather be a master prospector than be a wizard of speech and have no one to tell my story to.** 99
- Paul J. Meyer

Qualifying the Prospect

Establish a pattern for prospecting to avoid wasting a monumental amount of time calling on leads who are not prospects. When all you have is a name and address, you have only the possibility of developing a prospect. Exhibit 7.1 illustrates the process of moving a name from the status of lead to that of a qualified prospect. Truly qualified prospects are those who are a fit for you because they possess the necessary characteristics that make them logical buyers for your product or service. Apply a detailed screening process to each lead to increase your chances of successfully completing a sale.[4] The definition of the best prospect is this:

> **A Class "A" qualified prospect is one to whom you have been referred by a person the prospect respects, one who has the ability to make a buying decision and to pay for the product or service, and one about whom you have all the personal information you need to make a good presentation.[5]**

△ Exhibit 7.1

Action of the Salesperson in Developing Leads into Qualified Prospects · · · · · · · · · · · ·

Sales Lead

Prospect

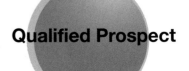
Qualified Prospect

Research needs, history, ability to pay, authority to buy, etc.

Evaluate information gained, add personal information.

To determine if you have a qualified Class 'A' prospect, use the **MADDEN** test to ensure that they: have money, are approachable, have desire, have decision-making ability, are eligible, and have a need you can satisfy.

MONEY

Separate the talkers from those who actually have the means to purchase. You will save yourself and your company many headaches by determining a prospect's ability to pay before spending your time and energy gaining a client who may quickly become more of a liability than an asset.

APPROACHABLE

Can you get an appointment? The president or CEO of a large company may grant an initial interview only to a senior level executive in your company. Do not hesitate to ask for such help when there is real possibility of gaining an important client. Individual prospects are often approachable only if you are willing to fit your time schedule into the unique time needs of their business or profession.

DESIRE

The prospect may be satisfied with a present supplier and have no desire to change. You can sell to such a prospect only if you create or discover a desire that will motivate the prospect to move from their present supplier to you. The prospect may desire to save money, enjoy a wider variety of services, receive more dependable service or quicker deliveries—all of which may have been the basis for selecting their present supplier in the first place.

DECISION MAKER

Be sure the person you visit is the decision maker. If you are unsure, then start with the head of the company. If you reach the CEO or COO, conducting business may be easier than you think. They earned the top spot by making tough calls and appreciate the tough call you've just made. A survey by McGraw-Hill's Laboratory of Advertising Performance discovered that over 90 percent of purchase decision-makers interviewed had not been called on by a salesperson within the previous two months.[6] Salespeople spend a great deal of time talking to people who are not in a position to make a buying decision. When you first contact a prospect, ask who else will be involved in making the decision and set up an appointment with all individuals at one time if possible.

ELIGIBLE

Determine whether the prospect is eligible to buy from you. Some prospects are already committed to a competitor and cannot buy. Others need a product with greater or smaller capacity than you can offer, or are in need of a service that is more or less extensive than yours.

NEED

Determine the need level for your product or service. To accomplish this you must ask questions and listen carefully to determine what the prospects' buying motives are in order to uncover their specific needs. Then decide if your company has the products that effectively satisfy those needs. Ask yourself—will the business your company gains be worth the amount of time you must invest to get it?

Methods Of Prospecting

While it may be true that *practice makes perfect*, this is only applicable to prospecting when you practice the correct methods. Incorrect practice on a musical instrument only produces an increased ability to make errors. This idea applies to prospecting—aimless, hit-or-miss prospecting, no matter how much of it is done, generally leads to failure. To streamline the job of prospecting and produce better results, master a number of different methods and use the ones that work best. The following is a list of eleven prospecting techniques discussed in this chapter.

1. **Referrals**—Names given to you by a customer, friend, or someone else who feels good about you and your product.

2. **Center of Influence**—A person who believes in what you are selling, influences others, and is willing to give you names and help to qualify them.

3. **Group Prospecting**—Bringing a number of people together at the same time and place and capturing their names and other information about them.

4. **Planned Cold Calling**—Calling on a lead without first making an appointment and knowing little or perhaps nothing about the person.

5. **Direct Mail**—Choosing a mailing list of individuals, businesses, or professional people who appear to be at least partially qualified and sending them a communication that requests a reply.

6. **Observation**—Prospects are everywhere, so keep your eyes and ears open. Scan local newspapers, trade publications, and the financial pages of major news magazines and papers.

7. **Civic Groups**—Membership in various civic groups such as the Chamber of Commerce gives you opportunities to meet people who can become prospects for a product or service.

8. **Networking**—Salespeople from different businesses share information about the sales climate and exchange prospect information.

9. **Directories**—Directories help identify possible prospects and provide information to determine whether they actually have the potential to become customers.

10. **Company-initiated Prospecting**—A company may provide initial prospecting for salespeople. This frees them to have more face-to-face interviews with qualified prospects.

11. **Web sites**—A company can market its services and find customers utilizing the power of the Internet.

12. Trade Shows

Referrals

The use of referrals is one of the most powerful prospecting techniques in sales. Level 3 Communications, a major telecommunications company, suggests that as much as 50 percent of its sales come from referrals. A *referral* is a name given to you as a lead by a customer, a friend, or even a prospect who did not buy, but felt good about you and your product. The factor that makes this prospecting method valuable is its leverage. Until the proper time to use that leverage arrives, a referral is just a lead like any other.

Once you qualify a referred lead by securing all the information needed to show that this person fits the pattern of prospects upon which you call, you are then ready to use the valuable leverage that is yours by reason of the referral. Those who provide referrals should be willing either to make an initial contact for you or to allow you to use their names. Referrals work because people are naturally fearful or skeptical of strangers, especially those who try to persuade them to make some kind of decision. People accept you and your product more readily if someone they know and respect has sent you.

Gain More Referred Leads. Salespeople do not have more referrals because they don't ask, or perhaps because they don't know how to ask. There are two reasons why people do not immediately provide referrals. The first is that they find it difficult to think of names. Basically, they simply do not want to exert the mental effort to decide who might be interested. The second reason is they consider themselves to be "conscientious objectors"—they claim they just do not give referrals. Sales professionals estimate that 20 percent of clients won't give referrals no matter how you ask. Another 20 percent of clients will always give referrals. It's the other 60 percent where a plan of action is essential.[7]

Exhibit 7.2 illustrates a step-by-step approach to use when you ask for referrals. Practice and rehearse it with your favorite clients or those who have given you referrals in the past.[8] Customers think of themselves as professionals, and they like to buy from professionals. Asking for referrals should become an automatic part of every presentation you make.

Δ **Exhibit 7.2**

. . . . **A Seven-Step Approach for Gaining More Referred Leads**

1. Ask for referrals with respect
Open the dialogue something like this, "I have an important question I want to ask you." This will capture your prospect's attention and indicate to them just how significant this is to you.

2. Ask for their help
Soften them up by saying, "I'm trying to build my business and I would value and appreciate your help."

3. Explain the course of action you propose
Tell them what will happen if they give you a referral, and also let them know that you will remain professional and report back to them.

4. Gain their permission to explore
You might give them another softening statement: "I understand how you feel." Then you can go on to say, "I was wondering if we could agree on who you know who might also benefit from the products I have to offer. Are you comfortable with that?"

5. Narrow their focus by describing your ideal prospects
Once you have been given names, make a first step toward qualifying them. Ask your client, "If you were in my place, who would you see first?" Ask why. Then find out which one to contact next.

6. Report back to them
Whenever you receive referrals, be sure to report back to them the result of your interviews with leads.

7. Thank them
Always offer thanks for giving you referrals regardless of whether they bought from you.

What to Ask. The principal thing you ask for in a referral is for your client to make it easy for you to contact a new prospect. The variable in each situation is how this contact should be made. What to ask for depends upon your client's need for control of the situation:

- Some customers want to handle the communication themselves.
- Others want minimal involvement. They prefer that you initiate the contact for them.
- Still others may have very specific instructions on what they want you to do or say with their referrals.

The best way to find out how much control your client wishes to have is to simply ask by using an alternate of choice type question: "Would you prefer that I call Mr. Evans, or would you want to personally call and talk to him on my behalf?" Here is a sample statement that can be used to make the client feel comfortable about giving you names:

"I'm not asking you to recommend me or my product. I am merely asking you to give me an introduction to some people you know. I will talk to them, as I have with you, in a professional manner and give them an opportunity to learn about me and my company."

The Million-Dollar Referral

Michael Twining, sales rep for a large distributor of agricultural products, has a clever way to secure more referrals. Whenever he gets a referral by an existing customer he quickly mails a handwritten thank-you note and includes a lottery ticket with the message—*Thanks a million for the referral. I hope you win a million!*

It costs very little and always creates a lot of good will and laughs on his next visit with that customer. Michael says, "It almost always gets me at least one more referral."[9]

When to Ask. Make asking for referrals a part of the selling cycle. A logical time to ask for referrals is right after the close. A customer who buys is sold on you and likely to feel good about giving you names. Sometimes, however, a customer wants to use the product or service before giving referrals. Often, salespeople go after referrals at the wrong time. They start asking for referrals before the ink on the contract is dry. You can't ask for referrals; you must earn them. The best referrals come from satisfaction, not a signature.

Centers of Influence

This method of prospecting is a specific application of the referral method. In both methods, you begin with a satisfied customer or with a person whose interest in you or your product has developed to the point of desiring to help you. The important distinction between the two is that a center of influence can give you far more prospects and is both willing and able to provide new names on a continuing basis.

The best sales tool you have is a person who believes in what you are selling, is influential with a number of people who are potential customers, and is willing to give you the names of these people and help you qualify them—that is the essence of a *center of influence*. When you have several centers of influence, you always have plenty of prospects. People respect the center of influence to the extent that an introduction from this source virtually assures you of an audience. Cultivate their friendship, sell yourself, and ask centers of influence to help.

Getting that person on your team can open doors that would otherwise remain closed. Think how you would react if such a person called you and said:

> *I had lunch this past week with Brian Hamblen, a business associate of mine. I think he is person you would like to meet, and I told him about you. He will be calling you this week; I hope you will meet him.*

Centers of influence are one of the most valuable assets you can have as a salesperson. Follow up every lead they provide, and then report your results to them and thank them. Find a way to show your gratitude by being of service to them. After all, a mutually beneficial relationship is rewarding to both parties.

Group Prospecting

Many companies use group prospecting with great success. The idea is to bring together a number of people, from eight to twenty or more. The group may meet in a home, a conference room in a hotel, or in an office. Your purpose is to inform prospects about your product or service.

Some direct sales companies use this method to find prospective distributors or salespeople. Among the well-known organizations that use this approach are Tupperware, Amway, Shaklee, and PartyLite Inc. Companies that use party-plan selling not only expect to make sales at the parties, but hope to find prospects who will agree to host parties at which new prospective customers and party holders are likely present.

A variation of this method is to look for groups of potential prospects and offer to be a guest speaker. Members of civic clubs may be ideal prospects for you, and they are always looking for speakers who have beneficial information for their members. If you establish your credibility, you may be able to close your speech with a brief presentation. Meet as many members of the audience as possible before and after the meeting, ask for business cards, and give them yours. If they were impressed enough to want you to call, you know you have a qualified prospect.

Planned Cold Calling

Some may say that prospecting is nearly a lost art. As a salesperson, you will stand above the crowd if you are not afraid to do a little cold calling.[10] Cold calling can be an enjoyable part of your day if you accept the reality of the situation. Each year 15 percent of all firms become dissatisfied with a supplier and want to change. This means that in one of every seven cold calls you make, a prospect is likely receptive to you.[11] Cold calling serves as an excellent supplement to other prospecting efforts if it is carefully planned. Here are some guidelines for cold calling:

Supplement Your Existing List. Because cold calling is designed to supplement your current prospect list, be careful that cold calls never take so much of your time that you neglect calling on qualified prospects and existing clients. Set aside a specific amount of time each week for cold calling, but never at the expense of more profitable activity.

Preplan Cold Calls. Develop several effective door openers and experiment until you find which ones work best for you. Give the prospect something related to your product or service, such as a newsletter, brochure, calendar, or share an idea that may save the prospect time or money. Your door opener should be something that causes the prospect to remember you when you later call for an appointment to make your presentation.

Stay Enthusiastic. Set a goal to turn every cold call into a warm call. When you make cold calls, the person you want to see is almost certainly not in or too busy to receive you. If you remain enthusiastic in spite of such responses, you make a positive impression on the receptionist. You may even get enough information to qualify prospects without meeting them. When you call again, you will be remembered; and receptionists exert a great deal of influence on who sees the boss. Impress them with your professionalism and you will find those doors to the buyers open more easily.

Golden Opportunities

Most salespeople would agree that cold calling is the toughest part of selling. But, at the same time, the rewards can be great. "When I started making cold calls I decided to call them warm calls because most prospects want to be treated with friendliness and spoken to in a positive manner," says Irby Stewart with Positive Communications in Thunder Bay, Ontario. Because he took this positive approach, Irby became the top salesperson across Canada selling Brian Tracy's two-day video seminars. Recently he developed another point of view toward cold calls. It struck him that he should be calling them *opportunity calls*. That's what they really are. Viewing cold calls as golden opportunities gives him even greater incentive for selling to clients and prospects. Now go out and create some golden opportunities for yourself![12]

Direct Mail

The success of direct mail prospecting depends upon the management of mailing lists. Some lists are better than others, and the best investment of your time and budget demands careful planning and analysis. The product or service you sell has a great deal to do with what kind of list you use.[13] The goal is a list of people or businesses that are already at least partially qualified prospects. Exhibit 7.3 has some suggestions for sources of direct-mail lists.

△ Exhibit 7.3

Suggested Sources for Building Direct-Mail Lists

Membership rosters
- Professional societies and trade associations (medical, accountancy, manufacturers, air conditioning, electricians)
- Country clubs
- Civic clubs (Kiwanis, Lions, Civitan, Optimist)
- Religious Groups
- Women's organizations (Altrusa, AAUW, Junior League)
- Special-interest groups (Audubon Society, garden clubs, environmental protection groups)
- Community business groups (Chamber of Commerce, Jaycees, Business and Professional Women)

Directories and telephone books
- White or yellow pages, depending upon need

People you have done business with in the past
- Examples include home builders, bankers, accountants, and auto service and repair companies

Develop a coding system to show which types of lists produce the highest percentage of responses. Code the names of people who actually respond. Even if you do not sell to them immediately, they have some interest in your product or service and might become active prospects at a later date.[14]

Ron Knox, a 35-year sales professional with Northwestern Mutual Financial Network, uses a systematic method of contacting existing clients and prospects. Ron sends out a cover letter attached to a newsletter to 400 clients and 100 prospects, four times a year. He has never received less than two reply cards back and often gets eight or more. Ron knows that this database marketing provides useful information in the form of a value-added benefit to his clients and prospects. He also knows that it keeps his name in front of them, and it gives people who've had recent changes in their situations the opportunity to review their insurance needs.

Power of Observation

No matter what methods of prospecting you elect to use, your own powers of observation provide many of your best prospects. Keep your eyes and ears open—prospects are everywhere. Exhibit 7.4 tells of one salesperson's success in using the newspaper for additional prospects. Wedding announcements, business promotions, reports of civic activities, winners of contests, lists of graduates, notices of new business openings, new partnerships or planned mergers—all these focus your attention on potential prospects. Clip an item, attach a personal note of congratulations, and mail them to the person or company featured.[15]

Δ **Exhibit 7.4**

Creative Observation in Prospecting ·

Denise Barnes, a telecommunications salesperson, read about Gary Granger, president of a local company, whose recent successes had been outstanding. A story in the Cleveland Plain Dealer mentioned that Gary was a 1980 graduate of Case Western Reserve University. This gave Denise an idea. She obtained a copy of the 1980 yearbook of that University and cross-checked with the local telephone directory to see which of the graduates still lived in the area.

Denise was successful in selling Gary a telephone communication system that would save his company $3,000 a month. As usual, she asked for referrals. But her observation and the initiative to make creative use of random information paid off in the personalized manner of her request. She asked Gary, "By the way, do you happen to know Bob Tight and Shirley Meggitt who were in your class at Western Reserve?"

Gary did, and he helped her arrange interviews with them. Denise sold both of them her service and eventually made sales to eight of the fourteen names she had found in the yearbook. A little extra effort and creativity paid rich dividends.

Joining Civic Groups

Membership in civic groups can give you opportunities to meet people who are prospects for your product or service. Their meetings provide you with regular times to meet more people and build relationships. Exhibit 7.5 lists tips for using membership in civic clubs as prospecting opportunities.

Δ **Exhibit 7.5**

Tips for Using Membership in Civic Clubs for Prospecting ·

- **Carefully select the groups you join.**
- **Assume leadership responsibilities to work for positive visibility.**
- **Set contact goals for each organization meeting.**
- **Follow up with contacts.**
- **Maintain an information file on the contacts made in each organization.**
- **Use "remeet" goals to help you develop closer relationships with people.**
- **Reach out to new members.**

In selecting groups to join, consider the kinds of prospects you need to meet. It is also beneficial to choose organizations to which decision makers belong. Set goals to meet a certain number of new people at each meeting and to reconnect, or establish stronger relationships, with a certain number of others. Keep an updated file of the organization's members as you meet and learn about them. Avoid actively selling at the meetings, but you may ask someone to tell you the best time to call to set up an appointment. Building relationships through these contacts lays the groundwork for active selling in the future.

Networking

Networking refers to the active cooperation between business people to share information about the business climate, specific happenings in the business community, and prospects.[16] It involves the 3 C's: *connecting*, *communicating*, and *cooperating*. In a sample of 1,500 job hunters, statistics indicated that 61 percent of these individuals found their employment through networks.[17]

Sharing information and names of prospects just makes sense. For instance, if you are a realtor involved in a pending real estate development, it could be to your advantage to alert a banker who may prove helpful to your client in arranging financing. You benefit, your client benefits, and so does the banker. When you regularly serve clients with your product or services, you have opportunities to learn about additional needs you cannot fill. Sharing your customers' names and information with other salespeople who can help is a tangible service to your customers.

Using Directories

Don't overlook directories as a source of prospects. The most accessible directory is the phone book. We are accustomed to looking there when we want to buy something, but telephone books also tell you where to look when you want to sell. They cannot replace other means of prospecting, but they are excellent supplements. Some directories are useful in identifying possible prospects; others are helpful in learning more about prospects to determine whether they have the potential to become customers. In this age of information technology, most directories are available electronically. Exhibit 7.6 is a list of directories with which you should become familiar.

∆ Exhibit 7.6

Use Directories to Identify Prospects

1. **Moody's Industrial Directory** is an annual publication with a wide range of statistical information about particular firms that might be prospects for your product or service. Names of executives, description of a company's business, and a brief financial statement for over 10,000 publicly held firms.

2. **Standard & Poor's Register of Corporations, Directors and Executives** is an excellent source of personal information about individuals in companies. You can use such information for qualifying prospects and for learning enough about them to plan an effective approach and presentation. This annual publication lists names, titles and addresses for 50,000 firms.

3. **Thomas Register of American Manufacturers**, published annually, provides information about who makes what, and where almost anything may be purchased. Information is also provided about the corporate structure of the manufacturer and about its executives.

4. **Polk City Directory** supplies detailed information on individuals living in specific communities. Polk publishes over 1,100 directories covering 6,500 communities throughout the United States and Canada. Your local chamber of commerce should have access to this directory.

5. **Trade Shows & Professional Exhibits** lists over 3,500 trade shows, including their location, when they are held, and attendance expected.

6. **Business List (infoUSA)** has 12 million businesses and 120 million households in their databases. They provide prospect lists (perfect for sales lead generation and telemarketing). On the web at: www.directoriesUSA.com.

Company-Initiated Prospecting

Company-initiated prospecting frees up time for valuable salespeople to concentrate on the top priority of all sales activity—face-to-face interviews with qualified prospects. This is where results are generated. Everything else is merely preparation for the sales arena.

Make the Most of Telemarketing. Telemarketing is an industry that has experienced incredible growth.[18] Some firms rely almost completely on telemarketing for leads; others use it as a supplement to other lead generation methods. However, one issue with telemarketing is its high cost. For smaller companies, the equipment, software, implementation, and training necessary to run a telemarketing center is simply too high. The good news is that more affordable solutions are beginning to be available. TeleMarketingKey, a provider of telemarketing solutions, develops solutions for all sizes of call centers, catering primarily to small and medium-sized organizations that require technology that both enables their agents to perform their duties and allows management to monitor and supervise the organization.[19] Additionally, more companies are outsourcing their telemarketing functions. When you think of outsourcing, you probably think overseas. There is a great deal of that, especially in India, Canada, Mexico and the Philippines. But, there is also a growing number of distributors and part-time agents domestically, even stay-at-home parents making calls during their free time. No matter the size or scope of operation, it is important that callers have the tools necessary to be productive, especially in remote locations, and that management can monitor their efforts and progress.

Personalization Through Internet Marketing. Reebok International makes its customers feel like they are the center of the universe—and they do this through personalization. Reebok designed a Web site that creates an interactive dialogue with their customers. Members can register their location, favorite sport, and such demographic data as age group and gender. Reebok then sends personalized emails to targeted groups such as female runners in the Northeast, for example.[20] Technology truly makes advertising a more effective prospecting tool.

Make the Most of Current Customers. A study of 183 company executives conducted by the Patrick Marketing Group (PMG) of Calabasas, California, found that 70 percent of them felt that expanding relationships with existing customers is the biggest factor challenging the success of their sales teams. These numbers suggest the importance of existing customers as sources of new revenue, says Craig Shields, senior marketing consultant at PMG. Firms realize that it is easier and less expensive to penetrate existing accounts and flush out their potential than to only prospect for new clients. It is estimated that *it costs 5 to 10 times more to go out and get a new customer* than to keep your existing customer base. Some companies take the initiative in furnishing salespeople with the names of past customers who are no longer active.[21]

Web Sites: Harness the Power of the Internet

Salespeople and small companies can set up a home page with a nominal initial expense and use these home pages to advertise their services, offer special deals, or tap into lucrative foreign markets. People can market their businesses inexpensively thanks to the online relationships they form.

Streamline the Sales Process. Suppose you need distributors to sell your product in Spain and Italy. A few years ago you may have sent a salesperson overseas, and the process may take months. Today you can use search engines to type in photography, bronze sculptures, or whatever product you sell, and in a matter of minutes have a number of solid leads to contact. Contracts can be emailed to the ones you select so they can make modifications and email or fax it back. Consequently, you spend a few days rather than a few months putting a team together.

Use Affiliate Program Marketing. The Internet is also a great prospecting tool, especially as a way to partner with others. Are there other Web sites that sell to the same types of customers that you do? If so, your products might complement what they're doing in a way that would allow for an affiliate arrangement. An innovative e-marketing tactic to drive traffic to your Web site is to target your marketing at specific groups of prospects that are likely to have an interest in your product. You can place an ad, and "pay-per-click," as it is commonly called.[22] You only get charged an advertising fee when someone visits your site. Google™ is the leader in affiliate marketing, with more pay-per-click clients than any other Web site. And unlike banner advertising, this approach allows you to only pay for results.

Turn Web Leads Into Online Sales. Used car sales have taken on a new form through online sales. The battle among the major online used car dealers, cars.com, eBay, AutoTrader.com, autobytel.com, and carmax.com, hinges on whose business model best suits dealers' advertising needs, as well as the buyers' ability to balance price with confidence in the transaction on each company's Web site.

The dominant online figure in the used-car market has become AutoTrader™, who has captured 30 percent of the online transaction market, according to J. D. Power. Rather than carving out a direct path between buyers and sellers, AutoTrader forged links with the traditional methods of selling cars via classified ads and used-car dealerships.[23] Not surprisingly, some car dealerships sense the threat of the growing popularity of online car shopping, and are now beginning to offer their inventories online as well. It truly is the trend in the automotive industry. A few years ago, physical dealerships would not have thought to have full-time salespeople devoted to online sales, but today more and more dealerships are stepping forward into the realm of Internet leads and online buying.[24] The forward thinking car dealers recognize this trend, and they refuse to get left behind.

Take advantage of the internet to quickly find more qualified leads.

Managing Prospect Information

Diligent prospecting is useless if you do not have a system for managing and using the information you find. The type of system used is not the primary consideration; more important are accuracy, completeness, and ease of use. When you use a computer, you can have multiple printouts and provisions for additional listings of names by any category you desire that can be added to your coding system.

Initial Recording of Leads

The initial information you need about prospects depends a great deal upon the product or service you sell, but it will, in all likelihood, include these items:

1. Prospect's full name, address, and telephone number (both business and home)

2. Name of company, address, and telephone number; type of business

3. Position in company

4. Family: spouse, names and ages of children

5. Personal information: hobbies, clubs and associations

6. Approximate income (if your product or service is to be sold to the individual rather than to the company)

Classification of Prospects

When you first find the name of an individual or company prospect, assign a classification to the name. One classification system uses the letters A, B, and C.

- **Class A** prospects are those about whom you have adequate information to make a presentation. You know they have the money to buy and the authority to make a decision. Ideally, you also have a referral from someone they respect.

- **Class B** prospects are those about whom you have inadequate information to make the best possible presentation. You may not know enough to be sure they need your product or service. You may not know whether they have the authority to make a decision or whether they can afford to buy. You may not have a referral to help open the door. When one or more of these items is missing, the proper action is research rather than approach.

- **Class C** prospects are people whose names you have found in some way, but about whom you have little or no information other than a name. They are leads, not prospects.

Prospecting activity involves not only finding new leads but also qualifying existing leads by adding information that allows you to move them up to Class A status.

Scheduling Contacts

When you have classified a prospect as Class A, determine when you will initiate contact, either by telephone, personal visit, or direct mail, according to the method of approach you choose. Use a tickler file arrangement of your prospect cards or computer records to see that you take the proper action on the date assigned. The same tickler file will help you schedule later contacts if your first attempt to schedule an interview is not successful. Once a prospect's name enters your file, it stays there permanently until you close a sale or determine that the person is not a prospect for your product or service. If you make a presentation and do not close, choose a time for a new attempt and schedule an appropriate time for contacting the prospect again.

When you discover that a person is not a viable prospect for you and will probably not become one in the foreseeable future, then that person can still be an important contact. The impression you have given by your professionalism may cause that person to recommend you to someone who will prove to be an excellent prospect. Passing on the information you have is the basis of networking among salespeople.

Automating Prospect Information

Professionals don't have time to organize prospect information on 3x5 file cards or loose-leaf binders. It would be difficult to go through handwritten or typed notes every time you're on the phone or in a client's office. However, as your client base grows, the need to interact with them and other individuals from the various departments within your own company requires the use of technology. This is why the most widely used software in selling is contact management programs. These programs were developed to help you collect, organize, classify, and keep track of prospect information. *Developing Partnerships Using Technology* describes some of the common features found in contact management programs.

Developing Partnerships Using Technology

CONTACT MANAGEMENT PROGRAMS: MAKING YOUR JOB A LITTLE EASIER

Pre-defined Fields. These are used for general entry information when building the database (name, company, phone, fax, e-mail, etc.). Some of the programs have fields for specialty items such as birthdays and other special occasions. You can also generate your own personal fields for contacts.

Keyword Searches. Search the entire database and find specific words, phrases, notes, names, or any information from the other fields. Information on any one of a countless number of prospects can be sifted through and found in a matter of seconds.

Synchronization. Now salespeople literally have prospects in the palm of their hands. They can transfer contact information to a handheld or take the entire database with them on a laptop. Information obtained in the field can be transferred back just as easily to an existing database or the office network server.

Journals and Histories. A great salesperson can locate every instance where a contact has been updated, reclassified, or added to the database. The program can also track what documents, email, and phone conversations a salesperson has had with each client. A running tally of time you spend with a prospect is only a few clicks away.

Email and Internet Integration. Contacts can be generated directly from email or from Internet submission forms. Thousands of new pre-qualified prospects can be added every day using these features.

Check out these Web sites for additional information:

www.smartcontactmanager.com

www.goldmine.com

www.saleslogix.com

www.bizforms.com

www.moneycafe.com

www.hotdata.com

With the widespread use of data mining, there is simply no excuse for making a cold call anymore. *Data mining* is the process of electronically searching through stacks of records to find useful information so that you can go into a call knowing about the prospect before ever meeting him. *Technology has created the solution*. Hotdata is one example. Simply type a company name into Hotdata, an intelligence-gathering tool that integrates or plugs into such leading contact managers as Act! and Goldmine, and find pertinent information about that company in seconds.

Applications for database technology are limited only by the creativity of its user. For example, you might begin your day by pulling up a list of follow-ups from the corporate database. Determine the best way to organize the day based on where you'll be, and what prospects or customers are in that area. Then generate form letters to go out to all the customers and prospects you visited the day before and print them on your own letterhead. In addition, you can generate call schedules and short-range forecasts, provide scheduled contact lists in chronological order and account summaries, expedite long-range forecasting and sorting by a variety of criteria (zip code, alphabet, amount of last sale), and prepare graphs showing trends in sales for your current customers.[25]

Too many sales teams fall back on product features, prepackaged pitches, and a narrow-minded focus on closing rather than focusing on being as thorough as possible in the initial stages of prospecting. A lot of salespeople fail to understand their clients' financial concerns and market struggles. As a result, some companies are teaching their sales teams that the best way to find prospects and keep them is to put themselves in their clients' shoes so they can offer their clients a real solution. This accomplishes more than merely establishing a solid rapport with prospects, it builds a relationship that will inevitably yield more success in the future.[26]

The single most important ingredient in the formula for success is *knowing how to deal with people.*

SUMMARY

- Prospecting is the skill that keeps salespeople in business. Once you have leads, qualify them to determine whether they are true prospects that have a need for your product and are in a position to make a buying decision.

- Make sure prospects pass the MADDEN test.

- Two of the most effective prospecting methods are referrals and centers of influence. When someone they respect makes the introduction, you have a built-in sales assistant—the influence of the person who provided the lead and the initial contact.

- Group prospecting is securing names of possible prospects at trade shows, through speaking engagements, or in any situation where you have the opportunity to meet a number of people. Cold calling also provides a supplemental source of new prospects.

- Networking is a valuable source of new prospects for salespeople who are willing to share information about their customers or clients. It's all about connecting, communicating and cooperating.

- Efficient management of information means that needed data is always at your fingertips. Utilize electronic filing systems to keep track of prospects as you record initial information, upgrade prospects, and schedule the time you want to contact each one.

REVIEW QUESTIONS

1. How does your skill in prospecting exert a direct effect on your ability to close a sale?

2. What characteristics make a qualified prospect?

3. What is a referral? How do you get referrals?

4. What is the advantage of having referrals from your clients?

5. What is a center of influence?

6. Name several directories that might be helpful sources of prospects. Where would you look for these directories?

7. What is observation prospecting? Name several places a salesperson might find prospects through observation.

8. How does networking work for salespeople? Why were women active in organizing formal networking groups? Is this an important activity for men as well as women?

9. What methods do companies use to provide leads for salespeople? Why would the company be interested in providing leads instead of having individual salespeople do all the prospecting?

10. What kind of records are needed for keeping track of prospects?

11. How long should a prospect's name remain in your prospecting system?

ROLE-PLAY EXERCISES

The following role-play exercises help build teams, improve communication, and emphasize the "real-world" side of selling. They are meant to be challenging, to learn how to deal with problems that have no single "right" answer and to use a variety of skills beyond those employed in a typical review question. Read and complete each activity. Then in the next class, discuss and compare answers with other classmates. Have some students take the role of the salesperson, and see how they would react. Remember, *"You learn more about a person in an hour of play than in a lifetime of conversation."* —Plato

1. Your sales manager has instructed you to find a way to update the company's method of recording leads and prospects. Go to a computer store and review the software available for salespeople to manage prospecting records. If possible, see a demonstration of a program in operation or get a brochure describing its features. Write a brief description of what it does to report back to your boss and give your opinion of its effectiveness. Have a sales meeting in the next class to discuss your findings. If your school has a computer lab with sample software, ask if they have a prospecting program or some type of filing program that could be used for that purpose by salespeople.

2. You decide to establish a professional business organization. Define its purpose and then write a profile of the type of people who would make good members for it. For a week, prospect for the organization on your campus. Consider using at least three methods. For example, you might ask a professor (a center of influence) to suggest students who fit the profile. You might find information in the student directory or other lists of people that would suggest prospects. Use your imagination, your powers of observation, and your creativity, and see how many prospects you can find in a week. Classify them as Class A, B, or C. Write a brief report on your experiences. You can also hold a screening for candidates with the students in your class. Which method worked best for you?

CASE STUDY

Case 7.1—Finding New Business

Gil Robinson studied the monthly report of his sales that had just come in from the home office. He knew things had been slow lately, but he had no idea that things had reached quite the low that the report revealed. The figures were in front of him in black and white. "Should be red and white except for the fact that black suggests mourning," Gil thought to himself. He decided going around feeling sorry for himself wouldn't do any good. What he needed was a big push to get back in the win column.

Just then the phone rang. His sales manager, Dick Porter, was calling. "Did you get your monthly report?" he asked.

"Yes, I did. Pretty sad, isn't it?" Gil said.

"It's kind of strange, too. The thing I don't understand is that the rest of the sales force is going great guns. What's causing your slump?" Dick wanted to know.

"Well, for one thing, I've lost a few customers. Plants are closing or moving out of my territory. None of my real big buyers, so I think things will start picking up pretty soon," Gil predicted.

"How are you doing with your steady customers?"

"Fine, no problems there," Gil answered.

"You know, we've set a pretty stiff quota for your territory," Dick said. "The way it looks, you're going to have to go some to meet it. Do you have any ideas about how to do it?"

"I've got a few ideas. I think things will get better soon."

"Okay, Gil," Dick said. "We're expecting a lot from your territory. Don't let us down."

After hanging up the phone, Gil turned to another item that had come in the mail. It was a listing of selected sales from all over the country. The home office had developed it to give salespeople an indication of what types of companies are buying which products. Gil glanced at it. "There's never anything in this to help me. Maybe I'll look it over later. Right now, I've got to get on the ball and find some customers to replace those I've lost."

1. What do you think is Gil's major problem?

2. What do you think about the conversation between Gil and his sales manager? Did they identify the problem? Did they find a solution for it?

3. How is Gil's problem related to prospecting?

Qualities of High Sales Performers...

1. **Exchange information** rather than present products. They tend to ask a variety of questions that force the customer to analyze, evaluate, speculate, or express feelings.

2. **Know when to close.** They advocate their products only after they have identified or created an important need and involved the customer in developing the solution.

3. **Sell to people, not organizations**, and demonstrate a strong commitment to meeting customer needs.

4. **Are perceived by prospects as genuine advocates** of prospects' needs, even while actively promoting the company and its products or services.

5. **Provide value added** to the customer. They act as a resource able to directly provide expertise to the customer.

6. **Regularly establish trust** within their own organizations by sharing information, encouraging participation in decisions, and recognizing the contributions of the internal staff to their success.

7. **Engage in behavior** such as maintaining eye contact, showing enthusiasm, asking questions about customers' needs, restating accurately and being prepared with effective responses to buyers' objections.

Preapproach & Telephone Techniques

- Recognize the importance of the preapproach in the sales cycle.

- Learn the objectives of the preapproach and the planning needed to make it effective.

- Study how to prepare for an effective preapproach.

- Understand how the preapproach fits into the sales cycle as an extension of prospecting.

- Discover effective methods for making telephone calls that are successful in leading to presentations.

- Understand the six-step telephone track and how to use it to make appointments.

See enough people. See the right people. See them at the right time.[1] That sounds logical enough! The pivotal part of this advice however, is the "right people." How can you be sure that you are investing your time in calling on qualified prospects? The answer lies in your diligence in collecting information about the leads you record in your prospecting system.

When someone gives you a referral, ask questions to learn what you need to know about that prospect. Research the prospect's business or industry and the company itself. Discover personal information that will help you know what kind of personality to expect. The various activities that provide this necessary personal and business information are called *presale planning* or the *preapproach*. The preapproach is the planning and preparation done prior to actual contact with the prospect.

In gathering such information, you learn on whom to call, why, when, and where. Seemingly insignificant details might be the key to the approach that spells the difference between a sale and a no-sale. Leave nothing to chance. For example, details such as the correct pronunciation of the prospect's name can be secured in advance. Roger Capps, an industrial salesperson, thought he was well prepared to call on an important new prospect, only to find himself sent on his way after less than a minute. The prospect, Mr. Hajovsky, had no time for Capps, who made the fatal error of mispronouncing Hajovsky's name. Capps could have avoided the lost opportunity by taking a few seconds to ask the receptionist for the correct pronunciation.

The sales cycle is a continuous process with no clear break between one phase and the next. In practice, you cannot separate the prospecting, preapproach, approach, and need discovery elements into different segments; rather, they blend together and become one. They are discussed separately for convenience, but the exact point where one phase ends and the next begins will likely never be the same. Exhibit 8.1 illustrates the absence of clear dividing lines between these steps in the relationship selling process.

Δ **Exhibit 8.1**

Four Phases of the Sales Process

The numerous types of selling vary so widely that few broad generalizations can be made about the amount of preapproach information to gather. Depending on the type of selling in which you engage and the product or services being sold, the preapproach differs considerably. At times, qualifying prospects can only be accomplished during the approach and need discovery process by asking questions, observing, listening, and interpreting verbal and nonverbal signals.

Preparation and Preapproach

Before engaging in the actual presentation process, sales professionals must analyze all the information they have available to them about a prospect to understand as much about them as possible. During the preapproach phase, sales professionals try to understand the prospect's current needs, current use of brands, and feelings about available brands.

In addition, they must identify decision makers, review account histories, assess product needs, plan a sales presentation to address the identified concerns of the prospect, and set call objectives. Salespeople also develop a preliminary strategy for the sales process during this phase, keeping in mind that the strategy may have to be refined as they learn more about each prospect.[2]

The type and quality of information uncovered during the preapproach is vital. Just like students dislike doing homework after school, many adults have a similar aversion to the groundwork and prefer to skip ahead to the "real work." However, the preliminary steps are a must. Successful sales professionals rarely even make a cold call without some sort of preparation.[3] When they are ready for a formal sales call, professional salespeople have studied and analyzed the prospect's personality, company, operations, needs, and financial position.

One of the most thorough ways to prepare is to develop a checklist of questions to answer before you make a sales call. Exhibit 8.2 presents a checklist designed to help gather the essential sales information you need before you are face-to-face with a prospect.

Δ **Exhibit 8.2**

Checklist of Sales Essentials for Collecting Preapproach Information · · · · · · · · · · · · · · · · · ·

- What business is the company in? What are its products and markets? Who are its primary customers?

- How big is the company? Where does it rank within its industry? Can this company give me enough business to make this call worthwhile?

- Who is the ultimate decision maker in buying my product?

- Who else influences the buying decision?

- How often does this company buy my type of product or service?

- How well is the company satisfied with its present supplier of similar products?

- What plans does the company have that could affect its future need for my product?

- What are the background and personal interests of each person concerned in the buying decision?

- Is the company's staff technically informed? Can I help them develop greater expertise?

- Do we (or can we) use their products or services in our company?

- Do any of our top executives know any of their executives personally?

Preparing for sales calls is time well spent; and most buyers are not receptive to those who skip this step. "If buyers perceive you as unprepared, you won't get that chance to call on them again," said Adrian Miller, owner of Port Washington-based Adrian Miller Sales Training. According to a recent Sales Industry Trends Report, 61 percent of executives expect salespeople to spend about 30 minutes preparing, and nearly 63 percent expect them to spend less than 20 minutes in preparation. The study included a survey of 141 sales managers and vice presidents at companies with sales of between $5 million and $50 million around the United States.[4]

According to their findings, the most important information a salesperson can gather is competitive insight, understanding who influences the buyer and industry trends. Other important factors include new and upcoming product and service launches, corporate directives, and share of the market. Leaders say the best way to get salespeople to invest in preparation time is through example, and by discussing strategies. It pays to do your homework.

Prepare for the Presentation

Do your research to find out about the prospect and develop a purpose for the call, linked to a potential client benefit.[5] Set a goal for each contact with a prospect, know what you want to accomplish, and how you plan to do it. There is much more to preparation than simply gathering and reviewing information. Rehearsal eliminates the stammering, nervous speech habits, and repetition that can result from lack of preparation.

Allow time in your daily schedule to prepare the sales approach and presentation you will use in each call. Decide how you can make the best possible use of sales literature and other tools provided by your company in this specific call. Plan how to incorporate visual aids into your approach and presentation for maximum effectiveness.

When preparing for a presentation, videotaping your sales talk allows you to see how you really look. "That's the best way to coach people," says Ken Taylor president of Decker Communication Inc. Videotaping also allows you to hear your use of "non-words" such as *um*, *uh*, and *you know*. Here are some rehearsal tips:[6]

- Practice your presentation with specific customers in mind.

- Videotape presentations to show sales reps their strengths and weaknesses.

- Make large, exaggerated motions until you feel comfortable making more natural-looking gestures.

Visualize Successful Selling

Salespeople can learn a great deal from the training habits of world-class athletes. Many track stars use visualization techniques to help them focus on a specific event. An integral part of their training consists of what are called "mental toughening sessions." They run the race over and over in their minds. Over a ten-year period, Edwin Moses won 122 consecutive races in the 400-meter hurdles. His power of visualization became so acute that when he mentally visualized hitting a hurdle, he actually felt the pain in his leg.

To further illustrate how powerful visualization can be, consider this amazing example. After the Vietnam War, a reporter interviewed an Air Force captain who had been a prisoner of war for over seven years. The former POW had just played a superb game in a golf tournament. When the reporter mentioned his surprise at the captain's skill after so long an absence, the captain said, "I've played this course perfectly for the last seven years." The reporter replied, "I thought you hadn't played golf in the last eight years." The captain said, "Well, actually I haven't physically played the game in the last eight years. However, for the last seven years in my cell as a POW I have been playing this course mentally."[7]

You can practice this same type of mental exercise. Positively affirm the feeling you want to create and visualize the outcomes you want to obtain. Think about what you will say and anticipate the prospect's responses. Create a mental image of the desired results, and then live it over and over in your mind. Practice out loud; your mind believes the sound of your own voice. *Remember that your mind cannot separate a real experience from an imagined one.*

It really pays to THINK BIG.

"WELL, I'D SAY THAT SALE WENT PRETTY WELL!"

Used with permission from *The Boxcar Millionaire*

Sources of Preapproach Information

When you know what information you need, you can identify a number of valuable sources for obtaining it. The information you gather will help you get in to make a presentation as well as guide you in preparing a strategy for the interview itself. For example, you can ask colleagues on your company's sales team for information they have on particular prospects. Current customers are also excellent sources of information, and they may be happy to share what they know. There is nothing wrong with calling on prospects without an appointment. At the very least, this cold call gives you the opportunity to observe their facilities and you learn something that validates them as, at least, partially qualified prospects. You cannot predict the most beneficial sources of information, so keep your eyes and ears open so you won't miss a great opportunity![8]

Here's a useful tip— read magazines and newsletters that are related to your customer's industry. You likely read publications that are pertinent in your field, so your clients probably also read publications relevant to their fields. This is a great way to uncover ideas to serve their needs better. However, just researching and reading are not enough. You must know what to look for.[9]

Here are six items to consider that may give you valuable information:

1. **Mergers**. Will new alliances give you better opportunities to see companies that have denied you access in the past?

2. **Personnel Changes**. Watch for new appointments by your customers, prospects, and competitors.

3. **Changing Product Lines**. Firms that drop or add products may be suggesting a new emphasis that gives you a reason to call.

4. **Advertising Plans**. Have your competitors or customers changed advertising agencies? Are they creating a new approach or pushing certain products? New advertising campaigns may signal a change in the company that elicits the use of your product.

5. **TV and Magazine Ads**. Television commercials and print ads are a source of invaluable clues. Look at the features being stressed and the image being portrayed.

6. **Sales Training**. The news media highlights new sales training endeavors. Is your customer or prospect developing a sales training program of which you can make use?

On a more personal level, there are numerous online sites that may make pounding the pavement a thing of the past.[10] Even your fingers don't have to do much walking. Just a few mouse clicks and you can find thousands of employment opportunities on the Internet. If you are seeking employment in sales, or in any other career for that matter, Exhibit 8.3 lists four online sources to assist you in gathering a significant amount of preapproach information.

Δ **Exhibit 8.3**

The Fast Track to Finding a Career

According to a survey of 100 executive recruiters conducted by executive job search and recruiting organization ExecuNet, 77 percent of recruiters use search engines to check the backgrounds of potential job candidates. Of those, 35 percent of recruiters have eliminated a candidate from consideration based on information they found online. For this reason, choose your words carefully so that you present yourself in the most accurate and best manner possible.[11]

Career Builder (www.careerbuilder.com)—Access is free to this Web site for job seekers. You can search opportunities by zip code anywhere in the United States. The site has the capability of notifying you via email of new listings that match your criteria.

Hotjobs (www.hotjobs.com)—You can narrow your search by keyword, region or by type of job. In sales, for example, options include client services, inside or outside sales, sales rep, sales engineer, and telemarketing.

Monster.com (www.monster.com)—Job seekers have access to interactive, personalized tools such as My Monster and Resume Builder. You can see real-time job postings and complete company profiles to guide you in your search for the "job."

Job Hunt (www.job-hunt.org)—Online job search and complete career resource and employment resources center. Job Hunt is an award-winning Web site with over 8300 of the best job sites and career resources.

Excellence in selling requires an awareness that the hardest work takes place during the preapproach, but all that hard work leads to the desired end result—a yes.[12] You must be prepared to answer the questions that are in the minds of prospects when you first contact them. Exhibit 8.4 lists ten questions that buyers have, although they don't often volunteer to ask you these questions.

Δ **Exhibit 8.4**

Ten Buyer Questions ·

1. What are you selling?
2. Why do I need it?
3. Who is your company?
4. How much will it cost?
5. Who else is using it, and are they satisfied?
6. What kind of a person are you?
7. Is your price truly competitive?
8. How does your solution compare to other alternatives?
9. Why do I need it now?
10. What is your record for support and service?

Building Self-Confidence

One of the most beneficial features of preapproach planning is that it builds personal self-confidence. Knowing that you are prepared gives you an added measure of self-confidence that is transmitted to the prospect. The opposite of this confidence is fear, and fear comes primarily from the unknown.

A definite plan for each prospect means you are more likely to be accepted. A purchasing agent for a large, international food processing plant who sees many salespeople described his reactions like this:

> *I turn away salesman after salesman because they come in like lost sheep. . . . They hope that somehow they'll stumble into an order. I get the impression that they figure I'll do the selling for them. I haven't got time for people like that.*[13]

Salespeople call on professional buyers whose job is to make sound purchasing decisions for their companies. These professionals expect to interact with another professional, not an unprepared amateur. If you walk confidently into the buyer's office and get down to business immediately without wasting the prospect's time with unnecessary questions, you increase the likelihood of a successful close. And by emitting an air of self-confidence, you add to your perceived value.[14]

Setting Up the Sales Interview

Preapproach involves doing research, studying a company's website, and discovering other companies with whom they currently do business. It also encompasses the methods used to set up the face-to-face interview itself. There is more to consider than simply picking a day and time. Below are some factors that must be addressed and thoroughly planned to ensure you walk into the most ideal situation when you meet with a prospect.

Timing

With a little research, you can determine the best time to call a prospect you have not previously met. For example, Powell Kenney, vice-president of Clampitt Paper Company in Fort Worth, sees salespeople only between 5:30 and 8:30 a.m. each weekday morning. He does not want his regular work routine disrupted by listening to sales presentations.

Ordinarily, sales calls can be scheduled for almost any time during the business day. Like Mr. Kenney, however, most prospects have a time when they are more receptive to your presentation. Some like to see salespeople the first thing in the morning. Others prefer to handle routine matters first. Fortunately, prospects have different preferences to the extent that salespeople can fill the workday with appointments.

If every buyer insisted on appointments before 8:30 a.m., salespeople would be in serious trouble. If a particular prospect does not seem to have a preference for a time of day to see salespeople, try to discover when most salespeople call on this prospect. If most call in the morning, schedule your call for late in the afternoon. Many executives work past 5:00 p.m. and will see you. In fact, they may well appreciate your diligent work ethic.

Gaining Entry

Before an actual face-to-face meeting can be arranged, you must choose a way to contact the prospect and set up the interview. Appointments can be set up in three basic ways. You may send a letter requesting an appointment, make a cold call, or telephone the prospect and schedule a specific time and date for the interview. Writing a letter for an appointment may produce no answer or may require several contacts to set a mutually convenient time. Cold calls have a low probability of finding the prospect available for an interview.[15] Often times, it requires a combination of all three methods to get an agreement to meet.

With email and instant messaging slowly replacing phones, it's getting tougher to set up a meeting in the first place.[16] But the telephone still works with a little diligence. Often times, you will have to wade through a complex automated system, but eventually, you will get through to someone. After you make contact, in many cases, a few minutes are all that are required to make an appointment. Good telephone techniques and habits are important to anyone in professional selling. Using the telephone successfully requires the same basic selling skills as a face-to-face call, plus some additional skills to meet the special challenges of telephone use. Finding a prospect in a bad mood or under a time constraint, the surprise element of a call, and the lack of visual contact are some of the elements that may prevent you from feeling as comfortable with the telephone as you do in a personal contact.

Many executives have receptionists or administrative assistants who screen their incoming calls and mail. These *gatekeepers* also do an excellent job of protecting and conserving the time of their superiors by determining whom gets in and when. It is important to build a relationship with these gatekeepers, because statistics show that approximately 60 to 80 percent of them have significant influence over the purchase of certain products and services. It is a mistake to view them as barriers to overcome, and the best way to get to the main buyer is to sell yourself at the door. Exhibit 8.5 outlines eight ways to build rapport with gatekeepers.[17]

Δ **Exhibit 8.5**

Building Rapport With Gatekeepers ·

1. **Adjust Your Attitude**. Be friendly, but not fake. Gatekeepers appreciate respect, and they can recognize insincerity.

2. **Honesty Is the Best Policy**. Don't lie to increase your chances of seeing the purchaser. Gatekeepers will inevitably discover your falsehoods, and once this happens the possible sale has ended before it has begun.

3. **Get Personal Information**. Find out the names of gatekeepers, their interests, and family names if you can do so without being too nosy. They appreciate being remembered by name.

4. **Sell to the Gatekeeper**. Gatekeepers have influence over buying decisions. So if you show them how their company can benefit by using your product or service, the chances of you making the final sale increase.

5. **Question Gatekeepers**. Ask them what are the needs and goals of their company, and they just might be willing to tell you.

6. **Be Thoughtful**. Remember to thank gatekeepers for their help, but also remember special occasions such as birthdays and holidays. Don't go overboard, and don't use these gifts as payoffs, gatekeepers are intelligent and know what's going on.

7. **Keep a Sense of Humor**. This keeps things light, and maybe this will encourage the gatekeeper to accept you in a favorable way.

8. **Be Patient**. It may take longer than you expect to get through the door, but if you keep your patience and persistence, a positive outcome is the result.

Telephone Techniques

Direct marketing expert Bob Stone defines telemarketing in this manner:

Telemarketing utilizes sophisticated telecommunications and information systems combined with personal selling and servicing skills to help companies keep in close contact with present and potential customers, increase sales, and enhance business productivity.

It is a marketing discipline that uses telecommunications technology as part of a well planned, organized, and managed marketing program that prominently features the use of personal selling, using non-face-to-face contacts.[18]

Telemarketing can be a key source of information on a company's prospective and current customer base, markets, inventory, distribution channels, and promotional efforts. When this information is combined with contact management systems, it can bring trained personnel into computerized contact with potential customers, and maintain that contact profitably.

Because of the ever-increasing cost of a sales visit to a prospect, for many companies the telephone call is replacing the unsolicited or cold call approach to make the initial contact with a prospect. Proper telephone usage helps you qualify prospects, budget time, and save money. In addition, good telephone techniques enhance your image and precondition the prospect to receive you favorably. Phoning for an appointment implies that you are courteous and considerate of the prospect's time. The phone call helps to create a selling situation because, just by agreeing to see you, the prospect tacitly indicates interest in your product or service.

Getting the Appointment: A Mini Sale

You must regard the use of the telephone to set up appointments as a true sales activity and not just a necessary evil. You must also remember what you are selling. The mini sale is selling the prospect on the idea of giving you an appointment; your purpose is not to sell your product or service on the telephone.

You can make a large number of inquiries in a fraction of the time it takes to make personal visits. You will likely find that personal visits made with a telephone appointment not only reduce waiting time, but prospects will likely be more receptive because those who are not really interested do not schedule appointments.

Making First Impressions

The quality of your voice, the hesitation in your voice, the volume, the strength of your speaking style all convey an image to another person. Do you come across as being sincere, honest, confident, strong, knowledgeable and likable? If you sound weak and tentative or use words like *well*, *sort-of*, *kind-of*, *maybe*, or *perhaps*, that says to the prospect, "I'm not one bit sure that this is going to a good investment of time for you." Some people even include phrases like, "Well, to be honest with you," which says to the prospect that you aren't always honest.[18] Consider how you would react to this type of telephone call:

> *Hello, Peyton... uh, my name is... uh Vince Young... uh I'm with the Tennessee Titans and... uh we've developed an...uh idea I...uh think you might find...uh interesting and...uh valuable. Uh...Peyton, are morning or....uh afternoon appointments more convenient for you?*

A salesperson with this type of delivery does not make a professional impression. Verbal hesitancy seems to signal a weak, unsure personality.[19] An essential element in telemarketing that helps overcome this is a script, whether it is general or written out word-for-word. Scripts are helpful in guiding the salespeople by capturing the prospect's attention. The first ten to thirty seconds of a telephone sales call are crucial; they go far toward determining whether your request for an appointment will be successful or end with a dial tone.

People buy from the people they like. Remember you're projecting your personality over the phone.[20] *How* you say something can be as important as *what* you say. Put a smile in your voice and the prospect can literally hear it. The most successful salespeople project positive voice qualities such as sincerity, courtesy, and confidence. A survey conducted for Jacobi Voice Development revealed the type of voice characteristics by which prospects are most annoyed. Exhibit 8.6 illustrates the most negative or annoying qualities.[21]

Δ **Exhibit 8.6**

Most Annoying Voice Characteristics to Prospects

Characteristic	Percentage
Whining and complaining	44.0%
High-pitched or loud tone	28.0%
Mumblers	11.1%
Too fast or too weak	8.5%
Monotone	3.5%
Strong accent	2.4%

Evaluate Your Telephone Voice

Your voice is your personality over the telephone. It makes an immediate impression that can portray you as friendly or distant, confident or timid, spontaneous or mechanical, and relaxed or nervous. So, how do you come across over the phone? Make a tape recording of yourself while on the telephone and evaluate the following attributes:[22]

Pitch. Is your voice too shrill or strained? Do you speak in a monotone? In normal speech, pitch varies. These variations are known as inflection. The more inflection you use, the more interesting your tone of voice becomes. Keep in mind that when you are under emotional stress, the pitch of your voice will tend to rise and become shrill or strained. Watch it! The pitch of your voice is a gauge of confidence and poise.

Volume. Check the volume or loudness of your voice. You may even get a friend to help you determine this. Is it too soft or too loud? Often when people are tired or upset, their voices fade, and they will be asked to speak up. Be sure to speak loud enough to be heard, but not so loud that you sound overly forceful.

Rate. If you speak too slowly you'll likely lose the attention of the listener. Conversely, your listener won't be able to follow you if you speak too rapidly. In either case, your message won't get through.

Quality. The quality of your voice is its most distinctive and individual characteristic. This is where the essence of warmth, understanding and "likeability" come into play. Smiling as you speak enhances your vocal quality. Being angry, upset or in a hurry negatively affects your vocal quality.

Articulation. The price of poor articulation is high, particularly in business. You must enunciate or pronounce your words very clearly or your listeners will misunderstand you. Faulty articulation and incorrect word pronunciation give your listener the impression that you are sloppy, careless, and lack knowledge.

The telephone may be one of the most powerful, efficient, and cost-effective business tools you have at your disposal. Telephone manners and etiquette are critical components of a professional image. Through experience, you'll develop your own telephone style. You'll also find customers and prospects responding positively when you and your employees smile, listen and show personal interest!

Organizing the Call

Inadequate preparation reduces the effectiveness of your delivery. Ask yourself these four questions to help you stay on track:[23]

1. *Why am I calling?* Do you want to make an appointment, check on a customer's need to reorder, or follow up an inquiry?

2. *What is my proposal?* Your plan should have two parts: 1.What do you want from the person you call, and 2. What commitment you will make. Jot down some notes and be specific!

3. *What would make this person want to grant my request?* Before calling, determine why the person you are calling will do what you request.

4. *How does my telephone script sound?* Identify those key words or phrases in your telephone sales call that you can emphasize to make your message more convincing.[24]

Before you ever pick up the telephone, go through a mental checklist to ensure that you are fully prepared. Exhibit 8.7 presents ten strategic checkpoints to consider when you are preparing to use the telephone to set up appointments.

Δ Exhibit 8.7

Key Points to Consider When Preparing to Use the Telephone

1. **Arrange a definite time each day to telephone.** Determine a specific number of calls to make during that time period.

2. **Arrange for privacy to avoid interruptions.** Make as many calls as you can in the allotted time. Your attitude is critical; without a positive attitude, using the telephone is mentally exhausting.

3. **Develop a well-written, structured script.** Know exactly what to say before you call. However, never make your call sound like a canned spiel. You can avoid sounding canned by doing one thing—practice, practice, practice!

4. **Verify that you are actually talking to the person that you intended to call.** Be sure you have the correct pronunciation of the name. Use the name several times during the call.

5. **Tell the prospect just enough to get the appointment.** You know a lot more than you need to tell at this time. Just peak his interest so that he agrees to a meeting.

6. **Show excitement and enthusiasm in your voice.** Give your voice the emotional feel of shaking hands over the telephone. Put a smile in your voice. You can even try placing a mirror by the phone to watch your expression.

7. **Never argue; be sure to ask for the appointment.** Always offer a choice of times so prospects can choose a time that is convenient for them.

8. **Sell your own name.** Ask the prospect to write it down so you are remembered when you arrive for the appointment.

9. **Be courteous.** Say thank you and begin sentences with phrases like, "May I ask ..." and "If I may...."

10. **Watch your language.** Choose your words carefully for greater impact. Repetition of nonfunctional expressions like, "I see," "uh huh," "you know," and "fantastic" are irritating and unprofessional.

Plugging Contact Management Into the Phone

Of all the daily administrative tasks performed by a salesperson, using the telephone to set appointments is certainly one of the most critical. With sales force automation, telephone time becomes much more efficient and productive. All of the leading contact management programs have some integration with the telephone. This powerful tool can help you maximize the use of your precious phone time. A salesperson can quickly review preapproach information gathered or any past conversations with the prospect or client.

This chapter's *Developing Partnerships Using Technology* accentuates how contact management programs assist the salesperson in setting up appointments for a personal visit with a prospect or client. These programs give salespeople an integrated system for organizing prospecting information. The information might include the size and date of the previous purchases, when you contacted them last, and what happened in that interview—and even have the computer dial the phone for you.

Developing Partnerships Using Technology

Integrate with a Contact Management Program to Make Appointments

With contact management programs salespeople working out of their virtual office now have a virtual assistant traveling with them. Contact management software dials, answers, screens calls, and finds files in the blink of an eye. New software, such as the Maximizer™, a sales and contact manager software designed to manage and profile customers and prospects, allows you to easily access your email for phone numbers, track every sale, and maintain relationships for repeat business.[25] Here are a few features available on these devices to help you make the most of your day:

Unlimited Information. A salesperson can easily review preapproach information gathered or any past conversations with the prospect or client. If a particular document or previous correspondence with an individual is needed, the salesperson can easily open the file to review a price quote, check inventory, or email.

Auto and Voice Dialing. Most programs are equipped with automatic dialing features. This requires a connection to the office phone system or modem. Instead of pounding away at the keypad, you can have the program dial the number. Calling is faster and more accurate, especially for international contacts with complex dialing codes.

Caller ID. New advances in technology are making sales calls more effective. Caller ID can recognize incoming calls. This allows for screening calls without needing an assistant. Contact management programs have these same advantages. The programs are able to pull up a contact's file whenever they call so it is right on the screen when the salesperson answers the phone.

Check out these Web sites for additional information:

www.treo.com

www.blackberry.com

www.smartcontactmanager.com

www.goldmine.com

www.maximizer.com

The Six-Step Telephone Track

The key to using the telephone effectively is to engineer conversations that sound like normal talk. They have to be two-sided, but simultaneously get people to sell themselves on seeing you. When you try to set an appointment by phone, you don't have the advantage of being able to show your prospect what a great product you offer. Instead, you need a careful strategy that allows the prospect to take an interest in what you're saying and agree to meet with you face-to-face. Use the six-step outline in Exhibit 8.8 to plan your appointment-setting calls so that the next time you talk to prospects, you're sitting face- to-face with them.[26]

Δ Exhibit 8.8

The Six-Step Telephone Track

Step I	Introduce yourself and your company
Step II	Take the curse off the call
Step III	State the purpose of the call
Step IV	Make an interest-capturing statement
Step V	Request an appointment
Step VI	Overcome resistance

Step 1: Introduce Yourself and Your Company

Most sales relationships depend heavily on initial impressions. When you place a call, the prospect will most likely make a judgment about you before your first twelve words are said.[27] How you introduce yourself, therefore, and what you say immediately thereafter are of vital importance. A weak or tentative opening puts you at a severe disadvantage throughout the rest of the call. Your opening words should tell who you are, indicate the company you represent, and confirm that you are speaking to the correct person:

> *Good morning . . . I am Bryce Damuth, sales representative for iDesign Inc. Am I speaking to Mrs. Teresa Ridings? . . . Good. Mrs. Ridings, . .*

Be sure the person you reach on the phone is someone who can make or influence a buying decision. Smile as you speak so that you transmit a warm, friendly personality.

Watch the rate at which you speak. Prospects instinctively pay more attention to someone who speaks at a moderate and energetic rate. A too rapid rate of speech seems nervous or sounds as though you are reading a canned pitch. If you are too slow, you come across as lazy or unconcerned, or the prospect feels that talking to you will be a long, time-consuming process.

Step 2: Take the Curse Off the Call

The telephone call is an interruption of your prospect's work. To sell people on the idea of granting you an appointment, you must detach their attention from what they were doing or thinking when the phone rang and attract it to what you propose. It helps if you think and talk about your call as a service you are offering rather than as an interruption for which you must apologize. You can take the curse off the call with a statement and a question to soften the impact of the interruption. For example:

1. *It will take just about a minute to explain why I'm calling. Is it convenient for you to talk now?*

2. *Mrs. Ridings, do you have a minute to speak with me now, or did I catch you at a bad time? . . . (If the prospect indicates the time is inconvenient) . . . When would be a better time?*

A prospect who is totally preoccupied with other matters may refuse to speak with you. In this case, calling back at a time the prospect suggests is far better for both parties. When you do call back at the suggested time, the odds will be greatly improved that your message will receive a favorable hearing.

Step 3: State the Purpose of the Call

Assuming the prospect does have time to speak, follow with a brief, hard-hitting, lead-in statement about why you are calling—just enough to capture the prospect's attention, but short of describing the benefit(s) you will present in a later step. Use these ideas to spark your creative thinking about possible lead-in statements you can use:

- Refer to a direct-mail piece you have already sent to the prospect.

- Mention the person who referred you to this prospect.

- Say that your company has designed a program or service to benefit clients like the prospect.

A letter, product literature, newsletter, or any other direct mail piece sent to a select sampling of prospects gives you the opportunity to call and inquire if they received it. This tactic gives you a purpose for calling and provides an acceptable type of lead-in statement. Here is a sample, and whatever the answer, you can use this beginning to move on to the next step:

Mrs. Ridings, thank you for taking a minute of your valuable time to speak with me. My purpose in calling is to find out if you received the newsletter I sent you last week describing a specialized investment service that my company has recently developed for professionals like you.

Perhaps the best reason you can give for calling is that a third party whom the prospect respects has referred you. The value of using a third party as an introduction is the immediate endorsement it provides. The prospect automatically assumes that you are reputable and reliable and that you deserve a hearing.[28]

In the majority of instances, a referral alone is enough to get the prospect to hear you out during this first telephone call. Then you must generate enough interest to motivate the prospect to agree to give you an appointment. Here is an example of how to use a referral as a purpose for calling:

Mrs. Ridings, we recently designed a new, interactive Web site for the DM Bass Company that was extremely well received by their customers and has doubled their online sales in the last month. The CEO, Martha Bass, was so pleased with the results that she asked me to get in touch with you and see whether we might also be helpful to you.

After you have established a legitimate purpose for the call, you are ready to move to the next step.

Step 4: Make an Interest-Capturing Statement

Once you have the prospect's attention, your task is to convert attention into interest so that you can expect a favorable hearing. Establish interest most effectively by promising a benefit or offering a service. Use product benefits, company services, or financial rewards to answer the prospect's unspoken question: "What's in it for me?"[29]

Offer the prospect a benefit from listening to you, offer a service, or offer to do something for—not to—the prospect. Be sure to say how long the actual personal visit will take, and assure the prospect that everything you have to say can be covered in that length of time unless the prospect wants to explore certain areas in greater detail. Here are three examples:

This call cannot be completed as dialed.

1. *Mrs. Ridings, we have designed a complete online package for companies similar to yours that could increase the effectiveness of your business from 10 to 25 percent with a decrease in the cost of your operations. It will take about 20 minutes for me to show you how.*

2. *The benchmarking results from our design department show that many managers have been pleased with the look and navigability of our custom designed web pages. Our clients report more online traffic and increased sales through their eCommerce stores. In fact one client, the Tom Black Center, saw their sales increase by $5000 in the week following the site launch.*

3. *Mr. Clay, we've found that most people are just waiting for an invitation to come into a health club, and we'd like to extend that invitation to you right now to come see how Total Fitness Gym is changing the way our members look and feel about themselves.*

Rather than making a statement, you may ask a question to capture the prospect's interest:

> *My company has an idea that could give complete protection to your entire plant and decrease your present costs. You are interested in cutting costs, aren't you?*

Most business people want to see their operations run more efficiently and would answer this question in the affirmative. You could then suggest that you have a specific plan and request a personal visit to discuss it with the prospect.

Step 5: Request an Appointment

Remember that your goal at this point is to secure an appointment with the prospect so that you can make a complete presentation. Avoid giving interview information over the phone; the more information you give, the more problems the prospect may see.

The prospect can easily say, "I'm not interested" over the phone. Then you have nowhere to go. The conclusion could be much different when you give an excellent presentation in person. Next time, try the "KISS" approach to setting the appointment: *Keep It Simple, Salesperson!* The telephone itself encourages brevity, so just ask for the appointment confidently and directly.

1. *I'm sure you agree that we should get together to discuss how we can accomplish this for you. Would this Thursday at nine be good for you? Or perhaps Friday morning would be better?*

2. *The best time for me would be tomorrow afternoon at 2:00 or Thursday morning at 11:00. Which would be more convenient for you, Mrs. Ridings?*

Notice that in each example the prospect was given a choice of times rather than asked, "When would it be convenient to see you?" which makes saying no far too easy. You simply want to create enough initial interest to set up an appointment. Resist every temptation to get into specifics on the telephone. You are selling an appointment, not the product or service.

After you have set up the appointment, be sure to say "thank you" and then allow the prospect to end the call. It is important for you to hang up last, because the prospect may think of something at the end and should hear your voice instead of a click.[30]

Step 6: Overcome Resistance

Using the telephone to set up appointments gives rise to two types of objections: An objection to receiving a telephone call and an objection to granting an interview. A prospect who was engaged in an activity of interest or importance may feel irritated by an interruption and prefer to resume that activity. This prospect's goal is to get you off the phone by refusing to become interested in what you have to say.

Prospects who do not want to grant an interview often fear that they cannot successfully defend their own ideas or decisions when faced by an experienced salesperson. They are afraid that they will buy. This type of objection can be overcome in three steps:

1. Agree sympathetically with objections to build the prospect's ego.

2. Switch from the prospect's objection to your idea or purpose for the interview.

3. Ask for the appointment.

Custom design the telephone approach to fit your needs in the six-step format presented above, and then practice it until it feels comfortable and natural. Internalize it rather than just memorize it. When you combine the six-step telephone approach with confidence and friendliness, you are likely to find yourself getting face-to-face with more responsive and receptive prospects.

Sample Telephone Script

Now that you know the reason for each step in the telephone track, let's look at a specific example that you can modify and use for your own purposes. The following is an example of a telephone script written by Ben Phillips, an agent with Northwestern Mutual Financial Network. Ben's example is a referred-lead telephone script. This is just one of five scripts he has developed depending upon the type of prospect he is calling. You will see how closely he follows the six-step telephone track.

Step 1: Introduce Yourself

Agent: Good morning, I am Ben Phillips with Northwestern Mutual Financial Network. Am I speaking with Mr. Boone? Good!

Step 2: Get Approval to Continue

Agent: Mr. Boone, it will only take a minute to explain to you why I am calling you today. Is it convenient for you to talk now? Thank you!

Step 3: State Your Purpose for Calling

Agent: Mr. Boone, as I mentioned I am with Northwestern Mutual. Our mutual friend Mrs. Smith is a customer of mine, and she felt that some of the ideas that I shared with her might also be of interest to you. Mrs. Smith has been pleased with the service that I provide and thought that it might be good to check with you to see if you too might benefit from my services.

Step 4: Capture Interest

Agent: Mr. Boone, I would like the opportunity to share with you how Northwestern Mutual is helping people just like you explore their family's financial security. It will take me about twenty minutes to show you the kind of work I do, and if you feel like some of the ideas I share with you would improve your situation I would consider it a privilege to help you in that way.

Step 5: Request Appointment

Agent: Mr. Boone, I am sure that you are interested in providing financial security for you and your family aren't you? Then I think we should get together for a few minutes and explore how our services may help you accomplish that.

Step 6: Overcome Resistance

Prospect: I already have insurance!

Agent: Great! Because our system takes into account your existing insurance. So we can take a look at your entire situation.

Prospect: I have enough insurance!

Agent: I am glad you mentioned that. Many people feel the same way, but a current review is nearly always beneficial. That way you will know that your program is staying current.

At the most, this script will take three to four minutes, and that's only if the prospect offers multiple objections, or in a better scenario, shows interest! It can become frustrating to repeat the same words again and again on the phone, but you must take care to ensure that you don't sound like you are on autopilot. You will hear no's, but you will also hear, "Yes, I'd like to meet with you." Persistence is the key—so keep smiling and dialing.

SUMMARY

- Planning and preparation are essential to securing an appointment for a personal sales interview.

- Your preapproach planning may utilize cold calls designed to meet the prospect and request an appointment, a letter to introduce yourself and your company, or a telephone call to request an appointment.

- The attempt to set up a sales interview is a mini sale in which the product is a live sales interview, and the purpose of the phone call is to sell the prospect on the idea of granting that interview.

- Save the detailed description of your product and its benefits for the actual face-to-face meeting. Keep the telephone discussion focused solely on getting the appointment.

- It is vital that you hang up last. The prospect may be thinking of something and should hear your voice instead of a click.

- The six-step telephone track for making appointments includes: Introduce yourself and your company, take the curse off the call, state the purpose of the call, make an interest-capturing statement, request an appointment, and overcome resistance

REVIEW QUESTIONS

1. What are the steps to follow in preapproach planning?

2. What information do you need about a prospect before you call to request an appointment for a sales interview?

3. What are the important sources for obtaining information about a prospect?

4. In what way may a telephone call to request an appointment serve to qualify the prospect?

5. What can you do to make sure your timing is appropriate for making a telephone call to a particular prospect as well as for the time you suggest for the appointment?

6. What advantages and disadvantages does calling for an appointment present in regard to the first impression you make on the prospect?

7. What is the six-step framework for making a telephone presentation?

8. How should a salesperson deal with prospects who say they are too busy for a sales interview?

9. If the prospect asks you to describe your proposition over the telephone, how would you handle the situation?

10. Who should be in control of the flow of the preapproach telephone call? How do you make sure control is in the proper hands?

11. Suppose that you telephone to make an appointment with a prospect. When the secretary answers, you say, "Mr. Steele, please, Joan Gray calling." If the secretary responds, "May I ask the nature of your call?" What answer would you give? If you give your answer and are then told that Mr. Steele is too busy to see you, what do you say then?

ROLE-PLAY EXERCISES

The following role-play exercises help build teams, improve communication, and emphasize the "real-world" side of selling. They are meant to be challenging, to learn how to deal with problems that have no single "right" answer and to use a variety of skills beyond those employed in a typical review question. Read and complete each activity. Then in the next class, discuss and compare answers with other classmates. Have some students take the role of the salesperson, and see how they would react. Remember, *"You learn more about a person in an hour of play than in a lifetime of conversation."* —Plato

1. Suppose you are a financial planner and learn from a friend that Joe Green has just received a promotion and a raise. These two items alone give you enough information to put Joe in your prospect file. What kinds of additional information would you attempt to get about Joe before meeting with him? Write a sample telephone script for obtaining an appointment with Joe. Then perform this script in groups of two or three in class.

2. You are a salesperson for USX Corp. and call on industrial customers. You work in a city for which you have access to newspapers, magazines, and other public information. During a one-week period, review these materials and any other available information and write a report for your manager in which you judge the quality of this information as a basis for assessing prospects.

3. An office supply salesperson uses the following telephone approach when in doubt about a prospect's authority to buy: "Mr. Crew, my presentation will take approximately fifteen minutes. I realize your time is precious and I want to be certain that you are the person with whom I should be talking. Are you the one I should see about purchasing office supplies, or does someone else have that responsibility?" In groups of three to four, have other students practice using this type of approach. What is the class reaction to this approach? Why?

CASE STUDY

Case 8.1—To Phone or Not To Phone

As Kevin Warren drove to his next scheduled stop at Baker Products, he thought to himself, "I wonder if that call was worth the time it took. I did get an order for some bubble pack, but sitting 25 minutes in the waiting room didn't add much to my commission. Oh, well, some days it goes like that." Kevin's company produces a complete line of packaging materials used by a wide range of manufacturers and wholesalers, so most firms that ship products are potential customers. Kevin was making a living but wasn't setting the world on fire.

Just last week, his sales manager mentioned that he should be making more calls per week. "You know the old saying, the more people you see, the more sales you make. Maybe your territory is poorly organized. Why don't you take a look?"

Kevin did take a look—and found nothing to criticize. He had divided the territory into segments to eliminate backtracking. Although he had not been able to do away with every lengthy drive, they were at a bare minimum. Parking in the visitor's lot at Baker Products, he took a few minutes to review his file to refresh his memory about their past purchases and his contact person there.

Then he went into the office and asked for Mr. Lewis. The receptionist said, "I'm sorry, but Mr. Lewis is visiting our other plants and won't be back for three weeks. I'll let you see his assistant, Miss Alexander." Kevin greeted her, "Miss Alexander, it's nice to meet you. I'm Kevin Warren; I've been supplying your company with packaging materials for a couple of years. According to my records, this is the month you usually order. Did Mr. Lewis mention it before he left?

"No, he didn't—at least not to me. I'm afraid I can't help you. Mr. Lewis will be back on the 17th. I know he'll be swamped for a few days. Can you come back after the 20th? Mr. Lewis should be able to see you then."

Kevin was committed for that time to another part of his territory, and he was almost sure he wouldn't be able to get back before his next regularly scheduled time in this part of his territory. Walking to his car, Kevin thought, "A thirty-mile drive out here and nothing to show for it. Now it's thirty miles back to the city, and it'll be too late for another call. I guess the boss is right; I need to make more calls. But even more than that, I need to make each call more productive, too. The boss suggested calling ahead for appointments, but I'm not very good at that. I've got to do something, though."

1. Are telephone calls to set up appointments the answer to Kevin Warren's problem? As he has not been successful with this technique previously, how can he make it work for him?

2. What else could Kevin do when a prospect is not available other than just come back later?

3. What other sources for ideas would you suggest for Kevin?

Case 8.2—Getting a Straight Answer

Barry West hung up the phone and slumped in his chair. "It happened again. I get more stalls than an old battery!" Barry couldn't understand why it happened so often. His line of business products, particularly the ultramodern microfilm system for indexing and filing documents, should have been of prime interest to the Merchant's National Bank trust officer to whom he had just talked. Before he had managed to tell Mrs. Blevins about more than one or two of the system's unique features, however, she cut him off, saying she couldn't consider anything of that sort until after the bank's planned remodeling project was complete and she knew just what space would be available.

The next call was no better. Davis Brothers Department Store should certainly have been interested in something in his line, but when he asked for an appointment he heard the same old story. When Ms. Kingsley, the office manager, asked the purpose of the appointment, Barry told her he wanted to show her all the various products he had to offer so she could see what she needed that he could supply. Ms. Kingsley replied that she really didn't know of a thing she needed at this time, that she was in the midst of an especially busy season, and that Barry should call at some later time if he had anything specific to show her.

"Maybe it would be better if I just dropped in to see prospects without any warning. Maybe they couldn't think of so many stalls that way," Barry mused.

1. Can you account for Barry's problem with stalls? What two principles of telephone use did he violate in these two calls?

2. Is he right in thinking he would do better by calling on prospects without an appointment? Is he likely to find that they would not offer stalls if he called in person?

3. Write out a plan of action for Barry to follow that could improve his results in gaining appointments by telephone.

"The **price of success is hard** work, **dedication to the job at** hand, and the **determination** that whether we win or lose, we have applied **the best of** ourselves to the task at hand."

-Vince Lombardi

The Face-to-Face Relationship
Model of Selling

CHAPTER 10

CHAPTER 11

CHAPTER 9

CHAPTER 12

CHAPTER 13

Consider this the "how to" portion of the textbook, the face-to-face segment of the sales cycle. The following chapters are the very heart of professional selling. It is the valuable time spent in the actual sales interview; and it is the time when a commitment is obtained and kept.

What happens in the opening minutes of a meeting is crucial to the overall success of the sales interview, and chapter 9 focuses on those opening moments—the approach. Chapter 10 is devoted to the art of asking questions and listening effectively. You will learn critical questioning and listening skills to help carry you through the entire sales interview. The SPIN® selling technique is explained and dramatized using a practical example. Chapter 11 then details techniques to use in the presentation itself. Units of conviction are the building blocks on which to build a meaningful sales presentation, and the five elements that comprise a unit of conviction are both explained and illustrated.

Chapters 12 and 13 present the psychology behind handling objections and closing the sale. You will be introduced to a plan to handle objections, and a portion of chapter 12 explains several ways to deal with the price objection. Chapter 13 stresses that closing the sale is the natural conclusion to a successful sales interview. The chapters in this section are:

9. Approaching the Prospect
10. Identifying Needs by Questioning and Listening
11. Making the Presentation
12. Handling Objections
13. Closing the Sale

First Impressions

You never get a second chance
to make a good…

FOLLOW the river and you will find the sea. Determination is the key.

INDIVIDUALS cannot consistently perform in a manner which is inconsistent with the way they see themselves.

REMEMBER…If you fail to plan, you plan to fail.

SOME people dream of worthy accomplishments, while others stay awake and do them.

THE single most important ingredient in the formula for success is knowing how to deal with people.

IF you don't take care of the customer…somebody else will.

MANAGE your time and your choices—and you'll manage your life.

PREPARE yourself for leadership. Be a living example of the excellence you expect from others.

RUNNING a business is no trouble at all as long as it's not yours.

EVERYTHING you say and do is a reflection of the inner you.

SINGIN' in the rain of life is better than letting it dampen your spirits.

SELF-ESTEEM, commitment, and action determine your outcome.

IF we could kick the person responsible for most of our problems, we wouldn't be able to sit for a week.

ONE way to avoid criticism is to do nothing and be a nobody. The world will then not bother you.

NO one is useless in this world who lightens the burden of another.

Approaching The Prospect

LEARNING OBJECTIVES

- Discover the purpose of the approach.

- Learn the importance of first impressions and ways to control them as a means of improving your performance.

- Understand how surface language affects your ability to establish rapport with a prospect.

- Examine the elements of the greeting and how to control them.

- Discover ways to get the attention and capture the interest of the prospect.

- Explore different types of approaches and the best circumstances in which to use each one.

You did your homework, and your prospecting and preapproach efforts uncovered potential clients. You successfully arranged a personal meeting with a prospect. So now what? What happens during the opening of the face-to-face encounter profoundly affects the success of the entire presentation and your ability to get a commitment to buy. The approach is the actual contact the salesperson has with the prospect. This is the point of the selling process where the sales professional meets and greets the prospect, provides an introduction, establishes rapport that sets the foundation for the relationship, and asks open-ended questions to learn more about the prospect and his or her needs.[1] The approach is important because it determines the character of your future relationship with a prospect, including how receptive the prospect will be to your presentation and whether the close will be difficult or easy.

Although the overall success of the interview depends on more than the approach, an effective approach creates a favorable buyer-seller environment. The approach is often overlooked or taken for granted. Although the approach is usually considered in the context of the first call on a prospect, every meeting with a new prospect or an established customer begins with an approach.

Salespeople tend to use the same approach over and over, but prospects and situations are not the same; instead, salespeople ought to make a practice of using various types of approaches that fit the needs of a specific situation, whether calling on new prospects or on old customers. An effective approach achieves four key objectives:

1. To make a favorable or positive impression on the prospect.
2. To gain the prospect's undivided attention.
3. To develop positive interest in your proposition.
4. To lead smoothly into the need discovery phase of the interview.

First Impressions

In his book, *Contact: The First Four Minutes*, Leonard Zunin says that the first four minutes of initial contact with a prospect are crucial. He suggests that four minutes is the average time the prospect takes to decide whether to buy from you. Impress the prospect with a show of good manners, clear enunciation, good grooming, and appropriate dress; when you look and act like a professional, the prospect, consciously or subconsciously, begins to trust you. People make quick decisions based on feelings, emotions, or hunches. The more positive their feelings, the more they hear and accept what you say. The opening moments of the approach must be designed to create an atmosphere of trust. The first ten words you speak tell volumes about you.[2]

The initial impression you make on a new prospect is much like a homebuyer who looks at the potential home for the first time. Sellers and their realtors go to great lengths to present the home in the best light possible through a process called "staging." Staging things as seemingly insignificant as the optimal location of the furniture and other items in the seller's home can make a difference between a sale or no sale.[3] Remember that this is a business meeting, not a personal lunch with a close friend. You must put your best foot forward from the beginning in order to ensure that the prospect hasn't said "no" in his mind before he ever hears your presentation.

> **Successful salespeople have a knack** for making other people feel important. It does not matter how knowledgeable they are about their product lines or how many closing techniques they have memorized. Unless they earn their prospect's trust and confidence, they are not going to make the sale—period.

A relationship salesperson must be able to work effectively with a prospect even in the presence of a personality clash. Look further than your first impression of a prospect before making an unalterable judgment.

Prospects watch and evaluate virtually every personal characteristic you have; so your approach must be impeccable. Positive first impressions count. There's something about a good initial person-to-person contact that instinctively leads to more sales.[4] Exhibit 9.1 presents some guidelines for making the first impression a favorable one. After all, *you never get a second chance to make a good first impression.*[5]

∆ Exhibit 9.1

There's Never a Second Chance to Make a Good First Impression ·

Visual Factors
- Correct any detail that could become a visible distraction such as a tattered briefcase, a messy car, or inappropriate grooming.
- Nonverbal communication is powerful. Pay attention to what the prospect sees in your body language as well as in what you wear.
- Don't wear jewelry such as lapel pins, tiepins, or rings that advertise your membership in a specific organization that may not be recognized or admired by some people.

Organization and Professional Habits
- Be prompt, or even early. Set your watch five minutes ahead if necessary.
- Present a clear agenda. State the purpose of your call right away. Make it clear that you are not there to waste the prospect's time.
- Be prepared with as much information as possible about the prospect (both the individual and company).

Building Rapport
- Be sure to pronounce the prospect's name correctly. A person's name is a personal identifier; mispronouncing it takes away some of the owner's status.
- If you pay the prospect a compliment, make it specific and of personal interest.
- Recall the importance of proxemics. Respect the prospect's personal space.
- Look for common ground like mutual friends, membership in the same religious or civic group, or similar hobbies.

Physical Actions
- Shake hands, maintain eye contact, and greet the prospect warmly, but never say, "How are you?" as it may sound contrived and insincere. Instead, open with a more specific greeting, including the use of the prospect's name.
- Refrain from personal habits like smoking or chewing gum, or from using careless language that might be offensive to some people.

Attitude
- Be enthusiastic. Enthusiasm is infectious if it is sincere.

Although first impressions may be dependable sign posts for the feelings you leave with a prospect, first impressions do have some weaknesses:

- They are likely to be based on feelings and emotions.

- All behavior traits do not show up simultaneously, and an initial short interview may not provide enough time for all traits (either favorable or unfavorable) to surface.

- The prospect may deliberately control behavior and allow you to see only certain chosen personality traits.

- Some event immediately preceding the interview may strongly influence the prospect's current behavior.

Be willing to wait before you conclude that you and a prospect are experiencing a personality conflict that cannot be overcome. Your job is to establish rapport, build confidence, and make the prospect feel comfortable. Do everything in your power to satisfy the needs of your prospects, and refuse to allow first impressions to prevent a mutually beneficial sales experience.

Surface Language

Surface language—including grooming, clothing, accessories, posture, and all other aspects of appearance—vitally affects first impressions, despite the fact that surface language factors actually provide limited or shallow insight into the true person. Salespeople must be sure the statements they make with their surface language are favorable because the impressions formed during the first few minutes of an initial encounter between two people will last indefinitely. Successful salespeople increase the odds in their favor by taking advantage of the power of first impressions. Visual impressions almost always come first. Fortunately, you can do a lot to shape the visual impact you make when a prospect first sees you.

Projecting an Image

"You want your clothes to command respect, inspire credibility and create trust—you must come across as the authority on the product that is offered," points out Sherry Maysonave, head of Empowerment Enterprises in Austin, Texas.[6] Your clothes speak volumes about you, your company, your work, and how you relate to customers.

When you know that you are dressed appropriately, you feel good about yourself. When you are confident and at ease, you emanate an air of competence that the prospect unconsciously accepts and interprets as credibility.[7] Total appearance is important because the prospect's initial attention is focused on you and not on your proposition. If you want to be successful, you must look successful. A salesperson who wears an obviously cheap suit, for example, creates a negative impression and sets up this line of thinking in the mind of the prospect:

- This salesperson is dressed cheaply. He must not be making much money.

- Because he's not making much money, he must be having difficulty selling his product.

- If the product is not selling, something must be wrong with it.

- I don't want an inferior product.

Look the Part. We must look the part of a professional to be viewed as one. In *Nice Girls Don't Get the Corner Office*, Lois Frankel says that research shows about 55 percent of our credibility comes from how we look. Personal appearance and behavior are the easiest areas to address on the road to greater success, yet all too often sales professionals choose to ignore this aspect.

Unspoken rules for appropriate dress extend into every aspect of professional life. Optometrist Jerry Hayes says, "Your appearance greatly affects how patients feel about you."[8] When we go to the doctor, we want the doctor to be dressed in a manner that projects his authority and knowledge. Would you trust a surgeon to operate on you who is dressed in shorts and a t-shirt? Of course not! So how can you expect a prospect to buy an expensive product or service if you don't, well, look the part? Dress in such a way that commands respect and credibility; but remember, everything in moderation.

Dress Conservatively. Your objective is to focus the prospect's attention on the benefits of buying your product or service. Anything that detracts from that focus works against you. Conservative dress gives the prospect the impression that talking with you is safe and that you are familiar and dependable. Although "conservative" varies from one region to another and from one industry to another, that variation is not extremely wide. Dressing conservatively suggests stability and dependability; following extreme fads of color, cut, and pattern may suggest just the opposite.

Corporate Casual dressing has become the norm in today's business world. This style is not intended to convey a lack of professionalism, just a more comfortable, perhaps less boring way of projecting one's best. "Professional" is the key word to remember when dressing business casual. But be aware that you do not dress too casually. Rather, make sure your clothes reflect your position and the message you wish to convey to your clients.

What do your clothes say about you?

Choose Accessories Carefully. Accessories are intended to enhance your appearance. Make sure they do not call attention to themselves. Jewelry should be simple—one good piece is more impressive than three or four cheap pieces.

- Jewelry that announces your association with some organization or belief (unless shared by the prospect) may call attention to itself and away from the purpose of your call.

- Accessories should be of good quality. High-quality pen and pencil sets and top-quality leather attaché cases make a quiet statement of your personal pride in your profession and mark you as successful.

- Avoid sunglasses or lenses that noticeably change color with shifts in light. People may not believe what you are saying if they cannot see your eyes. Hiding your eyes seems to say you are hiding something else as well.

Dress Appropriately. You should plan to dress as well as your prospect. People feel comfortable dealing with those who seem to fit into their own lifestyle; but don't use your age as an excuse to dress more "youthful" or casual. This is apparently a growing problem in the job market today. "It has gotten so crazy, a major pharmaceutical company called up and said, 'Help! People are wearing spandex to work!'" says Gail Madison, an etiquette and protocol consultant who regularly advises students at prestigious colleges on small but important details such as taking out their nose rings before a job interview or not dying their hair orange.[9] If your clothes are too formal or carry too much of an aura of power, you cause the prospect to feel overpowered; the result may be rebellion against what is perceived as your snobbish attitude. On the other hand, if you dress too casually or carelessly, wear distracting jewelry, or have an unusual hairstyle, prospects may unconsciously feel that you do not consider them or their business important. Exhibit 9.2 indicates what the clothes you wear say about your image.[10]

What does your clothing say about you? That you are sophisticated? Disorganized? Powerful? Your professional image should work for you, not against you. How you look goes a long way toward establishing your identity. Your clothes say much about your character and credibility.

Consider these style tips:

1. Clothes should be professional and understated. Flashy clothes detract from your image and take attention away from the work at hand.

2. Nothing you wear should be wrinkled, frayed or sloppy.

3. Always wear suits to meetings, as jackets give the appearance of authority.

4. The most powerful color is blue—this is why police uniforms are blue.

5. Keep your shoes shined; some men judge others by the condition of their shoes.

6. Make sure your socks match your suit and shoes.

7. Keep accessories simple such as ties, watches, and jewelry. Clients should be looking at you, not at your accessories.

8. Dress in line with your superiors, but never more casually than your subordinates.

9. Dress appropriately for your business. For example, bankers always look like bankers.

10. Be prepared for unexpected meetings. Have a spare sports jacket or blazer cleaned, pressed, and ready in your office.

The Proper Greeting

In order to increase the odds of making a good impression during the meet-and-greet, use the business etiquette *Rule of Ten*. The first ten words you speak should include a form of thanks: "Good morning, Mrs. Eubank. Thank you for agreeing to see me," or "Good afternoon, Brian. It's a pleasure to meet you."

Casual questions like "How are you?" or "How ya' doing?" have lost all semblance of meaning. How does the prospect respond? "Great" or "Just fine, thank you," but what if the prospect is not feeling great and what if business is not going great? If a prospect covers up real feelings with a conventional answer, a vague feeling of uneasiness results from the untruth.

How would you answer the simple question "How are you?" You may want to try the response used by Pat Shemek. When prospects or clients ask Shemek, "How are you doing," Pat replies, "Super duper." The clients have come to expect this response, and even look forward to it. Shemek's attitude seems to be—*fake it until you make it*! Come up with your own unique response delivered with a smile on your face and enthusiasm in your voice. Your customers will appreciate your positive attitude.[11]

A proper greeting isn't just about a friendly face or the proper words, but an appealing surrounding also helps. Sometimes this is out of your control, especially if you are meeting the prospect on his turf. However, if you have the opportunity to select the meeting location, find a spot that is warm and inviting, and one in which you will not have to shout in order to be heard. Salespeople often meet clients at coffee shops. These are great neutral locations, but avoid them around the busiest times of the day (early morning and lunch), or outside distractions will diminish any good impression you attempt to make.[12]

Geek Boy Services

Remember the movie, *The Revenge of the Nerds*? Well, now there is a company serving their needs. For about $1,000, Geek Boy Services, a Silicon Valley consulting service, provides total image makeovers to admitted computer geeks who want to spice up their plain T-shirt-and-khakis wardrobe. The consulting service also advises their clients on various nightclubs where they can go to try out their new looks and test their dating skills.[13]

The Handshake

Your voice inflection and how you shake hands are as important as what you say. You must project yourself as a leader, not insecure or apologetic. This signals to the prospect that you are confident and believe in what you sell. In order to have a leader's attitude, John Maxwell, the author of more than thirty books on leadership, says, "Leadership has less to do with position than it has with disposition."[14] What does your disposition say about you? Do you stand behind what you sell, or are you just trying to pay the rent? When combined with your tone of voice and facial expression, your handshake reveals to a prospect your mood. The business handshake is an essential selling technique to make a positive lasting impression. When the first handshake with a prospect is a firm one, you'll have the beginning of a strong business relationship.[15] Exhibit 9.3 presents more helpful guidelines for an effective handshake.

Δ Exhibit 9.3

Guidelines for an Effective Handshake ·

- Maintain eye contact for the duration of the handshake.

- You may wait for the prospect to initiate the handshake (to avoid offending those people who "do not like to be touched").

- If your palm tends to be moist from nervousness, carry a special handkerchief with powder and pat your hand several times just before entering the prospect's office. Be careful not to leave a residue of powder on your hand that might be transferred to the prospect's hand or to your clothes.

- Apply firm, consistent pressure on the hand and avoid limp-wristed, wet-fish, or bone-crusher handshakes.

- The hands should meet at an equal distance between you and the prospect in a vertical position. If you turn your wrist so your hand is over the prospect's, this nonverbal gesture implies the intention to be dominant. If you turn your wrist so that your hand is on the bottom, you are signaling a submissive nature.

The handshake is also an indispensable tool to consider when selling to customers around the globe. Several tips for international handshaking are presented in Exhibit 9.4.[16] The customs and mannerisms of our overseas partners are equally essential to understand and accommodate. Be sure to make use of this information as one aspect of surface language to assist you in establishing rapport with people, regardless of nationality or personality style.

Δ **Exhibit 9.4**

Shaking Hands Around the World

Three noteworthy tips when greeting international prospects and customers:

1. **Shake hands with everyone**. International etiquette demands that the salesperson shake hands with everyone that is in the room. Not shaking hands with someone will be noticed, and considered a personal rejection.

2. **Initiate the handshake**. An American saleswoman should extend her hand to a European male. Not doing so may cause her to lose credibility. Women should initiate handshakes, and shake hands with other women and men.

3. **Notice culture-to-culture differences**. Latin Americans tend to use a lighter, lingering handshake. In Arab countries, handshakes are limp and last longer than the average American handshake. Japanese salespeople shake hands with one firm gesture. The handshake is often combined with a slight bow.

Small Talk or Get Down to Business

In the initial face-to-face meeting, both parties may experience what might be called *relationship tension*. Prospects fear being sold something they do not want, and salespeople face the fear of being rejected. The opening few minutes of conversation are designed to find a comfort level for both parties so that rapport can be established. The purpose of small talk at the opening of the interview is to gain an advantageous, positive beginning that breaks the ice and eases the tension. Small talk may be a discussion of topics entirely unrelated to what you are selling. Al Angell, a successful sales professional in Boston, says this warm-up period usually takes him five minutes or more. Al calls this time "chit-chat with a purpose." He asks four basic questions that he feels are nonthreatening, easy to answer, and objective:

1. Are you a native of this area?

2. Were you educated there? (Based on answer to the first question.)

3. Are you a family person?

4. How did you happen to get into this business?

This type of socializing at the beginning of the interview eases tension and may give you some insight into your prospect's behavioral style. It warms up a cold environment and has the side benefit of providing additional information about the prospect. If the prospect seems withdrawn or even hostile, this warm-up conversation helps you determine whether that is the prospect's real personality or whether you have arrived on an especially bad day.

People love to tell you what they do in their spare time, talk about their accomplishments, or tell you about their families. This non-selling conversation is important. An ideal topic for initial chit-chat is one that relaxes the prospect, is of interest, and relates, if possible, to your objective so that you can move easily into the attention getter and then into need discovery.[17]

> **People have no confidence in salespeople** whose only interest is self-interest, who seek *to use* their clients instead of being *of use* to their clients.

Use of the Prospect's Name

People do not like to have their names forgotten, mispelled (sorry, I meant misspelled), or mispronounced. Typically, when we meet someone, we hear our own name, and then we may or may not hear the other person's name. In his book, *How to Win Friends and Influence People*, Dale Carnegie says, "A person's name is to them the sweetest and most important sound in any language."[18] If we forget a name or mispronounce it, we send out this message: "I care more about me and my name than I do about you and your name."

Imagine how a prospect feels when you say, "So you see, Ms. . . . ah . . . uh . . . excuse me (shuffle for prospect card or appointment calendar) uh . . . Ms. Hill, I mean, Lill." The prospect probably stiffens, the environment turns a bit frosty, and you may well walk out without an order.[19] Now recall how pleased you were when someone remembered your name after just a casual meeting several weeks previously. You would stand in line to do business with such a person.

Improving your memory for names is not as difficult as it may seem. Several books are available to help you devise a method to correct a careless memory for names. Exhibit 9.5 gives some suggestions for remembering names.

Δ **Exhibit 9.5**

How to Remember Customers' Names ·

Pay attention
Ask to have the name repeated (even spelled). It will impress the person.

Concentrate
Look for characteristics that distinguish this person from others.

Associate
Relate a characteristic with some gimmick to help you recall the name.

Observe
Study people regularly to strengthen your ability to see characteristics and practice your imagination.

Repeat
Use the prospect's name several times during the interview.

Gaining Attention and Capturing Interest

As the cartoon states, first you have got to get their attention! Develop a carefully constructed, attention-getting statement that focuses the prospect's full attention completely on you and your proposition; and remember that prospects are thinking, "What does this person want with me? Why should I allow my work to be interrupted?" Unless prospects want to listen, they won't—so give them a reason. Just as the newspaper uses a headline to make you take notice, you must also develop an attention getting opening that breaks through their preoccupation and focuses attention on the selling situation.

The two basic methods of getting attention are: 1. Through an appeal to the senses and 2. through the introduction of a benefit:

Appeal to the Senses. An appeal to the senses gets the prospect involved in the presentation. Be sure to use a little dramatization. Show something the prospect can see; hand the prospect something to hold.

First you've got to get their attention!

Introduction of a Benefit. Introduce a benefit by a statement that relates to the prospect's need for your product or service. Highlight the value of the product or service. The prospect always wants to know, "What's in it for me?" Phillip Proctor, vice president of sales and marketing for Associated Printing in Ft. Lauderdale, certainly knows how to get a prospect's attention. He routinely uses a corny but effective prop: A simple bag of bread with a note that reads, "Our clients say we're the greatest thing since . . . sliced bread."[20]

An effective attention-getting statement requires preparation. If you have done your homework in gathering preapproach information, you already know enough to have some idea about both the needs and the behavioral style of the prospect. If you spend a few minutes in small talk you gain further clues to confirm or adjust your preapproach information. Use what you know to plan an effective attention-getting device to introduce the heart of your presentation. Exhibit 9.6 suggests ways to gain prospects' attention by appealing to their behavioral styles during your initial exchange.[21]

Δ **Exhibit 9.6**

.... **Using Behavioral Styles to Choose an Attention-Getting Approach**

Expressive—Open in terms of long-range goals or implications.
Mr. Arnold, I would like to show you how our innovative service will help your department reach its long-term potential.

Analytical—Open in very specific terms.
Mr. Arnold, I would like to give you the background on our service and then list the ways in which I think it will reduce your overhead, increase your productivity, and improve your profit margin by ten percent. (Be prepared to do so.)

Amiable—Open in supportive, people-oriented terms.
Mr. Arnold, I am aware of some of the pressing concerns you must be facing at this time, and I feel our service will help you and your people overcome some of these problems.

Driver—Open in results-oriented terms.
Mr. Arnold, our service will help you increase your sales by fifteen percent in just six months. Are you interested? (Be prepared to prove your statement.)

Suit the Approach to the Person

Most people today have more work than they can hope to complete during regular working hours. Individual consumers, purchasing agents, engineers—anyone a sales representative might contact—feel time pressure and quite naturally regard you as an intruder. Prospects may react with resentment toward anyone who appears intent upon "stealing" precious time to engage in "small talk." How much or how little time you give to small talk or chit-chat depends on the behavioral style of the prospect, the circumstances of the moment, and the nature of your visit. If you sense that the prospect wants to get on with the interview, then move on.

Developing Partnerships Using Technology looks at laptops and PDAs available to today's salesperson—palmtops and handhelds. Some salespeople like to carry electronic copies of their approaches out on the field to review them before a presentation. The best way to take your approaches with you is on your handheld device. These portable devices also synchronize with a desktop or laptop system's contact management program. This synchronizing feature is incredibly useful to professionals for increased organization and efficiency.[22]

Developing Partnerships Using Technology

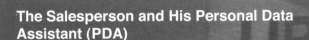

The Salesperson and His Personal Data Assistant (PDA)

Laptops. Bringing your laptop along is like taking a member of the sales team with you. But sometimes, the laptop is much too cumbersome to bring. To solve this problem, there are two other types of PDAs, both of which operate on special versions of Windows or other operating systems designed for smaller devices.

Palmtops. These mini-computers have considerable memory and storage capacity. They fold out like laptops into a keyboard with monitor. Most palmtops have LCD color screens. They also offer a pointing device, like a pen, to navigate on the screen. It's like having a smaller version of Windows Vista™ in your hand.

Handhelds. Normally these are the size of a notepad that fits in the pocket of a shirt. There is often no traditional keyboard; rather these systems are sometimes pen-driven. Some versions, such the Sony Treo™, have both a keyboard and a pen that controls a touch screen. Instead of typing, the devices "learn" your handwriting style, enabling you to write information in a blank space on the bottom of the screen. Handhelds use menu buttons or voice commands to perform specific functions.

Check out these Web sites for additional information:

www.palmpilot.com

www.store.palmone.com

www.pdastreet.com

www.psion.com

Types of Approaches

Because every prospect and every selling situation is different, you must have several approach methods available in order to use the one that best fits the particular circumstance. Learn the principles of each of the different types of approaches so that you can use whichever one is appropriate for a particular situation. How many approach techniques are enough? The answer is simple—you cannot have too many. The personality style of prospects, the mood they're in as you greet them, and your own feelings and mood that particular day suggest the need to have an opening for every occasion and every situation. You may have to deviate 180 degrees from the opening and presentation you had planned.

Self-Introduction Approach

This approach is commonly used, but it is the weakest approach to use alone. A smile, a firm handshake, and a relaxed but professional manner should accompany the introduction. Address the prospect by name (pronouncing it correctly), state your name and company, and present your business card. Although the business card is optional, it is a useful reminder of your name, and the prospect will not have to ask you to repeat your name. Here is an example of a typical self-introduction:

> *Good morning, Blakele. My name is John Andrews. It's nice to meet you. I'm glad you could come in to see our facility today." (Accompany this with a firm handshake and a smile to begin to establish trust).*

To increase the effectiveness of the self-introduction approach, follow it immediately with one of the other approaches. The consumer-benefit approach, for instance, is generally a good fit.

Consumer-Benefit Approach

Give the prospect a reason for listening and suggest a risk for failure to listen. The benefit statement should be unique and appeal to the prospect's dominant buying motive. It should be sincere and must never sound like a gimmick. Something new and different about your product or service that paves the way for the rest of the interview is a good choice.

> *Good morning, Mr. Carter. I am Kevin Davis with Lee's Gym and Fitness. I'm glad you stopped by to take fifteen minutes for me to introduce you to our facilities that will, first of all, give you 24-hour access—secondly, provide you with cardio, circuit, and free weights training, as well as give you access to professional certified personal training, and third—and probably the best part of all—is that it will help you reach and maintain your fitness goals.*

This example combines both the self-introduction and the consumer-benefit approaches. Because most business people want to offer value to their customers, presenting this benefit statement may well cause the prospect to seek more information. Such a statement often sparks questions from the prospect that lead directly into the presentation.

Curiosity Approach

The curiosity approach works best when you know something about the prospect. Used sensibly, this approach is an effective opener. Suppose you are selling a telecommuting software package so a sales force can get up-to-date information on their laptops when they are out in the field selling. You might say something like this:

> *Mr. Sherrill, have you ever been in a meeting when a written report analyzing a new competitive product is brought to your attention for the first time, and you want to share parts of it with your salespeople immediately? Do you know how much time you are losing by having to edit the report manually?*

People with certain behavioral styles, particularly analyticals and drivers, may find this approach offensive, especially if it sounds gimmicky.

Question Approach

The question approach quickly establishes two-way communication. It enables you to investigate the prospect's needs and apply the benefits of your product or service to those expressed needs. This type of approach suggests your interest in the prospect's problems and draws attention to the need to identify problems.

You may frame a leading question designed to obtain mental commitment from the prospect and at the same time show a major benefit. Here are two examples of how this might be done:

> 1. *Mr. Fisher, you want to have distinctive-looking, quality-driven reports and the most up-to-date pricing information to share with your customers, don't you?*

> 2. *Do you feel you could get more accomplished in meetings if you had complete and current information at your fingertips? Wouldn't you also like the capability to easily edit that information, thus enabling you to provide your customers the best support possible?*

Qualifying Question Approach

This variation of the question approach seeks a commitment from the prospect. This qualifying question approach asks the prospect to consider buying the product; it can help determine whether you have a prospect who is cold, lukewarm, or red hot toward your opportunity. Here are two illustrations of how this technique could be used:

> 1. *Mr. Armstrong, if I can satisfactorily demonstrate to you that the long-distance service provided by our company will save you at least $5,000 within the next three months, would you be willing to do business with us?*

> 2. *Mrs. Woods, I am looking for individuals who have the discretionary funds to invest in an opportunity that will produce a return on their investment of at least 15 percent. If I can show you the evidence to support this claim, would you be willing to invest with us?*

These may seem like bold questions, but if the prospect says yes, you have a sale—provided you can back up your statement with valid proof.

Compliment Approach

Opening with a compliment is like walking on eggshells, but this opening is highly effective if used properly. Follow the same guidelines you would use in any situation: offer compliments with empathy, warmth, and sincerity. The purpose is to signal your sincere interest in the prospect. Sources of information for the compliment will vary. Information from a person who provided a referral or from an item you saw in a newspaper or trade journal about the prospect can tell you about significant accomplishments that you genuinely admire. You can also see hints in the company office as you arrive, or see an item in the prospect's private office that suggests a potential basis for a compliment.

Camco Inc., with international headquarters in Houston, sells gas-lift equipment, well-completion systems, safety systems, and wire line tools and units to the oil industry. At a time when the oil industry is experiencing some instability, a Camco salesperson would be out of line to compliment a prospect on the company's "obvious prosperity." Instead, a compliment should center on some other commendable factor:

> *I have been impressed with your continuous emphasis on safety on your offshore drilling rigs. I noticed the recent announcement that your company ranked first in safety ratings last year. You must be proud of that achievement.*

This type of compliment not only builds rapport but also directs the prospect's train of thought toward safety and the related products that Camco has to sell. Whenever a compliment is used as an opening, it must be *specific*, of *genuine interest* to the prospect, and *sincere*.

Referral Approach

The referral approach is especially useful because it helps you establish leverage by borrowing the influence of someone the prospect trusts and respects. If you use a referral card signed by the person who provided the prospect's name, you can give it to the prospect to introduce yourself and your company. This approach enhances your credibility and increases the likelihood that the prospect will give you full attention. Here are two good examples:

1. *Miss Reid, your neighbor Ray Thornton has recently completed one of our courses in personal leadership. He told me that you are also interested in growing as a person and in becoming a better leader, and suggested that you would like to hear about what our company has to offer. (Give the referral card to the prospect.)*

2. *Mr. Evans, I am Chris Elkins with West Coast Gym. Rita Mitchell, who just signed up with us, suggested that I contact you. She thought you would like to have an opportunity to consider whether our gym facilities, personal training, and free tanning could also be of benefit to you.*

Product Approach

This approach consists of actually handing the product, or some physical representation of it, to a prospect to produce a positive reaction. The product approach provides a visible image of the product or service. This approach should focus on the uniqueness of the product and, as far as possible, allow the product to tell its own story.

Exhibit 9.7 is a great example of how Hills Bros. Coffee Inc. uses the product approach to appeal to the senses through demonstration. You can see how the innovative idea and personal touch really perked up coffee sales.[23]

Δ Exhibit 9.7

The Personal Touch *Perks* Up Sales

Hills Bros. Coffee Inc. sought to establish relationships with grocery store food buyers and convince them to carry a new product. When visiting buyers, the sales reps arrived with a colorful, custom-designed briefcase-style kit.

Inside the kit were a sampler jar and a can of the promoted coffee, along with a graphically coordinated set of imprinted promotional products—a napkin, coffee cups, and thermos that contained freshly brewed coffee.

After the buyers sampled and discussed the product, the salesperson presented the kit and promotional products to them. Orders were signed by over 80 percent of the grocers reached using this technique.

Bringing the product to the prospect stirs interest, permits a demonstration, makes a multiple sense appeal, and usually creates in the prospect a feeling of commitment to listen and to participate actively in the presentation. For example, a PDA or handheld device sales representative might say:

> "Mrs. Wampler, chances are, your busy field reps rarely have time to sit down. So why give them a computer that needs a lap? Our new lightweight, pen-based handheld helps them work better anywhere. Here, catch."

Sometimes you cannot bring the actual product with you because of size or other constraints, but you can use other devices to simulate the actual product. A piece of literature, a sample of the output of the machine, a small working model, a picture—any visual tool that the prospect can hold and look at helps to focus and hold attention. If you are selling a service, such as a time-management program, hand the prospect a letter from a satisfied client that identifies specific benefits of the program. Statistical data that shows the return on investment earned by satisfied clients can accomplish the same purpose.

Transition from the Approach

Whatever approach you decide to use, it should be directly related to your plan for beginning the need discovery phase of the presentation. The exchange of conversation in the approach phase allows you to move smoothly into the questions you plan to ask to discover the needs of the prospect. If your opening has involved "chit-chat with a purpose," the transition is fairly simple.

Any compliment you offer should relate to the general area of your product or service so that the presentation grows naturally from the opening. A consumer-benefit opening obviously leads directly into need discovery. A product approach immediately gets the prospect involved in examining your offering. The referral approach focuses upon your product or service the approval of someone whom the prospect respects; it emphasizes the referring person's belief that the prospect will be interested.

Because the actual presentation of benefits cannot begin until the prospect agrees to having a need for what you have to offer, whatever you can do to make need discovery seem a natural process will be helpful. Chapter 10 deals with the critical task of discovering needs by asking questions and listening. The degree of rapport established between you and the prospect during the approach determines how willing the prospect will be to answer your questions and accept your buying recommendation.

SUMMARY

- What you do and say in the initial moments of the face-to-face interview has a profound effect on the success of the close. Plan those initial moments carefully. The first 10 words out of your mouth are crucial.

- Be aware of the power of first impressions. You never get a second chance to make a good one.

- Proper dress and grooming give the prospect the feeling that you are competent.

- Appropriate choices in dress and grooming let the prospect focus on your sales message instead of on your physical appearance.

- The greeting is important to create a favorable first impression. Use the prospect's name often and begin with some "chit-chat with a purpose" to feel out the mood and behavioral style of the prospect.

- Use a firm handshake, maintain eye contact, and make use of voice properties that reflect confidence.

- Confirm or modify your impressions of the prospect's behavioral style and adapt your plans for the presentation accordingly.

- A good approach forms a natural transition into the need discovery phase of the selling process. A number of different types of approaches are available:

  1. The self-introduction
  2. Consumer-benefit
  3. Curiosity
  4. Question
  5. Qualifying question
  6. Compliment
  7. Referral
  8. Product

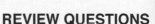

REVIEW QUESTIONS

1. What are the four objectives of an effective approach?

2. What are components of surface language? Why are these items called surface language?

3. What would you consider appropriate dress for calling on an insurance executive? A manager of a health and fitness facility?

4. What is the purpose of small talk? How can you use it to best advantage? For what kind of situation is small talk a negative?

5. Name and explain the nine types of approaches discussed in the chapter. Why does a salesperson need to master several approaches?

6. What are the advantages of bringing a product to the prospect? What are alternatives if bringing the product is not feasible?

7. Should the greeting you use be planned ahead of time, or should you depend largely on the inspiration of the moment? Justify your choice.

8. Under what conditions would you change the approach you had planned when you arrive for an interview?

9. List some guidelines for making a good first impression.

10. What are some weaknesses of evaluating a prospect totally on your first impression?

11. What can you learn about a prospect from a handshake?

ROLE-PLAY EXERCISES

The following role-play exercises help build teams, improve communication, and emphasize the "real-world" side of selling. They are meant to be challenging, to learn how to deal with problems that have no single "right" answer and to use a variety of skills beyond those employed in a typical review question. Read and complete each activity. Then in the next class, discuss and compare answers with other classmates. Have some students take the role of the salesperson, and see how they would react. Remember, *"You learn more about a person in an hour of play than in a lifetime of conversation."* — Plato

1. In the selling situations below, what would be an appropriate compliment you might pay to the prospect? How would that help you move into need discovery?

   • You are calling on a physician who heads a group practice of seven physicians to propose a medical insurance plan for the employees of their clinic.

   • You are calling on the purchasing agent of a large school district to sell school buses to the district.

   • You are calling on a middle-income, blue-collar worker in his home to sell homeowner's insurance.

2. Tour a local bank. Take notes about the dress of the men and women employees (other than guards). What similarities did you notice? What differences?

3. Interview a purchasing agent for a major corporation. Ask for some observations about the strengths and weaknesses of salespeople's approaches who call on that organization. Ask for the same observations from a retail shop owner. Ask them the best times for salespeople to call on them and why. In class, use the approaches in groups of two or three and discuss their effectiveness.

4. You are a sales representative who sells a number of paper products. Today you are calling on the owner of a large soda fountain to sell paper cups. Assume also that paper cups are not now in use at this facility. How would you begin your presentation? Act this scenario out in class in groups of two or three.

CASE STUDY

Case 9.1 — The Wound-Up Buyer

Milt Beck has good days and bad days. On the good days, everything goes smoothly and orders come easily. Some days he wonders if he should find a nice nine-to-five clerical job. But coming out of a tough interview with an order makes him realize he wouldn't trade selling for anything. Milt had one of the bad days recently. His sales manager, Allen Merton, had insisted he call on a prospect. "Milt," Al said, "I ran into a guy on the plane from St. Louis the other day who is a prime prospect for our degreaser. He's in the electrical business making armatures and windings. Our degreaser is ideal for removing grease and dirt from those items. His name is Walter Prince, and his company is Ideal Electric Products. Here's his card."

"Oh," Milt exclaimed, "he's the president of the company."

"That's the best kind of prospect," Al said. "When the top man says, 'I'll take it,' you know the order will stick. Let me warn you, though. He's a real talker."

So Milt drove the twenty-five miles to the Ideal plant. When he told the receptionist he had been referred to Mr. Prince by Allen Merton, he was asked to go right in.

"Say, that sales manager of yours is some live wire. He didn't waste any time sending you, did he? How's he doing?" the president said, as soon as Milt introduced himself.

"He's fine," Milt assured him. "You're right, he's a dynamic person."

"We had quite a conversation during the flight," Walter said, and then he was off.

He covered sports, politics, foreign affairs, and then taxes. He hardly paused for breath. Several times, Milt tried to turn the conversation to the degreaser, but every attempt just seemed to remind Walter of something else to talk about. Before long, Milt began to tell himself, "The chief will be some upset if I don't bring back an order. After all, he thinks he set it up for me. How can I get this talker to give me a chance?"

1. How would you deal with this type of prospect? Would you try to break in and insist that you get to business?

2. How long would you continue with this kind of talk with a prospect?

3. Give some suggestions for turning the conversation to business without alienating the prospect.

"The greatest motivational act one person can do for another is to listen."

CHAPTER 10

Identifying Needs By Questioning and Listening

LEARNING OBJECTIVES

- Understand the purpose of asking questions.

- Learn how to select questioning tactics appropriate for the sales situation.

- Study specific questioning techniques.

- Examine SPIN Selling and its applications.

- Understand the functions served by various types of questions.

- Appreciate the importance of listening in sales.

- Become acquainted with techniques for improving listening skills.

What is selling? Some may say selling is filling a need, while others says it's solving a problem. Some people say it's closing the deal as quickly as possible, and by any means necessary. None of those definitions really works for me. Selling is ultimately asking people what they do, how they do it, when they do it, where they do it, who they do it with, why they do it that way; and then, and only then, helping them to do it better.[1] *Telling isn't selling— asking is!*

The problem created by the misconception that *talking equals selling* lies in its assumption that every prospect uses the product or service for identical purposes and in the same manner. But in actuality, each prospect has unique needs. Of the many benefits you have to offer, only a few will be the key motivators for a particular prospect.[2] The challenge is to determine their buying criteria before beginning your presentation and then use only the specific benefits that address their particular situation.[3] In addition, customers are less likely to become bored and disinterested if they are actively involved in the presentation.[4]

Salespeople should become *Doctors of Selling*. Physicians know they must clarify the patient's problem and conduct a pragmatic diagnostic process before they can prescribe any treatment. Doctors of selling follow an identical process: They diagnose potential buyers fully to uncover any needs for the salesperson's product or service.[5] Your prospect has the right to expect the same professional attention.[6] If you went to your family doctor complaining of severe back pain, and the doctor—without asking any questions—wrote a prescription for a medicine to be taken three times a day for the next month, would you take it? Of course not! You would not believe the doctor could make an accurate diagnosis and prescribe the appropriate medicine without making a thorough examination and asking a number of probing questions about the problem. You would expect the doctor to understand your problem—not the problem of back pain in general—before prescribing for you.

Need Discovery and the Sales Cycle

The evolution of relationship selling has reached the point where, in many cases, the need discovery step in the sales cycle is more important than making the presentation, handling objections, or closing.[7] Exhibit 10.1 shows the relationship between need discovery and the other basic steps in the face-to-face sales process. At this point of need discovery—not in the close—the sale is most often lost. The dotted line around need discovery in Exhibit 10.1 is a reminder that this step is often skipped or given inadequate attention by the traditional salesperson. In reality, more time should be spent in the approach and in discovering needs than in any other steps of the process.

Δ **Exhibit 10.1**

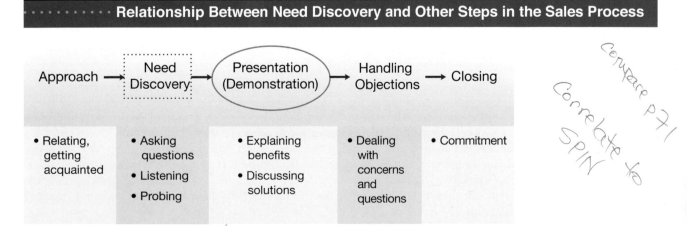

Relationship Between Need Discovery and Other Steps in the Sales Process

Consultant

Need discovery is the foundation upon which a successful sale is built. Telling prospects what they need is a mistake.[8] Asking questions that allow prospects to discover their own needs and share them with you sets you up as a sounding board for the solutions they "discover" while considering your proposal. Prospects are more receptive when they feel that the solution is their own idea. Successful sales interviews contain more requests for opinions and suggestions by the salesperson and fewer statements of disagreement and tension. And in successful interviews, salespeople control the direction of the interview by the way they ask questions.[9]

People are often unaware of a problem until they are questioned about it. Here is a case in point: A professor at a community college in Arizona conveyed an interesting story to the author of how an insurance agent sold him a policy by asking one simple question followed by an observation. The agent asked, "How much life insurance coverage do you have as protection for your family?"

When the professor replied that he had $75,000, the insurance agent shrugged his shoulders and remarked, "I guess you don't plan to be dead very long, then, do you!" This strong statement could easily offend some people. However, it caused him to realize for the first time the substantial disparity between what he had and the actual amount needed that would enable his family to maintain their current lifestyle, should something unexpected happen to him. The professor has continued to buy additional protection from this same agent as his family's needs changed.

Specific Planning of Questions

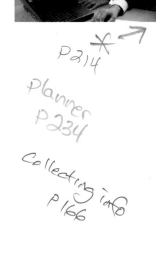

Asking the right questions is a skill all to often neglected. The majority of the time in sales situations, it isn't about asking just *any* questions, but it is about asking the *right* questions that help us to understand the perspective of the prospect, clear any misunderstanding, strengthen or break our assumptions, lead to new discoveries, and even close a deal.[10] You must retain control of the questioning phase of the interview so that you obtain the required information and do not detour into irrelevant areas. The old standbys—who, what, when, where, why, and how—are a vital part of the sales interview. Decide in advance what you need to know, and then plan what types of questions will elicit that information in the quickest and most efficient manner consistent with the prospect's social style and situation.

Because the sale is made in the mind of the buyer and not in the mind of the salesperson, using the questioning process to gain agreement on key issues is paramount. Then you must assist the prospect in prioritizing those issues and agree that those are the problems or concerns that must be addressed before they make a decision to buy. Prospects are more likely to buy if you establish points of agreement early in the interview. To accomplish this:

- Plan your questions in sequence to gain information in a logical order.

- Predict beforehand all the possible answers to each question so that you are never left wondering what to do next.

- Prepare a smooth transition from every possible answer into the next question.

Some salespeople hesitate to ask questions because they are afraid the prospect will refuse to answer. However, prospects that refuse to cooperate during the need discovery phase are unlikely to cooperate at the end of the sale either. Communication is a two-way street that demands participation by both you and the prospect. If you are to involve prospects in the sales process, you must be prepared to ask the questions that maximize participation. The right questions never materialize out of thin air. Your questions should attempt to achieve four objectives:

1. To discover the prospect's "hot button" or dominant buying motive.

2. To establish the purchase criteria or specifications.

3. To agree on a time frame for completion of negotiations.

4. To gain prospect agreement on the problem(s) before making the presentation.

John Zavitz understands the value of asking the right questions

John Zavitz is a Senior Account Manager for the Enterprise Mobility Sector of Motorola Inc. and celebrates 27 years of professional selling. He is responsible for identifying, cultivating and selling mobile computing, advanced data capture, wireless infrastructure and RFID solutions to a small but select group of Fortune 500 clients. These clients are comprised of retail, manufacturing, wholesale distribution, healthcare, and travel customers who do business worldwide. Through innovative technology, his team and partners help companies integrate, optimize and manage their operations to seamlessly stay connected as they move about their daily lives.

A key aspect of his day and job revolves relationship building with each of the clients… or as some would say, getting deeper and wider inside each account. Being visible and connected with each client allows him to ask "how and why questions" in order to dig deeper into situations and business problems where Motorola's solutions can assist their business to compete and win. Additionally, by coupling the "what is the impact of that issue" and linking the area to a financial impact, he can more readily find and show the return of investment for the business.

He considers each meeting as a mini-contract negotiation. John carefully plans every question, always listening and watching for things that could affect his ability to win the business.

For John, the questioning phase is the most time-consuming step in the sales cycle. John and his company are really in the outsourcing business. They are providing their clients with a unique system and the people and knowledge to manage that system. In John's words, "We become their telecommunications expert. Our contractual agreement may be established for a 5-to-10-year period." John's ability to diagnose each client's individual needs and recommend the correct solution is vital for this partnership to work.

Strategic Recommendations

As you select specific questioning methods, keep these four tactics in mind:[11]

1. **Avoid Technical Language That Might Confuse the Prospect**. An account executive selling ad space to a small business owner should avoid terms such as kerning, bodoni extra bold, mistral fonts, or bleed page unless certain that the prospect is technically sophisticated and would expect to use such terms. In the same way, using company stock numbers, codes, or abbreviations may confuse the client. Your goal is to promote understanding and not to demonstrate your own personal erudition.

2. **Establish a Clear Agenda**. Chapter nine presented four specific objectives of the approach: To make a favorable first impression, to gain attention, to create interest, and to serve as a logical transition into need discovery. This transition into need discovery requires that you

tell the prospect exactly what you intend to accomplish during the interview session. You are to provide a clear agenda for the sales interview. Always let the prospect know what you want to accomplish. You can set up the desired atmosphere by requesting permission to ask questions. Here are two practical **permissive questions:**

1. *I believe I can offer you a service that will be of considerable value to you, but in order for me to be sure, and to know a little more about your particular situation, would it be okay if I ask you a few questions?*

2. *The only way for us to know how my company can best serve your needs is for you to give me permission to ask a few personal questions. Will that be all right with you? Oh, and may I make some notes while we talk?*

3. **Phrase Each Question So That It Has One Clear Purpose**. An ambiguous question or one with multiple meanings creates misunderstanding between you and the prospect. Proceed logically, one topic at a time. Murphy's law operates here: Anything that can be misunderstood will be misunderstood. A corollary to this principle is equally important: Phrase each question to produce the maximum amount of information so that the number of questions needed to elicit the required information is as small as possible. Exhibit 10.2 gives a good example of how not to do it.[12]

P.212

Δ Exhibit 10.2

Focusing the Questioning Process

A real estate agent wants to find out how many children the prospect has, their ages and gender. Poor planning produces a scenario like this:

AGENT:	Do you have any children?
PROSPECT:	Yes.
AGENT:	How many?
PROSPECT:	Three.
AGENT:	How old are they?
PROSPECT:	11, 9, and 7.
AGENT:	Are they all boys or all girls?
PROSPECT:	Two boys and one girl.
AGENT:	What age is the girl?
PROSPECT:	She's the 7 year-old.

At this rate, the agent will be asking questions all day. Why not simplify the process with one straightforward question:

AGENT:	What are the ages and genders of your children?

4. **Use the "Repeat a Fact" Technique**. Sometimes a prospect will share a piece of information that may be buried in the context of other information or in an answer to another question. For example, let's say a prospect is discussing returns from last year and mentions a number like 15 percent. Repeat the number back to them, pause, and let them elaborate on what that number means to the company. There was a reason

the prospect told you this, so allow them the opportunity to reveal what that motive was and it may lead to a way you can help improve that number.[13]

The Spin Technique

Neil Rackham is president and founder of Huthwaite Inc. and the author of the book *Spin Selling*. His corporation's 12-year, $1 million research into effective sales performance resulted in the unique sales strategy, the SPIN® method: **Situation**, **Problem**, **Implication**, and **Need-Payoff** questions. Successful salespeople don't ask random questions. This model represents how relationship salespeople probe. These are guidelines, not a rigid formula. There is a distinct pattern in the successful call. The answers you get will be used during the presentation to help underscore how the benefits you give support, reinforce, and provide answers to the questions you have asked during need discovery. Its questioning sequence taps directly into the psychology behind the buying process. The questions provide a road map for you, guiding the sales call through the steps of need development until explicit needs have been agreed upon. You want to allow customers to discover for themselves the problems they have. People don't like to think, and certainly don't want to admit, their problems are that obvious.[14]

SPIN® Selling in Action

Let's take a specific example of a company and demonstrate the SPIN® method just as they might use it. A business with overdue accounts receivables has three options: It can hire a conventional percentage-based agency, a flat-fee agency, or do the collecting internally. Transworld Systems Inc. (TSI) is one of the largest collection agencies in the country. TSI works with over 40,000 clients helping them to recover their slow-paying and delinquent accounts without having to pay up to 50 percent of the collection as charged by a conventional agency. Many clients with a wide range of account balances have found the TSI system to be the only economical method of obtaining professional third-party collection results. TSI pays the money they collect directly to the client, the client maintains control of their accounts, and they do not have to pay a percentage. TSI has a low flat fee that enables clients to assign their accounts in the early stages of delinquency, thus providing the best opportunity for successful recovery. [15] Here is the SPIN® technique in action:

Situation Questions. These questions are designed to find out about the customer's situation. These are data-gathering questions. They ask about the prospect's general state of affairs or circumstances as it relates to the services TSI has to offer. They help the TSI sales rep get to know the prospects and obtain initial information about their background and situation. You are looking for a general understanding of the prospect's needs. The following questions have an important fact-finding role, are non-threatening, and help to build an atmosphere of trust and cooperation:

- Do you make the purchasing decision?
- How many active accounts do you bill each month?
- Do you do all the collection of overdue accounts internally?
- About what percentage of your customers do not pay their bills on time?
- Do you have out-of-state accounts?
- Is the billing and follow-up done in this office?
- Do you currently use a collection agency?

Problem Questions. Once the TSI sales reps feel comfortable about the buyer's situation, they move on to a second type of questioning technique. These questions explore needs, any difficulties they may be having, and dissatisfactions in areas where TSI's service could be the

Correlate to Exhibit 10.1

solution. The goal in this step is to have the prospect say, "I really do have a problem with the collection of my accounts receivables."

TSI wants to determine explicit needs or uncover the prospect's "hot button." Remember: The sale is made in the mind of the buyer, not in the mind of the TSI salesperson. Customers don't want to be told they have a problem; allow them to discover it for themselves. Whatever they say is true; when you say it, they doubt it! You're searching for areas where the services TSI offers can solve their specific problem. If you can uncover problems your service can solve, then you're providing the buyer with something useful. Ask these kinds of problem questions:

- Do you know how much it costs to do your collecting internally?
- Do you ever get mail back? Wrong address? No longer at the address?
- When do you consider an account to be a concern or problem?
- Do you ever get checks back NSF or ACCOUNT CLOSED?
- Do you have a service to help recover these checks? If yes, is it a guaranteed service?

Implication Questions. Implication questions build up the magnitude of the problem so that it's seen as serious in the mind of the prospect, and then the sales rep uses need-payoff questions to build up the value of the solution. Implication questions are the language of decision-makers, and if you can talk their language, you'll influence them. In larger sales you need to ask this third type of question. The phrasing of implication questions is critical because you want the prospect to discuss the problem and how it might be improved.

Attach a bottom-line figure to the implication questions. The TSI sales rep wants the prospect to agree that the implications of the problem are causing such things as loss of revenue, ill-will with some of its customer base, prohibitive cost of time and money in trying to do the collection themselves, and expensive percentage-based collection agencies. The prospects must see that the problem is serious enough that it outweighs the cost of the solution, namely, using the services of TSI. The TSI sales rep might ask these questions:

- Would it help if the money was paid directly to you? Last year we collected over $500 million for our clients and the money was paid directly to them.
- Do you know most collection agencies deposit the money they collect into their own bank account and hold it up to 60 days?
- Would it be important to you to recover a larger share of delinquent accounts and bad checks faster than a conventional collection agency and put the money directly into your hands and let it work for you?
- Is it safe to say that you would like to collect delinquent accounts quickly, without disturbing ongoing relationships with those customers?

Need-Payoff Questions. How would that help? What benefits do you see? Why is it important to solve this problem? Is it useful to solve this problem? These questions get the customer to tell you the benefits that your solution offers. These types of questions actually get prospects to name benefits and tell you why they should buy. These questions help you build up the value of your proposed solution in the customer's mind. You want to focus the customer's attention on the solution rather than on the problem. This creates a positive problem-solving atmosphere.

In the words of an eight-year-old named Quincy, "Implication questions are always sad; while need-payoff questions are always happy." That's because implication questions are problem-centered, while the following need-payoff questions are solution-centered:[16]

- Would it be useful to speed up the rate of collection, and at the same time be guaranteed that you will recover at least twice as much as you pay for our service?
- If you could create the perfect agency, what would you want them to do for you?
- If I can show you how TSI has been able to help others in your industry, and we can determine what kind of results you might expect, can we get started today? Let's take a look at your aging report.
- We automatically send out a report detailing the status of each account assigned for collection. Does this sound like something that would interest you?
- Do you want the account handled diplomatically or intensively? We have another division that handles the hard-core collection problems. Would you like to have that option?
- Would you like us to send a "thank you" card to the debtor after the account has been paid?

Common Questioning Techniques

The major types of questioning techniques are summarized in Exhibit 10.3. Questions are generally classified by the type of answers required and by the purpose they are intended to serve. Begin the questioning process with closed-end questions or fact-finding questions that are easy to answer and therefore not threatening to the prospect. If the first few questions are reasonable, the prospect begins to gain confidence and feel comfortable with the questioning process. The next questions then, although progressively more challenging, seem easier to handle.

Δ **Exhibit 10.3**

Types of Questions and Probing Techniques

General types of questions

1. *Closed-end questions*. Provide a series of responses from which the prospect selects one, are easy to answer, used to get feedback, and can be used to get prospect commitment.
2. *Open-end questions*. Identify a topic but do not provide structured alternatives for responses, usually begin with "how" or "what", cannot be answered "yes" or "no", and are designed to stimulate the prospect's thinking.

Classification of questioning techniques

1. *Amplification questions*. Ask prospect to expand on an answer; do not direct thoughts but encourage prospect to continue talking. (Double-check, nonverbal gestures, silence, and continuation questions)
2. *Internal summary questions*. Assimilate information presented, put it in perspective, and ask if the interpretation is correct; may repeat all of prospect's last response in the form of a question. (Reflective or internal summary question)
3. *Getting agreement on the problem*. Make a formal statement of the problem, get prospect to agree, and attempt to get commitment. (Formal statement of the problem)

Closed-End Questions. These questions are direct, fact-finding questions designed to reveal background information about the prospect's business and/or family. They ask an either-or question or request a choice from a series of suggested responses. Closed-end questions are usually answered with a very brief response, often a single word. They often ask for a yes or no response or a choice between two alternatives. They are directive questions for which you want specific answers:

- How many employees do you have working the day shift?
- With what interconnect companies are you familiar?
- Is a rear-window defogger important to you?
- Does your company pay the full cost of employee health insurance, or do the employees pay part of the cost?

You may also phrase closed-end questions to get feedback or to gain commitment:

- Would you like delivery Friday, or is Monday of next week all right?
- Are you responsible for making the decision to purchase from us or will there be others involved?
- Do you know what your customers do with your product after buying it?
- Do you prefer to pay cash, or would you like to arrange a monthly payment plan?

Closed-end questions may be used as a substitute for telling the prospect something. A question can sometimes make a point in a more telling manner than a statement because the prospect must think to answer it, and thinking makes a stronger impression than hearing. Consider these two ways to impart the same message:

1. *Our procedure will completely eliminate waste in your welding operations.*

2. *How much cost savings would you have if you used a procedure that completely eliminates waste from your welding operations?*

The first method tells the prospect something. The salesperson hopes the prospect is impressed, but that may not happen. Unless the prospect reacts strongly enough to the statement to break in with a comment, any skepticism is buried until some later point, where it emerges as a vague objection or stall like, "Well, we're not thinking of making any changes just now."

The question method, however, gains attention because the prospect has to think about an answer. Disbelief surfaces immediately where it can be dealt with instead of being postponed until later when the salesperson is trying to close. Exhibit 10.4 lists the various purposes served by asking closed-end questions.

△ Exhibit 10.4

Purposes of Closed-End Questions ···

- Uncover specific facts.

- Reduce prospect tension because they are easy to answer.

- Check understanding and receive feedback.

- Maintain control by directing the flow of conversation.

- Reinforce prospect commitment to a specific position.

Open-End Questions. These broadly phrased questions allow prospects plenty of room to answer as they wish. They call for explanations. Open-end questions encourage prospects to explain their needs by explaining their preferences, expectations, or judgments. Open-end questions tend to be general rather than specific. Use them when you want the prospect to talk freely. You can encourage the prospect to verbalize feelings by asking questions that begin with "What do you think?" or "How do you feel?" Talking out loud often helps people clarify and organize their thoughts. Real feelings are often not in the conscious awareness until they are verbalized.[17]

Open-end questions help you and the prospect sort out ideas and begin to make decisions. Here are some examples of questions that give prospects the freedom and responsibility to express their own thoughts and use their own information in the decision-making process:

- *What options would you want on your new Mercedes?*

- *How do you think I might be able to help you?*

- *In a perfect world, what would you like to see us deliver?*

- *What are five unique characteristics of your business?*

- *What benefits would you expect from our ten-week, self-paced time-management program?*

Open-end questions reveal attitudes that a salesperson must be aware of if the sale is to be closed. You cannot easily ask a prospect, "Are you motivated by pride?" but you can ask open-end questions designed to detect this emotion, and you then have the answer to the direct question you cannot ask. Exhibit 10.5 lists the properties of open- end questions.

Δ Exhibit 10.5

The Properties of Open-End Questions

- Allow the prospect to move in any direction.
- Cannot be answered with "yes" or "no".
- Ordinarily begin with "how" or "what".
- Designed to stimulate the prospect's thinking and increase dialogue.
- Help determine dominant buying motives (rational or emotional).
- Uncover the social or behavioral style of the prospect.

Classification of Questioning Techniques

The questions salespeople ask can be classified by the purpose they are intended to perform. Three basic classes of questions can be used: Amplification, internal summary or reflective, and questions to gain agreement on the problem. Either open-end or closed-end questions may be asked for any of these purposes, depending upon the situation. If one type of question does not provide all the information needed, another type can be used to get a more specific response or to elicit a better sense of the prospect's point of view.

Relationship selling is more than a process in which two people sit together in a room and take turns talking. As the salesperson, you must be certain that the prospect knows what you are talking about and understands it. You must also be sure that you understand the prospect, know that person's needs and desires, and be certain you can satisfy them. You need feedback, and asking questions is the method for receiving feedback.

Be careful how you phrase the questions you ask. Place the responsibility for not understanding on yourself rather than on the prospect. "Do you understand what I said?" or "Did you get that?" or "Are you with me?" seems to imply that the prospect may not be too bright. You must take responsibility for any possible misunderstanding by asking, "Have I explained this clearly enough? Is there some part I need to clarify or go over again?"

Amplification Questions

Ask probing questions and listen to your customer.[18] These questioning techniques encourage prospects to continue to provide enlightening information and encourage them to explain the meaning of a statement made. Amplification questions help both salespeople and prospects. At times prospects may not make themselves clear; they may wander off the subject or may stop talking before you can fully understand their position. In a subtle manner, these techniques ask the prospect to expand on or clarify the meaning of a statement and help identify the frame of reference used. There are four types of amplification questions:

Double-Check Question. A double-check question is a means of giving feedback to the prospect. It involves taking the information the prospect has provided, rephrasing it, and handing it right back. A prospect might tell a motor freight salesperson, "Every Tuesday and Thursday the whole yard is backed up with trucks for the entire afternoon." The salesperson might offer feedback by saying, "Now as I understand it, you find that your loading platforms get badly jammed at peak hours." This statement is actually a question because it evokes an answer. It serves the dual purpose of clarifying the salesperson's impression of the situation and solidifying the prospect's opinion.

Nonverbal Gestures. Visual cues such as nodding the head or leaning forward show that you are listening, believe the prospect is on the right track, and understand what the prospect is saying. You may also inject appropriate words or phrases to encourage the prospect to continue: "You don't say?" "Is that right?" "That's interesting!" You may imply a question by the nonverbal choice of silence accompanied by a slightly raised eyebrow or furrowed brow.

Silence. Silence is a powerful sales tool. When prospects avoid telling you the whole truth, the knowledge that they are being less than honest makes them uncomfortable. Your silence convinces them to go ahead and tell you the whole story. Silence allows you to slow down and relax the pace of asking questions. Some prospects want to think and contemplate longer than others before responding to your questions. Give people time to reply at their own pace. Silence also gives you valuable time to formulate your own next question or comment.

Continuation Questions. Continuation questions encourage prospects to keep on talking by making a positive request for more information. Such questions do not push for a particular response or for agreement; they just encourage more communication from the prospect. Here are two examples:

1. *What additional thoughts do you have on that topic?*
2. *Could you tell me in a bit more detail why you feel that way?*

Exhibit 10.6 lists the advantages of using amplification questions.

Δ Exhibit 10.6

Advantages of Using Amplification Questions · · · · · · · · · · · · · · ·

- Encourage the prospect to continue to provide revealing information.
- Allows the salesperson to rephrase what the prospect appears to have intended.
- Invites the prospect to expand or clarify any point of disagreement.
- Narrows down generalizations and clears ambiguities.

Internal Summary Questions

Probes designed to get prospects to think, see, and consider your interpretation of the situation may be called internal summary or reflective questions. Summarize what you understood the prospect to mean. You want to assimilate the information provided, place it in the perspective that suits your purpose, and ask if the interpretation is correct.

You achieve this by repeating all or part of the prospect's last response in the form of a question or by rephrasing the entire idea expressed by the prospect, feeding it back in a slightly different form, and asking for confirmation. Consider the following example in which a company president explains why the firm may not be able to sponsor an in-house blood drive. Note how the salesperson empathizes and rewords or echoes the president's remarks but suggests the process can be accomplished without disruption:

> **Prospect (company president)**: My company has always felt the need to support the charitable activities of organizations like yours. But where do we draw the line? I am constantly besieged with requests for my company's time. We have only so many hours a day.

> **Salesperson (donor consultant)**: I certainly understand how you feel. If I were in your position, I'd probably feel the same way. I sense that the blood donor program is something you wholeheartedly endorse. But with only so many hours in the working day, humanitarian concerns take a back seat to the realities of the business world. However, if you thought this could be accomplished with a minimum of time lost, and you felt your employees really wanted to do it, it could be done. May I tell you how we manage it?

These types of questions are useful throughout the interview. Every salesperson knows about summarizing the key benefits just before asking for the order: "Now, as I see it, we've agreed that a complete line, with these particular items featured, will move for you with the proper promotion. Am I right about that?" Such summary techniques are especially useful during the close.

The summary question may be used to underscore points on which you already agree. An occasional summary of the points to which the prospect has already agreed will fix them firmly in the mind of the prospect and demonstrate just how wide an area of agreement there is between the two of you.

Getting Agreement

In *Open the Mind, Close the Sale*, John Wilson says that the salesperson's failure to confirm the problem is one of the biggest mistakes in selling. The underlying purpose of asking questions is to determine whether the prospect has a problem or need that you are capable of solving. State the problem in your own words and get the prospect to agree, "Yes, that's it." Never begin the actual presentation phase of the sales interview until the problem has been clearly established in the minds of both you and the prospect. Begin the formal statement of the problem by using such phrases as these:

- *Let me attempt to summarize what we have been saying.*

- *As I understand it, here is (are) the problem(s) we must solve.*

- *Based on your answers to my questions, I see the problem as . . .*

After you pinpoint the problem, you must seek confirmation. Get the prospect to agree by following your summary of the problem with questions like these:

- *If I show you some comparisons demonstrating that my company can save you money without sacrificing quality, would you commit to our program?*[19]
- *Is that a fair statement of the way things stand?*
- *If I can satisfactorily demonstrate a solution to these concerns of yours, would it be enough to earn your business?*

If the prospect agrees with the problem statement, you are ready to present the specific benefits of your product or service that can solve the problem. Even if the prospect disagrees with your summary of the problem, you have both learned by sharing information.

Listening

Everybody wants the secret to closing more sales, but it's no secret. If you're not closing sales, you're not listening to the customer. Salespeople are so busy telling their prospects or customers all the wonderful things that their products or services will do for them instead

of being quiet and letting the prospects tell them what they need.[20] Prospects are not patiently sitting at their desks waiting for you to call so they can buy your product. People are not easily sold, which is why you must do more than mechanically go through your script. Prospects can sense insincerity, and they will know if you are not really listening to them and giving only scripted generic response. Listen— your prospect will reveal his needs and show you how you can help him.[21]

Eighty percent of waking hours is spent communicating, about half of that listening. Effective listening is not just hearing what the prospect is saying. Faulty listening results in misunderstanding and lost opportunities.[22] Research indicates that 60 percent of misunderstandings in business are due to poor listening.[23] Fortunately, improved listening skills can be learned. When a salesperson listens intently to prospects, they are likely to have a very positive reaction when it is the salesperson's turn to speak. Actively listening to prospects not only increases the effectiveness of the interaction, it also greatly increases the chance of making a sale.[24]

To succeed in professional selling, you must be able to offer a product or service that satisfies the buyer's needs. Presenting features and benefits is not always enough. How they are presented may be as important as what is presented. Listening is the key to finding ways to present benefits that enhance the possibility of a close. Effective listening helps sales professionals catch verbal and nonverbal signals indicating a prospect who is interested in buying their product or service. "Unfortunately, good listening skills usually require a change in our behavior," says Barry Elms, CEO of Strategic Negotiations International.[25]

Psychologists claim that listening uses only about 25 percent of our brain. The other 75 percent either thinks about what to say next or stops listening if the conversation is boring or of no interest. Exhibit 10.7 is an example of the kind of listening that destroys any credibility you have or ever hope to establish.[26]

Ed Milligan called on the drugstore every week to fill inventories and check new items. He always greeted the owner with a big smile and the question, "Good to see you. How's the family?"

The storeowner answered, "Fine," and Ed always replied, "Terrific. Let me show you what we have for you this week."

Wondering if Ed really cared about his family, the owner decided to give a new answer to Ed's standard question. When Ed showed up on schedule the following week and said, "Good to see you. How's the family?" the owner said, "Well, my mother-in-law jumped off the cliff, the children are lost in a forest, and my wife had to go to a leper colony."

Without missing a beat, good old Ed answered, "Terrific. Let me show you what we have for you this week."

Improving Listening Skills

To improve your listening skills, practice these five mental activities as you listen:

Avoid Prejudgment. Not only should you allow the speaker to complete a message before you comment or respond, but you should also wait until you have heard the entire message before judging it. Making value judgments colors your thinking and creates emotional blind spots that can block your ability to make a solid buying recommendation. Jumping to conclusions is a common fault of poor listeners. As the cartoon indicates, assuming you know what is coming next can seriously damage your understanding of the actual meaning intended.

Be Patient. Listen more and give "verbal nods" of encouragement. This allows speakers plenty of time to answer questions and encourages them to express their ideas. Speak at the same speed as the other person: Matching speed is a rapport builder. In addition, find the person's mental rate of speed and then adjust or modify your thinking to that rate. Even though the speaker is saying something exciting, wait until the message is complete and you are sure that you understand it all before you contribute your own thoughts.

Take Notes. Remembering everything a person says is difficult. Use the pen-and-paper approach to selling. Divide your notepad into two columns. On one side note what the prospect says. Then in the other column sketch out your proposal to meet those expressions of needs, requirements, or desires. The mere physical action of writing down a few key words reinforces your memory and understanding. You can go back to the prospect's own words to help you show your product's applicability to the problem.[27]

Reinforce. Anchor, in your mind and in the prospect's, the points made by the prospect. Use your own reinforcing responses to achieve this purpose. If the prospect says the mileage per gallon a car gets is important, respond, "Yes, that is very important." Later, tell what mileage the prospect could get with your car. If the prospect says, "Our secretaries spend too much time making copies," respond, "That has to be a problem." Then later emphasize how your copier cuts secretaries' time by copying on both sides of the paper in one operation and by running more copies per minute.

Capitalize on Speed of Thought. We can process about 600 words a minute, but even a fast talker gets out only 100 to 150 words in that time.[28] Thus you can think about four times as fast as the average prospect talks. All that spare time is valuable. The poor listener uses it to fidget impatiently, to think about what happened earlier in the day or what will happen later, or to plan what to say as soon as the prospect takes a breath. Successful salespeople have a plan to follow for using this time profitably:

- *Anticipate where the prospect is going*. If you guess right, your thinking is reinforced. If you are wrong, compare your thoughts with those of the prospect; look for the point the prospect is making.

- *Mentally summarize the message*. Pinpoint problems, misconceptions, attitudes, objections, or misunderstandings. What you learn can be an excellent guide to the items that should be stressed in the presentation and at the close.

- *Formulate a response*. Be careful not to formulate one before you hear everything the prospect wants to say. Listen, understand, and then turn the prospect's words to your advantage.

- *Listen between the lines*. Nonverbal messages are as important as verbal ones. Watch facial expressions, body movement, and position; listen to the tone of voice and volume changes.

SUMMARY

- Asking questions is the primary tool for identifying problems. Need discovery lays the groundwork for the presentation and close. When you ask the right questions, prospects clarify problems in their own minds as well as in yours.

- No standard set of questions is universally applicable. The product or service, your preapproach information, and the prospect's behavioral style help determine the questions you ask.

- Questions may be either closed-end or open-end. A closed-end question asks for a yes-no response or a choice between alternatives. Open-end questions ask for opinions, explanations, or judgments.

- Ask questions according to their structure: Amplification, internal summary, and questions designed to gain agreement.

- Listening is one of the most neglected skills in any type of training program. Taking notes focuses your attention on what the prospect is saying and avoids prejudgment of ideas. Reinforce what you hear by comparing the prospect's ideas with your own.

- People can think at a rate much faster than they talk. Use this spare thinking time to anticipate where the prospect is going, mentally summarize what you hear, form a response, and refine the message as your listening continues.

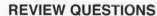

REVIEW QUESTIONS

1. What factors determine a salesperson's ability to formulate the right questions?

2. What is the difference between manipulation and consultation? Which is most useful to the successful salesperson? Why?

3. What kinds of questions allow the salesperson to discover the prospect's behavioral style? How does this information aid the salesperson?

4. What tactic is useful as a transition from the approach into need discovery?

5. Who should control the needs-assessment phase of the interview? How is control maintained?

6. What is the purpose of the open-end question? Formulate an open-end question that might be used to sell investment property.

7. Describe in detail all the instruction you have had in school, at home, or elsewhere in listening skills.

8. In what situations do you find it hardest to listen? Easiest? What makes the difference?

9. Is listening easier if a visual factor is added? For example, do you prefer to talk to someone in person or on the phone when you have something serious to discuss?

10. Educators say learning that involves more than one of the senses is more effective. Explain how this applies to listening and taking notes, to simultaneously listening and looking at visual aids, and to listening to radio versus watching television.

ROLE-PLAY EXERCISES

The following role-play exercises help build teams, improve communication, and emphasize the "real-world" side of selling. They are meant to be challenging, to learn how to deal with problems that have no single "right" answer and to use a variety of skills beyond those employed in a typical review question. Read and complete each activity. Then in the next class, discuss and compare answers with other classmates. Have some students take the role of the salesperson, and see how they would react. Remember, *"You learn more about a person in an hour of play than in a lifetime of conversation."* —Plato

1. You are a salesperson for lawn mowers in a retail store. Pair up in groups of two. Have one student play the salesperson, and the other play the part of a customer. List questions you could ask to determine what type of mower a particular customer needs.

2. Pair up in male-female teams of two. Assume that you want to ask your partner for a dinner date at a restaurant and list some questions that you could ask to find out what kind of restaurant to suggest to make the best impression. Avoid closed-end questions like "Would you rather go for pizza or eat at a fancy restaurant?"

3. You sell automatic garage-door openers. Your prospect has never had one. Prepare a dialogue asking questions that would lead this customer to recognize a need for an automatic opener and create a desire to own one.

CASE STUDY

Case 10.1 - The Pause That Sells

Ken Simpson was elated. He called his sales manager and gleefully reported, "I have an appointment tomorrow with the head buyer for the Pilot Company, the largest department store chain in this area—you know, the one with the big garden centers in their suburban branches. If I get the contract for our power mowers, snow blowers, and garden tractors, you'll have to tell the plant to go on overtime!"

The sales manager congratulated Ken but warned him to spend some time preparing his presentation. This opportunity was not the time to go in poorly prepared. Ken assured his sales manager that he would be ready. No way did he intend to muff this chance!

The next morning, Ken was confident he could make the biggest sale of his career. He started by mentioning his company's excellent reputation for high-quality products. Then he told about the performance record of their power equipment, their high manufacturing standards, and their rigid specifications for raw materials and parts. And on and on and on. He finally asked his first question: "With your reputation for selling only high-quality merchandise, don't you agree that our outstanding line of lawn and garden equipment would fit right in with your image in the high-income, suburban area?"

The answer left Ken almost speechless. The buyer said, "Your company's promotional campaign has made me quite familiar with your line. But while you were gushing about how good your outfit is from your point of view, I was never able to get a word in edgewise. I want to know about markup and service centers. I don't want to hear about quality-control procedures; I want to know about the result of your procedures. You know, I see a lot of salespeople like you. You know your product, and I admit we want to handle the best line we can get. I still have two weeks before I have to choose a line of power mowers, tractors, and snow-removal equipment to recommend to the buying committee. If you can come back and will promise to answer my questions, I'll give you another appointment."

1. Ken's mistake is obvious. Correcting it, however, may not be as simple as it seems. What would you suggest he say to the buyer right now?

2. If he makes another appointment, how should Ken prepare?

3. What should Ken tell his sales manager about this interview?

Case 10.2 - The Silent Treatment

Della King sells custom business forms as well as a complete line of stock forms applicable to almost any firm with large-volume paperwork. Her first call on Harry Thompson, purchasing agent for a large community college, was frustrating. He was the silent type. Della thought to herself, "This guy must have adopted that old slogan that says even a fish would stay out of trouble if he kept his mouth shut."

Della was sure the college could benefit from using the custom design service her company offered for printing all sorts of student information forms: invoices and bills, grade records, and transcript forms, as well as administrative forms like requisitions and purchase orders. After she completed her standard presentation, Della asked for an order. Harry spoke for the first time, "We've got enough inventory of forms to last through next semester. Call on me next time you're in town. If you'll excuse me, I have a meeting in the president's office in two minutes."

All Della could do was say good-bye and leave. Back at her car, she noted on Harry's prospect card: "A real clam. Find a way to get him to talk." A month later, she was back again. She checked over the points she could make about the service her company offered and thought to herself, "He's the purchasing agent; he can at least suggest some problem that we could address. I've got to get him to talk." As she approached his desk, he silently waved her to a chair. "It's good to see you again, Mr. Thompson," Della began. His only reply was a grunt. Determined to get him to talk, she asked, "Mr. Thompson, do people in your organization ever complain about the difficulty of reading the last copy in your multiple forms?" His only answer was a shrug.

1. What might happen if Della tried the silent treatment by asking a question and then just waiting until Harry actually said something? Is he likely to be uncomfortable with a protracted silence?

2. What other option can you suggest for Della to use in getting Harry to talk enough to reveal some need or buying motive?

"People are delighted when we introduce new ideas that make them laugh out loud, reflect, and reconsider what they thought they knew to be true,"

-Sam Horn

Making The Presentation

LEARNING OBJECTIVES

- Understand how to make a presentation.

- Learn how units of conviction help prospects reach a buying decision.

- Discover effective tactics for making a sales presentation.

- Study different methods for involving the prospect.

- Understand the significance of using a demonstration.

- Examine the different types of sales aids available.

- Recognize the value of using technology in making presentations.

With the ever-increasing popularity of online buying, some experts say that salespeople are soon to be corporate relics on the road to extinction. This is simply not true! Relationship salespeople will continue to prosper in the future if they understand one simple concept: There is a big difference between presenting data versus information. In the past, traditional sales reps simply presented data—facts and figures that can often confuse or complicate a presentation if their significance is not explained. How "data dense" are most sales presentations? Here are some interesting and surprising facts about most sales presentations:

- The typical salesperson presents six to eight features or benefits during the sales presentation. Twenty-four hours later the average prospect remembers only one benefit.

- In 39 percent of those cases they remember the one benefit incorrectly.

- In 49 percent of the cases they remember something that wasn't mentioned at all.

Prospects demand a product that does what they want it to do, explained in a language they understand.[1] The future of professional, relationship selling is going to be based on real-time value and how well sales professionals become trusted advisors in guiding clients to solutions to their problems. The future belongs to those sales pros that can present and share their knowledge, offer wisdom, and create value in a way that benefits the prospect.[2]

Developing a Persuasive Presentation

Strive for Passion, not Perfection. More often than not, customers buy because of the rapport building established over time. "Selling is all about relationship building. There are hundreds of competitors chomping at the bit," says Diane DiResta. It all comes down to the way you present yourself and your product or service, and the value you create for the customer. Sales presentations must be listener-centered. People want to have their problems solved. People-reading skills help salespeople adapt to their prospect's social styles.

Mark McCormack in his book *What They Don't Teach You at the Harvard Business School* said there are three fundamental selling truths: (1) If you don't know your product, people will resent your efforts to sell it. (2) If you don't believe in your product, no amount of personality or technique will cover that fact. (3) If you can't sell your product with enthusiasm, the absence of it will be infectious.

Nobody buys from a dispassionate seller; if you don't believe in the product, no one else will. The more options a sales rep creates for the prospect, the greater the chance for a sale.[3] Don't worry about making the perfect presentation. It probably will not happen! Besides, the prospects are looking to you for knowledge of what you're selling and how it can help them solve a problem or become more successful. You must truly believe in what you're selling and show some passion when doing it—that is far more important than perfection.

Calling on Regular Customers. If you are calling on the same person or dealer on a regular basis, you may tend to give the same old presentation over and over or even skip the presentation entirely and merely ask, "What do you need today?" If you are unwilling to put some real work into your selling and are content just to "take orders" all your life, your best opportunity to become rich is to win the lottery! Vary your presentation. Provide new ideas to help your customer make money, save time, or increase efficiency. Plan to use ideas like these:

"The true perfection of man lies not in what a man has, but what a man is."

—Oscar Wilde

- Give the customer a new advertising or merchandising idea.
- Help the customer develop an overall marketing plan for improving the business.
- Tell some new product fact that the customer needs to know.
- Share a piece of industry or trade news of personal interest to the customer.

Begin with Planning

Everything important begins with planning. Over the last few decades, sales professionals strived to find ways to quantify best planning practices and ways to target key prospects. The best salespeople learn to dutifully target, segment, and measure inputs, outputs, and performance. AC Nielsen has built a multibillion-dollar business of gathering and distributing sales data to analyze and report with perceived expertise; and consumers and management eat it up. Some even refer to this research and planning as a science.[4] This may seem like an overstatement to some, but effective planning, in fact, has become highly methodological and even scientific in its approach.

Exhibit 11.1 is one man's account of the results he suffered from his failure to plan his immediate future. Random, haphazard action never leads to success in any worthwhile endeavor, and in this respect, selling is no different from any other undertaking. How well you plan what takes place during the sales interview plays a major role in the success you achieve when closing time arrives.

Δ Exhibit 11.1

Failing to Plan My Immediate Future ·

I am writing in response to your request for additional information. In block #3 of the accident form I listed "not planning my immediate future" as the cause of my accident. I trust the following details will be sufficient.

I am a bricklayer. On the date of the accident I was working alone on the roof of a new six-story building. At the end of the day, I discovered about 500 pounds of bricks left over. Rather than carry them down by hand, I decided to lower them in a barrel by using a pulley that was fortunately attached to the building at the sixth floor.

Securing the rope at ground level, I went to the roof, swung the barrel out, and loaded the bricks. Then I went back to the ground and untied the rope, holding it tightly to ensure a slow descent of the 500 pounds of bricks. Block #11 of the accident report shows that I weigh 135 pounds. Due to my surprise of being jerked off the ground so suddenly, I forgot to let go of the rope. Needless to say, I proceeded at a rapid rate up the side of the building. In the vicinity of the third floor, I met the barrel coming down. This explains the fractured skull and broken collarbone.

Slowed only slightly, I continued my rapid ascent, not stopping until the fingers of my right hand were two knuckles deep into the pulley. Fortunately, I had regained my presence of mind enough to hold tightly to the rope in spite of my pain.

At approximately the same time, however, the barrel of bricks hit the ground and the bottom fell out of the barrel. Devoid of the weight of the bricks, the barrel now weighed approximately 50 pounds. I refer you again to block #11. As you can imagine, I began a rather rapid descent down the side of the building.

In the vicinity of the third floor I met the barrel coming up. This accounts for the two fractured ankles and the lacerations of my legs and lower body. The encounter with the barrel slowed my descent enough to lessen my injuries when I fell onto the pile of bricks. Fortunately only three vertebrae were cracked.

I am sorry to report, however, that as I lay there on the bricks, in pain, unable to stand and watching the empty barrel six stories above me, I again lost my presence of mind and let go of the rope. Now the empty barrel weighed more than the rope, so it came back down on me and broke both of my legs.

I hope these details explain sufficiently that my accident was caused by failure to plan my immediate future.

In reality, planning and preparing for the sales presentation begin when a name is first recorded in your prospect files. As information is gathered about the prospect, you are subconsciously planning how to approach this person, what features and benefits are most appropriate, and what kind of close is likely to be most effective. The final step of preparing for the sales interview is to crystallize all your plans and decide exactly how to proceed with making the presentation. You really need a clear, focused objective for your message, and that's partly determined by the type of individual or company on which you are calling.

When planning your presentation, here is a good rule of thumb to follow: When you are developing a brand new sales talk, plan on spending one hour of preparation time for each minute of presentation time. For example, if you are speaking for twenty minutes, you should invest twenty hours in research, development, organizing, outlining, fleshing out, and rehearsing your presentation. It sounds like a lot of time—and it is—but it's necessary if you want to deliver a dynamite presentation. If you invest the time to construct a superb, researched presentation, you'll be able to deliver the same or a similar version to other prospects. As Dr. Norman Vincent Peale said, "I give the same mashed potatoes for each speech, I just change the gravy."[5]

Call Objective

The most successful salespeople have specific objectives for each sales interview. In many instances, the call objective is to present your product or service and secure an order. In others, your objective is to discover the prospect's needs so that you may prepare a proposal for later consideration or to persuade the prospect to set up a presentation to a group of people who are jointly charged with the responsibility for a buying decision. In these latter instances, you will probably plan several interviews that, taken together, contain all the elements that may be considered parts of "the presentation." The difference is that you accomplish the various steps in successive interviews rather than in a single meeting with the prospect.

Whether you intend to complete the presentation and the close in a single call or in a series of calls depends upon the type of product or service you sell and the size of the expected order. The single-call close is appropriate for selling items that can be ordered upon the decision of one person; if a buying center is involved, multiple calls are usually necessary.

Tanis Cornell is a Global Enterprise Manager for Network Appliance, a leader in the data storage industry. She manages one of their Top Enterprise Accounts, AT&T. Tanis has a team of 25 people either partially or totally dedicated to selling and supporting this one account. Her approach to selling a major account involves a complex interview process. The sale may be closed on any one of the calls, but often it requires many more than 4 calls. Here is her system:

1. **Initial call**. Develop rapport and establish a need. Judge how far to go by how quickly a relationship is established. Take notes all along to help build a trust level.

2. **Survey call**. Interview all key decision makers to get information. The decision is ultimately based on three factors: cost, quality, and service. Discover which one is most important to this client.

3. **Proposal call**. Present a buying recommendation. Recognize the fact that this is a joint or buying center decision, and give each person what that individual needs to reach a decision. Use trial closes.

4. **Closing call**. Get verbal and/or written commitment.

5. **Follow-up calls**. Continue meeting with executives, managers, and department heads until a solution is reached. Consider each meeting as a mini contract negotiation.

Sales Call Planning Sheet

Many companies, especially those whose product or service entails extensive research into customer needs, require salespeople to prepare a presentation plan in written form. The plan reveals the need for any additional information, makes it possible to check needs and goals against suggested solutions, and makes sure you have a clear picture of the entire situation before arriving for the personal interview. Exhibit 11.2 is an example of a sales call planning sheet that may be used for this purpose.

Δ **Exhibit 11.2**

Sales Call Planner ·

1. Company Name _____

2. Type of Company _____

3. Address _____

4. Individual(s) to contact
   _____ (position)_____
   _____ (position)_____

5. Background and profile of buyers _____

6. Major competitors to be aware of
   _____ (sales rep) _____
   _____ (sales rep) _____

7. Objective for this particular call _____

8. Best time to see buyer _____

9. Expressed needs or problems _____

10. Strategies and tactics useful for this situation _____
    a. Best approach to use _____
    b. Specific fact-finding questions _____
    c. Features and benefits to stress _____
    d. Anticipated objections _____
       (and techniques to answer them) _____
    e. Closing techniques to be used _____

11. Sales tools to take (audiovisual, flip-chart presentation, etc.) _____
    _____

12. Results of this sales call _____
    _____

Presentation Styles

As long as people have been attempting to analyze the selling process, a running controversy has raged over the use of "canned" presentations. Opponents point to presentations that are obviously memorized, and delivered in a hypnotic manner likely to produce a mesmerized listener in the shortest possible time. Supporters of memorized presentations point to the many advantages of knowing exactly what to say and when.

The question is not likely to be settled once and for all because the difference lies more with the salesperson than with the method of delivery itself. In deciding how you will deliver the message you want the prospect to receive, consider the advantages and disadvantages of three basic choices: The memorized presentation, the outline presentation, and the extemporaneous presentation.

Memorized Presentation

Some companies supply their salespeople with a printed presentation and require them to memorize it. A few words of caution are in order when considering the use of a memorized presentation. Even though it is memorized, the presentation should never sound memorized. A memorized presentation should be practiced and its delivery polished until it becomes natural. It should be internalized to the point that it is a normal, personal message. The memorized presentation must be used as a framework or guide to lead you and your prospect through the sales process. Most companies that make use of a standardized presentation provide a list of suggested questions to help discover buying motives, suggest options to use in different types of circumstances, and caution the salesperson to remain flexible. A well-prepared, memorized presentation offers a number of important advantages, especially to new salespeople.

Quick Productivity. If the salesperson is new to the company or to the selling profession, they can memorize a good presentation in much less time than one can be developed. Using a standardized presentation gets the salesperson into production quickly. Enough sales can be made during the initial learning period to supply basic income needs while they gain knowledge and experience.

Reliable and Proven Effectiveness. The memorized presentation makes sure you give the right information to the prospect. Nothing vital is omitted, and nothing erroneous is inserted. The presentation a company supplies to salespeople has usually been tested and refined over a period of years in actual selling situations.

Internalize, don't just memorize.

Confidence Building. Using it is a confidence builder for the inexperienced salesperson. When you know the presentation has worked for others with no more experience than you have, you feel capable of using it successfully. When you succeed in closing a sale with the presentation, you gain even more confidence. Each success builds on the previous one, and you are earning and learning at the same time.

Memorizing your presentation as well as your answers to the most commonly asked questions or objections prevents you from committing pitfalls from which you may never recover. Neil Rock, a district sales manager for pharmaceuticals giant GlaxoSmithKline, said, "I had a representative talking to a group of ten neurologists, and she began to answer a question she didn't know. Her response was a hesitant, 'I think the answer is…' "[6] Salespeople are not expected to know every last detail about a product, but starting a response with, "Um, I think…" is not an option. You have to be confident in your answer. By memorizing your presentation and learning the answers to common concerns, you can attain that much needed confidence and set yourself apart.

Outline Presentation

The outline presentation takes a great deal of thought and preparation. With this presentation technique, exact words are not planned in full detail. You know what content will be presented at each stage of the presentation but are confident enough of both knowledge and skill to believe that the right words will be available as needed. This is the same process that most experienced public speakers use.

Using an outline presentation successfully depends upon the development of numerous units of conviction that are thoroughly internalized. The outline is built by considering all the information available about the prospect. Most salespeople who use an outline method follow the same general outline for most presentations. They may, however, have several approaches or openings from which to choose, numerous features and benefits to present, and all sorts of evidence to present—all of which can be combined and recombined to meet the needs of the specific situation. Ideally, you make the choice in advance and know which pieces of material will be used. The use of the outline presentation generally calls for more judgment about people and broader product knowledge than the memorized presentation.

Many companies, especially those whose product or service entails extensive research into customer needs, require salespeople to prepare an outline presentation in written form. Any type of written plan you use reveals any existing need for additional information, enables you to check needs and goals against suggested solutions, and makes sure you have a clear picture of the entire situation before arriving for the interview. Procter & Gamble is one company that recommends its sales reps follow an outline plan for presentations. Exhibit 11.3 is an outline for a presentation written by one of its sales managers in Cleveland, Ohio.

Δ Exhibit 11.3

Procter & Gamble Sales Plan

Purpose of the Sales Call

Sell 40 cases of Folger's one-pound for display.

Background of Account

Chain store with $100,000 weekly volume. Store is allowed to select displays in addition to headquarters' displays. Store's current need is to increase dollar volume per customer transaction. Manager has also expressed concern with labor cost. This particular store has a back stock of eight cases of canister creamers.

Summarize the Situation

The store manager said several weeks ago that they want to increase dollar volume 7 percent in the next three months by increasing the average amount of each customer transaction. I want to suggest a way to sell more Folger's coffee to help achieve this goal.

State the Idea

My idea is for the store to display 40 cases of one-pound Folger's coffee with eight cases of canister creamers from the store's back stock.

Explain How It Works

Last year's records show that the store displayed 30 cases of Folger's one-pound coffee during this time, and it sold out quickly at regular shelf price. Now in the cold months, coffee consumption is the number one dry grocery item. Capitalize on customer appeal of Folger's, which has proved popular in the past, and enhance it with an appealing display with the canister creamers. Store now moves 10 cases weekly, and a special display will move 40 cases easily. I'll help build the display and save time and labor for the store.

Reinforce Key Benefits

Show calculations of contribution this display can make to help reach the 7 percent increase desired. $2,678.40 in sales on coffee. Add the quality image created by Folger's TV advertising. The related item display will increase movement on creamers that are now sitting in back stock. The result is an increase in the average per-customer sale, which is the goal.

Suggest an Easy Next Step

Ask for a decision on which truck to send the 40 cases of Folger's and suggest Tuesday.

Extemporaneous Presentation

Some highly successful salespeople, particularly those who have many years of experience, may be heard to say that they "don't prepare" for a sales presentation. Actually, their preparation time is distributed in a different way than that of the less experienced salesperson, but they do prepare.

The extemporaneous presentation follows the same principles that any other presentation would incorporate, but experienced salespeople who use the extemporaneous approach are master people watchers. They understand people; they ask questions and listen. They are experts in discovering problems and identifying dominant buying motives. They know their product so thoroughly that they can seize almost magically upon the one feature or benefit that will best appeal to the prospect. They possess such charisma that the air of trust and credibility they create makes objections nonexistent and painlessly places the client's name on the order form. People love to buy from them. As a result, these master salespeople spend most of their "preparation time" in gathering additional information about the prospect rather than spending time in consciously matching features and benefits to prospect qualification information. This step is almost automatic and subconscious as a result of their long experience.

You can use the extemporaneous presentation when you have paid your dues over a period of time. It takes up-to-the-minute product knowledge, intensive prospecting, thorough preapproach qualifying of prospects, and a full background of selling experience upon which to draw. Although salespeople who use the extemporaneous method sometimes claim not to prepare, listening closely to presentations made by these masters shows that they have, over time, developed some uniquely personal tactics for conducting a sales interview. Many of the same phrases and sentences appear over and over—because they work! Conscious preparation, for these people, consists of learning about the particular prospect. Then automatically the tactics, the procedures, and words themselves surface from the well of experience and provide the "extemporaneous" inspiration that accomplishes the goal.

Product-Analysis Worksheet

Prospects have neither the product knowledge you have nor an understanding of the type of service you are prepared to render. You must not only know all the facts about your product but also be able to relate your knowledge directly to the specific needs of the prospect. If you can quote prices, catalog numbers, shipping dates, delivery schedules, and credit terms but have no solid, convincing evidence of the product's value to offer upon which the prospect can base a buying decision, you are afflicted with what has been called the *salesman's curse:* "You know your product better than you know how your client's business can use it."[7] A salesperson who suffers from the "salesman's curse" is in the same league as a math student who can recite all the formulas in the algebra book but never knows which one to use to solve the problem. Before you can expect a signed order form, you must figure out how to improve your customer's business and then find a way to persuade the prospect that the solution you offer is the best possible. You can do this by preparing *units of conviction*.

Units of Conviction

Units of conviction are concise, carefully prepared "mini-presentations" used as building blocks to construct the information you present. When the individual units of conviction are combined, they form what is referred to as a *product-analysis worksheet*.

Preparing a written product-analysis worksheet helps you evaluate the various characteristics of your product so that you are better able to present it to your prospects. When you prepare units of conviction and add them to your store of available options, they become a permanent part of your selling arsenal. A single unit of conviction consists of five elements:

1. A feature of your product or service

2. A transitional phrase

3. The benefits the feature provides

4. Evidence to support your claims

5. A tie-down question to gain the prospect's agreement

Features and Benefits. *Features* are the tangible and intangible qualities of the product or service you sell. Features are facts that are the same no matter who uses the product or service. The tangible features of a product include observable factors such as color, size, capacity, speed of performance, material from which it is made—anything that can be detected through one of the five senses.[8] Intangible features are also important: the service given by the company, price, delivery, availability of service, and even the service and support that you promise.

Benefits, however, are the value or worth that the user derives from the product or service. Of the numerous benefits a product or service has to offer, only four or five will be key motivators to a prospect, and these will be different for each prospect.[9] Your task is to find out which ones are the key motivators.

Every feature of your product has numerous benefits. Remember, *one feature does not equal one benefit*. Examine the insert that follows and challenge your mind to perform some mental gymnastics to prove this point.

Every feature of your product has numerous benefits. Here's an exercise to give your mind a healthy benefit workout: What are the benefits of a 270-horsepower engine in a luxury car? They could include a smoother ride, power to spare when passing a slower car, quick acceleration away from a hazard, the feeling of being in charge, less wear and tear, higher resale value, etc. The point is, one feature does not equal one benefit. List your product's top ten features, and then come up with at least five different benefits for each feature. Remember, features only justify the price; benefits justify the purchase. This gives you 50 new ways to close more sales.

Transitional Phrase. The ability to translate features into benefits is one of the strengths of a relationship salesperson. Even if you know which feature can fulfill the buying motive, you cannot expect the prospect to make the connection automatically. You must make the verbal transition. The prospect does not know your product as well as you know it and has to have features and benefits connected by transitional phrases. Some salespeople call these *bridges*.[10] While the actual words may vary, they are all designed to accomplish the same purpose: To connect, in the prospect's thinking, features and benefits. These phrases all serve the purpose of answering the prospect's question, "What's in it for me?" Some common transitional phrases are:

"This is beneficial to you because . . ."

"This lets you . . ."

"This heads off all the problems of . . ."

"What this means to you . . ."

Begin preparation of units of conviction by listing in writing all the features of your product or service. If you sell more than one major product, make separate lists for each one. Then go back and list all the ways the first feature can benefit your prospect. If you neglect this preparatory step, you will find yourself confronting prospects who listen to the features you describe and ask, "So what?" and you will have no appealing answers. When you have prepared units of conviction in advance, finding the right one is just like reaching into your briefcase and pulling out a sample; you know what is there and all of it is at your fingertips for instant use when you need it.

Exhibit 11.4 shows an excellent features and benefits chart prepared by the Intersystems Ensemble™, a line of integration software used in hospitals to increase productivity by adding rich Web interfaces and more adaptable workflow systems.[11] Notice the positive language and use of words and phrases like "reduces costs," "reliable," and "provides" in the benefits.

Δ Exhibit 11.4

Unique Features and Benefits of Intersystems Ensemble Software

Features
1. Messaging engine

2. Advanced abstraction technology

3. Rapid integration & development environment

4. Data transformations

5. Business activity monitoring

6. Adaptable workflow engine

Benefits
1. Rapid and reliable solutions with publish/subscribe, event driven, and content-based routing; ease of modification and management of routing rules using a graphical rules editor for programmers and business analysts.

2. Provides an efficient representation of different programming models and data formats; enables access to multiple database management systems as a single "federated" database.

3. Works with languages and tools already familiar to developers; simplifies and accelerates modeling and automating of business processes for business analysts and developers.

4. Speeds project completion by eliminating barriers raised by differences in semantics and data schemas between applications or services; reduces the learning curve and speeds transformation development.

5. Immediate awareness of business events and changes in key performance indicators; Reduces costs and speeds execution of business strategies.

6. Better task execution accountability; tasks can be reused easily in any business process.

Evidence to Support Claims. Just as you present benefits to head off the prospect's question "So what?" about the features of your product or service, you must present evidence to support the claims you make to head off the questions "Can you prove it?" and "Who says so?" Even if you have been unusually successful in establishing a high degree of credibility and trust with the prospect, you are unlikely to be looked upon as an all-knowing sage with all the answers whose statements are to be accepted without question. You must be prepared to back up what you say with: (1) demonstrations, (2) testimonials, (3) facts and statistics, (4) samples, and (5) examples or case histories.

1. Demonstrations. Show the product being used. The demonstration is especially effective for some types of prospects if they have hands-on use in the demonstration. Audio and stereo salespeople encourage prospects to listen to their speakers to hear the high definition sound. Furniture salespeople suggest that prospects sit on the furniture and experience its comfort. Some office machines are left with the prospect for several days' trial.

2. Testimonials. The best possible testimonial is for one of your satisfied customers to call the prospect ahead of time and suggest that you be given an appointment. At this time, your customer expresses satisfaction with the product or service; this predisposes the prospect to accept what you say. Other types of testimonials are also effective with the right type of prospect. Use customers' letters expressing their pleasure with your product and the service you have provided. Such letters are easy to get. Just ask for them! You may even write the testimonial yourself and ask the prospect to read and sign it to save the client's time and make sure the letter is worded to fit your needs. When a client thanks you for some help, just say you would appreciate a letter saying the same thing. This kind of testimonial is especially helpful when it comes from a person who has influence in the community or with the particular prospect or when it is written on the letterhead of a respected company. You may have pictures of your clients using your product, with their signatures on the back.

3. Facts and Statistics. Call attention to manufacturer's ratings, such as the energy ratings of air-conditioning and heating units and the estimated mpg ratings of automobiles. Show earnings of stocks or other investment vehicles over the past five years. The U.S. Census Bureau projects that the 65-and-older group will grow 75 percent by the year 2050. Hispanics over 65 will increase by 150 percent, faster than any other ethnic group in that age bracket. This type of niche marketing information is useful to a wide variety of companies in various industries.[12]

4. Samples. A sample of the product itself or of the material from which it is made gives the prospect something concrete to use as the basis of decision- making. Supermarkets offer customers a taste of a featured food: Cheese, sausage, pizza—anything that can be served from a small table, cooked in an electric frying pan, or stuck on the end of a toothpick. The demonstrator then displays the food item and asks the customer to try it. A salesperson for operating room scrubs for hospitals might give the purchasing agent a swatch of the material from which they are made to feel as the quality is described. Samples are intended to provide an appeal to one or more of the five senses.

5. Examples or Case Histories. The use of examples or case histories is another way to present the satisfaction of other clients and customers. You may tell the prospect about other people whose circumstances are similar and how you were able to solve their problems or how they are enjoying some benefit from using the product. Use these guidelines when planning this type of evidence:

- The case history must be authentic. It should be about someone the prospect knows or can contact for verification.

- Use many details to let the prospect know you are intimately familiar with the situation.

- Back up the example with pictures, personal letters, newspaper articles, and other evidence.

- Relate it directly to the prospect's circumstances.

The evidence used to back up the features and benefits you present must be as carefully tailored to the needs, problems, and personality of the prospect as the features and benefits themselves. For example, use cost-saving evidence for a prospect who is especially interested in economy; but use testimonials from prominent people for a prospect who is largely motivated by the desire for status. Use everything you know about the prospect as input for every step in the sales process.

The Tie-Down. The "tie-down" is an essential step in building units of conviction, although it usually consists of no more than a single question that asks for the prospect's agreement. Your goal is to translate features into benefits for the prospect, to provide the necessary evidence to prove your points, and to gain a commitment to act. Here are some examples of tie-down questions:

- *Considering these facts, you agree with me that this is a safe tire, don't you, Ms. Craft?*

- *I believe you will agree with me, Mr. Sanders, that this is a better way for handling this process than your present method, won't you?*

- *I think you can get an idea of the enormous advantage you will have with one-tenth of a minute billing, can't you, Ms. Grimmett?*

The tie-down is important throughout the presentation to check on understanding and agreement and to make sure the prospect is ready to proceed to the next point. One of the functions of the tie-down is to ask a series of questions, all of which the prospect can be expected to answer yes. Then when you attempt a close, the prospect more easily says yes again. Suppose, however, that you ask, "You agree with me about this, don't you?" and the prospect says, "No, I don't." Where are you now? You are in a better position than you were before you asked the question because you now know you have a problem. Had you not asked this question and found out about the lack of agreement, you would have pushed on to the close and to failure. Now you are warned about the existence of a problem and can go back to find its source and correct it, ask another tie-down question, and move forward again when agreement is reached.

Exhibit 11.5 is a complete unit of conviction developed by a long-distance telephone service for their sales force to use. Notice the tie-down at the end—the question that leads the prospect into agreement.

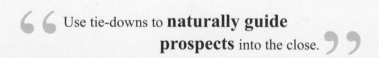
Use tie-downs to **naturally guide prospects** into the close.

Δ Exhibit 11.5

Unit of Conviction: Long-Distance Telephone Service ·

Feature	We offer one-tenth of a minute billing on your long-distance telephone service. A lot of other companies bill in full minute increments.
Transitional Phrase	What this means is...
Benefit	On a call of 3 minutes and 6 seconds, for example, other companies would bill you for 4 minutes. We would bill you for only 3.1 minutes. This will provide you with a significant cost savings on your monthly telephone bill or will give you the luxury of increased service at the same cost.
Evidence (Facts and Statistics)	Here's an illustration of the extra savings you could receive: If a call is billed at the rate of 25¢ per minute, our charge would be approximately 78¢ for 3.1 minutes. The same call, when billed at 4 minutes, would cost you $1.00—an increase of 22¢. Of course, not all calls would save you this much because some would save you only three-tenths or one-tenth of a minute instead of nine-tenths of a minute. But for someone whose business relies as heavily on long-distance as yours, the savings could be enormous. Even a few cents saved per call would be a sizable amount.
Tie-down	I think you can get an idea of the enormous advantage you will have with one-tenth of a minute billing, can't you, Mr. Carter?

Effective Presentation Tactics

You have the option of approaching the task of telling your story to the prospect using a variety of sales tactics. Which tactics you choose depend upon what you have learned about the prospect during preapproach qualification, what you observe in the opening minutes of the interview, what you personally want to do, and what kind of environment you find in the interview location. The only limit to the number of different presentation tactics is your own creative imagination. The most common tactics are presented here; you will use all of them at one point or another as they fit into your sales activity. You will probably find yourself developing your own personal mixture of tactics—a blend that fits your personality, your product, and the needs of your prospects.

Participation

Every presentation—no matter how it is organized or what other method is used—must get the prospect involved in the selling process. When prospects are shut out of the presentation process or choose to remain aloof, say nothing, and contribute nothing, they also buy nothing.

The prime tactic for gaining the participation of the prospect is asking questions and then listening to the answers. Plan the questions to be asked during the presentation to gain maximum participation by the prospect.

Beyond asking questions yourself, you should encourage prospects to ask questions about any benefit of the product you present or any factor involved in its application or use. Their questions prevent misunderstanding and give you the opportunity to direct your presentation to the problem or need that is most important to them.

Demonstration

Showmanship sells if it is more than mere carnival hoopla. There is a big difference between showmanship and *show-off-manship*. A well-timed dramatic touch seizes and holds the prospect's attention. A demonstration is an effective method of adding showmanship to the presentation while achieving the purpose of the presentation. A good demonstration provides you with these benefits:[13]

1. Catches the buyer's interest

2. Strengthens your selling points

3. Helps the prospect understand the proposition

4. Stimulates your own interest

5. Cuts down on the number of objections

6. Helps you close the sale

The value of a demonstration is that it involves more than one of the physical senses in the selling process. Remember these three points when determining how you will deliver your message to the prospect:

Use a hands-on demonstration to capture the prospect's interest.

1. If you rely solely on "telling" the prospect about your product, only the auditory sense is involved. If you add a demonstration, you include the visual sense.

2. If you involve the prospect in the demonstration, you add the sense of touch. The more of the senses you can involve, the more quickly the prospect absorbs the information that leads to a sale.

3. People remember 20 percent of what they hear and 20 percent of what they see. But they remember 50 percent of what they see and hear. By mapping your information out visually, you unquestionably increase how much your clients retain.[14]

Here are four principles to follow in using a demonstration as a part of your sales presentation:

Concentrate the Prospect's Attention on You. The CEO of a large corporation once called a meeting of his associates in his office. When they came in, he was juggling several tennis balls. Finally, he tossed aside all but one and said, "We all have many things on our minds—like these tennis balls. But we must put them aside and concentrate on one problem at a time or we'll waste time trying to juggle them all." This demonstration illustrates the situation when you go to call on a prospect. You must focus the prospect's attention on one thing—what you are saying. A planned demonstration is an excellent tool for accomplishing this purpose.

Follow the "Tell 'Em Three Times" Rule. At the beginning of a presentation: 1) tell prospects what you're going to be sharing with them 2) then tell it to them during the demonstration and finally 3) at the end, tell them what you just told them. This is probably the oldest rule in speechmaking—and with good reason. Because it works. It makes it easier for your listeners to follow the details and easier for you to stick to the point.[15]

When you fill your prospects in on the agenda and key points in your introduction, you send a signal as to what "files" your audience should open in their minds. When you cover the points in the body of your presentation, you place the data you wish them to comprehend and retain in those "files" they have opened. When you repeat the salient points at the end, you are essentially hitting the "save" button and reinforcing the data already presented. Remember that your prospect, unlike the reader of a written document, cannot "re-read" a passage they did not comprehend or look up a word not understood.[16] Consequently, a built-in redundancy is necessary to have your message understood.

Get Your Prospect Into the Act. Invite the prospect to operate your device, taste your food, smell the fragrance, feel the depth of the tread on the tires, or listen to the quiet sound of your machine in operation. If you are selling an intangible, hand the prospect photos, charts, or a prospectus. Get as many senses as possible involved. The Gulf Coast Regional Blood Center in Houston asks a prospect to put a thirty-letter word puzzle together. The sales representative hands the prospect a small box full of letters that, when properly arranged, spell: **WILL YOU HAVE BLOOD WHEN YOU NEED IT?** This demonstration dramatically illustrates how crucial a company-sponsored blood drive is to the community and to individuals. Read exhibit 11.6 below to see how one salesperson gets her prospects involved in the demonstration.[17]

Δ **Exhibit 11.6**

Not Another Boring Presentation ·

Here is an example of how Amber Sherrill, a salesperson for a shipping services and supplies company in Los Angeles really gets her prospects' interest:

Amber: *You can forget about damage to your merchandise when you ship in our cartons. Watch this.* (Amber slams a sealed carton that her company makes on the floor several times and then proceeds to hit the carton with a metal chair.)

Upon opening the carton, Amber exclaims: *Glass, as delicate a piece of merchandise as you'll ever ship, is still in perfect condition. Here, let's take a look.*

(After the prospect examines the glass, Amber continues): *This protection is provided by the specially designed, double-corrugated walls that give the utmost in protection.*

Amber says that few prospects can say no to such a visually appealing demonstration of such a strong product. She states, "Anyone can say a box is strong. I prove it, and I get the prospect involved in the process."

Paint a Mental Picture Using Metaphors. Metaphors imply comparisons between otherwise dissimilar things without using the words "like" or "as", often creating a dramatic visual image. Remember, "facts tell, stories sell." Painting a mental picture is a hook that grabs prospects and reels them in. Steve Becker, west regional manager for Amersham Life Science, has used this creative metaphor with prospects:

Picture yourself in a desert without a canteen. In the distance you see a water well. There's a bucket with a rope nearby. Now, would you jump into the well headfirst or would you use the bucket and rope? What my firm can do for you is supply you with the bucket and rope—the tools you need to succeed.

Metaphors, analogies and similes can bring special life to sales presentations. These are effective ways to reinforce concepts, while building rapport and winning people over to your way of thinking.[18]

Presentation Sales Tools

Sales aids fall mainly into the categories of audio, visual, or audiovisual. Many people are visually oriented. That's why exciting, illustrative slides, overheads, and computer-driven programs are effective presentation tools. Sales aids are used primarily to help the prospect visualize or otherwise experience the benefits of the product or service or to help you organize the presentation so that your prospect receives an ordered, logical message that is easily remembered.

The Organizer or Flip Chart

Companies may provide their salespeople with standard visual sales kits in the form of a small flip chart suitable for standing on a desk or in the form of a ring binder. When such an organizer is provided, a planned sales presentation usually accompanies the visual and is coordinated with it. The presentation and visual help you cover all the features and benefits and overcome objections. The organizer not only provides additional input for the prospect but also prompts your memory about what to cover next and keeps the interview on track. A well-designed organizer has these characteristics:

1. It is built around user benefits.

2. It fosters two-way communication because you can concentrate on listening attentively to the prospect rather than worry about what to say next.

3. It increases the closing rate by leading naturally to that point.

4. It helps you tell the complete story in less time.

5. It helps the interview get back on track after an interruption by reminding both you and prospect what was being discussed.

Although the company-prepared organizer is a good beginning tool, most successful salespeople develop additional visuals that are useful for their personal style and type of selling. Here are some of the visuals you can prepare for yourself:

1. Letters from existing customers expressing satisfaction with the product, the company's responsiveness, and your personal service.

2. Business cards of existing clients, preferably with a note thanking the salesperson for service.

3. Pictures of clients actually using the product.

4. Pictures of product installations in customers' plants or offices.

Exhibit 11.7 gives guidelines for preparing visuals.[19]

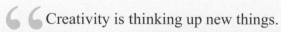

" Creativity is thinking up new things.
Innovation is doing new things. "

-Theodore Levitt

Δ **Exhibit 11.7**

Guidelines for Preparing Visuals ·

- Keep your visuals simple.
- Don't use complete sentences. Text should be in short phrases.
- Leave plenty of white space and place text in a similar location on each slide or overhead.
- Use colors that are functional, not decorative. Colors should be easy on the eyes (use red sparingly).
- Never put the whole presentation on a visual and simply read it to the prospect.
- Tables or charts with complex data must only be used for groups that need to study the information closely.
- Each chart or graph should present only one idea at a time to ensure clear understanding.
- Use *line charts* to show how several variables change over time.
- *Bar charts* show relationships between two or more variables.
- *Pie charts* are used to show relationships among parts of a whole at a given point in time.

Audiovisual Presentations

For presenting complicated equipment or processes and for presenting to a group instead of a single prospect, audiovisual aids are especially helpful. However, they may also be effective with one-on-one sales presentations. Some of the most common audiovisual presentations involve computers, video, or slides. Computers can be used to produce multimedia presentations on a laptop screen or a portable video projector.

Current technology is rapidly producing hardware that enables salespeople to use audiovisual aids under almost any conditions. Presentation software gives professional salespeople the ability to create, modify, and customize their presentations easily and inexpensively. Numerous software packages produce graphs, charts, or other artistic renderings of data. Salespeople find such graphics useful in sales presentations. For instance, sales reps for ABC's TV stations now use laptop computers and the Internet to generate charts and graphs showing up-to-the-minute demographics, Nielsen ratings, and product-usage data. They can put together a thirty-chart presentation in less than two hours. A salesperson can communicate a message quickly, accurately, and dramatically with graphics like these.[20]

Developing Partnerships Using Technology illustrates several options for computer-based presentations. Just a few years ago, the only tools a marketer had to prepare a visual-aid presentation were flip charts, slides, and overheads. Today, salespeople have a variety of presentation tools at their disposal.

Developing Partnerships Using Technology

Customizing Graphical Presentations with Your Laptop Computer

Presentation Software. Echo 3 has a presentation manager and media library management system that makes every video, slide, overhead, brochure, electronic presentation, and audio file created by a sales organization available with a few keystrokes. Instead of reinventing the wheel each time they present to a prospect or client, salespeople can access existing presentations done by their peers and customize them for a particular presentation.

Smart Phones. Cell phones with Internet access and handheld computers are a must for salespeople. These tools can give you an edge on the competition by communicating with clients quickly and more effectively, accessing product and order status information, and staying on top of your schedule.

Pen-based Computers. These are especially effective for individual presentations. It works much like a pen and paper, except it's a computer LCD screen with a pen-shaped stylus. With the touch of the pen, the salesperson can bring up any information the prospect may need. The system reads your handwriting and translates it into text that can be edited, manipulated, and saved. Many larger companies—especially in the financial services sector—now supply these to their sales forces.

Check out these Web sites for additional information:
www.info@echo3newmedia.com

www.maximizer.com

www.saleslogix.com

www.microsoft.com/outlook/

Spice Up Your PowerPoint Presentation. Salespeople should try to put some sparkle in their presentations; but avoid turning them into a three-ring circus. In other words, use some bells and whistles without going overboard. A little color and some type-font changes can spruce up a presentation. There are a lot of electronic devices and special effects available today to create what is anything but a boring slide show. For example, liven up your PowerPoint presentations with tools to grab your client's attention such as spinning titles, TV-style transitions, and animated photographs.[21] You should try to make the presentation interactive, fun, and as concise as possible without eliminating main points. Exhibit 11.8 discusses another new and innovative idea for your presentations.

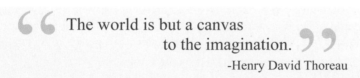

> " The world is but a canvas to the imagination. "
> -Henry David Thoreau

Δ **Exhibit 11.8**

VOI Protocol—Voice on the Internet ·

A new technology called Brainshark™ uses the power of voice mail with the convenience of a PowerPoint presentation. You upload PowerPoint slides onto the Web site, then call a special telephone number and record your message to be delivered in synch with each slide. You use your telephone keypad as the record, play, rewind, and erase buttons. Once the slides are narrated, you can forward the presentation to a prospect or targeted audience. Tony Swierkot, marketing manager for Ricoh Company Ltd. in Canada, used it to send a presentation to Ricoh's sales force. The sales reps were delighted because the technology allowed them to actually hear the presentation from one of their own sales managers.[22]

Mimio™ is a portable tool produced by Virtual Ink Corporation. What is it? It's a durable plastic arm that, when attached via suction cups to any regular whiteboard, turns it into an electronic interactive whiteboard.[23] Hook up your computer and flip on your projector, and the whiteboard basically becomes a large computer screen where you can run a PowerPoint presentation, access the Internet, or take notes that are automatically saved onto your computer. Need to do some computations for your clients? Simply pull up an Excel spreadsheet, tap on an empty cell, jot a number on the board, and the moment you stop writing the number will pop into the cell as if you've just typed it there.

Situational Selling

Master salespeople have a specific plan for every sales interview, but they never feel slavishly bound by that plan. Relationship selling requires flexibility. No matter how much you learn about a prospect before you appear for the interview, you can never be absolutely sure what kind of situation to expect when you arrive. Instead of finding a calm, receptive prospect ready to listen and evaluate your product, you may find one who is angry, resentful, or emotional. If planning has been adequate, you can shift gears and make a different kind of presentation, switch to another purpose for the interview, or even delay the presentation until a better time.

Bill Hamilton finds his handheld computer ideal when making sales calls. This way he doesn't walk into a buyer's office "lugging equipment" during the initial call. Instead, he can reach into his pocket and be prepared to take an order, calculate it, offer "what ifs," and make any changes right on the spot.[24] The ability to exercise this type of flexibility is called *situational selling*—fitting yourself to the situation and making each contact with the prospect beneficial to your ultimate purpose of closing a sale.

The Setting

Where the sales interview takes place is often a vital factor in determining its success. The prospect's own office is usually the best place if interruptions can be controlled. If the prospect has a private office, the door can be closed and calls can be held. The prospect feels at ease and in control in familiar surroundings and is not required to put forth effort or travel time to accommodate you. You are a guest and automatically a person to be treated politely and with respect.

If your information tells you that this prospect customarily tries to control every interview and every person, however, you might decide that meeting at a place where you are the host or even on neutral turf would give you more potency. Some salespeople make effective use of what is called a power lunch. Inviting the prospect to lunch at a carefully selected restaurant gives you an opportunity to present your product or service with several distinct advantages:

- You are away from an office where interruptions may occur.

- You are the host, and the prospect, as your guest, feels obligated to listen politely.

- The atmosphere is nonthreatening.

- Relaxing over the meal relieves some of the stress of making a decision.

Interruptions

No matter how carefully you schedule an interview, your best-laid plans often go astray. Asking the prospect at the beginning of the interview if the secretary could hold all routine calls until later can prevent many interruptions. This tells the prospect that you believe the interview is more important than routine matters, but that you know some important duties could take precedence over the interview.

When preapproach information indicates that a particular prospect's duties involve continuous supervision of a work group's activities or that the prospect does not have a private office, consider arranging the interview away from that environment. When an interruption does occur, your sense of timing will tell you whether the discussion can be resumed or whether scheduling a later interview would be better.

If you decide to continue, summarize what has been said up to the point of the interruption. If a problem or need has been identified, state it again and ask a question designed to gain the prospect's agreement. Review in more detail the last major point made in your presentation, and again check for agreement or commitment by asking a question. Be sure the prospect is back on track and is following your planned path of reasoning. If you decide to come back later, attempt to set up a time for the interview. If the interruption is caused by some real crisis that demands the prospect's immediate attention, say you will come again later and leave so that the prospect may give full attention to the urgent problem.

When you do come back, begin the presentation all over. You can safely assume that the interruption has probably completely erased the effect you had built. Preface points with phrases like these: "You will remember that we discussed," "As I told you the other day," or "I believe you told me that." Intersperse your remarks with questions that check on what the prospect remembers, and you can quickly discover what needs to be repeated in depth and what can be quickly reviewed.

Let's review in detail what we discussed last time.

SUMMARY

- You can memorize a presentation or use an outline that allows you to present each of your selling points in an orderly and systematic way.

- Personalize each presentation to the needs of the prospect. One of the most important tactics available is prospect participation.

- One way to choose what you will present is to develop units of conviction. Each unit of conviction includes:

  - A feature of your product or service

  - A transitional phrase

  - The benefits the feature provides

  - Evidence to support your claims

  - A tie-down to gain agreement

- Sales aids include all sorts of visuals and audiovisuals. Many people are visually oriented, which is why exciting, illustrative slides, overheads, and graphics are effective presentation tools.

- Interruptions represent anything that distracts the prospect's attention from your message. The setting of the sales interview requires that you be prepared to take advantage of any situation. You must learn to control these distractions and transform them into buying opportunities.

REVIEW QUESTIONS

1. Describe the types of evidence that may be used to back up a claim.

2. Define "salesman's curse." Why is it a problem?

3. How does a salesperson learn to personalize units of conviction? Why is this important?

4. Distinguish between a feature and a benefit. Why is it important to know both?

5. What is a tie-down and why is it an important part of the sales presentation?

6. How can a novice salesperson prevent a memorized sales presentation from sounding memorized?

7. Why must the prospect become involved in the selling process?

8. What are the pros and cons of using a well-designed organizer as an integral part of your sales presentation?

9. What self-prepared visuals could be used by a salesperson selling a landscaping service?

10. How can a salesperson get back on track after an interruption?

ROLE-PLAY EXERCISES

The following role-play exercises help build teams, improve communication, and emphasize the "real-world" side of selling. They are meant to be challenging, to learn how to deal with problems that have no single "right" answer and to use a variety of skills beyond those employed in a typical review question. Read and complete each activity. Then in the next class, discuss and compare answers with other classmates. Have some students take the role of the salesperson, and see how they would react. Remember, *"You learn more about a person in an hour of play than in a lifetime of conversation."* - Plato

1. Choose three products advertised in a magazine you read. Name two features with corresponding benefits for each product.

2. Prepare a short demonstration of some product to share with the class. Suggestions: food items, cleaning products, laptop computer, small appliance or tool.

3. Visit several stores to shop for a MP3 player, some new make-up, a waterbed, or some other product that could be demonstrated. Report on the demonstration techniques used by the salesperson and evaluate them.

CASE STUDY

Case 11.1 - Words That Sell

Anita Watson is a designer-salesperson for a leading manufacturer of office furniture. She tells how a personal shopping experience early in her sales career showed her why she seemed to be floundering and put her on the road to success.

When her old TV quit, Anita and her husband decided the time had come to get high definition. They went first to a store that carried a well-known brand. They knew it would be expensive, but they were quality-oriented and more interested in value than in price. Right away, Anita saw a flat screen that would fit perfectly into the decor of their den. They hunted up a clerk (notice she didn't say salesperson) and here was the entire sales pitch: "This is a very good set. It has a clear picture and vivid color. It's a good buy." Both Anita and her husband reacted the same way. Almost in unison, they said, "Let's look around some more."

The next store they visited also handled a top brand. They saw a beautiful TV with a bigger screen than the first one they had liked. Anita's husband—a rabid football fan— said, "Boy, the Cleveland Browns and their dog pound will really look great on that big screen." Anita watched the salesperson approach and hoped he would be wishy-washy, too. The set was obviously the most expensive in the place, and she had forgotten they wanted a new surround sound system. "There goes our budget," she thought to herself.

However, this salesperson's approach was different. "I can't blame you for admiring that amazing flatscreen. It will blend into any contemporary room. But I'm sure you are also interested in bright, true-to-life color and digital sound. XYZ's screen gives clear pictures and true sound with just one press of a button. Here, let me show you." He turned on the set and let it do the rest of the selling job almost by itself. Then he added the final touch: "You may think that we have a special antenna or booster here at the store, so I want to assure you that if you don't get the same performance with a regular antenna, we'll take the set back and refund your money." That evening, Anita thought about the two salespeople they had met. Her sales had not been very good lately, and if the old TV had not conked out, they probably would not have considered spending money on a new one. So Anita tried a little trick that had worked for her before. She sat down in front of her dressing table and talked to herself in the mirror. "OK," she lectured herself, "you heard with your own ears what a terrible sales talk does even when the customer wants to buy. Then you heard a top-notch professional use a few colorful words and demonstration. And you bought! What have you been saying to your prospects?"

Anita replayed her interview with a real estate agent who was moving to a larger, plusher office in the new bank building. Anita had looked at the plans for the office space and figured she could concentrate on the top of the line. She recalled saying, "Obviously, Mr. Keller, you believe in doing things right. I have just the right furniture for this fine office. Not only is it stylish, but all pieces are made from quality material. It's not only comfortable, but it's practical, too. I can do the whole job for you, including sales offices, secretarial and filing needs, and an attractive reception area. Take a look at this catalog and tell me which style you prefer."

Anita looked herself straight in the eye. "And which did he prefer? None, of course. So what are you going to do about it?" Obviously, Anita found a good answer because she is now one of the top salespeople in her company. In fact, prospects sometimes call the company and ask for her to come talk about furniture for a redecorating project because they have heard from business acquaintances what a good job she did for them.

1. What kinds of measures do you think Anita took to transform her sales performance? Name several ways she could have solved her problem.

2. Suggest some resources a salesperson in Anita's position could use to improve her ability to make a good presentation.

Case 11.2 - The Glad Hand

A common problem of salespeople is dealing with a person who acts as a buffer to keep them from seeing the real decision maker who can buy their product or service. The buffer is usually pleasant, listens politely, asks a few questions, accepts brochures, and then says good-bye in a friendly manner. You could visit with the buffer a dozen times and be no closer to an order.

Pam Davis, a veteran salesperson of graphic arts services, seems to meet a lot of these buffers. For some reason, advertising executives, the prime prospects for graphic arts services, seem to be among the foremost users of buffers. Just last week, Davis called on the Mercury Manufacturing Company, a firm that does a large volume of advertising. She asked for Mr. Warner, the advertising manager. The receptionist called his office and then said, "Mr. Warner is not available, but his assistant, Mr. Bailey, will be right down."

"Here we go again," Pam groaned inwardly. The assistant was an affable young man with a firm handshake. He listened politely as Pam explained the services her firm provided: engraving, retouching, illustrations, and finished artwork. He agreed that Mercury's extensive ad program called for such services, but said they were satisfied with their current suppliers. Pam showed him her portfolio of samples of her company's work, but he said again that they really didn't need another supplier but would be glad to take her card and call her if they need anything.

"The old brush-off again," Pam said to herself. "I'd really like to have a slice of their business. They do more advertising than any other manufacturer in the area."

1. What is the major problem, and what options does Pam have?

2. Could Pam have had a better result with better planning prior to making this call?

CHAPTER 12

Handling Objections

LEARNING OBJECTIVES

- Develop a positive attitude toward objections.

- Understand why prospects have sales resistance.

- Learn how to uncover hidden concerns or questions.

- Know the basic strategies for overcoming sales resistance.

- Become familiar with the six-step plan for dealing with sales resistance.

- Learn specific techniques to overcome objections.

- Discover tactics to handle price concerns.

The problem with the word objection is that it conjures up an adversarial relationship between the salesperson and the prospect—someone must win and someone must lose. Just mentioning the word may send some sales veterans into a state of panic or anxiety. But what many fail to understand is a "no" and an objection are two vastly different things. The most successful salespeople look positively at the objections prospects offer. Objections move prospects nearer to the close and reveal what they are concerned about. An objection often reveals the key to closing the sale.

> ❝ **Always bear in mind that your own resolution to succeed is more important than any one thing.** ❞
> **-Abraham Lincoln**

If the prospect has been properly qualified, objections are really buying signals. Offering an objection is another way for the prospect to say, "Here are my conditions for buying," or "I want to buy as soon as you answer a few more questions or reassure me that buying is the smart thing to do." Welcome objections! They are the verbal and nonverbal signs of sales resistance that give you the chance to discover what the prospect is thinking. These objections later become leverage for closing the sale.[1]

Objections actually indicate that the prospect is interested in what you are saying. Successful sales presentations, those that end in a sale, have twice as many objections as those presentations that are unsuccessful.[2] Qualified prospects will not raise objections to a proposal in which they have no interest. They simply wait and say no.

Defining Objections

An *objection* is anything the prospect says or does that presents an obstacle to the smooth completion of the sale. Sounds simple enough, right? It's not quite that easily defined due to the fact that sales resistance, or an objection, contains elements of both logic and emotion. When people really want something, logic goes out the window and emotion takes control, and the heart tends to rule the head when it comes to making decisions.

Objections are a normal and natural part of almost every conversation—not just in sale situations, but whenever people discuss any current topic. Without this resistance to buying, there would be no need for salespeople.[3] A purchasing decision usually involves risk. To ease the fear of risk, people object, raise concerns, or ask questions in hopes of getting answers that will convince them that the buying decision is in their best interests. Objections are so common that research indicates a prospect will say "no" at least five times before they actually buy.[4]

The first task in answering an objection is to calm the prospect's emotions by proving that you are open to reason. Pause before responding; then acknowledge that you respect the prospect's opinion and find the views expressed worthy of consideration.[5] People are open to changing their opinions and attitudes when they are convinced that others value their opinions, understand how they can feel that way, and grant them the right to those opinions.[6] Show a measure of empathy; thus, the key to maintaining a positive sales environment is to *disagree without being disagreeable*.[7]

Your purpose is to remove the objection without being objectionable. Arguing with a prospect, particularly in response to objections, is one of the easiest and most disastrous mistakes you can make. Remember that relationship selling is a win–win proposition. The negotiation process is not a battle that you win and the prospect

There is a vast difference between a "no" and an objection.

loses; rather, it is a situation of mutual cooperation and mutual benefit. You may well win the argument and prove that you are right, but lose the sale in the process. People who are forced to agree seldom actually change their minds. Never force a prospect into making a decision; prospects are more likely to stay sold and come back to you for repeat business if the decision to buy was their idea.

Types of Objections

The difficulty with objections is that they have the tendency to sound like obstacles that will stop the sale. When the prospect objects, you must understand what type of sales resistance is being offered before you can handle it effectively. Sales resistance may be separated into four general categories: the *searcher*, the *stopper*, the *hidden objection*, and the *stall* or *put-off*.

The Searcher

The first type of objection is called a *searcher*, which is a hidden request for additional information.[8] Some prospects object simply to get more information, even though they have already mentally decided that they want to buy. The customer just wants to be convinced that buying your product or service is the right thing to do.

Handle Searcher Concerns With Finesse

Responses to Four Common Searcher Objections:

1. **I'm not interested.**

    There is no reason why you should be interested until I show you how my service can help you make money and solve your problems. May I show you how the product can do that for you?

    Do you mean you are not interested at this time, or at all? I'll call back in four weeks; hopefully, things will be less hectic for you.

2. **I don't have the money for this.**

    I can certainly respect that. If I could show you two ways the product will pay for itself, would you be interested?

    If you did have the money, would you want it? Good! Allow me to present some facts and statistics illustrating just how affordable our product really is.

3. **We are satisfied with what we have now.**

    What do you like most about the product you are using now? Then demonstrate how your product is better.

    You don't like to change without a good reason, right? I can certainly understand that. Here are five reasons why more and more managers are switching to our online sales training material.

4. **I really like the competitor's product.**

    I am not surprised to hear you say that. Their product does have some interesting features. I know some of my happiest customers are people who used to own that other company's product.

The Stopper

Prospects often have legitimate reasons why they feel unable to buy. One type of valid objection is what might be called a *stopper*.[9] Even Houdini couldn't solve this one. The stopper is an objection to which no satisfactory solution can be found. For instance, if you can promise delivery no sooner than six months from now and the prospect absolutely must have the product in three months, you cannot—or at least, you should not—make that sale. Not every prospect is a fit for your product or service. This is inevitable, and if you encounter such a situation, simply recognize this and move on to a more qualified prospect with a real need for what you sell and the ability to buy.

The Hidden Objection

A third type of sales resistance is called the *hidden objection*. This kind of resistance is often more difficult to overcome. They can be defined as hidden problems or unspoken hesitations, which, if they are not addressed, can delay or prevent a sale.[10] The prospect refuses to let you know the real concern. Many times the reasons are actually quite personal, so the prospect prefers not to reveal it or has a vague feeling that cannot be articulated easily. Exhibit 12.1 pictures the hidden objection as an iceberg lurking below the surface. Just the tip of the iceberg is revealed. You know the prospect has a hidden objection when the answers fail to make sense.

△ **Exhibit 12.1**

The Hidden Objection

The reasons for not buying are not logical based on the interview up to that point. That means the prospect likely has other reasons for objecting that are not directly related to something specific in your presentation or your product. For example, a prospect may simply not feel comfortable revealing these four real concerns:

1. "Circumstances have changed since you first qualified me. Recent family problems have caused severe financial hardships, and I do not have the ability to pay for your product."

2. "I find this whole situation distasteful, and I don't want to deal with you. I don't like you, but social convention prevents my being blunt enough to tell you so."

3. "I really don't know what my objection is. It just doesn't feel right. Quite frankly, the product looks like a cheap imitation to me."

4. "I really wasn't in the market for your product. I just wanted to hear what you had to say for future reference."

The Stall or Put-Off

When the prospect offers a *stall* or *put-off* objection, look for the true meaning behind their words. Oftentimes, the prospect is simply trying to avoid making a decision.[11] However, you should rarely experience a stall if you have properly qualified a prospect at the beginning. The stall could mean that you have not presented a compelling enough reason to buy. A stall is a classic sales killer unless you can create a sense of urgency to buy NOW.[12] The stall is actually the prospect's way of saying, "I really don't want to think about your proposition right now because I would then be forced to make a decision." Here are some examples of how stalls are phrased by prospects:

1. "I have to leave in fifteen minutes; I have an important meeting."

2. "Just leave your literature with my secretary. I will look it over in the next day or so and then call you."

3. "I must talk this over with my partner."

How you handle a stall is really a test of your attitude. If you believe you have a qualified prospect whose needs will be satisfied by your product, then you do not allow a put-off to put you off. Here are some suggestions for responding to the stalls given above:

1. "We are both busy people. Can I have five minutes to show you something that would save you hundreds, perhaps thousands of dollars?"

2. "Mr. Ray, I thought that I had adequately covered the points summarized in the literature. Obviously, I have not made myself clear at some point. Would you tell me what I have not explained to your satisfaction?"

3. "I certainly understand wanting to involve your partner in a decision like this. Can we ask him to join us now, or may I drop by his office this afternoon?"[13]

The Heart of Sales Resistance

The relationship salesperson must get to the heart of the prospect's objection before it can be negotiated successfully. Before you can assemble the appropriate facts, logic, and evidence to resolve a vaguely stated objection, you must know the basis for the prospect's point of view.[14] To make intelligent responses to customer resistance, you must know the underlying circumstances.

Most objections that an experienced salesperson hears are not original. If you have been selling for any length of time, your chance of encountering an objection you have not heard before is remote. Eighty percent of buyers will give you the same five or six objections. You should therefore be ready to handle each one in advance, and have practiced them in a training course or sales meeting first.[15] Adopt the attitude described by Ana Barber, a top sales representative for Sportswear International in San Jose, California. When Ana hears an objection, she says to herself, "Hot Dog! Another sale!" Ana knows she has the knowledge and experience to answer every legitimate objection. Prior preparation and a servant's heart allow relationship-oriented sales pros like Ana Barber to adapt such positive attitudes toward objections.

To deal effectively with the objections you hear, develop a worksheet to categorize them and the responses you use to answer them effectively. Write out your responses word for word, commit them to memory, and practice delivering each one so that it becomes a responsive, intrinsic action. Polish and refine your responses; keep a record of how they are received. You will soon be able to choose the best possible response from your prepared list for each situation you encounter. Exhibit 12.2 lists six basic categories of buyer resistance with examples of what the prospect might say or, in the case of hidden objections, might think.

Δ Exhibit 12.2

Categories of Buyer Objections

Product Objection

- The materials are not up to industry standards.
- The product is poor quality.
- The product won't hold up over time.

Objection to Salesperson (Hidden)

- You are poorly prepared.
- I don't like you.
- You have tried to dominate me from the moment you arrived.

Company Objections

- Your company is not very well known; I prefer to deal with a large, established company.
- Wasn't your company charged with some unethical sales practices?

Aversion to Decision Making

- See me on your next trip.
- I want to think it over.
- We don't have room for your line.

Service Objection

- I can't live with your delivery schedule.
- We need same-day response on all service calls.
- Your maintenance contract doesn't meet our needs.

Price Objection (Possibly Hiding Real Objection)

- I can't afford it.
- Your pricing structure is out of line.
- I'm going to wait until prices come back down.

When To Answer Objections

A lot more has been said about how to overcome objections than about *when* to answer them, but choosing the proper time to answer them is just as crucial as the answer itself.[16] In determining when to answer an objection, you must consider the type, why it has been raised, the mood of the prospect, and in what phase of the interview it is raised. Timing is important in any negotiation. Prospects introduce an objection at a time that favors their position. Why shouldn't you choose to handle it when the timing favors your position? Normally, there are four logical times for responding to the buyer's concerns:

1. **Anticipate and forestall objections**
2. **Postpone the answer until later in the presentation.**
3. **Answer it immediately when it is raised.**
4. **Do not answer an excuse.**

Anticipate and Forestall Objections

Every product or service has both strengths and weaknesses. Because no product is perfect, a prospect may well identify a negative feature or shortcoming in what you sell. Hoping that the prospect will fail to notice a negative feature is futile. Instead of waiting for the prospect to raise a specific objection, anticipate the objection and forestall or answer it in the presentation before the prospect can ask. Just as companies want to stay ahead of the curve in technology and product advancements, you must strive to stay ahead of the "objection curve."[17]

Weave into your presentation factual answers to anticipated objections, so they are answered before the prospect verbalizes them. Anticipating objections requires a well-thought-out, planned presentation delivered from the prospect's point of view and focusing on value. Don't just identify potential roadblocks; spell out how to overcome them as well. The more obstacles you remove in advance, the easier it is for others to welcome your suggestions.[18]

As an example of how you might forestall objections that come up over and over again, consider the two objections Fred Bass, a venture capitalist in Phoenix, was constantly hearing from prospects: "I don't have the money" and "I have to talk this over with my (partner, wife, agent, etc.)." After the opening, get-acquainted chit-chat, Fred gets down to business by saying:

> *Mr. Timberlake, I am working with professional athletes who have enough discretionary income that they can invest at least $75,000 in a business venture they are convinced is sound and who can also make their own investment decisions without consulting someone else first. Do you fit into these conditions?*

This opener is perhaps a bit forceful, but Fred prefers not to spend 45 minutes presenting his proposition and then hear one of these familiar objections. Of course, dealing with an objection early in the presentation does not guarantee that it will not be raised again. However, you are at an advantage in such a situation for two reasons:

- The objection has much less impact the second time.
- You may recall the original answer, expand upon it, and then move on into a close or back into the presentation if necessary.

Postpone the Answer

Some answers to objections are better postponed. This tactic is logical when you are planning to cover that very point further along and the prospect has simply jumped ahead. To answer early might disrupt the flow of the presentation and make the answer less effective. For example, the prospect may ask about price. "How much is this going to cost me?" This often occurs before you have had the chance to establish the value of your product. If you answer immediately, the price may seem too high because the prospect has not yet learned enough about the product to make a value judgment. The price may depend upon options selected; in that case, you cannot quote an accurate price. You may need to build a better foundation before risking a confrontation with the prospect.[19] You can postpone answering an objection by saying something like this:

That's an excellent question, and I can certainly understand why you want to ask it. Let me write it down so I won't forget to answer it. And if you don't mind, let's postpone the answer until later. I have some information we need to consider first. Is that all right?

> **"Nothing will ever be attempted if all possible objections must be first overcome."**
>
> **- Samuel Johnson**

Salespeople often get price questions early in the interview. Here are two ways to postpone the premature price question:

1. I can appreciate that you would be interested in the price, and I assure you we will discuss it completely, but before we even consider the price, I want to be sure that my service can satisfy your needs. Will that be all right?

2. Mr. Winehouse, your concern for price is quite understandable. The actual amount paid for the product, however, will depend upon the options you ultimately select. Let's consider the price for the system after we establish the specific features you will require. Is that fair enough?

The price question should be answered near the end of the presentation, after need, value, and benefits have been discussed. Should the prospect absolutely insist that you answer immediately, then by all means do so. You do not want to risk the question remaining in his mind to block out everything else that follows.

Answer Immediately

Most valid objections should be answered when they are raised unless you have a logical reason to postpone them. If you feel the objection is valid and postponing an answer could cause problems, then obviously it should be handled immediately. Answering an objection right away prevents it from festering in your prospect's mind and blocking out the more important information you are presenting. Never answer until you are sure of the real concern, and once it is discovered, answer in 30 seconds or less. Answer questions briefly and honestly; be congenial and intelligent.[20] A sincere and immediate response conveys professionalism, respect for the prospect's point of view, empathy, and listening skills. The right answer removes the resistance and promotes the sale.

Do Not Answer an Excuse

A final alternative is to simply not answer an excuse. After all, some issues don't have a worthwhile answer. On some sales calls, prospects raise concerns that have nothing to do with your discussion. They say things that have no relevance to the point you are trying to make. In reality, they are offering excuses for not buying rather than valid resistance. Never try to answer an excuse. By acknowledging excuses, you may actually turn them into real objections in the prospect's mind. If you must reply to excuses, suggest to the prospect that you will answer them at the end of the presentation. If the question is a serious objection, the prospect will repeat it later. Exhibit 12.3 summarizes the factors to consider in choosing the best time to deal with objections.

Δ **Exhibit 12.3**

Timing Considerations for Objections ·

Anticipate the Objection and Answer It Before It Arises

• This option should be considered only when you are fairly certain that the prospect will bring up the objection.

• Anticipating the objection prevents a future confrontation and shows your objectivity.

Postpone an Answer Until Later

• Postponing an answer allows you to present many more benefits that have the effect of reducing the significance of the objection.

• Postponing an answer allows you to maintain control of the interview by keeping to your agenda rather than to that of the prospect.

• Postponing an answer gives you time to think about how you will answer it.

Answer the Objection Immediately

• Answer immediately so the prospect can concentrate on the rest of the sales story.

• Answering the prospect immediately shows them your sincerity.

• An immediate answer prevents prospects from inferring that you are unable to answer.

Do Not Answer an Excuse

• Not acknowledging an objection is one way to separate it from an excuse. The serious prospect will repeat it.

• By not answering, you suggest that the excuse is not relevant and imply that bringing it up again is not necessary.

A Six-Step Plan For Identifying Objections

Why do salespeople need specific plans to handle objections? The answer rests in maintaining control. If you allow a prospect to derail you from your presentation with every question or comment, you lose the power; and when this happens, your perceived value decreases—and so do your chances for making the sale.[21]

You can best handle prospects' objections successfully by first identifying them, and then placing them in the proper perspective—then the well-handled objections become powerful aids. To handle them skillfully, you need a definite negotiation strategy so that you react naturally to buyers' concerns. Knowing that you have a strategy gives you confidence; then you can welcome objections instead of shuddering at the very thought that the prospect may not go along with your proposition. The six-step plan presented in Exhibit 12.4 should be internalized so that you use it instinctively and automatically.

> **Wars are not won by *fighting* battles.**
> **Wars are won by *choosing* battles.**
> -General George Patton

△ **Exhibit 12.4**

······················· **A Strategic Plan for Overcoming Buyer Concerns**

1. **Listen carefully and hear the prospect out**. Learning to listen is not difficult, just unusual. We were born with two ears and one tongue. Listen twice as much as you talk. The buyer will tell you what you need to know. Just listen!

2. **Confirm your understanding of the objection**. The key is to clarify and classify the objection. What type of objection is it and into what category does it fall?

3. **Acknowledge the prospect's point of view**. Prepare the prospect for your answer. Don't just tear into your answer. After all, the buyer must have a reason for stating the objection. Show concern for his or her feelings. Practice empathy.

4. **Select a specific technique**. No one technique works best for all prospects. It must fit your behavioral style as well as that of the prospect.

5. **Answer the objection**. The answer must satisfy the buyer if a sale is to result, and it must be complete. Get a commitment from the prospect.

6. **Attempt to close**. If the close is not completed, continue the presentation. After answering a major objection, ask for the order. The worst that can happen is that the buyer will say no. If that happens, continue with the presentation.

Plan to overcome (answer and resolve) objections.

Hear the Prospect Out

Be happy when the prospect raises an objection, because it provides the information needed to complete the negotiation. Never interrupt a prospect who is expressing an opinion; rather, listen carefully to what the prospect says. Observe the prospect's verbal and nonverbal behavior, and listen to what is not being said. Recognize the prospect's right to express opinions and concerns. The prospect is really telling you what to do, and their objection is actually saying to you:

"Give me more information."

"Go over that service agreement again—it wasn't clear."

"Reassure me one more time that this is a good decision."

Simply paying attention is the first step in becoming more responsive to your prospect's objections. Active listening will help you to better respond to what your prospect is really saying. If you really listen, then you can pinpoint what the source of the objection is. This type of listening, called active listening, will help you to better explain the ways your product or service can be of value to the prospect.[22]

Confirm Your Understanding of the Objection

Restate the prospect's objection to make sure you understand just what it is; this is a critical negotiation tactic. Use your own words and repeat what the prospect was saying to clarify and classify the real objection, and to indicate to the prospect that you understood what was said. In addition, you give yourself time to formulate an answer. Restating the objection in a sympathetic manner dissolves the prospect's defensiveness and helps you avoid the temptation to argue. Say, "Now as I understand it, your position is... ," and then explain the prospect's position in your own words. When you prove you understand, the prospect is ready to listen to you.

Your purpose in this phase is to evaluate and isolate the stated concern. Determine whether the reason given for not buying is the real reason, simply an excuse, or a statement hiding the actual objection. You may decide to answer immediately, not answer an excuse, or seek more information. If you need more information before you can answer, ask questions until you have the information you need. There are a number of questions you might ask the prospect that can help you isolate the real issue and confirm your understanding.[23] They include:

1. Other than that, is there any other reason that would prevent you from purchasing?

2. I am glad you brought that out into the open. Is this your only concern?

3. If we can work together to find a solution to this important concern, would that help you make a purchase decision?

It may help to ask the prospect to explain the objection. At times, the prospect may not know fully what they are objecting to, and explaining it will help clarify the issue for both you and the prospect.

Acknowledge the Prospect's Point of View

All successful negotiations find points of agreement with the prospect before you begin to answer an objection. Agree as far as possible before answering, and take responsibility for any misunderstanding. If the prospect indicates a bad experience with your company or your predecessor, believe it. Find a way to cushion your response so that it has a chance of convincing the prospect. After all, prospects believe they have good reasons for not buying and give you those reasons. Instead of arguing directly, soften your answer and say something like this:

1. I can certainly understand how you feel, Mr. Keenan. Others have had much the same feeling when I first presented the concept to them. (Then provide a plausible explanation.)

2. I appreciate your concern, Mr. Keenan, and you do have a relevant point. Thank you for bringing it to my attention. (And you really should appreciate it.)

Select a Specific Technique

In the next section of this chapter, five techniques are detailed for use in formulating answers to the types of sales resistance you may encounter. Not all of them work all the time. In deciding which of the techniques to use, take these factors into consideration:

- The prospect's behavioral style
- The stage of the negotiation process in which the objection is raised
- The mood (argumentative or receptive) of the prospect
- How many times the objection has come up
- The type of objection (searcher, excuse, stall, product or service)

You must decide quickly on the technique you will use and avoid showing that an objection has upset you. Keep in mind that far too many variables operate in a given selling situation to guarantee that every objection can be answered satisfactorily.

Answer the Objection

Negotiation is persuasion, not manipulation. Avoid explanations that merely cloud the issue and cause prospects to feel that you are trying to pressure them. The answer, however, must be conclusive; don't close off your answer with the question still up in the air. Present only as much information as required to gain the prospect's cooperation and commitment. Minimize the objection by not dwelling on it. Say just enough to dispose of it to the prospect's satisfaction.

Be honest and factual, and do not promise anything that you, your company, or your product or service cannot deliver.

Prospects have their own needs, viewpoints, and ways of looking at things. Be sure to consider the prospect's ego and help the prospect to win. Your answer should include a benefit and should be shaped to fit the behavioral style of that prospect. Finally, confirm that your answer satisfied the prospect. Gain agreement by suggesting, "Am I correct in assuming that I have completely satisfied you regarding...?"

Attempt to Close

Closing opportunities exist at various times throughout the entire negotiation process. Recognizing those times and capitalizing upon them is up to you. When you have successfully answered a major objection, you have created an opportunity to close, especially if you are near the end of the presentation. Attempt a trial close before continuing with the presentation. The trial close gets a prospect's reaction without exerting any pressure for making a definite decision. It may be used at any point in the sales presentation to test the water to see whether you have presented enough information for the prospect to make a decision. Typical trial closes start with "If you were to buy," "In your opinion," or "How do you feel about..."

If you receive positive buying signals from the prospect at this point, you can attempt to close. If the close proves unsuccessful, get back on track and continue the presentation until another opportunity presents itself.

Five Techniques For Negotiating Objections

Keep in mind that with any technique you must produce evidence to prove the validity of what you say. Techniques do not establish belief and credibility; that is your job. Techniques are merely vehicles for organizing your answer and your support for it.

After an objection has been clarified and classified, you are in an excellent position to respond by using one or more of the following techniques.

1. Feel, Felt, Found

This practical technique overcomes a stall or a very personal concern. It can offset prospect hostility, pacify an unhappy customer, or inform someone who does not yet clearly understand the value of the product or service. Answer the prospect with this language:

> *I can understand how you feel.... I have had other customers who felt the same way until they found out....*

This approach serves several purposes. It shows prospects that you understand their concerns, and it reassures the prospect that having this kind of objection is normal. Now the stage is set to introduce information that can change the prospect's way of thinking. This technique says that other people who are now customers had similar misgivings but changed their minds after they found out some new information. These new facts allow the prospect to reevaluate your proposition. The following example illustrates how a bank executive in a sales role might use this negotiation technique with an unhappy client:

Banker: Good afternoon, Mr. Reznor. I am Jay Arnold with Third National Bank. I have been assigned to your account and would like to ... (suddenly interrupted!)

Client: So Third National is playing musical chairs with its loan officers again. It took Lily Allen six months just to learn about my business needs and now I have to train someone new. Why can't you people give me a banker who will stay with me?

Banker: I certainly understand how you might feel that way. Some of Lily's other clients have indicated that they felt the same way. However, the bank has found that someone with Lily's experience is an invaluable asset to our Problem Loan Division.

I have previously worked with firms in your line of business (mention them and provide testimonial letters) and from my review of your account, I feel I have a pretty good understanding of your operation. (By the way, here are my credentials.)

A word of caution when using this method: The feel, felt, found technique is commonly used in a vast number of industries, and if you are dealing with a seasoned professional, he or she may likely recognize that you are using this "technique" and get annoyed if they are aware of what you are doing. Then again, they might be impressed and even have a good laugh with you, not at you, as they will know what you are trying to accomplish.[24] Here is an example of how to rearrange your words slightly in these situations:

> *"Mr. Blunt, I do understand how you must feel. Frankly, lots of my customers have felt the same way when they first heard about our program, but what they discovered after further discussion was the benefits heavily outweighed the limitations."*

2. Compensation or Counterbalance Method

At times, a prospect may buy in spite of certain valid objections. The prospect may be partly right or may have misunderstood a portion of what you said. Accept and admit any truth in the objection. Admit that your product does have the disadvantage that the prospect has noticed and then immediately point out how the objection is overshadowed by other specific benefits of the product. Your job is to convince the prospect that the compensating benefits provide enough value that the disadvantage should not prevent the prospect from buying. By admitting the objection, you impress the prospect with your sincerity and sense of fair dealing. Then you can select the real strengths of your offering to offset the prospect's negative feelings.

A good way to deal with this situation is to provide documentation such as statistical evidence, a third-party endorsement, or the case history of someone who faced a similar situation. This method works because the prospect is approached positively with an acknowledgment of expressed concerns, and then given a series of logical, compensating benefits to counterbalance the stated objection.

3. Ask "Why?" or a Specific Question

This method is helpful not only for separating excuses from real objections but also for overcoming objections. You can use questions to narrow a major, generalized objection to specific points that are easier to handle. If the prospect says, "I don't like to do business with your company," ask, "What is it that you don't like about our firm?" The answer may show a past misunderstanding that can be cleared up. If the prospect complains, "I don't like the looks of your product," ask, "Why do you object to its appearance?" The objection may be based on a relatively minor aspect that can be changed or is not true of all models.

4. Deny the Objection

One way to answer buyer resistance is simply to assert that the prospect is wrong. This technique must be used with caution or it will antagonize prospects. You can sometimes tell prospects they are wrong but you have to be careful how you do it. You could win the argument but lose the sale.

The denial technique is useful when the prospect clearly has the wrong information. Either a portion of the presentation was misunderstood or someone else has supplied incorrect information. Point out that the prospect's information is wrong, but not by means of a direct, frontal assault. Present the denial sympathetically, thoughtfully, and with dignity. Listen attentively to the buyer's concern, and then begin by saying:

> *I don't believe I fully understand what you are saying.*

This response allows the buyer time to cool down emotionally and perhaps to soften the statement. It also gives you the opportunity to regain your composure. After the prospect repeats the incorrect information, respond in this manner:

> *I don't know how you could have gotten that impression. I really must have stated my position poorly; please let me correct it for you.*

> *A bit more forceful statement would be: Fortunately for me, that is not the real situation. I have some other information that does not support what you just told me.*

Your attitude is critical when using this technique. Your goal is to earn the prospect's respect and avoid an angry reaction. However, you do want the prospect to know that you will not be intimidated. Sometimes a direct denial is your only recourse. There are times when you must fight fire with fire. A direct denial is a high-risk method of dealing with any objection, but it is necessary at times, even if you lose the sale.

A successful salesperson can agree with prospects while still showing them that their concerns need not prevent a purchase.

5. Boomerang Method

The *boomerang method* allows you to agree with prospects yet show them that their objections need not prevent a purchase. This method is often used in a situation where the point to which the prospect is objecting is actually a sales point in favor of buying the particular product or service. The boomerang method involves agreeing with the objection and then making another statement that translates the objection into a reason for buying. For example, a sales representative for Blue Bell Inc., located in Brenham, Texas, might hear this type of objection:

> *"Blue Bell Ice Cream is too new to this area. My customers will not buy something they have never heard of before."*

> Then turn the objection into a sales point: *"There is no question that our ice cream is new to your area; that's why we are eager to build consumer awareness for the product. We intend to spend over $100,000 to tell your potential customers about our ice cream. Blue Bell uses its advertising messages to presell the product for you. If you agree to carry the product, we will generate a great deal of customer demand (and increase store traffic) for you."*

The boomerang method works well when the prospect lacks complete information or perceives a drawback that actually may not exist. Be careful of the image you project when using this technique. If prospects feel that you are directly challenging them or perhaps patronizing them, then you could be in for a real battle. In that case, you might as well pull out your boxing gloves because you will have more use for them than you will for your order book.

The *tongue-in-cheek method* is an adaptation of the boomerang method. It uses a bit of humor that may soften up the prospects and turn away their anger. A salesperson for Strickfaden's Nursery in Sandusky, Ohio, used the technique this way:

> **Prospect**: "I'm not going to buy any more shade trees from you; every time I plant one I have too much dirt left over!"

> **Salesperson**: "Yes, that is a concern. But the way to solve your problem is to dig your holes a little deeper."

Handling Price Objections

One type of objection surfaces so frequently that it requires additional examination: The Price Objection. Your prospects and customers want as much for their money as they can get. While that's not unexpected, you can't provide value-added service at reasonable prices if you give up too much at the negotiating table. How many times each week do you suppose a salesperson hears, "I just think your price is too high." To succeed in selling, you must see this type of sales resistance for what it is and overcome it.

The price objection is more difficult to pin down because it can mean many different things. The final price paid for a product or service depends upon the type of discounts available, advertising and promotional allowances paid by the seller, service after the sale, free trial periods, warranties or money-back guarantees, sales support service and training, delivery charges, and myriad other price-related variables. Then, too, the prospect may not really be objecting to the price but may just be hiding the real reason for not buying. When prospects says, "I can't afford it" or "Your prices are just too high," they may just be saying, "You have not convinced me that the value I will receive is worth the price I have to pay to get it." Often the buyer's concerns or questions about price represent an incomplete sales job!

Your company priced the product or service so it would sell. Never be afraid to ask the full value for your offering, but be prepared with solid evidence to support the price you are asking. Do not be defensive or apologetic. You must believe that the price you are quoting is actually much less than the value your product will give the prospect. If your product has exclusive features that are not readily apparent, convert them to benefits and sell those benefits as this classic example of Ma McGuire in Exhibit 12.5 illustrates.[25]

∆ Exhibit 12.5

Sell Benefits to Overcome the Price Question·····································

Two farm wagons stood in a public market. Both were loaded with potatoes in bags. A customer stopped before the first wagon.

"How much are potatoes today?" she asked the farmer's wife, who was selling them.

"A dollar and a quarter a bag," replied the farmer's wife.

"Oh, my," protested the woman, "that is pretty high, isn't it? I gave one dollar for the last bag I bought."

"Taters has gone up," was the only information the farmer's wife gave. The housewife went to the next wagon and asked the same question. But Ma McGuire "knew her potatoes," as the saying goes. Instead of treating her customer with indifference, she replied:

"These are specially fine white potatoes, madam. They are the best potatoes grown. In the first place, you see, we only raise the kind with small eyes so that there will be no waste in peeling. Then we sort them to grade out culls so you get only full-sized, good potatoes. Then we wash all our potatoes clean before sacking them, as you see. You can put one of these bags in your parlor without soiling your carpet—you don't pay for a lot of dirt. I'm getting $1.50 a bag for them—shall I have them put in your car or will you take them now?"

Ma McGuire sold two bags, at a higher price than her competitor asked, in spite of the fact that the customer had refused to buy because she thought the price was too high!

Ma McGuire certainly understood how to sell value. People have a perceived price-quality relationship. They do not mind spending money when the quality and value of the purchase have been successfully established.

Three Methods for Overcoming the Price Question

A product often has hidden qualities, and the prospect cannot see these qualities and does not fully appreciate them until they are pointed out. You usually get what you pay for. A low price is probably low for a good reason. Competitors can undersell you only temporarily because they have the same basic costs, they are cutting corners somewhere with lower standards of product quality, service, or delivery. A bargain price can turn out to be quite expensive.

You must face the fact that you will not always have the lowest-priced product or service to sell. Be prepared to justify your asking price and show that it is fair. Understand and be able to apply the differential competitive advantages you have in product, source, people, or service superiority.[26] There are a number of negotiation tactics that can help you overcome the price obstacle. You may respond to the question of price by using one or a combination of the following methods.

1. Price Breakdown

The price that sounds intimidating in its entirety often sounds much smaller when you break it down into weekly or monthly payments and compare it to how the customer normally spends extra money. If the prospect is really objecting to the absolute magnitude of the price, then a logical response is to break the total cost down over a period of time. Here is an example of how you might use this technique:

> *I am glad you mentioned price, and I can certainly appreciate your concern. The $3,000.00 does seem like an awful lot of money for a Bose car stereo system. But just imagine, for the price of a daily cup of coffee and a newspaper, you will enjoy your terrific new sound system during that hour-long commute you said you make to and from work every day. What a small price to pay for the increased enjoyment and relaxation that comes from owning such a magnificent system. You may just decide to take the long way home on some evenings!!*

Compare the one-time price of your product to the amount of money the prospect will save after years of using it. The clearer you make the distinction between what your prospects pay and what they get, the easier for them to recognize your product's great value. That's your job—to establish value, not price.[27] Talk about the initial and ultimate costs. Look at the *price-cost-value* comparison from two perspectives: *Price* represents the initial amount paid for the product; *cost* is the amount the buyer pays as the product is used over time.

2. Presumption of Exclusivity

What can you do when the price for your company's product is higher than that being asked

You can be confident when your firm does quality work.

by a competitor? Stress those features that are exclusively yours. What does your product have that the competition cannot offer? No two products are exactly alike. You will find strengths and weaknesses in any offering. Analyze your competitor's offering to see why the same product has a lower price. If your analysis indicates that you are offering more, then your task is to drive home those exclusive features. You may have to show more interest in the prospect than the competition that concentrates only on price. Go out of your way to isolate other needs of the prospect for which you can provide assistance.

If your company has a higher price, then it must be because you offer more to your customers. Identify your superior advantages and convince the prospect that the extras can be obtained only from you. In other words, justify the price with facts. Determine what the prospect wants more than anything else from your product and then identify the features that satisfy those wants. This is what Mack Hannan calls the *presumption of exclusivity*.[28] Concentrate on those features until the prospects feel that only with you can their needs be completely satisfied.

Now, consider this example of how one cellular phone salesperson's lack of product knowledge and his product's unique features prevented a sale. A prospect was not convinced that the newest arrival in the cellular company's product line was offering him a better deal, and was reluctant to change wireless providers. With every objection and question that the prospect posed to Ron, the sales rep, it became evident that the prospect knew more about the various options and offers in the cellular services than Ron did. "Really?" Ron would say, "That's their new scheme?"

For every answer, he went into a huddle with his boss, who appeared equally clueless. The prospect thanked him for his time, and left without purchasing. The prospect had the upper hand because Ron did not understand the concept of the presumption of exclusivity. A visionary salesperson will be able to not just anticipate knowledgeable prospects, but be so educated about his own industry and product line, that he can show his product's unique features in such a way that prevents objections from even surfacing.[29]

If a prospect gives you a hard time about price, stop selling price. Show what the money buys. Make the price seem unimportant in comparison to the value received. You may proceed something like this:

> Mrs. Harvey, allow me to share some information with you. The lower price of our competitor may not be the best buy for you. Let's look at the quality of our product and why we are more expensive. We pay our employees a fair wage, purchase superior-grade raw materials, and have a multimillion-dollar advertising program that has made our product nationally known.
>
> Our price includes training for your people; our staff is skilled at maintaining and upgrading the product over time. You will have easy availability of parts and a one hundred percent guarantee. We stand behind our product. We don't fight your complaints; we settle them promptly and equitably. The price paid for a solution to your problem should be based on what gives you the best solution. Don't you agree?

Draw the picture clearly and convincingly. Sell quality and exclusivity when the prospect argues price. If you sell the exclusive features properly, the prospect is not even thinking about price by the end of the presentation. Most buyers are fair-minded if you show why your company must get the price it does.

3. Comparison

Be prepared to present logical reasons for the price you are asking. One way you can do this is to compare the quality of your product to that of the prospect's company. For example, you could stress that both are selling superior products:

Mr. Beckham, your own company makes a high-grade product that commands an exceptionally high price, and deservedly so. Your tool-and-die products warrant their outstanding reputation because of the top-quality materials used to make them. Our high-viscosity, high-grade motor oil is naturally suited for your machines. Oh, you can buy less expensive brands than ours, but you would not be satisfied with their performance.

Acknowledging the superior nature of your prospect's product and suggesting that the prospect's company and your company are two of a kind makes considerable sense. This approach elevates your product to the same level of pride the prospect's company has in its products.

If you choose to make comparisons, be sure you have facts to substantiate your claims. Case histories and testimonials are useful for this purpose. For example, Dick Randolph sells X-ray equipment to hospitals and clinics by focusing on company performance and referrals to build trust. "My customers are more concerned about what happens after they sign a purchase order than the actual price," says Randolph, account manager at NXC Imaging. He provides prospects with current customers and a referral list encouraging them to contact any or all of them. Randolph uses his company's reputation to build trust and justify the higher price.[30] A demonstration could also work effectively to show a comparison. Let the prospect see personally how your product compares to other alternatives. Visual evidence and verifiable case histories produce powerful comparisons, regardless of what you are selling.

Always remember when dealing with price objections that your prospects know it is unwise to pay too much, but it is actually worse to pay too little. Your customer may pay too much and lose a little money, but when they pay too little, they could lose everything, because the thing that was bought was incapable of doing what it was bought to do. The common law of business balance prohibits paying a little and getting a lot—it can't be done. So be patient with your prospects and focus on the benefits if they still seem fixated on price.

SUMMARY

- Success in handling objections depends on your attitude. If you assume that the sale is over when you hear an objection, it will be. If you regard an objection as an invitation to continue negotiating, you are likely to enjoy a successful close.

- Buyers offer objections for a number of reasons, most of which are psychological. Objecting to something enables them to avoid the risk of making a decision that has potentially unpleasant consequences.

- Some objections are valid and indicate either a logical reason for not buying or a need for you to present additional information before the prospect makes a buying decision.

- Classify and clarify the objections according to their type and apply the appropriate plan to overcome them.

- The six-step strategic negotiating plan for dealing with buyers' concerns gives you the opportunity to handle whatever objection you encounter.

- Experts in overcoming objections record the objections they hear, study them to determine which ones they hear most often, and develop logical answers to use whenever these objections come up.

- You will not always have the lowest-priced product to sell. Apply the competitive advantages you have in product, source, people, or service superiority and respond to the question of price by breaking the price down, employing the presumption of exclusivity, or by using comparison.

REVIEW QUESTIONS

1. How does a salesperson sometimes cause a specific objection to be raised? What can be done to prevent this?

2. Who is responsible if prospects misunderstand part of the presentation or are not convinced that the product is applicable to their needs? Give examples of how objections reflecting these conditions are likely to be stated.

3. If you were selling homes in the price range of $200,000 to $250,000, how would you anticipate and forestall price objections?

4. In deciding when to answer objections, what factors would lead you to choose to answer them before they arise, postpone the answer until later in the presentation, answer them immediately, or ignore answering at all?

5. List the six steps in the strategic plan for handling objections.

6. List and discuss several strategies for coping with price objections.

7. How can an objection be considered a buying signal?

8. What are some underlying causes for psychological sales resistance?

9. Why might a prospect raise objections even when that prospect has already mentally decided to buy?

10. In what phases of the relationship sales cycle does negotiation play a part? Describe its purpose in each.

ROLE-PLAY EXERCISES

The following role-play exercises help build teams, improve communication, and emphasize the "real-world" side of selling. They are meant to be challenging, to learn how to deal with problems that have no single "right" answer and to use a variety of skills beyond those employed in a typical review question. Read and complete each activity. Then in the next class, discuss and compare answers with other classmates. Have some students take the role of the salesperson, and see how they would react. Remember, *"You learn more about a person in an hour of play than in a lifetime of conversation."* – Plato

1. You are ready to move out of the dorms and into your own apartment, but must first ask your parents for permission. Make three columns and list in the first the objections your parents might raise; in the second, note a technique that might be used to overcome each objection; in the third column, write out the specific answer you could give using that technique. Break up the class into groups of three, with two of the students playing the role of the parents, and act out the scenario.

2. Go to three car dealers and attempt to get the price of an automobile near the beginning of the sales encounter. What techniques, if any, did the salesperson use to postpone the question of price?

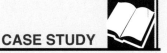

CASE STUDY

Case 12.1—Copy Cat

Bob Hawkes woke at the first shrill ring of the telephone. He groped for the light switch in his motel room and grumbled, "Who could be calling at this time of night?" It was his sales manager.

Bob's sales manager had called to say that he had learned that the chance of selling the new Faxmatic Total Copy System to the Sullivant Broadcasting Company was about to evaporate. Sullivant was about to sign with a competitor. "You'd better get there fast," the sales manager warned Hawkes.

"Chief, I've already seen Sullivant and shown him slides of the Faxmatic System. He liked it and asked me to come back early tomorrow."

"Yes, but did you research...?"

"It's all done. They now have their Monthly Program Guide printed outside. I found out it's Sullivant's pet project and he writes the program notes. Why are you so uptight about this guy? You've called me four or five times about him. Don't worry, I'll do the best I can."

"Okay, but remember, no special price deals without consulting me first."

Early the next morning, Bob, briefcase in one hand and a copy of Sullivant's Monthly Program Guide in the other, walked into Sullivant's office. Sullivant was absorbed in a stack of financial reports. "Why the gloomy frown?" Bob wondered. "Something's wrong."

"Didn't you get my message?" Sullivant growled.

"What message?" Bob asked.

"I had my secretary call your home office a few days ago and cancel our appointment."

"But why?" Bob was bewildered.

"After you were here last week, I discussed your copy system with two of my key people. One says we should sit tight and not spend any more money we don't have to. There's a point there, especially in this unstable economy. The other prefers another product. It's an import, but it costs less."

"And what is your opinion, Mr. Sullivant?"

"Well, I'll be frank with you. Of all the products we've seen, I'm inclined to agree that the import does offer more quality features for less money."

Bob could see his sale going down the drain. "But, Mr. Sullivant, the last time I saw you,"

"I know," Sullivant agreed hesitantly. "But now I'm not so sure, considering its price. That's why I've decided to think it over."

1. As Bob doesn't know what competing system Sullivant is considering, how can he effectively counter Sullivant's objection that it offers more than the Faxmatic System?

2. What should Bob's next move be?

Case 12.2—Computer Savvy

Karen Burgess sells a line of computer terminals that are compatible with most mainframe computers. She was certain that Ed Sommes, manager of a regional insurance office, was sold on the purchase of a dozen new terminals that the accounting clerks would need because the company was adding new software to replace their old batch system that had used only two data entry clerks to enter all documents. Now, all the accounting people would be entering data directly instead of preparing written documents to be entered by someone else.

Karen summarized the benefits she had presented. "Our terminals are especially adapted to accounting needs. One of their best features is that the ten-key pad is designed in two models: One for right-handed operators and one for left-handed. Because the pad plugs into either side instead of being part of the keyboard, you can order the kind you need. When you have a new clerk who needs the other kind, you replace only the ten-key pad and you are ready to move. You could even stock a right-hand and left-hand pad as spares and have instant flexibility. The non-glare screen is easy on the eyes, yet sharp and clear for ease of reading. The special tilt adjustment gives people of different heights just the angle they need. And our service people are on 24-hour call with radio dispatching whenever you have a problem."

But before Karen could ask the closing question, Ed broke in. "I've got to admit your units look attractive, but with the capital outlay for the new software, I need to hold down my cost for terminals to the minimum. Just how much would a dozen new terminals set my budget back?" When Karen quoted the unit figure, Ed sighed. "That's almost ten percent more per unit than the price your competitor offers. I don't see how I can justify that much at this time."

1. Put yourself in Karen's situation. Your prospect has just told you that your price is too high. How would you handle it?

2. Would knowing the competitor's line help to give you a clue about how to handle the objection?

Closing the Sale

- Develop productive attitudes and a professional perspective toward the close.

- Know the function of the close.

- Discover the importance of reassuring the prospect.

- Appreciate the value of persistence.

- Gain knowledge of how to deal with rejection.

- Develop a sense of timing in knowing when to close.

- Recognize buying signals.

- Study the different types of closes.

Finding new prospects, successfully making appointments through referrals and other prospecting techniques, establishing trust, and effectively explaining features and benefits can be difficult enough. But when it comes time to close, the results can be crushing, especially to inexperienced salespeople. After all, even the pros often have trouble wrapping up the deal.

A *close* can be defined as a question asked or an action taken by a salesperson designed to elicit a favorable buying decision from the prospect.[1] It is always related to the specific objective you identified for the interview. Closing the sale is not really difficult for the salesperson who is conducting a professional sales interview held under favorable conditions, including the presence of a qualified prospect.

Although closing a sale is actually quite natural, far too many salespeople have adopted such a distorted view of the close that they dread trying, even though the close is their only reason for being there. In fact, in 63 percent of all sales interviews, salespeople fail to ask for the prospect's business.[2] The usual scenario goes like this:

> *Well, Dr. Gill, that's about all I have to tell you. Is there anything else you would like to ask me? No? Okay, I guess I'll call you again in a few weeks. Have a good day. I enjoyed talking with you.*

Then the salesperson is standing outside the prospect's office wondering, "What happened? I thought sure I had that order. What did I do wrong?" The usual answer is that the salesperson did not do anything wrong. The salesperson just did not do anything.

> **Many of life's failures are people who did not realize how close they were to success when they gave up.**
>
> -Thomas Edison

Always Be Closing

Closing is not a separate event tacked onto the end of a sales interview—it is something that happens all along during the course of the presentation. Closing might be easier to understand if someone had devised a better name for it. The word close suggests something that occurs at the end of a process, so salespeople seem to feel that it is an isolated segment of the selling process that must be approached in some exact manner to produce success; but the opportunity to close may occur at any time during the sales interview. The wise professional watches for and takes advantage of every closing opportunity. Take the order as soon as you can get it!

Closing begins the moment you speak the first word to the prospect and continues throughout the whole process until the order is signed, sealed, and delivered. You close on many points: the prospect's agreement to grant an interview, confirming the existence of a need, permission to make a survey or an on-site visit, permission for a trial installation, and acceptance of your explanation of product benefits.

The sale has actually been made or lost long before the time arrives to sign the agreement. The final step should be just a formality—a necessary step, but not one that requires making weighty decisions. Unless you complete the selling process by asking for the order, the only title you deserve is *conversationalist*. Ultimately, it's a simple concept; you must close from the beginning. Don't confuse this idea with the hard sell. A cutthroat approach alienates many potential customers. Instead, explain your agenda. Tell the prospective customer exactly what you're selling and how it can benefit their business. Being up front about your intentions promotes an honest, mutually respectful and rewarding discussion, paving the way for a smooth close.[3]

> **By meeting the prospect's expectations and desires from the start, the close will occur naturally.**

Failure at the close is the result of inadequate completion of the prior steps in the sales process: Inadequate prospecting, incomplete qualifying of the prospect, or too little probing to determine the prospect's needs. As a result, the presentation has focused on the wrong features and benefits, or the wrong evidence has been supplied to support claims for the product. A prospect's failure to buy, then, does not automatically brand you as a poor closer. Studying your entire performance to find the weak link in the chain is necessary. Focusing only on closing as an indicator of sales skill is like expecting to hear Tiger Woods say that putting is all that matters in golf. Of course, that final putt that wins the championship is the most obvious success moment, but secure agreement throughout the sales process and the final step is the easiest one.

Functions of the Close

Even when all the steps leading to the close have gone well, the prospect may still hesitate. Logically, the prospect would gladly sign the agreement when a professional salesperson has a good product or service to offer, has presented meaningful benefits, has a carefully planned strategy for servicing the prospect's account, makes an impressive sales presentation, and successfully answers all of the buyer's concerns. However, the moment of decision is difficult for most people. Buyers take many risks: They must live with the purchase and pay for it; they may be forced to justify the buying decision to someone else; they may be responsible for an important impact on the company's productivity or profitability as a result of the purchase. Risks are threatening to most people. Of course, you may also feel some strain at the moment of decision. You may be asking yourself, "Have I told the prospect enough? Did I find the real need? Did I read the verbal and nonverbal clues correctly? Is this the best moment to close? What if the answer is no?"

Learn the art of diagnosing prospects to find their real needs—and then fill them.

The *salesperson-prospect* relationship is much like the *doctor-patient* relationship. The patient knows something is wrong and looks to the doctor for advice about diagnosis and treatment. The doctor guides the patient to a course of action to which the patient gladly agrees. Closing a sale requires a similar guidance of the prospect by the salesperson. Just as a doctor urges the patient to follow the treatment closely, a salesperson must make wise decisions about the prospect's needs.[4] If you believe that the decisions you recommend are in your prospects' best interests, then you must support buyers and help them make the decisions that will solve their problems.

Reassure and Close. Consider how the prospective buyer is probably feeling and thinking. Do you remember the first time you jumped off a diving board? You thought, "The board is too high; I can't swim that far; I'll choke on some water; I think I see sharks." You thought about all the possible bad consequences. Perhaps a friend in the water encouraged you to try. When you finally jumped, you discovered that the water was fine, just as your friend had said. In the sales situation, you are the friend in the water, you know how the prospect feels and you offer the needed reassurance: "Come on in; you'll be glad you took that first dive; I'm here to help if you need me." Your attitude must be that you respect prospects and their decisions, whether or not they decide to jump in. You continue to reassure them until they finally make a decision. The next time you advise them to make a buying decision, they will trust your recommendation more readily.

Wife: Honey, do you have difficulty making decisions?

Husband: Well, yes and no.

Once prospects agree that they can benefit from using your product or service, your responsibility is to guide them to a close. You must never be discouraged by a no. If you honestly believe that a sale is an exchange of mutual benefits, then a no should set up this train of reasoning: The prospect is asking me to explain once more that this decision will work, so I will continue to reassure and close. Do not be discouraged when the buyer hesitates. People do not like to make decisions; without assistance and reassurance, some simply cannot make decisions at all.

A Closing Consciousness

The most important factor in successfully closing a sale is not having the lowest price or the best product. Your attitude is the crucial factor. You must have an absolute belief in what you are selling, and you must expect to be successful. If you assume that you will successfully close the sale, the prospect interprets your confidence as reassurance that the product will provide the needed benefits. Your positive attitude makes the difficult decision, "Yes, I'll buy" much easier. All they have to do is say, "Yes, you're right" when you recommend that they buy. Confidence is contagious; it infects prospects and draws them to your side. Confidence at the close allows you to ask for the order in a straightforward manner.

Indecision is the graveyard of good intentions.

> *Mr. Sherrill, we have agreed on the capacity of the printer, its speed capabilities, and the cost of supplying paper, and we have clarified your questions regarding the service contract. We could significantly speed up the process if we could settle now on a delivery date. Is Friday okay with you?*

Closing is only frustrating if you have not identified customer needs, shown the right mental attitude, made a memorable presentation, and were perceived as a genuine help.[5] If you and the prospect have together defined the problem and worked out a solution, then the final question, the close, is nothing more than the last step in a sequence. After all, you have provided a quantity of solid information and helped the prospect study the existing situation and work out solutions to personal and/or business problems. You have been working for the prospect as an unpaid business consultant. The close is payday.

When you maintain a positive mental attitude, a high level of self-confidence, and belief in your product, you create an atmosphere within which you can handle the day-to-day rejections that are inevitable in the world of selling. Steve Simms, noted author and speaker, reveals how to *shake off the shackles of rejection*. Simms says that when prospects fail to follow your buying advice, you know that the rejection is seldom directed toward you personally but is instead a reflection of their own differing opinion about what will best fill their needs or a result of their personal hesitancy to make a decision that they perceive as a risk. In other words, you have lost nothing except a little of your time, but the prospects who say no have lost the opportunity to benefit from

The art of closing is not the process of persuading, but the art of making decisions with which people agree.

using your product or service and of being your personal customer. The bigger loss is theirs. Take the following attitude tips from Donald Trump on NBC's series, *The Apprentice*:[6]

- **Be Positive**. People like being around those who give off good energy. Sam got fired in large part because no one could stand to be around his prickly personality. (Although nodding off at the conference table as his colleagues toiled on the ad campaign didn't help.)

- **Have the Courage to Speak Your Mind**. Don't mistake being positive for going with the flow. For example, during a negotiating challenge, Kwame, a former investment manager, knew the price of gold is inflexible, but wasted time haggling over it anyway. Expertise is worth nothing if you don't use it.

- **Stand Up For Yourself**. As "The Donald" says, "If you don't stand up for yourself, no one else will." He fired one of his favorite candidates, Kristi, because she didn't defend herself when her team told Trump she'd been a poor project leader. Trump told his aides afterwards, "If you don't fight for yourself, the accusations must be true."

Persistence

Diana Smith, a representative for Jim Stephenson and Associates, Inc., says, "You should push, but never be pushy." Smith calls on Houston homebuilders to convince them to use her company's line of plumbing supplies in their construction projects. She suggests that, "making repeat, meaningful calls demonstrates to prospects that you are not going to give up. *The idea is to be graciously tenacious—without being obnoxious.*"[7] Focused persistence involves asking whether doing this today will get you that tomorrow.[8] Successful salespeople like Diana Smith never take no for an answer unless it is in everyone's interest to do so. If the business is worth having, it is worth going after repeatedly—with repeated calls or repeated attempts to close during a single call. The extra effort often makes the difference between success and failure.

By permission of Syndication International Ltd., London.

Gerhard Gschwandtner, founder and publisher of *Selling Power* says that, "When you are at the point where you think it's not worth it, that's when you need to redouble your efforts. Customers are looking for someone who is dependable, who is persistent and who will do what it takes to get the best solution implemented within the customer's organization." When sales are slow and you feel like every step is an uphill battle, that's when you shouldn't quit. Salespeople who redouble their efforts will be rewarded handsomely by the payoff. "The pain goes away the minute you are victorious," says Gschwandtner, "but if you give up, the pain will persist for the rest of your life."[9]

How often do you ask prospects for their business? The answer often given is "one more time." Realistically, you should be prepared to ask at least four or five times. A study of several thousand salespeople demonstrates how important persistence really is:

1. 48 percent of those interviewed quit after the first contact with a prospect.

2. 73 percent give up after the second contact.

3. 85 percent quit after the third contact.

4. 90 percent give up after the fourth contact.

The most dramatic statistic from the study shows that the 10 percent of salespeople who continue past the fourth contact, end up with eighty percent of the business.[10] Selling should be a side-by-side, step-by-step process, involving both prospect and salesperson, in which the salesperson earns the right to close. When you understand the problems faced by prospects, stay with them through the problem-solving process, watch for buying signals, and time the close to fit the prospect's behavioral style, your chances of a successful close skyrocket. Opportunities to close occur a number of times during the sales process; recognize them, persist, and ask for the order. Exhibit 13.1 describes the kind of persistence needed for success in sales.

Δ **Exhibit 13.1**

Persistence

One of the best examples of persistence is a story you probably loved as a child: *Green Eggs and Ham.* This Dr. Seuss classic describes the attempt of the "salesman," Sam I Am, to induce a wary "prospect" to try a meal of green eggs and ham. When his first straightforward offer is rejected, Sam I Am tries one assumptive close after another: "Do you want them here or there? Would you like them in a box or with a fox? Do you want them in a house or with a mouse?" Finally, the prospect tries green eggs and ham and is surprised to find them quite delicious. His no's seemingly never registered with the persistent Sam I Am. If you have not read *Green Eggs and Ham* lately, visit the children's section of the library and learn the story's important lesson about persistence.

Dr. Seuss, *Green Eggs and Ham* (New York: Random House, 1960)

Dealing With Rejection

Many would-be salespeople leave the profession because of their inability to cope with the day-to-day sense of rejection they experience. They interpret a prospect's refusal to buy as a message that says, "You are personally worthless." Mary Crowley, founder of Dallas-based Home Interiors, Inc., would often tell her salespeople what Eleanor Roosevelt was quoted as saying: "No one can make you feel inferior without your permission." She feels that this concept is especially important for not only her people, but all sales reps, to internalize.

> ❝ My great concern is not whether you have failed, but whether you are **content with your failure.** ❞
> **-Abraham Lincoln**

[handwritten margin note:] OMG Cpl P'll when you have done your very best, you may still experience disappointments, but you will not be disappointed in yourself.

Sales professionals must learn to deal with rejection by keeping a positive attitude about themselves and how they make their living. True, they feel disappointment if they fail to close, but successful salespeople focus in on the sense of accomplishment they feel when they do close a sale.[11] To keep from being overwhelmed, accept the fact that rejection exists, see it for what it really is, and never make the mistake of allowing it to serve as a measure of your own self-worth.

What is a good *batting average* in selling? Professional baseball players who average .300 (three hits for every ten times at bat) or more for a full season are a small minority of players in the major leagues. Imagine failing to get a base hit 70 percent of the time. Consider some of the great names in baseball history:

- **Babe Ruth hit 714 career home runs, but struck out 1,330 times.**
- **Cy Young won 515 games, but lost 313.**
- **Ty Cobb stole 96 bases one year but was caught stealing 38 times.**

Baseball fans ignore the failures and instead concentrate on the successes of their favorite players. The attitude of all true professionals is, "I may have failed, but that does not mean I am a failure."

A salesperson who never hears a 'no' is not a salesperson, but merely an order taker. Rejection is as much a part of sales as getting dressed in the morning, and salespeople who can't or won't deal with it had better find another career. The first thing to remember when handling rejection is that you just can't take it personally.[12] Refuse to permit anyone else to make you feel bad about yourself. Exhibit 13.2 describes nine specific tactics for coping with rejection.[13]

Δ Exhibit 13.2

Nine Tactics for Dealing with Rejection ·

1. **Remind yourself that you are not alone.** Remind yourself of exceptional salespeople and how many hundreds or thousands of rejections they had to face on their journey to success. You see, you are not alone!

2. **Forgive yourself.** When you make mistakes, forgive yourself. Mistakes are great learning experiences, but to benefit from them you have to keep moving forward. Continue to generate, gather and harvest prospects. The more prospects you have, the better you feel.

3. **Give yourself a pep talk.** Replace negative thoughts with positive ones such as, "I'm a great salesperson, and after they hear what I have to say, they'll want to buy from me."

4. **Refuse to give up**. Remind yourself constantly that persistence is key to success, and that rejection may not be pleasant but you won't let it stop you. Stubbornly refuse to let it get to you!

5. **Remember you are important because of who you are, not what you do**. Remind yourself of the difference between self-worth and performance. Never equate your worth as a human being with your success or failure as a salesperson.

6. **Engage in positive self-talk**. Separate your ego from the sale. The prospect is not attacking you personally. Say to yourself, "This prospect doesn't even know me; the refusal to buy cannot have anything to do with me as a person."

7. **Positively anticipate rejection and it will not overwhelm you**. Expect it, but don't create it. Think in advance what your response to rejection will be.

8. **Broaden your definition of success**. Instead of looking at outcomes, or being attached to how things turn out, look at success as getting out there in the first place.

9. **Commit to routinely attracting more customers than you need**. "No, thanks" is much easier to handle when you have a steady flow of qualified prospects streaming in. If you aren't in this position, be sure to revisit your marketing plan and recommit to daily marketing actions.

When To Close

Most of the sales you make will not close themselves. The true superstars of selling do not find it necessary to ask overtly for orders. The good salespeople openly ask for orders approximately ninety percent of the time before sales are closed.[14] The closing curve shown in Exhibit 13.3 illustrates how the closing process works. The will-buy line (WBL) shows that some sales will be closed almost at once, others are easy sales, and that most can be closed with an interest-building presentation. A few can never be closed. The key is recognizing the spots at which a close can be made—when the buyer gives a buying signal. The appearance of a buying signal is the critical moment during the presentation when a successful close is more likely.

Δ **Exhibit 13.3**

The Closing Curve

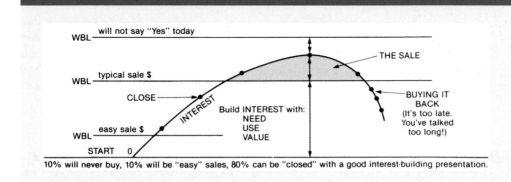

10% will never buy, 10% will be "easy" sales, 80% can be "closed" with a good interest-building presentation.

When you sense the psychological moment to close do so immediately. A delay of even a few seconds may give prospects a chance to change their mind.[15] If you fail to recognize these critical moments at which the prospect is most nearly ready to make a buying decision and continue to talk past them, the close becomes steadily more difficult. After a critical point is passed, you must buy back the prospect's readiness to decide. In other words, you must once again convince the prospect that buying is the proper decision. Talking too much and overselling is a much greater danger than underselling. Your attempts to close early and often eliminate the possibility of going past the point at which the prospect is ready to buy.

The professional salesperson guides and directs the prospect's behavior. As you reach the point where the final decision is to be made, it's just as important for you to know when to ask for the order as it is for you to know how to ask.[16] Instead of just watching passively for signs of interest, you must create situations in which interest can be generated and revealed.

The best psychological moment for closing may occur at any time during the presentation. When it does come, prospects signal in some way that you have convinced them and they are ready to buy.[17] You never have only one possible moment to close. You may be in the early stages of the presentation, you may have completely exhausted all the selling points you planned to present, or you may be somewhere in between.

Recognizing Buying Signals

A *buying signal* is anything the prospect does or says that indicates readiness to buy. Buying signals are all around us if we learn to recognize them.[18] Unfortunately, it's all too easy to become focused on your presentation that you overlook these signals even if they are obvious. Buying signals occur quickly and may be verbal, nonverbal, or both. Genuine buying signals show that the prospect has moved from evaluating your proposal to an appraisal of it.

A buying signal may come in the form of a question. A prospect may ask you to repeat some point or benefit previously discussed or stop you right in the middle of the presentation to ask how long delivery will take. However a buying signal comes, take advantage of it and close immediately. Always remember that when the prospect is ready to buy, you will receive a signal.

The CHEF Technique

Just as the experienced chef in a fine restaurant knows precisely the right ingredients to blend to produce exquisite cuisine, similarly professional salespeople can exhibit chef like characteristics as they try to translate the combination of gestures fed to them by their prospects. With the traditional method of selling, salespeople were taught to close, close, close. They were told to spend most of their time closing the deal. Trainers taught salespeople fancy closes to handle and overcome objections. Over the years, a new school of thought has evolved: the school of possibility. Imagine what would be possible if all the objections you typically hear at the 'closing table were prevented and defused throughout the course of your presentation.[19]

In addition to this new mindset, it is essential to decipher prospects' physical buying signals to determine your level of effectiveness through the presentation in bringing them to a point of decision. Use the **CHEF** method to identify these verbal and nonverbal buying signals.[20]

Cheek Or Chin. When prospects touch or stroke their chin or cheek they are signaling satisfaction and gratification. Leaning forward and nodding the head in agreement says, I'm almost persuaded. In this instance, ask if you've answered all their questions, move quickly and ask for their business. Prospects that tighten their jaw muscles or cover their mouths suggest that they are not receptive to what you have to say. This is a critical time to ask questions to open them up.

Hands. Open and relaxed hands, especially with palms facing upward, are a sign that prospects may be ready to buy. Rubbing their palms together signals that they are already assuming ownership. Those individuals who steeple (like a church steeple) their hands together are indicating confidence or superiority. When the prospect's hands are fidgeting or forming a fist, they're more than likely skeptical, or worse yet, irritated. You must stop talking and find out what is wrong!

Eye Contact. Maintaining consistent eye contact with you indicates that the prospect is probably paying attention to what is being said, and the handling and examination of any visuals shows the intensity of that commitment. This is a good time to request a buying decision. When the pupils of the prospect's eyes are dilated this signals relaxation, and you are on the right track. However, rolling or squinting of the eyes often means irritation or confusion. In addition, the rate at which a prospect blinks can indicate anger or excitement. A raised eyebrow can mean the prospect doesn't believe what you are saying.[21] Something is wrong and you had better find out what that something is. If you sense this you might say, "You seem a bit uneasy with this. Please tell me what concerns or questions you have."

Eye contact, or the lack of it, can signal to the salesperson a prospect's level of interest.

Friendly Prospects. Prospects who are smiling, relaxed, or engaging you in conversation are telling you that you've earned their trust. A prospect indicates readiness to purchase by saying, "It sounds good, but I ought not to buy." Give this prospect another reason to buy. Reassure and ask for a decision. When prospects turn unfriendly, try to be sensitive and empathetic. After all, the basic reason for becoming experts at relationship selling is to *create an atmosphere within which an act of trust can take place!* People like to buy from people who are like them.

The Trial Close

A *trial close* asks for an opinion; a *closing question* asks for a decision. A trial close, by asking for an opinion, serves as a thermometer that tells you whether the prospect is warm, hot, or cold to your proposition. It is designed to help you read the prospect's feelings and predict probable reactions. In Chapter 11, the tie-down question was discussed as one element in a unit of conviction. The tie-down and the trial close are used for basically the same purpose. When you get the prospects agreeing with you throughout the presentation they are much more likely to agree with you when you ask the closing question, that is, when you make the formal request for their business. You want to be careful not to talk past the sale. Close when the prospect wants to buy.

Many salespeople think of closing as the last phase of a sales call. If they do, they may not get all the sales that they should. During every sales call there will be a number of opportunities to close the sale. How do you know the proper time? When in doubt, test the prospect with trial closes such as:

1. "Is this what you're looking for?"

2. "Can you imagine how this will boost your productivity?"

3. "Do you have the necessary budget for this?"

4. "What else do you need to make a decision?"

5. "Does this sound like something you would like to do?"[22]

Although it resembles a definite attempt to close, the trial close is used to probe and to reveal how far along the prospect has gone in the decision-making process. You do not need to ask a closing question if you know the prospect is not ready to buy. The time to ask for the order is when the prospect is fully ready to buy. You can, however, ask for an opinion at any time.

A Closing Question

A closing question, in contrast to the trial close, is designed to produce an answer that confirms the fact that the prospect has bought. Look at these two examples:

1. Would it be better for you to receive shipment of a full month's supply right away, or would you prefer to receive half at the end of this week and the other half in about ten days?

2. We can have the product on your dock next Monday. Is Monday a convenient delivery day for you?

When you ask a closing question, say nothing else until the prospect gives an answer. The pressure of silence is enormous. *Silence* is golden because of what it brings you in terms of the information you need. Never miss the opportunity not to say something.[23] If you can remain silent after asking the closing question, only two outcomes are possible: 1) The prospect says yes or 2) the prospect gives a reason for not wanting to buy. In either instance, you are better off than you were before you asked the question. If the answer is yes, you have a sale. If the prospect gives you a reason for not buying, a concern has surfaced that you can convert into another opportunity to close.

Technology and Closing. Computer technology can make closing the sale quicker for salespeople. It may eliminate the need to return to the office for price approvals or price calculations. Saving time is also possible when several individuals must approve a price or bid before the salesperson can close. For instance, the Falconite company sells cranes and lift equipment to industrial and commercial users. In the past, days or weeks might pass before all the individuals involved study, make corrections, and approve a bid on a large purchase. Today, the bid is sent to each person's electronic mailbox. Each one makes changes and returns the bid to the salesperson with applicable comments or notes. The changes are incorporated and the bid is sent back for final approval. Less than a day may be required for complex bids even though all those whose approval is required are at widely separated locations in the field.

Developing Partnerships Using Technology examines how computer networks shorten the selling cycle and facilitate the purchasing function. Computer-to-computer systems link customers and suppliers, providing a one-stop communication tool for the salesperson. These systems are referred to as Electronic Data Interchanges.

Developing Partnerships Using Technology

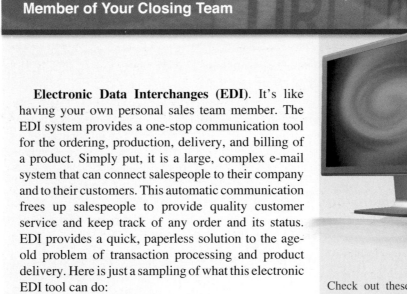

Make an Electronic Data Interchange a Member of Your Closing Team

Electronic Data Interchanges (EDI). It's like having your own personal sales team member. The EDI system provides a one-stop communication tool for the ordering, production, delivery, and billing of a product. Simply put, it is a large, complex e-mail system that can connect salespeople to their company and to their customers. This automatic communication frees up salespeople to provide quality customer service and keep track of any order and its status. EDI provides a quick, paperless solution to the age-old problem of transaction processing and product delivery. Here is just a sampling of what this electronic EDI tool can do:

1. Shorten the selling cycle and simplify the purchasing function between the salesperson and his clients.

2. Allow automatic replenishment of inventory on a just in-time (JIT) basis.

3. Recording of all production, ordering, and delivery communication.

4. Automatic processing of information through computers without human interference.

Check out these Web sites for additional information:

www.edi-network.com

www.cticomm.com

www.truecommerce.com

Types Of Closes

There are a multitude of closing strategies, and as a professional, you should become familiar with as many types of closing techniques as possible. One or two standard closes are not enough in the competitive selling arena that is filled with many different kinds of buyers, all with varying needs and personalities. You need a specific close for every occasion and for every type of prospect. If you attempt to use the same close for every prospect, you will walk away from much of the business that should be yours. The sales plan for each interview calls for a specific type of presentation strategy; your plan should also extend to the type of close you use. Just as circumstances often dictate some changes in your presentation, however, they also point up the need for shifts in your closing plans. Your sales call plan should provide the preferred closing routine to fit with the presentation you expect to deliver. Be sure to plan some alternative closing routines you can use in the event you find it is necessary to modify your presentation.

For example, an insurance agent had prepared a comprehensive insurance program to present to a client. Upon arrival the agent finds an excited prospect who shares information that he and his wife are actually expecting triplets. This prospect's needs have changed dramatically in just 24 hours. The presentation now becomes a work session to devise a new program, and the close the agent anticipated may not be appropriate. A master salesperson with a full repertoire of closing techniques merely chooses one that fits the revised situation and moves on as though nothing unusual is occurring. The various closing methods shown in Exhibit 13.4 and described here are not the only methods available. Most of them are subject to combination with other methods to fit your unique personality, your product, and your market. Learn the principles upon which these techniques rest and adapt them to your needs.

Δ Exhibit 13.4

Successful Closing Techniques

1. **Assumptive close**— Throughout the presentation, assuming that the prospect will buy allows the prospect to make the decision more easily by presenting opportunities to make smaller or easier choices. Common assumptive closes include the continuous-yes close, the physical-action close, the order-blank close, ownership close and the alternate of choice close.

2. **Impending-event close**— Stress the urgency to make a decision because something is about to happen that means the opportunity to buy with the present advantages may be lost.

3. **Direct close**—Make a straightforward request for the order. Many buyers appreciate a no-nonsense approach, but be mindful of each prospect's behavioral style and use this approach only with those who welcome such tactics.

4. **Summary close**—Review the features and benefits of the offering with particular emphasis on selling points that generated the most prospect interest earlier in the presentation.

5. **Call-back close**—Most sales are not closed on the first attempt. Offer to call back on a prospect with a specific purpose in mind and with new information.

6. **Trial-order close**—Either guarantee the prospect's money back or offer to absorb all expenses if the prospect tries the product or service and decides not to keep it.

7. **Balance-sheet close**—The salesperson takes an active part in the decision-making process to help the prospect understand that the reasons for buying heavily outweigh the reasons opposed to buying.

8. **Never-the-Best-Time Close**—This close is ideal for prospects who are sitting on the fence and unable to make a decision by showing them that delaying will either get them no advantage or may even be to their disadvantage.

9. **1-2-3 Close**—For those prospects who are "straight shooters" and don't want you to have to woo them into buying, this can be an effective close. You simply summarize the best benefits in sets of three and ask a closing question.

Assumptive Closes

In a sense, every close is assumptive. You do not attempt to close until you have received one or more buying signals from the prospect and have reason to believe you have a better than even chance of success. When you enter every sales interview with a positive expectation of success, you are assuming that the prospect will buy at the close. Your attitude throughout the interview is assumptive. Say, "When you use this product" and "As your program progresses." Avoid words like *if* and *should* because they are conditional and block closing action.

The assumptive approach to closing establishes a positive environment in which the prospect can more easily say yes. These closes work well with indecisive buyers who tend to be nervous about making a final decision. Present them with minor decisions that give them the opportunity to appear decisive in a small matter while they are actually painlessly making the big decision at the same time. The closes described below are common assumptive closes.

Continuous-Yes Close. By asking a series of questions throughout the sales presentation, all of which are designed to be answered in the affirmative, it becomes more difficult for buyers to say no when they've already said yes a number of times. That is why you must get agreement on minor points before you ask for the order.

These questions begin in the need discovery phase. For example: "I'd like to ask you a few questions that help me understand your particular needs. Would that be okay with you?" Yes. Continue them during the presentation: "Do you like the idea of our billing in six-second increments on all your long distance calls?" Yes. During the closing phase you may ask: "Are you satisfied with the comprehensive service contract that we offer?" Yes. "Does the financing of this telecommunications system seem fair to you?" Yes. "Then it seems we can go ahead with our plans to begin the installation process." Yes. These are all closed-end type questions, so you must be confident that you will receive an affirmative response before you ask them. When the final closing question is asked, the prospect is inclined to keep on agreeing with you. You have a sale.

Physical-Action Close. The physical-action close is quite simple, but can be most effective. Without directly asking for the prospect's order, begin taking some action that assumes the sale is completed. For example, you can begin filling out paperwork and ask the prospect for a signature when you finish. A retail salesperson may simply begin wrapping the merchandise or move to the cash register to ring up the order. If the prospect does not object or stop your action, the sale is made.

Order-Blank Close. Begin to ask the prospect a series of questions and write the answers on the contract or agreement form. You might ask, "Do you use your complete middle name or just an initial?" Continue to fill out the information and then ask for a signature. "Now that we have reached agreement, I know you will want to expedite delivery. Just indicate your approval by placing your name right here."

Ownership Close. With this assumptive close, you act as if they already own what is being sold. Talk about your product and what they are going to do with it. Discuss how it already fits into their lives. Do not talk about whether they are ready to buy or have already bought it. Just act as if it has always been theirs.[24] Here are some examples:

- Now where will you put your new wardrobe?

- What will people say about your car?

- What do you like most about your camera?

The ownership close uses an assumptive principle, acting as if they already owned the product. This seeks to create mental closure on the principle of already owning it.

Alternate of Choice Close. In general, people like to exercise their freedom of choice and salespeople like to lead their buyers toward an easy agreement. This well-known close consists of giving the prospect a choice between two positive alternatives. Here are some suggestions:

1. Would delivery be convenient on Thursday, or would you prefer Friday?

2. Do you prefer to pay cash or is our monthly payment plan more convenient for you?

3. Where would you like the order sent—directly to your warehouse or to the main office?

The idea behind the alternate of choice close is to offer the prospect a choice between buying A and buying B instead of a choice between buying and not buying. The question is not "Will you buy?" but "When?" or "Which one?"

Impending Event Close

This close uses the sense of urgency that is suggested by some impending event that will affect the terms or the effectiveness of the buying decision. Use this close with discretion. It must be based on truth and must not seem manipulative. The most common inducements are concerns that prices are going up or that resources will be in short supply.

My company has announced that prices on this product will go up about five percent next month because of an increase in supplier costs. If I can call your order in now, you can stock up before the price increase becomes effective.

Never use this close deceptively! Whatever the impending event is, it must be real and in the prospect's best interests to take advantage of an order placed now. Because this close is often abused by unscrupulous salespeople, prospects are likely to be skeptical of it. When you have good information to work with, you can prevent a customer from running short of inventory or from facing an unexpected price increase, and this gains the appreciation and the loyalty of the customer. Properly applied, this close can work wonders for your long-term credibility.

The Direct Close

The direct close is a straightforward request for an order. Once you have covered all the necessary features and benefits of your product and matched them with the buyer's dominant buying motives, you can ask with confidence, "May I have your business?" This type of close is quite common when selling to industrial buyers. Many buyers appreciate a no-nonsense approach. Of course, be mindful of the buyer's behavioral style. Amiables, for example, could find this approach threatening.

Be sure to keep the direct close positive. Avoid the word don't. "Why don't we begin next week?" and "Why don't you try the product for a while and see what happens?" are open invitations to additional objections. Insertion of a negative into the close may implant doubt where none existed, and the prospect may try to tell you why not. Use positive statements like these:

1. May I schedule delivery for next Tuesday?

2. It comes in five-pound, ten-pound, and twenty-pound bags. I suggest you take five of each to begin.

3. Let's run your first ad beginning Friday of this week.

When you use this type of closing statement, then you and your customer can make positive plans together.

The Summary Close

One of the best closing tactics is to summarize the major selling points made during the presentation. This method is especially good when the prospect must defend a purchase to someone else. The repetition of benefits at this point overcomes the prospect's tendency to forget or overlook points previously identified as important to satisfying existing needs. Review the benefits and ask the prospect to confirm again that they are important. Avoid mentioning any new benefits during this close. Bring up additional points only if the summary fails and you need additional ammunition to answer new objections.

Concentrate in the summary close on those items that were of most interest to the prospect and that related directly to the dominant buying motives.[25] For example, the sales representative selling advertising space in a consumer magazine might use the summary close like this:

Mr. Hardwick, let's review the major points on which we have agreed:

1. An ad in our magazine will give you maximum effective circulation coverage.

2. Your ads will enjoy high readership.

3. We saw that businesses similar to yours have had a great deal of success advertising with us (indicate testimonials or case histories used during presentation).

4. Our marketing staff will help you develop ads for all the media you use, not just our magazine.

5. You'll receive free artwork and layout help. These services are included in our basic price.

This summary puts into capsule form the highlights of your sales story. It gives both you and the prospect an opportunity to reconsider what was covered throughout the sales interview.

Give the prospect an opportunity to agree that the summary is correct. Once agreement has been expressed, the prospect is in a positive frame of mind, and the time is ripe to get some sort of formal commitment. The summary close must be combined with some other closing technique to complete the sale. For example, you might use the alternate of choice close like this:

Mr. Hardwick, with all of these major benefits available, you can see that advertising with us is a sound investment. Do you want to run your first ad on October fifteenth, or would November first be better for you?

Call-Back Close

Many sales opportunities are lost every day because salespeople take the prospect's decision not to buy as permanent. Studies show that many accounts are won by salespeople who call five or more times on the same prospect. Each time you return, you must present new information or ideas that will stimulate the prospect to buy. If you have the same old story told in the same old way, you probably will not make a new impression. If you walk into the prospect's office and say, "Well, have you thought it over?" the prospect's natural tendency is to restate the original objection: "Yes, and I still feel it is not a good time to spend that much money." In other words, "No deal." Here is an effective plan for a call-back situation:

1. **Approach**. Begin by giving a reason for calling back: "Coach Blevins, after I left the other day, I realized that there is some information I did not give you that has real bearing on your situation." Be sure you do have something different to present—new data, additional proof material in the form of testimonials, or whatever. Be sure it is pertinent and logical.

2. **Review**. Next, review the whole presentation. Begin with, "Let me review briefly the items we talked about last time." The last meeting may be fresh in your mind, but the prospect will not remember ten percent of what you presented. Throughout the review, use phrases like *as you remember, you will recall,* and *we said that* to suggest points of agreement from the previous meeting.

This approach may not always work, but you know that you cannot sell to someone without face-to-face contact. Being there gives you the only opportunity you will ever have to sell this prospect.

The Trial Order Close

This technique involves asking the prospect for a trial order with no obligation. You either guarantee the money back if not completely satisfied or absorb all expenses and make the offer free. Prospects like it because they can simply refuse to pay for any unsatisfactory merchandise. Their risk is low and yours is minimal because only a small quantity is shipped with the possible result of establishing a satisfied customer who will give you repeat orders. Sometimes salespeople call this the *puppy dog close*. How could you ever return a puppy to the pet store and get your money back after the children have played with it for a week? By then, everyone is in love with it.

Suppose you are selling personal leadership training materials to a career counselor, and the prospect says something like this: "I have never used material like this in my teaching or counseling activities. Let me think about it before I decide." Respond with this trial order close:

> *"I can certainly appreciate that. One thing we do that might be helpful to you is to make the program available on a fifteen-day, satisfaction-guaranteed basis. This enables you to work with the material firsthand and see if it is something that would be useful in your career counseling and training. We encourage you to listen to some of the tapes, go through the manual, and try it out in some actual counseling situations. After you have done that, if you find that you can use it in your library, then just hang on to it and we will bill you next month. In fact, you can even spread the payments out over six months; that would mean just $43 per payment. But if you find that you can't use the material or that it's not suitable for your situation, we'll understand. All we ask is that you return it to us. Is that fair enough?"*

Follow this statement with one of the assumptive closes to get the prospect to take action that will allow you to actually enter the order.

The Balance-Sheet Close

This practical, decision-making format is familiar to most prospects, and they will feel comfortable as you use it. The procedure involves using a blank sheet of paper with a line drawn down the center to form two columns. In the first column, list all the reasons for making an affirmative decision in favor of your buying recommendation. These are the assets. In the second column, list all the questions or concerns about a buying decision— the liabilities involved in saying yes. The closing process is an analysis of the two columns to show the prospect that the reasons for buying heavily outweigh the reasons for not buying. Give the prospect the opportunity to express agreement with your conclusions.

As you build the balance sheet, resist the temptation to hurry. As you list each advantage for buying, pause and allow time for the prospect to absorb the idea. Be sure that you have many more ideas in favor of buying than opposed to it so that the number of reasons will be so impressive that you won't have to deal with the relative weights of individual reasons.[26] To use the balance-sheet method, you can begin like this:

Mrs. Hillman, the decision you are about to make is important. I know you want to be sure you are making a sensible choice. So that we will be sure to make the decision that is best for you, let's look at all the reasons in favor of buying this product and any questions or concerns about it. We can then determine which side weighs more and make your decision accordingly. Let's begin with the ideas that favor a positive decision today. Is that fair enough?

Take out a sheet of paper and begin to list the reasons for buying. Be sure to avoid the word objection. Instead of talking about the prospect's objections to buying, state them as concerns or questions to be answered: "You expressed concern about delivery schedules." When you use the word objection out loud, you are setting up the prospect and yourself as adversaries; if you are adversaries, one of you must win and the other must lose. Exhibit 13.5 shows a partial balance sheet for selling a mutual fund.

∆ Exhibit 13.5

The Mutual Fund Decision ·

Reasons for Buying

1. This fund has grown faster than savings accounts.

2. Diversification lowers risk.

3. Professional management lowers risk.

4. Blue chip portfolio lowers risk.

5. Stocks are a hedge against inflation.

6. You can quickly redeem or borrow on shares.

Questions or Concerns

1. Higher risk than a savings account.

2. Less liquidity than a savings account.

Never-the-Best-Time Close

When people are procrastinating or indecisive over whether they should buy now or buy later, show them that delaying will either get them no advantage or may even be to their disadvantage. You can discuss what they will miss by not having it over the coming period. If you have some, give examples of people who waited for the best moment, which never came.[27] Here is what this close may sound like:

- If you leave it until next year, you'll have one year less to enjoy it.

- The best time to buy is when you need it—which I'd say is now, wouldn't you?

The never-the-best-time close works by reframing delaying tactics as value-destroying procrastination.

1-2-3 Close

In this close, you summarize in sets of three items and word it as, We will give you this, that, and the other. The three items may be features of the product, benefits, or add-on "sweetener" items such as bonuses or rebates. There are two ways to do this: the items may either be closely related (to reinforce a single point) or may be relatively separate (to gain greater coverage, especially if your presentation is long or your product is complicated). Most customers ideally want the impossible: products that are free, perfect, and available immediately—the classic business measurement trilogy of cost, quality, and time.[28] That is why this close can be effective; you are naming a bundle of benefits, the flawless "trifecta" of reasons to buy your product. Here is how to phrase this close:

- This product is cheaper, faster, and more reliable than the competition.

- The houses here are better-looking, better-built, and better-equipped than those in the other development.

- If you buy today, we will give you free insurance coverage, pay the sales tax, and provide a full tank of gas.

The 1-2-3 close works through the principle of triples, a curious pattern where three things given together act as a coherent triple threat that, when grouped together, give a compelling message.

Getting Creative with Closing

It is always a good idea to have as many of the closes memorized as possible. But salespeople should also be coached and trained to use an adaptive approach to selling.[29] Highly adaptive salespeople use a little creativity to close the really tough prospects. The following list is a few out-of-the-ordinary strategies you can use to influence customers to put pen to paper:[30]

1. Looking for one phrase to reassure customers that you will always do right by them? Try this: "I will spend your money as if it were my own."

2. As you close, hold up a $50 bill, tear it in half and give one half to the customer. Then hold up the remaining half and say, "If you can find a better value for your money, I'll give you the other half."

3. Put it in writing. Print up a list of services you can personally guarantee to the customer: "I will return all phone calls the same business day," "I will always treat your time as a precious commodity," for example. Offer this sheet to customers in exchange for their business.

After the Close

Once you have closed the sale and have completed any necessary paperwork, you have no further business with the prospect at this time. Learn to leave gracefully. Don't become afflicted with "*lingeritis*." You may be tempted to stay and enjoy the company of a new customer you especially like. You feel like celebrating a successful sale. However, the customer has other work to do, and so do you! If you linger, you invite second thoughts and perhaps even regret. Leave while the client still has good thoughts about you and your efficient, professional manner. Thank the client for the order, say you are looking forward to meeting again, and leave.

SUMMARY

- Closing the sale is a natural conclusion to a carefully prepared and well-conducted presentation to a qualified prospect. Successful closing is often a matter of attitude.

- Learn to recognize buying signals. These enable you to close at the earliest possible point in the presentation. Learn the CHEF technique.

- The most threatening element in the sale for many salespeople is the fear of rejection. Develop a plan for dealing with rejection.

- Both verbal and nonverbal clues point to the prospect's readiness to buy. The buying signals often suggest the type of close that would be appropriate.

- Close when the prospect is ready to buy.

- One effective tactic is a trial close that asks for an opinion rather than a commitment; this allows the salesperson to determine just how ready the prospect is to say yes!

- Use words like when or as during the close. Avoid words such as if and should because they are conditional and block closing action.

- The summary close consists of restating the major selling points made during the presentation. This repetition of benefits overcomes the prospect's tendency to forget or neglect main points.

- The balance sheet close works well because it also allows you to present a summary of the main selling points, but in a pro and con format. Many of us tend to think this way and this close is well received by the analytical and amiable social styles.

REVIEW QUESTIONS

1. Discuss some strategies for handling the feeling of rejection that salespeople tend to experience from missing a sale.

2. Why do many prospects naturally say no when a close is attempted?

3. Why do many salesperson dread the close? Why is this fear unfounded?

4. When should the salesperson decide what kind of close to use? Why?

5. Should the planned close ever be changed in the course of the interview? Why or why not?

6. Timing is crucial in closing. Is attempting a close before the prospect is ready more harmful than trying to close past the critical point? Why or why not?

7. Distinguish between a trial close and a closing question. When is each appropriate?

8. What is the purpose of reassurance in connection with the close?

9. How many times in one interview should a salesperson ask for the order? How many times should you call on the same prospect to ask for an order?

10. What is the difference between persistence and pushiness?

11. Describe some typical verbal and nonverbal buying signals.

ROLE-PLAY EXERCISES

The following role-play exercises help build teams, improve communication, and emphasize the "real-world" side of selling. They are meant to be challenging, to learn how to deal with problems that have no single "right" answer and to use a variety of skills beyond those employed in a typical review question. Read and complete each activity. Then in the next class, discuss and compare answers with other classmates. Have some students take the role of the salesperson, and see how they would react. Remember, *"You learn more about a person in an hour of play than in a lifetime of conversation."*—Plato

1. Assume you are making a sales presentation to a prospect about the purchase of a flatscreen television. Write a possible trial close and a closing question that you could use.

2. Visit a furniture showroom or store that sells exercise equipment. What sorts of attempts to close the sale were made? Could they have been improved? If so, why, and how?

CASE STUDY

Case 13.1—Sales Power

Linda Parker, representative for a leading cosmetic maker, leafed through a business magazine directed to retail drug stores. She noticed an ad for a new, low-priced home-permanent kit being introduced by one of her company's competitors. "Here we go again," she thought. "These prices are going to look good to stores who love to advertise low prices on popular items to build up store traffic." So Linda was not surprised to meet a price objection the very next day from the proprietor of a leading independent store who was in fierce competition with cut-rate stores in the neighborhood.

"I can't understand you big outfits," the druggist said. "There's no reason to keep prices so high on home permanents. You're probably making a huge profit on them by now; you should have recovered your research cost long ago."

"I can assure you there's no inflation in our prices," Linda said. "We use only the very best and therefore the most expensive ingredients. Our formulas are more expensive to put together, but that's why they produce a faster, longer-lasting permanent for the customer. And we're continually improving the product; so research is still important. I doubt if we'll ever stop research on this type of product because perfection isn't possible, and current hair styles call for new techniques all along."

"But those less expensive brands are all right," the druggist complained. "With this type of product, an appealing price brings people into the store, and we sell a lot of impulse items that are real profit makers. If we could feature a well-known brand like yours at a low price, we'd get better results. So if you'll give me a break on the price, I'll reorder. Otherwise, we'll just have to go with the new product. I'll still want some of your other products, but at present prices, you'll have to forget about permanents in this store from now on. My competition is giving me fits with price cuts as it is."

1. If Linda's company has a strict policy against special deals, a special price offer to this customer is not an option. Can you suggest other concessions or special help Linda might offer to convince this customer to continue to buy the more expensive item she offers?

2. Can Linda convince this customer that price is not the primary consideration for all customers?

Management Aspects:
Personal and Organizational

CHAPTER 15

CHAPTER 14

CHAPTER 16

The service you give the customer after the sale has been completed can be as important, or even more important, than the sale itself. Keeping current customers happy and regaining lost clients is the focus of chapter 14. The customer absolutely defines quality in every transaction. Great salespeople don't talk customer service—they live perfect service.

Chapter 15 shows you how to get better control of your time and your activities. The chapter really is all about personal organization and self-management. You cannot manage time, but you can manage yourself and your personal activities. Administrative ability on the part of the salesperson is fundamental to success. Statistics indicate that only about 20 percent of a salesperson's time during a typical day is spent in face-to-face interviews with prospects.

Finally, chapter 16 details job responsibilities of the sales manager, and provides a useful introduction for classes in sales management. The chapters in this section are:

14. Service After the Sale
15. Personal, Time, and Territory Management
16. Sales Force Management

WHAT IS EXCELLENCE?

Excellence is never an accident. It is achieved in an organization only as a result of an unrelenting and vigorous insistence on the highest standards of performance. It requires an unswerving dedication to continuous quality improvement.

Excellence is contagious. It infects and affects everyone in an organization. It charts the direction of programs. It establishes the criteria for planning. It provides zest and vitality to the organization. Once achieved, excellence has a way of penetrating every phase of the life of an organization.

Excellence demands commitment and a tenacious dedication from the leadership of the organization. Once it is accepted and expected, it must be nourished and continually reviewed and renewed. It is a never-ending process of learning and growing. It requires a spirit of motivation and boundless energy.

Excellence inspires; it electrifies. It potentializes every phase of the organization's life. It unleashes an impact that influences every program, every activity, every committee, every individual. To instill it in an organization is difficult; to sustain it, even more so. It demands adaptability, imagination and vigor. But, most of all, it requires from the leadership a constant state of self-discovery and discipline.

Excellence is an organization's lifeline. It is the most compelling answer to apathy and inertia. It energizes a stimulating and pulsating force. Once it becomes the standard of performance, it develops a fiercely driving and motivating philosophy of operation.

Excellence is a state of mind put into action. It is a road map to success. Success is getting what you want. Happiness is about liking what you get. Successful people form the habit of doing what unsuccessful people don't like to do.

Excellence in life is important—because it is everything. The quality of a person's life is in direct proportion to their commitment to excellence regardless of their chosen field of endeavor.

Service After the Sale

- Examine the purpose of total customer service.

- Determine what constitutes service quality.

- Know when and how to service.

- Understand your role in servicing.

- Appreciate how to upgrade and cross-sell current customers.

- Develop a systematic plan for follow-up activities.

How do you sell your products or services and keep them sold when there are so many others fighting to do the same thing? *Total customer service* is the answer. According to Dun and Bradstreet, the single, most important reason for the failure of businesses in America is lack of sales. And this refers to re-sales and up-sales as well as initial sales. So your company's job is to create and keep a customer, and your job is exactly the same.[1] Remember, no matter what your official title may be, you are a salesperson for yourself and your company. And the best way to increase your value as a salesperson is to build a loyal customer base through first rate service. The customer absolutely defines quality in every transaction. Don't talk customer service—live perfect service.[2]

> ❝ **The best way to hold your customers is to constantly figure how to give more for less.** ❞
>
> **– Jack Welch**

Because meeting and exceeding customer expectations is so vital to success, companies must develop customer service strategies. This usually involves segmenting customers because they generally have different service needs. So you must inform specific customers what kind of service they can expect, and the key to success is exceeding what you promise. Keeping customers happy, and coming back, takes more than smiles and thank-you's. It takes outrageous service. Allen Endres of the Juran Institute explains, "Customers have an increasing rate of expectation for services and a decreasing tolerance for poor service, and as a result are more likely to migrate to the vendors who provide the highest-quality service."[3] To effectively use service as a competitive weapon, you must surpass customers' expectations.

Second-Mile Action

Be willing to give your customers more than they demand, more than they expect, and even more than you feel they deserve. Exhibit 14.1 depicts one salesperson with such an attitude. Act from the desire to serve—not the desire to gain. When you make this your policy, you will do whatever you must to be of service to your client. That means that you sometimes deliver an order in your own car so that you get it to the customer sooner than your company could deliver it.

Δ Exhibit 14.1

Second-Mile Service

Going the second mile may involve a service for the customer that is unrelated to the business. "Big Jack" Frazier, who sells industrial chemicals, had a regular client in Waco, Texas, whose son was a student at San Angelo State University. The student's mother had typed a term paper for the son. Because Jack was leaving Waco for his regular trip through West Texas, he offered to take the paper to the student so it would be sure to arrive on time. Going through San Angelo was a bit out of his way, but he was happy to do it.

Paul J. Meyer, founder of SMI International, once had a client who made a hobby of collecting rocks containing fossils. When Meyer was on a vacation trip one year, he found a rock with a particularly interesting fossil on it. He packed the rock carefully and mailed it to his client. That kind of extra service, when given from sincere interest, pays rich dividends. Exhibit 14.2 highlights a company who truly understands the value of second-mile service.

∆ Exhibit 14.2

Doing The Right Thing ·

One company that understands the importance of second mile service is John Laing Homes. CEO Larry Webb sets the bar high with a simple credo: Do the right thing. The company places top priority on near-constant communication with buyers. "It's a lot more important today than a few years ago," says Vic Goochey, operations vice president in the Inland Empire division of the company.

George Hammond, vice president of Laing in Colorado Springs, pioneered a new standard for response time to warranty service requests: 15 minutes—that's 15 minutes for a phone call or visit from a customer-care representative after the request is received. Now the whole company aims for it.

Inland Empire division president Terry Neale came up with an innovative idea to raise customer satisfaction scores. He budgets $100,000 a year and one of his best customer service reps to keep Laing's homeowners even happier than they already are. The rep calls home owners, makes appointments to stop by, and then gives them gifts and asks if he can do touch-up painting or preventive maintenance. He also drops off a gift certificate and walks the house looking for something to do. "We think we're doing pretty well with customer service and trade relations, but we're only scratching the surface of what we could do."[4]

Ascertaining your client base's level of satisfaction and keeping a constant flow of feedback is the best way to know if you and your company are consistently going the extra mile. Benchmarking, in which organizations evaluate various aspects of their processes in relation to best practices, is an excellent method of performing "preventative maintenance" in your processes and interactions with customers and prospects.

The Hylant Group, an insurance brokerage with revenue of more than $100 million, decided it needed a formal process for determining the level of client satisfaction with its products and services. It retained the services of Active Retention, a company that specializes in retention, renewal, and cross-selling. Active Retention's two hallmark products are the Client Service Review™ and the National Benchmarking Module™. The Hylant Group conducted a client survey first and then began the benchmarking process. "When we were out with clients, we'd ask, 'How's it going?' Our approach was basically opportunistic, as opposed to inviting feedback in an organized fashion," says regional vice president Richard Hylant of their traditional feedback methods. With the new benchmarking strategies in place, "We were able to see exactly how we stacked up with other participants in the program," vice president of sales John McDermott said. "In some cases the results were surprising, and in other cases they weren't. Overall, our loyalty factor was very strong, at 95 percent, and the majority of that was favorable or exceptional. That was very gratifying."[5]

It pays to go the extra mile. Here are a few additional ideas that could be seen as going the extra mile in the eyes of the customer:[6]

1. Offer to pick up or deliver goods to be replaced or repaired.

2. Give a gift of merchandise to repay for the inconvenience. The gift may be small but the thought will be appreciated.

3. Reimburse for costs of returning merchandise such as parking fees or gas.

4. Discounts on office supplies, car rentals, or express shipping.[7]

5. Acknowledge the customer's inconvenience and thank him for giving you the opportunity to make it right. Make the wording of the apology sincere and personal.

6. Follow up to see that the problem was taken care of. Don't assume the problem has been fixed unless you handled it yourself.

Moments of Truth

Awareness of *quality service* by your customers and prospects can be a great advantage. Salespeople are far more likely to make a sale when they can truthfully say, "If you buy from me, I will never let you down. Servicing your account is my top priority." Jan Carlzon, president of Scandinavian Airlines (SAS), writes in his book *Moments of Truth*, "Each of our 10 million customers come in contact with five SAS employees. Each contact lasts about 15 seconds. Thus, SAS is *created* in the minds of our customers 50 million times per year, 15 seconds at a time."[8]

Customer service is like a daily election

and customers vote with their feet.

Those 50 million *moments of truth*, when customers are made aware of service quality, are the moments that ultimately determine the success of SAS. All employees must realize and care that their work affects customers' perception of service quality and even product quality, no matter how far they are removed from the "front line" or from direct communication with customers. Customer satisfaction is measured as moments in time. Plenty of customers do not come back unless the service you provide is consistently better than service provided by competitors. You must create a trust-bond relationship. Sixty-five percent of a typical firm's sales volume is done by loyal customers who return to buy again and again because of the service quality provided.

There are many ways a service organization can determine when service recovery efforts are likely to be needed. For instance, one simple method is to provide customers with an opportunity to voice their dissatisfaction by providing customer response cards, or supplying a toll-free telephone line, email address, or Web site. Such means make it easy for an unhappy customer to express a complaint. For example, Holiday Inn posts a toll-free number in its rooms for travelers to use if they wish to complain to company executives rather than to the hotel property.[9] Exhibit 14.3 spotlights one company who has truly created trust as well as a place for themselves in their customers' hearts.[10]

Δ Exhibit 14.3

Charity Begins at the Call Center ·

VIRTUATel, a division of Interactive Voice Response Ltd who specializes in the development of hosted and on-premise voice automation applications, has put a new spin on customer feedback. They give their customers an incentive to send in their comments and opinions by donating money for every customer response survey that is called in. The donations go to Beacon Care at Home, a charity that provides care and support for patients at home, particularly at night, towards the end of their lives. Alan Weaser, a director and co-founder of VIRTUATel comments, "I'm sure our clients are pleased that the opinions they're gathering are helping a good cause."

Service Techniques That Support Relationships

Value Added

Jim Jewett, author of *Discovering Fast Track Success* and founder of Telco Research, an international telecommunications company, attributes much of his company's success to the ability of his salespeople to engage in value-added thinking. He defines this concept as "seeking out every possible opportunity to add customer value."[11] Recognizing value added is much easier than defining it. When you are in the position of the customer, you recognize value added when you receive it—and you remember it! Here are a few examples of value-added service:

- Salespeople from Caterpillar Tractor promise that their customers will receive ordered parts within forty-eight hours anywhere in the world. This after-sale service is both appealing and highly successful. The promise is not an idle one; if the delivery is not made within the forty-eight hours, the part is free.

- The air conditioner in your car goes out, and you take it in to the service department of the car dealership to be repaired. They find they must order a part that will not arrive for two days. You mention to the service manager that you really need to get the car fixed before the weekend because you are planning a trip. Two days later when you take the car in to have the new part installed, the mechanic finds that the wrong part was shipped and they will have to reorder. The service manager asks you to wait for a minute and returns with a set of keys and says, "Here, we want you to use one of our demonstrators for the weekend. The new part will be here early Monday morning, and you can pick up your car by noon."

When an automobile service department repairs your car's air conditioner, that isn't service. It's what you paid them to do. When you are provided with a car while they wait for a replacement part, that is service—and you remember it. The delay in getting the part was not their fault, but they knew the delay was not your fault either. Their concern was helping you have a comfortable trip. One weekend's use of a demonstrator was a small price for the dealership to pay for the kind of goodwill that will bring you back to purchase a new car next year.

One company that understands the power of value added service is Ameribanc National Ltd. Not only do they offer value to their customers, their products themselves give their clients the opportunity to offer free value-added incentives to their own customers. Ameribanc sales agents actively market a flat-rate, no-risk gift card program to the 500-plus merchants a month that buy their innovative, free terminal program they can access online. These merchants can offer loyalty rewards and gift cards to their customers that they can then redeem on the Ameribanc terminal. And Ameribanc differentiates itself from other loyalty reward programs by offering customization services unique for each client. In other words, their merchants can select which rewards they wish to offer to their customers, rather than having a generic list of gift cards and vendors from which to choose. And this customization feature comes at no extra charge—now that's value added![12]

The automobile industry estimates that a brand-loyal customer represents a lifetime average revenue of $140,000 to the manufacturer. Carl Sewell estimates the lifetime value to his Cadillac dealership in Dallas of one satisfied buyer at well over $300,000. Home improvement retailer Home Depot determined its typical shopper's lifetime value to the store to be $25,000. The professional salesperson has numerous opportunities for follow-up activities that determine whether particular customers will reorder as well as whether they will tell others of their satisfaction or provide referrals to other prospects. The relationship sales rep is sincerely and unselfishly helpful to clients and prospects alike. Sometimes value-added service costs nothing except thoughtfulness and a few minutes of time.

Herb Kelleher founded Southwest Airlines to set itself apart from other airlines. Since inception the company has been known for its low fares and attention to customer service. Southwest has maintained a high level of customer satisfaction not just because of its flights, but also because of its value-added service. Exhibit 14.4 shows how Southwest Airlines adds value to its service and develops a loyal customer base.[13]

Δ Exhibit 14.4

· Going Above and Beyond

At 9:00 p.m. one Christmas Eve, customer service agent Rachel Dyer was working the ticket counter at Southwest Airlines when a man with a cane approached her. In a faint voice he told her that he had to go to New Orleans. It seems that his sister-in-law had dropped him off with some cash and a plastic bag full of clothes, and told him to go to New Orleans where he had some relatives. Confused and worried, the man explained that he'd also recently undergone bypass surgery.

Dyer responded by reassuring him that they would work everything out. She booked him on the earliest flight to New Orleans the next morning, got him a hotel and a meal ticket for dinner and breakfast, and tipped a World Services employee to take the man to the airport shuttle. Dyer bent down to explain his itinerary to him and told him everything would be okay. He told her, "Thank you," then bowed his head and started to cry.

In Southwest's monthly employee newsletter, Dyer wrote, "I am so proud to work for a company that not only allows but encourages me to help people who really are in need. I truly believe the success of this company has to do with the fact that it was founded and is run by kind, honest and loving people."

Get More From Current Customers

Managers are telling their sales forces to get out of the office and start building personal relationships with their customers. Chick-Fil-A founder Truett Cathy knows how important the customer base can be for business. "We can outperform [the competition] because we teach our employees the importance to be kind to customers. Your customers become cheerleaders for you, and you have to do little advertising. They're worth more than TV and radio," Cathy says of his customer base.[14] Thus, not only can current customers be sources of additional income themselves, they can in essence become part of your marketing team!

Sell current customers more of what you're already selling to them. Other departments may have a need. Sell them upgrades, enhancements, or additional products. Needs change over time. Sell your current clients something new. Keep them up-to-date on new products. Sell customers on you. Strive to become a trusted member of their team and opportunities will present themselves.[15]

Upgrading or Up-selling. Upgrading, also known as *up-selling*, is the process of persuading the customer to purchase a better-quality product or, perhaps, a newer product. Upgrading is largely a matter of selling your company and pushing the quality factors of your product and customer image. You ask for the upgrade because the newer or higher-quality product will serve the needs of the client better than the less expensive version of the same product. Most firms have products that vary in quality and price. And most buyers like to have choices when making a purchase. The only way you can succeed in upgrading is to believe one hundred percent in what you're doing, think ahead, service your clients, and create win-win relationships.

The cornerstone of selling—especially when trying to upgrade a client—relies on continuously qualifying the prospect throughout the buying process. It's ultimately the customer's choice and you don't want to oversell, but giving them options is just logical. You want to sell to the real needs of the prospect. Salespeople need to remember they don't sell products—they sell results. Sadler Evans, account executive for Comcast Cable Advertising of Huntsville, Alabama, says he is "more of a consultant instead of just a salesperson scrambling to make his monthly numbers."[16] Evans attempts to upgrade his clients to the point where he thinks the advertising schedule will work. One of his clients wanted to start out at $600 per month, but Evans was convinced that at least $750 was needed for the advertising to be effective. The client took his recommendation. It worked, and now the company is a really solid account, spending about $2,500 per month.

Cross-selling. *Cross-selling* is the process of selling products that are not directly connected to the primary products being sold to new and/or established clients. For example, cross-selling occurs when in a conversation with your bank's loan officer about a loan for expanding your business, you casually mention how expensive it is to keep your two elementary school children in a private school. Several days later, you receive a note in the mail from that same loan officer with materials describing how a limited trust fund could be used to help pay college expenses and offering the bank's services to help set it up.

Cross-selling and upgrading have become increasingly important to many companies in this information age. Customers have to be convinced that what you have available is going to solve a problem or save them money before they're even willing to talk. "To be truly customer-focused you have to make as many channels available as your customers are demanding," says Ann Vezina, vice-president of customer relationship management at systems integrator EDS. To do the best job of fostering lifetime loyalty, you need to know exactly what your customers are thinking. The ideal scenario goes like this: When a customer contacts our customer service hotline via email or telephone, the agents in our call center can call up a comprehensive record of every interaction, no matter how, why, or when. And the most profitable callers are identified and directed to the most knowledgeable agents right away. Our agents get a view of our customers that is so granular they can *cross-sell* and *up-sell* products to our customer base.[17]

It really does pay to go the extra mile for the customer; not just for their benefit, but for yours as well. In fact, the payoff of exceptional, consistent customer service can be summed up in four primary categories, called the "Four R's." They are:[18]

1. **Referrals**. Loyal customers encourage others to choose your company or product over the competition, saving you the substantial cost of acquiring new customers. Where yesterday's "word of mouth" could influence a dozen individuals, today's "word-of-mouse," via email or blogs, can influence thousands.

2. **Retention**. Customers who continue to do business with you provide a solid base for success. Your most loyal customers should cost you the least to service because they are not as sensitive to competitive pressures.

3. **Reputation**. Loyal customers speak well of you to others. They increase public support and positive interest from investors, suppliers, future employees, the media, and even regulatory bodies.

4. **Revenue**. Loyal customers give you a larger share of their business, which increases overall revenue and the recognition that comes with success. As mentioned previously, cross-selling and up-selling to existing customers can be the primary growth strategy for an organizations and is particularly lucrative with loyal customers.

Retain Or Win Back Unhappy Customers

A customer calls and launches into a tirade, complaining and whining about everything. Who needs an account like this? But then you stop, catch your breath, and think, "When clients are rude it's usually because they are having a problem with some aspect of our product or service." No matter how badly clients behave, avoid responding angrily. You must learn not to take their rudeness personally. Maintain a positive attitude and an even tone of voice. This serves to disarm them and they will generally follow your lead. For all the steps you may take, some may inevitably be unhappy with whoever services them. Sometimes a resolution isn't always to the consumer's satisfaction—this isn't a perfect world.[19]

Restate the client's concerns to demonstrate that you were listening. Employ empathy by putting yourself in their shoes and seeing it *from their perspective*. Remember that this customer is reacting to a real or perceived problem with your product or service that they feel has let them down. Thank the customer for bringing the issue to your attention and then recommend a plan to solve it while the client is still on the phone. Make sure your proposed solution meets with the customer's approval. Lastly, follow up with a personal visit to ensure the issue has been resolved and the client is completely satisfied. This tends to build a stronger relationship and greater loyalty with clients.[20] The following is a list of additional ideas to keep your customers smiling no matter what the circumstance was surrounding the sale:

When a customer is angry, try to see things from their perspective.

1. **Be genuine in your efforts**. First and foremost, customer service can't be lip service.

2. **Be proactive**. Anticipate any further problems and their needs every step of the way and take care of those needs.

3. **Communicate thoroughly and frequently**. Don't give your customers the chance to call you to inquire about a late order or faulty merchandise. Be the first to communicate with them.

4. **Go the extra mile to do what's not expected**. Consumers can be a pretty jaded bunch. If you go above and beyond to offer what they need but least expect, you're sure to gain many, many fans.

5. **Create a memorable experience**. In today's business climate, "good" is as good as dead. You have to be the best to succeed, so you have to do whatever you can to leave an impression in your customers' minds.

6. **Be professional**. This is the best medicine for an upset customer.[21]

Service in Response to Needs

When you are practicing ongoing service, you can anticipate complaints and handle them promptly before they become serious sources of customer dissatisfaction. A customer who is dissatisfied with a product or service tells an estimated nine or ten other people. Always respond immediately to the possibility of a complaint or to one that is actually expressed. The salesperson who assumes that a customer must be satisfied because he has voiced no gripes over an extended period, is living in an unreal world. "Unless those dream customers called me to order goods or praise my products or service, I wouldn't let too much time go by without visiting them. Complaints can be customer-saving opportunities," says Ray Dreyfack.[22]

Technical Assistance Research Programs Inc. (TARP), based in Washington, D.C., conducted research among manufacturing concerns that produced overwhelming evidence of the value not only of "handling" complaints but also of going out of the way to encourage and then remedy complaints. TARP's key findings include these:

- Of unhappy customers, only four percent of them complain to company headquarters. For every complaint received, the average company has 26 customers with problems, six of which are "serious," who do not complain.

- Among customers with problems, complainers are more likely than non-complainers to do business with the company again, even if the problem isn't satisfactorily resolved.

- Between 54 and 70 percent of complainers will give repeat business if their complaint is resolved, but a staggering 95 percent are repeat customers if they feel the complaint was resolved quickly.

- Dissatisfied complainants tell 9 or 10 people about their experience. 13 percent recount the incident to more than 20 people. Customers who have their complaints satisfactorily resolved tell an average of five people about the treatment they received.[23]

Retaining Existing Customers

Service after the sale is critical to retaining existing customers, particularly in technical selling. In many technical sales, up to fifty percent of the sale involves the follow-through stage of the selling cycle. More technical sales are lost through inadequate follow-up than from any other cause. When so much time is invested in making a sale, attempting to save time by neglecting follow-up is a costly mistake. A bad buying experience can be a bitter and enduring memory. There is no substitute for salespeople asking their customer base how they feel about the service the company is providing.

All the efforts to retain customers is certainly not without benefits. Customer retention results from customer satisfaction. The average business loses about 15 to 20 percent of its customer base a year, forcing them to put money and effort into attracting new customers. It has been estimated that reducing customer defections by as little as five percent can double a firm's profits.[24] The banking industry is one area that recognizes the importance of keeping and communicating with current customers. *MoneyFind* of Campbell, California, is a company aimed at helping banks and their lending arms retain clients by better identifying which customers need what products—and when.[25]

> "**Those who enter to buy support me**. Those who come to flatter please me. Those who complain teach me how I may please others so that more will come. Those only hurt me who are displeased but do not complain. They refuse me permission to correct my errors and thus improve my service."
>
> **-Marshall Field**

Win Back Angry Customers

No one enjoys losing a customer. Winning back a customer who has turned to a competitor helps your feelings as well as your sales records. The first step in regaining a customer is to discover why you lost the account. Almost 80 percent of former customers leave because they feel they've been badly treated.[26] It is your responsibility to mend this relationship. Exhibit 14.5 gives some of the most common "excuses" given by salespeople for losing accounts. If you put aside such excuse-making, then some real soul searching can show you why the account was lost.

Δ **Exhibit 14.5**

Excuses Salespeople Give for Losing Accounts

- If it isn't price, then it's because the competition uses unfair or unethical tactics.

- My company fails to back me up; delivery is late, or quality deteriorates.

- That customer is just too difficult for anyone to get along with.

- The customer never cared about anything but price, so I was helpless.

- I just don't have time to make all the service calls I'd like to make.

- There can't be anything wrong with my sales techniques. I'm doing exactly what I've been doing for years.

You will find helpful questions to ask that relate directly to the product or service you sell. Listen carefully to what the customer tells you in answer to each question. Do not contradict what the customer has told you, argue, or become angry yourself, no matter how angry or unreasonable the customer may seem to you.

When faced with an angry customer, you have two choices. One, you can walk away and consider the account lost; or two, you can resolve the conflict and further reinforce the relationship.[27] If you listen politely, ask additional questions, and probe for hidden feelings, the mere act of telling you what is wrong often defuses the negative feelings of the customer. The former

satisfaction that was experienced in doing business with you surfaces and the customer may be quite happy to consider reestablishing your relationship.

Do your best to glean every bit of current information you can regarding this angry customer, along with what you know of your relationship with the customer in the past, in order to decide what went wrong. Here are some possible reasons that you might lose an account:[28]

Something You Have Done. No one is at top effectiveness all the time. Without intending to do so, you may have said or done something that offended the customer or damaged your credibility in some way. Exhibit 14.6 illustrates a sure-fire way to offend a customer and destroy a relationship. The old slogan for Arpege perfume began, "Promise her anything, but...." For you, the "but" must be followed by "don't promise what you can't deliver."

Δ Exhibit 14.6

Destroying Credibility with the Customer ·

YOU WANT IT WHEN?

Something You Fail To Do. Failing to tell the full story about what the product can or cannot do, failure to keep the customer informed about product or delivery changes, failure to meet promises, failing to follow up or waiting too long to follow up—all these omissions destroy the customer's faith in you, your product, and your company.

Something The Company Does. If the company delivers only a portion of an order, substitutes some items in the order without telling the customer or makes errors in billing, the customer may become dissatisfied enough to change suppliers.

Something The Company Fails To Do. The company may fail to meet the promised delivery schedule without warning, fail to provide necessary training and technical backup as promised, or fail to meet maintenance agreements.

Take some time for problem solving. Until you discover and acknowledge the real problem, you cannot solve it. Sometimes the answer is unpleasant. If the problem lies in your actions or attitudes, you must accept responsibility so that you are free to solve the problem and regain the account. If you deny your obvious responsibility, you escape into excuse making and are blinded to the options available for regaining the customer's goodwill. When you know what the problem is, you can plan strategies for rebuilding the account.

A Systematic Plan For Follow-up

Your tracking system for servicing should be as well-organized as your prospecting system. Set up a rotating tickler file by dates of expected contact for each account. Use a card file or computer program. The file method chosen should list the customer's name (company and individual with whom you deal), the date of each service contact, and the form it took (telephone call, letter, visit). Whatever organizing system you choose, be sure to have a specific, written plan for servicing. Your plan should include these four elements:

1. Stay Informed

The process of buying and selling does not end with the purchase—unless you intend for the current purchase to be the only possible transaction you will ever have with this customer or with anyone this customer can influence. Service is the *marketing concept* in action. Service is the activities you do to keep customers sold permanently. The sale is not complete until the customer is satisfied. You have a responsibility that goes far beyond closing the sale. You may carry the responsibility for customer satisfaction a long time after the sale has been made. It is not enough to "pass the buck" to a service representative; tell your customers how to get in touch with them and be prepared to help them make initial contact. Giving the customer the name of a person to contact when things go wrong is an excellent idea. If something goes wrong, your client has the right to expect you to help him put things right.[29]

Frequent service calls on existing customers help you keep up with personnel changes in their company. If you meet new personnel early, a relationship can be developed and your credibility established before you ask for a new order. Make sure you do not continue to send mail addressed to a buyer's predecessor. Keeping up with personnel changes not only helps you solidify your presence with the existing company client but also gives you an ally in the company where the former employee now works.

You also learn about anticipated changes in the company structure when you make frequent service calls. Perhaps a merger or an acquisition is about to take place. Your customers may be planning to introduce a new product line that will increase their need for your product or service, or they may be expanding their whole general operation as a result of increased sales. All of these conditions affect you as a salesperson, but you will not hear of them while the information can help you unless you are there. It takes days, weeks, even months to get a customer. Regaining a lost customer after poor service will be much more expensive than keeping a current customer satisfied.[30]

GAINING A NEW CUSTOMER COSTS FIVE TIMES MORE THAN
KEEPING A CURRENT ONE.

2. Make Phone Calls

The telephone is one of your best service tools. It allows you to give the customer personalized attention with less investment of time for both you and the customer than would be required by a personal visit. Customers respond positively to the fact that you are interested in them and how the product is meeting their needs, and they are also pleased that they did not need to spend half an hour in a personal visit with you. Here are some of the items of service you can handle through phone calls:

- Verify delivery
- Check for problems
- Inform the customer of price changes or possible shortages
- Check customer's inventory level

A Variety of Communication Devices. "Make it possible for your customers to reach a live person—even when you aren't available," advises Eric Harris, sales manager at Benefit Partners in Roseville, California. His job is to offer independent insurance agents or brokers and their customers access to a wide selection of health insurance plans. The brokers need fast, accurate information when they call, and for that reason Harris' phone does not have voice mail so that callers can always talk to a live person. If their specific rep is not available, brokers talk to another member of the sales team who can answer their questions.

The telephone isn't always enough. Use a variety of communication media to make sure you reach your customer and that your customer can reach you.

When you secure a new client, learn the person's schedule, best times to call, email address, fax number, cell phone number, other office telephone numbers, and even his home telephone number. Exhibit 14.7 illustrates the value of having the necessary information and the trust of your client.[31]

Δ **Exhibit 14.7**

Telephoning a Client on a Sunday Afternoon ···

Robert Lowcher, account manager of Time Distribution Services, called a customer at home on a Sunday, and it paid off for both of them. Lowcher said, "When John F. Kennedy Jr.'s plane went down, most people were uncertain if he was dead." However, Time magazine assumed he had died and planned a memorial issue in his honor. The buyer he called usually ordered 5,000 copies for his stores, but that would not be nearly enough because this issue would be a big seller if indeed their assumption proved correct. Lowcher talked to his buyer

on Sunday afternoon and told him about the special issue and that the deadline for ordering extra issues was that evening. The customer ordered 25,000 copies and sold 90 percent of them that next week. Lowcher says, "If I hadn't been looking out for my customer and built a relationship based on trust, both of us would have lost out."

3. Determine Call Frequency

Decide how often you will call on each customer. Base this on your experience with each customer and with customers in general in your business. Consider account penetration (current and potential volume) and customer need. Rate your accounts as A, B, and C, much as you rate prospects, according to how much business you can expect to develop with each one and how many referrals that customer can generate for you that will produce business in addition to what that account provides. Also consider the personality and needs of the customer and determine what care is needed to maintain goodwill and a solid relationship. Decide also whether calls will be by telephone, in person, or a combination.

4. Send Mail (Letter or Card)

When your customer has no specific problems or need to reorder, keep your name before the customer with direct-mail items like these:

- New promotional material your company produces that will help the customer use the product more successfully.

- Information about new products from your company that might interest your customer.

- Your company in-house newsletter that could include trade information, promotional articles, and stories that might interest your customer (Be sure to write a few words of greeting).

- A letter with a self-addressed business reply card on which the customer can check the level of satisfaction (excellent, good, fair, poor) with your product.[32]

Give close attention to the effectiveness of each type of service contact you offer to your customers or clients. Discard methods that do not work, and repeat methods that do. Keep your service records as meticulously as you do your data on prospecting. Know what you have done for each customer, what you plan to do next, and when.

Hallmark keeps in touch with their customers by regularly sending personalized cards. They developed a division called Hallmark Business Expressions that caters specifically to businesses and consulting services. The salespeople send welcome cards to new customers, as reminders of their purchase and to begin the relationship. Scott Robinette, the director of business development for Hallmark Business Expressions, says, "We don't attempt to get a sale. When we send a card to a customer we do so with the intent of developing a relationship." In the future, the company plans to send cards to clients marking their "anniversary" as customers. Exhibit 14.8 illustrates how a thank-you card and a follow-up phone call paid off for a creative salesperson.[33]

△ Exhibit 14.8

It Pays to be Prompt

Thank each client you visit promptly! This is what Julie Puckett, a sales rep with Home Buyer Publications in Fairfax, Virginia, does. And it is something worth emulating. Before Julie travels on business she addresses an envelope to each customer she plans to visit. After each appointment, and while the details are still fresh in her mind, she immediately creates a handwritten card thanking them for their time and expressing how much she enjoyed the meeting. The note is mailed that day in their city!

By the time she returns home to make follow-up phone calls, the clients have received the "thank you" cards. Puckett says, "It's surprising how often my customers refer to my note and express appreciation for its timeliness." It doesn't surprise me! It may seem like a no-brainer, but it certainly is effective for her.

SUMMARY

- The right kind of customer service brings you repeat business over time. A buying decision is a one-time action unless you turn it into a habit with effective follow-up and follow through procedures.

- Service after the sale adds value to what you sell by showing the customer that you are willing to take care of any problems. Service after the sale can be more important to your client than the actual sale itself.

- Sell current customers more of what you are already selling to them. You do this by cross-selling or up-selling to your customer base.

- After sale service gives you an opportunity to keep up with personnel and other company changes so you will know who to contact for reorders and what additional opportunities you have for supplying this customer.

- Service is an ongoing activity. It is never too soon or too long after the sale to provide service.

- Plan, execute, and track any personal visits, telephone calls and mailings to your customers and measure how effective they were.

- Service is the key to winning back lost accounts. No matter what causes the loss of an account, that loss is a signal for renewed service activity. Contact the former client with sincere concern and interest.

? REVIEW QUESTIONS

1. List ten elements of service after the sale and give a concrete example of each.

2. What is meant by value added in connection with selling? Can you give an example of a time when you experienced value added as a customer?

3. Think of a situation in which failing to keep up with personnel changes could cause loss of sales for a salesperson.

4. List some types of problems a customer might have that you, as a salesperson, could solve before they become serious by following a regular servicing program.

5. What is the salesperson's responsibility if a piece of machinery or equipment is installed and then is found to be defective or has some part missing?

6. Discuss the importance of service as an ongoing activity.

7. Explain how you would go about setting up a systematic plan for follow-up activities.

8. Describe some of the particular services that are beneficial to buyers for a retail business.

9. Is prospecting for new customers or servicing existing ones more important? Justify your answer.

10. Describe some specific servicing activities that could be used to win back a lost client.

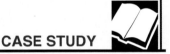

ROLE-PLAY EXERCISES

The following role-play exercises help build teams, improve communication, and emphasize the "real-world" side of selling. They are meant to be challenging, to learn how to deal with problems that have no single "right" answer and to use a variety of skills beyond those employed in a typical review question. Read and complete each activity. Then in the next class, discuss and compare answers with other classmates. Have some students take the role of the salesperson, and see how they would react. Remember, *"You learn more about a person in an hour of play than in a lifetime of conversation."* – Plato

1. Contact the manager of a major grocery store chain. Find out what services salespeople perform in the store. For example, do they build product displays, check inventories, or suggest price changes? Ask the manager what these salespeople do well and how they could improve.

2. Interview the purchasing agent of a local hospital. Ask what kinds of servicing needs arise during the course of a year. Find out if the agent has ever changed to a different supplier because of a servicing problem. With what kinds of salespeople does the purchasing agent prefer to form long-term relationships?

CASE STUDY

Case 14.1 - The Unjust Comment

Marty Silva sells a line of industrial fans in a large metropolitan area. Because he doesn't travel long distances, he is in his office the first thing every morning to make calls to set up sales interviews and to prepare for the day's sales activity. One morning just as he walked into the office, the receptionist stopped him. "There's a Mr. Morton on the phone and he sounds angry. Will you take the call?"

"Sure," Marty agreed, "he's my customer." Picking up the phone, he said, "Good morning, Mr. Morton. What can I do for you?"

"You can tell me how I'm supposed to install that circulating fan you sold me without mounting brackets. What kind of slipshod operation ships a thing like this without brackets?"

Marty was confident that the fan couldn't have been shipped without brackets, but he wisely didn't tell the customer his thoughts. "I certainly can't blame you for being upset, Mr. Morton. I'll check with our shipping department right now and I'll be in to see you this afternoon."

"Well, okay." The customer sounded a little less angry. "But maintenance had scheduled the installation for today. They're so busy that I'll probably have to wait awhile to get on their list again. I still think it was stupid on someone's part. Do what you can, Silva. Come in anytime you can get here today."

After hanging up, Marty looked at his appointment schedule. At 2:00 he was supposed to be in Westdale, all the way on the other side of the city. He didn't see how he could get to Morton's shop before closing time. He decided to check with shipping right away, though. The traffic manager, Carl Todd, suggested looking at the receiving slip. Sure enough, Morton's receiving clerk had checked off the items— including brackets, mounting(2)—and signed the receiving slip. "They must have lost them over there," Carl suggested. "Tell them to look around."

1. Marty now has proof that the brackets were delivered. Should he call the customer and tell him that his own operation is stupid and slipshod? Should he call and politely ask the customer to have his receiving people give another look for the brackets?

2. Does he have other options to consider?

3. Should he keep his promise to put in an appearance at Morton's shop today? What about his other appointment?

Case 14.2 - Shortcut to Profit

Sometimes salespeople who have built a good volume of business and a sound relationship with a customer forget to be as energetic in sustaining that business relationship as they were to establish it in the first place. Ron Beebe, who sells industrial safety equipment, tells about how he learned an important lesson.

"I suppose it's natural to gradually become complacent with a good customer and, as a result, lose a lot of good business you could have had by staying on the ball. I remember when I sold my first order of safety glasses to a large manufacturer I had been calling on for months. I followed that order through the factory, checking all along the line to be sure the customer got what was specified. As soon as the first batch was delivered, I made a special trip to the plant to be sure the order was right. Soon I was selling them hard hats, safety shoes, and ear protectors. Before long I was no longer giving such close attention to their orders. I just assumed everything was going fine. Even when I got a complaint, it seemed routine to me. But one day I learned a real lesson about keeping buyers informed.

"I had been selling ear protectors to this customer for two or three years. In the meantime, our company developed a new model that is adjustable to fit any shape or size of head. It can also be worn with various types of safety hats without discomfort. But as long as this buyer seemed satisfied with the old model, I figured I wouldn't rock the boat by showing him anything new. But my complacency backfired. One day I mentioned that they must be low on ear protectors since they hadn't ordered any for some time. That's when I got the big shock. He told me they were buying from another supplier whose product was adjustable and fit under safety hats. This cut the number of ear protectors they had to keep in inventory and solved the comfort problem when protectors had to be worn with hard hats."

"I guess I blew this one,' I admitted. 'We've had a model like that available for over a year. I didn't know you wanted to change styles,' I finished lamely.

"How could I know I wanted to change if I didn't know the model existed? We are always looking for better protective devices. And another thing, you haven't given me a new catalog for ages. Just because we've done a lot of business together doesn't mean we're married to you,' he told me in no uncertain terms. Now my problem was not only to regain the ear protector business, but to be sure I kept the business for other items, too. I won't ever forget that painful lesson!"

1. What suggestions can you give Ron about regaining the ear protector business?

2. How should Ron apply this lesson to his overall selling strategy?

Personal, Time, and Territory Management

LEARNING OBJECTIVES

- Discover how to develop an effective time management attitude.

- Recognize the need for organizing your activities and surroundings as a means of controlling your time.

- Develop a procedure for getting organized.

- Establish an effective organizing system for all activities.

- Learn how contact management and mapping programs increase productivity.

- Examine the need and the process for managing travel time in your sales territory.

The term *time management* is a contradiction. Because every minute has sixty seconds and every hour has sixty minutes, time itself cannot be managed—it can only be used. What can be managed, however, are you and your activities. So in actuality, time management is really personal organization as well as self-management; and it involves three areas:

- Self-management (also known as self-discipline)

- Planning and organizing

- Systems and techniques to form routines

Time itself is a precious commodity. Although a continuous supply of time is available, it cannot be stored for future use, and it cannot be reclaimed if it is wasted. When you realize that life itself consists of time, the value of time becomes clear. We loudly denounce attitudes or practices that show a lack of respect for human life, but we don't seem to notice when we throw away priceless hours in useless activity or idleness.

Manage your time as you would manage your money.

Use your time instead of simply spending it. Time is made up of a series of events. The key to managing time is controlling these events to your advantage.[1] Time control and self-management can be learned; you have the ability to control your present thoughts and actions and to decide how to use your time. Here are some symptoms of time mismanagement. See if any of these sound familiar to you:[2]

- Letting papers pile up on your desk and emails pile up in your in-box.

- Delaying decisions, thus frustrating both your superiors and your coworkers.

- Getting farther behind every day.

- Working late and having to work weekends.

Most of us can relate to some or all of those symptoms; so, here is an easy visualization exercise that may help you get a better grip on time's worth. Pretend that the president of your bank informs you that you have been chosen to receive a special prize: Every day for the rest of your life $86,400 will be deposited into your account. The only stipulation is that it must all be spent every day. Anything left at the end of the business day goes back to the bank. You can't hold anything over from one day to the next. Those first weeks are exhilarating. By the end of the first month, you have received over $2 million. After a while, however, you begin to have trouble spending that much every day. Think how you would feel the first time $20,000 slipped away from you and went back to the bank because you failed to spend it all. You would quickly realize that using this much money every day calls for some serious planning.

This imaginary scenario is not entirely fantasy. The old adage is true: *Time is money*. Every day, 86,400 seconds are deposited in your account and into the accounts of everyone else. You cannot save any unused time for another day. How many of your 86,400 seconds go back to the "bank" unused depends on your skill in planning and managing your time. The important questions are these:

1. How will you spend your time?

2. How will you invest your time?

3. How much time will go to business, to service for others, to family, to leisure?

4. How much time will be reserved just for you, for the things you want to do?

 Time flies. It's up to you to be the navigator.
-Robert Orben

A Time Management Attitude

Your most important asset is time, and how you use it is crucial to your success. Renowned speaker Ira Hayes once said:

> *"The inability or lack of desire to become organized is responsible for the vast majority of failures. It is why otherwise bright people turn out to be only mediocre performers and achieve only a small degree of the success that they rightfully could achieve. A disorganized desk, car, or way of life leads to rushing around and confusion and generally results in a poor attitude which makes people around you question the advisability of doing business with you."*

Everybody has the ability to manage his or her time. The *desire* is the variable that makes the difference, and taking charge of your life depends on your personal choices. Like most success factors in selling, time management depends on attitude. The first line of defense to protect your time is to identify precisely how it can be eroded, and then learn effective means for managing it.[3]

Nearly everything that we think, say, or do is governed by patterns of behavior that we develop over the years. We develop most of them early in life and rarely change them. The only way to lose a habit is to stop practicing it. Stop practicing negative habits and start practicing positive ones, and your life will improve automatically.[4] If you want to achieve high-quality results in professional sales, establish healthy habits and patterns. The people who most efficiently control their time have the best idea of what they want to accomplish.[5]

In sales—more than in many other professions—the management of time is a matter of personal choice and responsibility. Here's an idea to try: Get to work by five o'clock in the morning three times a week, and you'll gain an extra day. You will realize a great feeling of satisfaction at eight o'clock when you have already finished what would have taken you at least six hours to do during normal working hours because of the interruptions.[6]

"The average American worker has fifty interruptions a day, of which **seventy percent have nothing to do with work.**"

-W. Edwards Deming

Mental preparation is necessary to win the race against time. Developing a time management attitude helps to overcome life's obstacles. Just as Olympic champions practice diligently and relentlessly to perfect their athletic techniques, you can practice time management techniques and maximize the benefits to be enjoyed from both professional and personal pursuits.

You can let the whole subject of time management assume such proportions that the mere thought of attempting to master it becomes frustrating. It is estimated that the typical salesperson spends an average of only two hours a day in productive selling. However, just increasing the time spent with a customer doesn't do very much for you, it's what you do with the time that's important. Focus your time so that it matches opportunity. Perhaps it is a better strategy to target five large accounts, rather than target 50 accounts and divide your time trying to get each one of them. You don't have enough time or enough protection, and competitors swoop in and take them away.[7]

Keep a positive perspective toward time and your use of it. Here are some suggestions for establishing the kind of time attitudes that will bring you success:

1. Make a list of the activities you want to complete during the next week to achieve the results you desire.

2. For an entire week, keep an hour-by-hour record of exactly what you do with your time. Summarize your record and compare what you actually do to the list you made of what you want to do to achieve your goals. (Exhibit 15.1 illustrates a form you can draw to use for this purpose.)

3. At the end of each day and at the end of each week, take a personal accounting of what you have accomplished compared to what you set out to do.

4. List the five habits or attitudes that were the biggest obstacles to the achievement of the results you wanted. Write out a plan for changing these habits or attitudes. Conduct another time analysis study three months from now and compare the two. Determine whether you are making progress in replacing these habits or attitudes with new ones.

Δ Exhibit 15.1

Daily Time Survey

	Prospecting	Telephone for Appointments	Sales Interviews	Travel	Reports and Paperwork	Meetings	Sales Training	Servicing Accounts	Preparing for Interviews	Studying Product Info.		
6 am												
7 am												
8 am												
9 am												
10 am												
11 am												
12 pm												
1 pm												
2 pm												
3 pm												
4 pm												
5 pm												
6 pm												
7 pm												
8 pm												
9 pm												
10 pm												

Conducting a detailed personal time-analysis study at least twice a year is a good habit to establish. Just as you schedule a regular medical checkup (or at least you should), plan for a time management checkup to keep you aware of how well you are using your time resources.

Getting Organized

Many professionals have the skills to be successful, but they are often held back by their bad habits. If you are disorganized or inefficient, the first step towards organization is to determine what type of "time abuser" you are. There are three types:[8]

1. **Procrastinators**—Do you leave assignments until the eleventh hour and then throw yourself into a panic, working round-the-clock in a vain attempt to meet a deadline?

2. **People Pleasers**—Do you chronically take on more and more responsibility out of a fear of confronting authority and eventually commit too much time to unproductive projects?

3. **Perfectionists**—Do you take more time than is allotted to satisfy extremely unrealistic but deeply internalized standards of excellence?[9]

Once you identify what type or types you may be, and before you can gain any measure of control over your time, you must lay the groundwork for effectively handling the onslaught of information you encounter every day. The following techniques can help you:

Remove the Clutter

"Simplicity is the ultimate sophistication."

~Leonardo DaVinci

You can think more clearly and more creatively if you remove as much clutter as possible from your life and your living space. Remove unnecessary papers from your work area—your desk, your attaché case, and your car. Even if the stacks of paper are neat and appear to be well organized, they promote a subconscious psychological tendency to review and think through the items in sight. According to a national Harris Interactive survey by Cambridge Home & Office Accessories in Stamford, Connecticut, more than 84 percent of salespeople polled are *pilers*—they regularly stack up their paperwork instead of filing it.[10]

In a few seconds you can think through all of the tasks or in completions that are represented by a sizable stack of paper. For all practical purposes, however, your mind does not differentiate between doing a task physically and doing it mentally. If you mentally review a big stack of paper a dozen times a day in the process of deciding which one to tackle next, or which one to avoid, you are exhausted long before the day is over. Once you decide to dispense with clutter, tackle the job at once. Follow this plan to eliminate the disorder from your surroundings and your life:

1. **Collect the Clutter**. Gather up all the clutter that affects you and take it to one convenient work area. Empty your car, bedside table, pockets, and any other cubbyhole where you stick things that are waiting to be done. Dump all the clutter into one container.

2. **Sort the Clutter**. Divide the clutter into two categories: Time-critical material (that is, items with a specific due date) and "someday" material (that is, items that need to be addressed but have no specific due date). Removing clutter allows you to think more clearly and creatively.

3. **Deal With Priorities**. Deal first with the time-critical items. Provide a series of thirty-one folders to represent the days of the month. (This is commonly called a *1-31 file*.) A computer master calendar is just as handy and can quickly retrieve each day's notes or retrieve items by subject. You may still need the 1-31 file to collect reports, memos, and other written items. Examine each of the items you have identified as time critical. If it involves a meeting or a specific hour of the day, write it on your calendar. Then put each item in the folder for the day that

the first action must be taken to meet the due date. Each day check the appropriate folder as you make your daily to do list. Then each item will be accomplished on time.

4. **Set Up Categories for the Rest**. Now begin to organize the *someday* material. Set up two convenient files—the stacked in-out file boxes are helpful. Label these files *reading* and *projects*. Go through your someday items and sort them in the two files according to their nature. Pull out a reading item to take along when you are going somewhere that might involve a wait, and then use waiting time to catch up on reading. The material in the projects box may then be sorted into folders for each separate project.

Handling Interruptions

To handle interruptions properly, you must first determine whether an occurrence is truly an interruption or part of your job. Only when you understand this difference are you able to control your attitude toward the people and the circumstances that threaten to get in your way as you are doing your job. Once you determine that an interruption is part of your job, decide whether it is more important than what you are currently doing or whether it should be postponed. This will help you keep your priorities straight and reduces procrastination.[11]

Interruptions typically fall into three categories, each of which you can handle with the right attitude. Exhibit 15.2 lists the three types of interruptions and examples of the most common ways that people experience them.

Δ Exhibit 15.2

Types of Interruptions

People	Paper	Environmental
• Superior	• Notes	• Telephone calls
• Associate	• Memos	• Visual distractions
• Subordinate	• Correspondence	• Comfort factors
• Client or customer	• Periodicals	-temperature
	• Messages	-light
	• Projects	-clothing

People Interruptions. People interruptions are the most frustrating because they are the most difficult to solve, and who the person is makes a difference in the way you respond. If your superior interrupts you, remember that that person probably has the right to interrupt you. If you are working on an item of extreme importance with a tight deadline or are due to leave for an appointment with a prospect, however, you can properly ask respectfully whether your superior might wait until your project or call is completed. It's okay to say "no" to your superiors.[12] As your work is presumably important to the success of the organization, and therefore to your superior as well, most bosses consider such a request to be a mark of both effectiveness and self-confidence on your part.

When a client interrupts you either by phone or in person, adopt the attitude that this contact is not an interruption. You do not automatically put your full day at the disposal of a client's whim, but you do give full attention while the client is talking and then do whatever is necessary to take care of the situation.

Paper Interruptions. People who work in a disorganized environment experience both confusion and frustration when confronted with necessary paperwork. They feel confused

because they have no automatic method for handling the item; they spend too long thinking about how to handle it. Then, because they dislike feeling confused, they become frustrated with the repeated inroads made on their time by additional paperwork. Before very long, disorganized people decide they just hate all paperwork. Salespeople are often among those who say they hate paperwork because they feel that it is less important in producing their income than their direct selling activities.

Howard Langejans, vice-president of Orion Research, equips all salespeople with laptop computers. Using this equipment, they enter orders and call reports directly into the computer by phone from wherever they might be. They can also access the computer to find new leads that may have come in. The only paperwork left is the expense report, and Langejans adds, "Salespeople don't mind that kind of paperwork because it brings them money."[13]

Environmental Interruptions. Distractions in your work space can wreak havoc on your productivity if not properly addressed and controlled. Instead of feeling overwhelmed by environmental distractions such as frequent phone calls, schedule a specific telephone time each day to set up appointments for sales presentations and to take care of other sales-related business.

Email is one of the newest and most treacherous time zappers. Some organizations have tried email-free-Friday. Others have attempted to ban it altogether. The starting point is to ban any casual use of email. Next, take the time to audit incoming mail and don't be afraid to be selective. Try to set aside specific periods to deal with it. Turn the sound off on the computer, so you are not alerted every time a message arrives.[14] Then the remainder of the day is free for those vital selling contacts. When you have a particularly important piece of work to complete, take everything you need to do the job and go to a place where you can work without any kind of interruption.

> **Ordinary people** think merely of **spending time.**
> **Great people** think of **using it.**

An Organizing System

The challenge for salespeople is to discover the methods that work for them, and typically this will be different for everyone. What's important is that you take the guesswork out of the sales process and replace it with a defined business process. Recognize that success is a percentage game; sales is a profession in which there can never be 100 percent success. Just because you have a clean desk and an organized filing system won't guarantee you will make more sales; but it certainly won't hurt. If you find a certain system that works for you, just keep doing it—in other words, repeat successful behaviors.[15] This is a secret of success at any level of competition. Selling is not a game that requires perfection. You only need to figure out ways to stay ahead of the competition. Identify the behaviors that will consistently improve your performance and you will be well on your way to creating a powerful sales discipline.

In order to be on your way to staying ahead of the competition, you must first remove the unnecessary disorder from your environment. Once you remove the clutter and the incompletions from your work area and get a firm grip on controlling interruptions, two simple tools will help you organize your activities.

1. The Master Calendar

Many salespeople prefer a pocket-sized book that is always available to note an appointment. Whatever its size, the calendar should list only specific time commitments such as appointments with clients and meetings to attend. All the information needed for those specific commitments is collected in the 1-31 file folders or recorded on your computer master calendar until it is needed for the appointment or other commitment.

2. Daily To-Do List

The second time-organizational tool you will need is a daily to-do list. Be sure to prioritize each item on your list. Highlight those activities completed, and carry forward the uncompleted items.[16] A story about Charles Schwab, former president of Bethlehem Steel, shows the impact of this simple tool. Schwab called in consultant Ivy Lee and proposed a challenge, "Show me a way to get more done with my time, and I'll pay you any fee within reason."

"Fine," said Lee, "I'll give you something in twenty minutes that will increase your output at least fifty percent."

Lee then handed Schwab a blank sheet of paper and said, "Write down the six most important tasks that you have to do tomorrow and number them in order of their importance. Now put this paper in your pocket, and the first thing tomorrow morning look at item one. Work on it until you finish it. Then do item two, and so on. Do this until quitting time. Don't be concerned if you have finished only one or two. You'll be working on the most important items. If you can't finish them all by this method, you couldn't have finished them by any other method either; and without some system, you'd probably not even decide which was the most important."

Lee continued, "Use this system every working day. After you've convinced yourself of the value of the system, have your men try it. Try it as long as you wish and then send me a check for what you think it's worth." Several weeks later, Lee received Schwab's check for $10,000 — an impressive sum at the time.

As much as we may want to, no one can alter time. The trick to managing your time is to manage not your time, but your *activities*. Keep a daily to-do list of what needs to be accomplished and use the list to make sure your moving the sale forward.[17] The value of a to-do list is apparent, but it becomes even more valuable when you use it not only to identify needed tasks but to establish priorities for them. Putting top priorities first is the only way to be sure that your activities are making a direct impact on your goals. Sales success depends on establishing and steadfastly pursuing a series of goals. When you develop specific and measurable growth goals, you gain the determination and drive it takes to succeed.[18]

Charles A. Coonradt, president of Western Leadership Group, says, "In the absence of clearly defined goals, we are forced to concentrate on activity and ultimately become enslaved by it." Using a to-do list helps you develop the automatic habit of attaching a when to every thought, idea, commitment, or promise. Exhibit 15.3 is an example of a format you can use for your to-do list. If you are using a computerized master calendar, you can print out your daily to-do list. The form is not nearly as important as the practice!

Δ **Exhibit 15.3**

To-Do List with a Daily Plan to List Appointments ·

Priority	Done	Date_____ Important	Priority	Done	Date_____ Imperative

The Integrated System

The 1-31 reminder file, the master calendar, and the to-do list together constitute a place your mind can trust and a place where you can store all the reminders that must surface at a given time in the future. You can safely forget about incomplete tasks until they surface in your system. Together these organizing tools form a system that makes organization of your daily activities an automatic process. At the close of each day's work, transfer any leftover items from today's to-do list to the new list for tomorrow. Then consult your 1-31 file and your master calendar to find all the items you have scheduled for tomorrow. Note any specific times associated with those items, such as the time for an appointment or meeting. Now you are ready to begin work tomorrow without even thinking about what to do first. You are ready to begin your day with the task of highest importance.[19]

Identifying Priorities

An important concept for good time managers to understand is the *Pareto Principle*. It states that 80 percent of the value (or the frustration) of any group of related items is generally concentrated in only 20 percent of them. In other words, "a minority of the input produces a majority of the results." The principle, named for the Italian economist who proposed it, holds true for many areas of today's experience. For example:

In Measuring Value, You Receive...

80% of:
- Sales
- Productivity
- Profit
- Referrals
- Commission Income

From 20% of:
- Customers
- Activity
- Products
- Clients
- Orders

In Measuring Frustration, You Experience...

80% of:
- Absenteeism
- Errors
- Servicing Problems

From 20% of:
- Employees
- Workers
- Customers

Likewise, 80 percent of your success comes through the achievement of the top 20 percent of your goals. In managing your time effectively, you must recognize that which items you complete, not how many items you complete, determine your success.

To identify the special 20 percent of your activities that have the potential for producing the greatest success, practice establishing different categories of priorities.

"A" priority items are the most pressing. They include the items that must be done by a specific date if you are to reach one of your major goals and items that would damage the reputation of your company or your personal credibility if you failed to accomplish them.

"B" priority items are any items that can be done at any time within the next week or month without causing any repercussions.

"C" priority items would be nice to do at some time when you have nothing else pressing to do, but you would suffer no real loss if you never got around to them.

Obviously, you want to give first attention to your "A" priorities and carefully number them in the order of their importance. Your goal is to complete as many "A" priorities as you possibly can each day and then supplement them with any "B" items you can.[20]

Time Goals

Once you have established the habit of using a to-do list, begin to record next to each item your estimate of the amount of time you will need to complete it. Estimating the required time lets you judge whether you can complete everything. If you can't, you have the possibility of getting someone else to help before you fail to complete some vital item. Time studies have shown that even people who know which items are most important and set priorities still waste an average of fifteen minutes between items of work in simple procrastination or in trying to decide what to do next.

A second benefit of estimating completion times is to help in avoiding procrastination. A deadline—even an informal estimate of the time required—pushes you to complete the work in the allotted time. Northcote Parkinson is noted for his observation that *work expands to fill the time allowed* for its completion. Something about a stated time allotment seems to establish a mental set that causes you to use just that amount of time. If the time is short, you work efficiently and push for completion. If the time allowance is too generous, you procrastinate, spend extra time getting ready to work, and find a dozen small interruptions to make sure you don't finish too early. By estimating times for completion, you eliminate the tendency to procrastinate.

Positive Attitudes Toward Time

Anyone who expects sales success should also expect hard work and long hours. If you always seem to have more work than working hours, though, you may be due for a refresher course in time management. These techniques can't give you more time, but they can help you make the most of what you've got. Follow them to help you get—and keep—time on your side.

Place a Time Limit on Meetings. If you or your salespeople tend to dread meetings, maybe it's because they drag on too much and accomplish too little. Knowing your meeting lasts only an hour should help keep things moving. Before each meeting, decide on a limited number of topics to discuss and a limited time period for discussing them. Exhibit 15.4 looks at how two top executives learned to reign in abuse of meeting time.[21]

Δ **Exhibit 15.4**

Meetings: The Best Way to Avoid Real Work ·

As the new executive vice president at Barnhart/CMI, a marketing and advertising firm based in Denver, Cheryl Akright's first order of business was to cancel all of the company's regular meetings. ''It was ridiculous,'' Ms. Akright said. ''Every person in the company was in some type of meeting three to four times per day.''

Samuel J. Palmisano, chief executive of IBM, was concerned about how many meetings his company's sales representatives attended each week, Specifically, he was concerned that more than 30,000 members of the company's sales force were spending six hours a week, on average, preparing for and attending meetings. The company is so serious about its new rule on meetings that top executives must now approve any unscheduled sessions. Executives at IBM estimate that the sales force has doubled the time spent with customers as a result.

Set Deadlines and Beat Them. When you've got a lot to do and not a lot of time to do it in, deadlines can help you to stay on schedule. Prioritize your tasks, and then draw up a schedule for completing them. Don't make the mistake of waiting to start on a task just because the deadline seems far away. Chances are, something will come up to fill the extra time you think you have.

Take Advantage of Your Peak Time. To be most efficient at the jobs you like least, tackle them at the time of day when you feel most productive. Pay attention to your moods and work output throughout the day to find out when you're most productive, and save your worst jobs for when you're at your best.

It's Okay to Say No. When it comes to time management, many of us are our own worst enemy. You'll never have enough time to finish your work if you're always biting off more than you can chew. When people ask you to take on extra projects, they are putting a monkey on your back. *If you agree to take on too many jobs for others, you are soon carrying an impossible load of monkeys and accomplish nothing.*

Don't Overload on Overtime. If your workweek consistently exceeds a reasonable number of hours, ask yourself why. Identify the tasks that take up the most time and look for ways to complete them more efficiently. Also, compare the number of hours you're working to what you're actually getting done. A too-small return on your time investment indicates a problem.

Do Some Delegating. Don't feel guilty about delegating responsibility—if you take on a job that someone else could handle more effectively, you're not making the best use of your company's resources.

Put It in Writing. To remember phone numbers, important dates or anything else, write them down. Freeing your mind of clutter helps you think more clearly, and concentration is key to productivity.

Cultivate Helpful Relationships. Create and keep lasting relationships that result in people gladly working to assist you, and this can be one of your most powerful time-management strategies.

Ultimately, it's all about balance. If you are going to be an effective time manager, you need to balance the driving forces with the limiting forces in your life. Live within the zone between these two pressures so that you can be your most effective all the time.[22] Time is like talent—you can't create more of it, you just have to make the most of what you've got. You need self-discipline from the time you wake up in the morning until you go to bed that night.[23] Spending your time more wisely starts with paying attention to how you spend it. Once you decide to take control of your time, you'll have the power to stop squandering it.[24]

Managing Travel Time

Organize your time before you hit the road, not while on the road.

One of the most important considerations for field salespeople is protecting their time for making those vital sales presentations. Travel through a territory is, in a sense, nonproductive although necessary time. Linda Meyer, sales director for Oakstone Publishing Company in Ohio, says, "Organize your time before you hit the road, not while on the road."[25] She plans for time blocks—how long it will take her to write letters, do reports or recap a meeting. Look at your time as a 24-hour cycle of fragments. Travel time must be kept to a minimum.

As you learned earlier, the Pareto Principle says that 80 percent of your business will come from 20 percent of your customers. Thus, you must determine how much time and energy each account receives. Scott Gander, a sales rep for Geneal, a company selling restaurant supplies, divides all accounts into A, B, C and D accounts. He tries to spend 40 percent of his time helping A's, 30 percent with B's, 20 percent with C's, and 10 percent with the D's—the D accounts are only interested in price.[26] Be sure to categorize your accounts in a priority ranking such as:

"A"—High-volume, repeat customers.

"B"—Moderate sales volume, but reliable customers.

"C"—Lower volume accounts.

"D"—Accounts that cost you more time and energy to service than you receive in profits.

Outside salespeople travel through time and space, so it will help if they set themselves in motion on the most efficient route between customers and prospects. Sales professionals pay close attention to the routing and scheduling of their calls. They take into consideration the proper mix of accounts on each trip. Prioritizing is useful for determining a profitable mix of account visitation and servicing. A common mistake is to call on "D" accounts simply because they are located near "A" accounts, and require little travel. These customers do not need to be called on with the same regularity as the "A" accounts. Instead use your time to prospect for new high volume, repeat customers.[27]

Computer Mapping Systems

It's a safe bet that most sales managers have spent considerable time with markers and paper maps to plot their salespeople's positions. Mapping systems is a rapidly growing market of sophisticated products that put numeric data into visual form, making the data much easier to understand. These products create computer-generated maps of geographic areas of interest to both sales managers and their salespeople. This software is used to balance sales territories, optimize driving time, and then target new markets and new accounts. This desktop mapping software lets managers do in minutes what used to take hours, or even days to complete.

The PDA—Your Travel Companion

Wherever your travels take you it helps to know where to eat, where to stay, and what to see. Now all of this information is available in a handheld computer. Use the AvantGo Internet Information Service™ (www.avantgo.com) and download the information to your Personal Data Assistant, or PDA. AvantGo choices include a mapping program for getting you from point A to point B and RestaurantRow. com that organizes restaurants based on ZIP code. The maps that are generated are so precise that large buildings, tunnels, bridges, and even historic landmarks are indicated. And it will even phone or e-mail a reservation on your behalf through the channel's concierge service.[28]

Unless you have intimate knowledge of all the ZIP codes in every sales territory, it's impossible to know which areas border one another, and which don't. "You can look at a spreadsheet, but there's no substitute for looking at them nicely mapped," says Richard Bohn, president of Denali Group. "You can simply visualize the territory more easily that way."[29] Spreadsheets and databases tell you how much and what kind, while mapping software tells you where.

Dave Delmonte, sales engineer for Steel Heddle, uses a product called TripMaker™ that simplifies his trip planning. Delmonte types in his point of origin, his final destination, and any stopover points. In seconds, the digital atlas generates the appropriate map and compares alternate routes side-by-side. The program can help track expenses and budget costs for hotel, gas, meals, and also includes information on 2,800 restaurants and 12,000 hotels.[30]

Strategize Your Sales Calls

Like a leaf blowing in the wind, many salespeople leave the office with no idea where they're going. They go where the wind blows and when the wind changes direction, so do they. The solution to this is a quality contact management system coupled with a good mapping system.[31] The goal of all the various mapping programs is to minimize your *travel time* and maximize your *selling time*.

For example, Gabriel Smith, outside salesman for Apple™, uses a mapping system called BusinessMap™ to plan his road trips more efficiently. Smith covers a Southeastern territory that spans seven states, requiring him to spend 70 percent of his time on the road. He says, "If I know that I will be visiting a customer in Alabama, I can map out my route so that I can call on customers on the drive out there as well as on the way back."

The uses of computer mapping systems are limited only by your creative imagination. For example, when prospects ask you for referrals, really impress them by trying this: Use your mapping system to place the prospect on a map, and then use the system to draw a circle that identifies every one of your customers in a 25-mile radius. By doing this, you provide your prospect with a comprehensive and organized list of referrals who are nearby. Proximity is important when providing referrals to potential customers.

This mapping technology also enables a sales rep to get a list of every potential customer in a geographic area and map it against a display of the company's existing accounts. The result is an up-to-date analysis of how well you have penetrated your territory and the opportunity that remains. Maximizing travel time is an obvious and critical competitive advantage for today's traveling sales professsionals.[32]

Developing Partnerships Using Technology examines mapping programs and GPS (Global Positioning Systems). Getting lost is no longer an excuse, and there is no need to be flipping through an atlas on the side of the road. Just plug in your computer, and type in the address you wish you find, and let your GPS do the rest.

Developing Partnerships Using Technology

Here are some of the features found on most quality mapping programs:

a. **Detailed maps** with street names and geographic markings.

b. **Zoom-in** capability for more detail.

c. **Suggested routes** by the shortest, fastest, or most scenic routes.

d. **Hotel listings** by price range, wireless internet, pool, tennis courts, health club, and other amenities.

e. **Restaurant guides** searchable by cuisine, price range, or if credit cards are accepted.

f. **Toll-free numbers and websites** for car rentals and airlines, as well as information on toll roads.

g. **Assistance in tracking expenses** and budget costs for your hotel, gas, and meals.

h. **Available printouts** with written and picture directions and detailed maps.

Check out these Web sites for additional information:

www.google.com/maps

www.infousa.com

www.randmcnally.com

www.delorme.com

www.microsoft.com

www.travroute.com

www.yahoo.com

www.mapsonus.com

Territory Routing Patterns

You may not realize it, but traveling in your territory involves more strategic planning than merely getting from point A to point B. Two popular scheduling or *routing patterns* have been developed and are used by field salespeople to cut travel time in their territories and maximize face-to-face selling opportunities, and they are:

The Cloverleaf Pattern—Exhibit 15.5 illustrates how this travel pattern might look. The starting point may be your home or the district or regional sales office location. One "leaf" is covered at a time. Each leaf or quadrant could take a day, a week, or longer to complete. A new leaf is started on each subsequent trip, until the entire territory is covered.

Δ **Exhibit 15.5**

The Cloverleaf Pattern

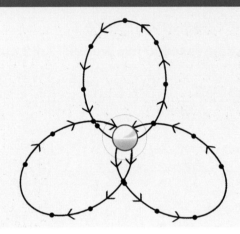

The Hopscotch Pattern—Exhibit 15.6 is a graphic illustration of this travel pattern. You begin at the most distant point from your home base and make prospect and client calls on the return trip. Depending on the size of the territory (some sales reps have territories that encompass several states), you may fly out to the starting point and drive back. Outside salespeople can vary this pattern and cover different directions on subsequent trips.

Δ **Exhibit 15.6**

The Hopscotch Pattern

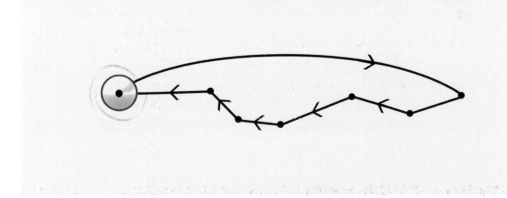

Two other routing patterns are the *Circular Pattern* and the *Straight-line Pattern*. Dividing the territory into several segments and scheduling appointments for a single day in one segment of the territory makes considerable sense. Controlling your schedule in this manner does not preclude flexibility to meet an important prospect or client regardless of location; occasionally, you will choose to readjust your plan for an important reason. Without a plan, however, you are so flexible that you are soon all bent out of shape.

The great dividing line between
success and failure
can be expressed in five words; "I did not have time."

-Franklin Field

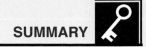

SUMMARY

- The ability to manage time efficiently and effectively is fundamentally a matter of attitude. *Time is money.* If you seek advancement and a comfortable income, managing time properly is one of the best skills you can develop.

- Interruptions are ultimately just time wasters, so handle them with planning and control. Interruptions come from everywhere—including people, paper, and environmental factors.

- A workable system for time management includes at least three elements:

    1) A master calendar for scheduling commitments.

    2) A daily to-do list to record activities to be done each day to reach your goals.

    3) A reminder file to hold items that will become important at a specific later date.

- Personal Data Assistants (PDAs) allow you to download mapping software onto your laptop or vehicle navigation system to make getting around and tracking appointments more convenient.

- Use mapping systems and territory routing patterns to balance sales territories, optimize driving time, and target new markets and accounts.

REVIEW QUESTIONS

1. Write a hundred-word statement giving your opinion about the importance of effective time management and its possible impact on your future in professional selling.

2. What three activities must your mind perform that affect how you use time? How does a system for time management make each of these tasks easier?

3. Describe an effective method for handling incomplete tasks.

4. How does a cluttered desk or briefcase affect time use? What kind of impression do you think a cluttered office or briefcase gives your prospects?

5. How does the appearance of a salesperson's car and briefcase affect professional credibility?

6. Describe the necessary elements of an effective organizing system.

7. Explain how a computer can be used to help with time management.

8. What three main sources of interruptions cause time problems? Give some strategies for handling each type.

9. What can be done to limit the time needed for telephone calls?

10. How can the time needed for travel in the sales territory be kept to a minimum?

ROLE-PLAY EXERCISES

The following role-play exercises help build teams, improve communication, and emphasize the "real-world" side of selling. They are meant to be challenging, to learn how to deal with problems that have no single "right" answer and to use a variety of skills beyond those employed in a typical review question. Read and complete each activity. Then in the next class, discuss and compare answers with other classmates. Have some students take the role of the salesperson, and see how they would react. Remember, *"You learn more about a person in an hour of play than in a lifetime of conversation."* - Plato

1. You begin to realize that there is a lot of your day that is unproductive. Write a list of the most important activities you perform every day. After each item, estimate the amount of time you spend on that activity each day. Now keep a detailed record of how you use your time for the next three days. (Use a form similar to Exhibit 15.1.) Compare your estimate with what you actually spent. Can you identify some ways you could improve the use of your time to increase your ability to reach your goals? Compare your records with other students in class and discuss ways to improve your time management and productivity.

2. Select a product or service for which you might be a salesperson. Secure a map of a metropolitan area, a county, or a group of counties that could logically be an assigned territory for you to sell. This may be your home area, where you are attending college, or some other area for which you can secure necessary information. Divide the map into segments to show how you would organize the territory for best time management. Write out a territory management plan giving attention to each of these considerations:

   - Where the best prospects are located in the territory.
   - How many segments are needed in the territory.
   - How the territory can best be divided to minimize travel.
   - How you determined where to draw segment lines.
   - How often each segment should be visited.
   - What percentage of total time should be given to each.

CASE STUDY

Case 15.1 - Making Time for the "Little Guys"

Carol Puckett has had quite a wait in the reception room of the Seaboard Hardware Works. After about twenty-five minutes, she was thinking to herself, "I can't hang around here much longer. This is still a pretty small outfit, and they've never bought very much. Maybe I should cost this out. I might even be losing money. On top of that, they can be pretty demanding. Guess I'll cut out; I'll be around this way again in a few weeks, anyway. I've got a lot of miles to cover today."

Just then, the switchboard operator spoke up. "Ms. Puckett, Mr. Griffin can see you now. Do you know where his office is?"

"Yes, I do, thank you. I'll go right in."

"Sorry to keep you waiting," the manufacturing manager said, "but our production committee meeting took a little longer than usual. It's always that way when you're trying to get started on a new product."

"How is business these days?" Carol asked. "Things are pretty hectic, but it's better that way than being too slow, "Mr. Griffin replied. "I'll buy that," Carol replied.

"Speaking of buying, you should be about ready for a reorder on those special fasteners, if they worked out as we thought they would."

"Haven't had any complaints from assembly so far," Griffin answered.

"Good," said Carol. "Shall I just repeat the order?"

"Yes, that should do it," Griffin said.

"Okay, delivery will be four weeks."

"Let me see," Griffin replied. "We're getting a little low on these, according to our running inventory report. Could you make that three weeks?"

"As I was saying," Carol answered, "four weeks is normal. But I suppose that if you really need them sooner, I can give it a try."

"If I didn't need them, I wouldn't have asked," Griffin said with an edge on his voice. "If you can't deliver, say so. There are plenty of other fastener suppliers around."

"I assure you that I'll take your request right to the top if I have to. I'm going to be calling the office in a short while anyway. I'll have it checked out with our production control manager and call you back this afternoon," Carol promised.

"Well, okay. But you can certainly make a partial shipment earlier than four weeks, can't you?"

"Probably. However, these are a special design, and that means a completely different machine setup. Once the setup is made, production goes along pretty fast. The schedule for all of our other products and previous customer orders is really the determining factor in our lead time. But I'll try my best. What I mean to say is that if we can make any shipment at all in less than four weeks, it'll probably be a complete one," Carol explained.

When Carol phoned the plant, the sales manager, after agreeing to push Seaboard's order through in three weeks, asked Carol to come in to see him the next day. The unusual request made Carol somewhat apprehensive. Field salespeople usually went into the main plant only for a full or district sales meeting.

The next day, after the handshake and the invitation to sit down, Carol asked, "Why did you ask me to come in? Is something the matter?"

"That's what I want to know," the sales manager said. "Just before you called I was checking your call reports. Contrary to what most of you bird dogs think, I do read the reports. Anyway, I noticed a strange sort of pattern. You seem to be doing very well with your major accounts. But what I can't find is any evidence that there's been any growth in the smaller ones. It just stands to reason that some of these must have grown since you hit the territory. There are some in the electronics field, for example. And, of course, the two that make safety equipment must be benefiting from the Occupational Safety and Health Act."

"I guess it's possible that some will grow," Carol replied. "But the way I figure it, and with the amount of business they're giving me now, I just can't give them the time it would take to build them up."

"Still, you should be thinking about their potential for the future. As a matter of fact, it is quite a coincidence that you should have called about that Seaboard order. Did you know that they're taking over the Flatley Company?" the sales manager asked. "They're in your territory, too."

"No, I didn't," Puckett admitted. "And I was at Flatley last week, too. Neither of them gave any hint of anything in the works. How did you find out?" "Just between you and me," the manager whispered, "I read it in the paper. But, seriously," he went on in a normal tone, "things like this can change a situation overnight.

1. Is the sales manager nitpicking, or is Carol neglecting an opportunity to increase sales? Support your answer.

2. Did Carol miss anything in her conversation with Griffin that should have given her a clue to the Flatley takeover? Was there a clue of any other kind she missed?

3. What ideas can you suggest that Carol might list for the sales manager?

"Leadership is a potent combination of **strategy** and **character**. But if you must be without one, be without the strategy."

-Norman Schwarzkopf

Sales Force Management

LEARNING OBJECTIVES

- Examine the function of sales management in a company.

- Understand what is required of a sales manager.

- Learn the differences in qualifications between sales managers and salespeople.

- Determine the specific responsibilities of the sales manager.

- Examine the distinctions of various compensation plans.

- Discuss the recruitment and selection process of salespeople.

- Study orientation, training, and motivation practices used by managers.

Sales force management plays a vital part in the overall success of any company. If salespeople do not sell the company's products or services, no amount of effort in sales or marketing planning will produce success. Although the failure of an individual salesperson to sell may occasionally be attributed to lack of ability or unwillingness to work, the failure of an overall sales force is more likely to result from a basic sales management problem: *The salespeople were improperly recruited, selected, trained, compensated, or motivated.* The costs associated with managing a sales force are often the largest single operating expense item for a company.

Exhibit 16.1 shows the actual dollar investment ten different companies make in every salesperson they hire.[1] The cost of hiring and training a single salesperson ranges from a low of $5,000 to a surprising $100,000. When it comes to team leaders the costs can escalate rapidly. One Senior VP estimated the cost of losing a single product development team leader at $29 million, due to the necessity of getting a product rapidly to market.[2] In addition, the time invested in training a new salesperson ranges from eight weeks to two years. You begin to get a clear picture of just how truly critical are the recruitment, selection, and training processes. And when you add in the *turnover factor*, you begin to fully understand that companies must have a process in place that provides them with salespeople who are committed and loyal for the long run.

Δ Exhibit 16.1

Cost of Hiring and Turnover Vary Widely

Company	Number of Salespeople	Cost of hiring and training per salesperson	Time invested in training a new salesperson	Average annual turnover
AC Delco	500	$100,000	24 mos.	3%
AT&T	10,000	$20,000	6 mos.	35%
Boise Cascade	1,400	$5,000	18mos.	15%
Brown-Forman	435	$100,000	24 mos.	5%
General Electric ICS	12,800	$100,000	6 mos.	12%
Lucent Technologies	10,000	$30,000	6 mos.	6%
Mark IV Industries	282	$25,000	6 mos.	2%
Reynolds and Reynolds	1,200	$25,000	6 mos.	10%
UPS	3,038	NA	8 wks.	5%
Zellerbach	750	$50,000	6 mos.	14%

The sales function is the responsibility of the sales manager, who is involved with all aspects of selling, including planning, organizing, controlling, and evaluating the sales force. The sales manager is the link between individual salespeople and their customers and the organization's upper management. In a smaller firm, the sales management function may be assigned to the marketing manager. A larger, more diversified company may have several sales managers classified by geographic area, customer type, or product line, and each may report to a district or regional manager who, in turn, reports to the chief sales executive of the company.

Both sales ability and management ability are required regardless of how broad or how limited the sales manager's job may be. The management ability required of a field salesperson is primarily applied in the area of personal time and activity management. The sales manager needs excellent management ability in addition to the basic sales abilities that everyone in sales needs. The amount of time spent in actual *sales activity* versus *administrative activity* changes at each level of management. The manager who directly supervises field salespeople spends more time in actual selling activities than in administrative duties, but a chief sales executive who is separated from field salespeople by several levels of sales management may be almost completely involved in administrative activity.

Managing In Today's Business Climate

Marketing and sales companies historically used the 4P's—*Product*, *Price*, *Place*, and *Promotion* to formulate strategy. Now a fifth P is needed: *People*. A sales manager's job is no longer to rule over the sales force using the traditional authoritative management style. Individuals entering the sales world today have a different set of values. They have more education and sophistication, desiring managers who listen, encourage, teach, coach, and give them a voice in how they are managed. If the sales environment does not meet these requirements, they will search for one that does.

According to Dr. Ken Blanchard, co-author of the *One-Minute Manager*, young sales professionals are foregoing other aspects of the job, including financial considerations, to work in a caring, supportive environment. In a recent study by the Families and Work Institute, 3400 randomly selected men and women ranked their three most important job considerations, which were:

1. **Open Communication**. Information is power; do not withhold information as a way to abuse your management position. Tell your sales force everything you know that is pertinent to their job. Involve them in the decisions that affect them.

2. **Effect on Personal and Family Life**. The explosion of two-wage-earner families and the growing number of families with single parents makes it more stressful to juggle all the demands of work and home life. Problems that did not impact the work place a generation ago, such as sick children or scheduling a day-care provider, means managers must find new ways to allow for greater flexibility and autonomy in individual jobs.

3. **Nature of the Work**. Workers want to feel their job is important to the success of the company. A wise sales manager takes every opportunity to let the sales force know how critical their efforts are in meeting company goals. Saying "thank you" frequently is easy, and best of all, it's free.[3]

The sales manager's challenge is to walk the fine line between pleasing top management and keeping the sales force motivated. Sales managers must be coaches, facilitators, and cheerleaders for their people. Their main concerns must be how to shape a more supportive work environment and to find ways to help each salesperson be more productive.

Sales Managers and Technology

Sales managers have an increasing array of options to choose from as they communicate with their remote sales forces: Cell phones, teleconferences, Web processing, email, videoconferencing, voicemail, instant messaging, text messaging, and of course the standby, face-to-face.

Videoconferencing. In today's global marketing economy, the salesperson must sell to a more diversified and physically spread-out customer and prospect base then ever before. Finding the time and resources to have a face-to-face meeting can be difficult and expensive. One of the truly amazing technological innovations is the modern advent of videoconferencing.

Videoconferencing is the combination of a telephone call and a video camera. It allows the salesperson, sales manager, or customer to have a "face-to-face" meeting that is so critical to success in professional selling. Videoconferencing is far less expensive than flying to a business or sales meeting. A skilled sales manager can conduct an interactive meeting with sales reps in offices from New York City to Perth, Australia. No expensive plane tickets are necessary, and the sales reps never have to leave their territories.

Internet conferencing takes this process one step further. With videoconferencing you need a special room and equipment. For Internet conferencing all you need is an Internet account, computer, camera, and microphone. This enables the sales manager to conduct a meeting with his salespeople who might be anywhere in the world. And the salesperson can connect with customers no matter where they happen to be located. Internet and videoconferencing enables companies to conduct sales meetings around the world.

One sales manager who attempted to use the technology had it flop so badly that he now uses the equipment as a plant stand. However, Eli Lilly and Company has had considerable success using it. Eight of their major sales offices keep in regular contact with headquarters using videoconferencing. For Christopher Roberts, manager of business communication technologies for Eli Lilly, this technology makes sense. He says, "You're able to keep people informed without taking them out of the field."[4]

Maximize Your Investments. As you prepare for a sales conference, here is an idea to consider. Suppose you are bringing in your salespeople from all over the country to one central facility for two days of meetings. Prior to the conference with your sales reps, use a tool called Group Mind Express™ from Catalyst Consulting. Here's how it works: Send an email to each salesperson that includes a link to a site that contains a survey you wrote. When your salespeople go to the site, they answer the questions and the site immediately displays the results to date for the entire survey—showing them where they stand on the issues you raised compared to their colleagues. This allows you to quickly see the concerns that are most important to them. Using this type of tool for surveying your sales force prior to a critical sales meeting will help you zero in on the topics that are of critical interest to them once you actually all come together. This is one way to maximize your twin investments of time and money.[5]

The Sales Manager As a Leader

Pushing yourself to greater heights of leadership is not just a good suggestion—it's crucial for your company's survival. It's not enough to just say, "Keep up the good work." Managers must create a motivational culture that challenges and inspires positive change in their salespeople.[6] The pressure is on everyone in this economy, so managers must be ready to step forward and lead a sales force toward success. One of the keys of leadership is *motivating people*. Sustained motivation comes from day-to-day motivation—and that has to come from sales managers who are leaders themselves.

The best leaders know that one-on-one talks can help employees overcome problems.

Sales may be the lifeblood of a company, but some smaller companies don't have a formal sales manager position—and others delegate that responsibility to an already overworked producer, one who may be great at acquiring business but lacks the skill and will to lead others. "Our agency was profitable, but growth was not meeting my expectations," says Ralph Hartwell, founder of the Hartwell Corporation (THC) in Idaho. THC shuffled the sales manager job among various executives, so no one was consistently responsible for setting sales goals, monitoring progress, or achieving results.[7] Hartwell finally recognized the importance of having a solid leader in order to break through to the next level of success. Bob Nelson, author of *1001 Ways to Energize Your Employees*, says, "For today's employees, you can't light a fire under them. You have to light a fire in them."[8] Exhibit 16.2 gives sales managers powerful tips on how to motivate employees and then keep them motivated.[9]

> **"Effective leadership is putting first things first. Effective management is discipline, carrying it out."**
>
> -Steven Covey

Δ **Exhibit 16.2**

Tips on Motivation ·

Motivation is Caring *not* Scaring. Fear should never be used as a motivation strategy. It may get managers what they want now, but it will set them up for what they don't want in the future in the form of employee anger, resentment, and lack of enthusiasm and commitment.

Motivation Blossoms in the Right Atmosphere. When employees feel nurtured, appreciated, acknowledged, and respected, they'll give 100 percent of their time, effort, and commitment in return. The job of the manager is to create a work environment that provides employees with the opportunity to attain their goals and experience what they value most in their professional lives.

Walk the Talk. Modeling the behavior leaders want from their salespeople is the most effective way to change any behavior. If they want motivated employees, they need to become a role model for motivation.

The Law of Attraction. The *law of attraction* states that whatever we focus on we bring to ourselves. If sales managers focus on the lack of motivation in employees, they will find more and more examples of it. When they seek to learn more about motivation and create an atmosphere that fosters it, they will find more examples of motivation in the workplace.

Ongoing Commitment. Motivating employees is an ongoing process because people are continually growing and changing. As they achieve something they want or value, they then seek to achieve more of the same. If motivation is not kept on the managerial front burner, sales managers see the fires in their employees slowly fade and die out.

Despite the widespread use of Total Quality Management techniques in many of today's corporations, a high failure rate of total quality management improvement programs exists— 60 percent to 67 percent—according to recent studies.[10] These failures occurred not because of basic flaws in the principles of TQM, but more so because of ineffective implementation systems. So, what can a sales manager do to ensure his techniques are successful? Here are five leadership skills that a sales manager can use to more effectively put TQM fundamentals into practice.[11]

1. Provide employees with a sense of mission.

2. Create a work environment where salespeople feel free to stretch their talents.

3. Give immediate feedback on what salespeople need to improve on so they don't have to guess.

4. Offer praise and reward in an appropriate way so that individual salespeople are recognized as well as the team as a whole.

5. Help and support employees in developing their talents and careers.

These skills are the basis for the sales manager's approach to the task of sales management. You must remember that leadership isn't an event; it is a process. Sales managers must be able to diagnose what their people need and remain flexible enough to provide for those needs.

Based on the leadership skills outlined above, Exhibit 16.3 recommends a new management style. To maximize a team's performance, sales managers must break away from the traditional management style and develop the winning style of management that will help their companies gain a competitive advantage. The idea is to lead, not to simply tell people exactly what to do. You develop people and ask how they think a task should be handled. The winning manager takes the sales force to the next level—after all, they can't accomplish that without the help and support of their salespeople.

Ask yourself, *Why do America's corporate giants invest many hours annually in supervisory and management development?* It's because they recognize that competent and consistent staff supervision is the principal ingredient of an effective and efficient organization; but in order to achieve this, supervisors and managers need to be skilled in communications, planning, scheduling, evaluating job performance, coaching, counseling, team building, handling employee problems and problem employees, resource allocation, and conflict management.[12]

"The key to management lies in always providing value to the people who work under you." This is the definition of strong leadership according to Edward Berube, president of Conseco Insurance Group in Indianapolis.[13] Sales managers serve as *champions* to the people who report to them.

Δ **Exhibit 16.3**

· Traditional vs. Winning Managers

Traditional Managers	Winning Managers
1. Stick to their old ways and resist change.	1. Thrive on, and relish, change.
2. See themselves as cops or bosses.	2. Think like a coach or team leader.
3. Make all the decisions on their own.	3. Believe in group decision making.
4. Are reluctant to share information.	4. Are eager to share news and information.
5. Demand action, effort, and long hours.	5. Expect progress and results to occur.
6. Neglect career-planning discussions and assume company will do that for them.	6. Take initiative for planning own career and assist sales staff in planning theirs.

Adapted from: Dr. Wolf Rinke's book Winning Management: Six Fail-Safe Strategies for Building High-Performance Organizations

The qualifications that produce success for an individual salesperson are not necessarily the same as those needed for success as a sales manager. On one hand, a salesperson must possess a strong sense of self-discipline coupled with a fondness of independence. A sales manager, on the other hand, is continuously involved in interaction with a diverse clientele both inside and outside the organization. The freedom enjoyed by salespeople to arrange and manage their own time and activities is not as likely to be available to the sales manager who is held accountable for the overall effectiveness of a number of salespeople. Managing yourself and your own time is not the same as directing and managing other people's time and energies. Choosing the best salesperson for promotion to sales manager does not always work. A manager's job is to do whatever is necessary to achieve consistent production and growth, both personally and in all members of the sales force, and to build top-performing producers while maintaining a profitable business.

Determining Sales Force Organization

In building and maintaining an efficient sales force, the sales manager performs at least six distinct managerial functions, as shown in Exhibit 16.4. This model serves as a basis for the information presented next and illustrates the complexity of the sales management function.

Δ Exhibit 16.4

The Job of the Sales Manager ·

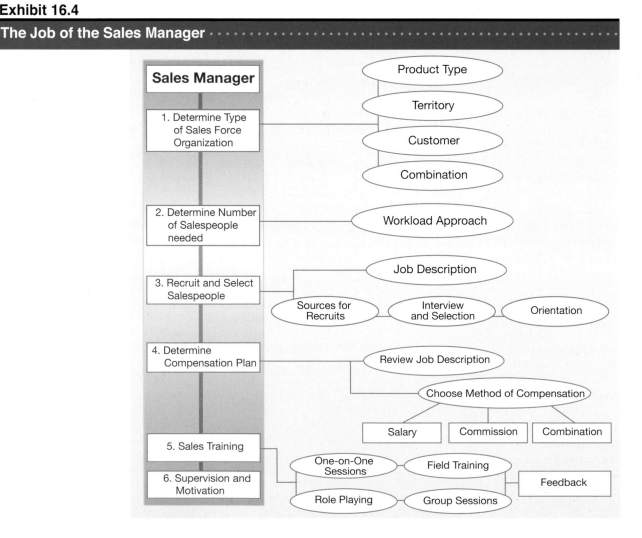

As the exhibit illustrates, the first task that must be performed by a sales manager before the first sale is ever made is determining how to organize his sales team. Organizing the sales force within imposed budget constraints is one of the sales manager's major concerns. No precise rules apply for choosing the organizing strategy to follow. Exhibit 16.5 depicts the three basic types of sales force organization models.

Δ **Exhibit 16.5**

Types of Sales Force Organization

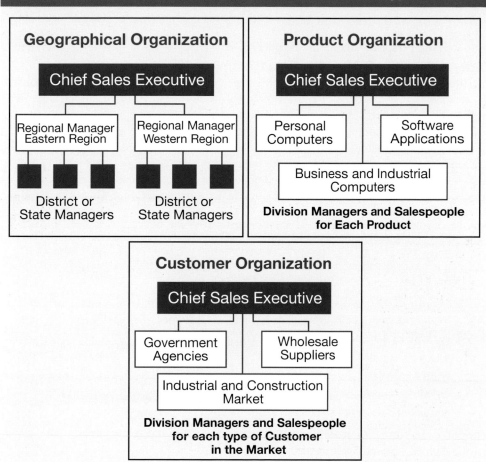

Product Organization. When this plan is used, salespeople specialize in the sale of a relatively narrow line of goods or services. This organization is effective in a company that sells expensive, complex, or technical products that require high levels of product knowledge. It is also effective when buying patterns vary greatly among the various parts of the product line. Product organization is expensive because of the time, effort, and human resources needed for specialization.

Bertelsmann AG decided to reorganize their company along strict *product lines*. According to Michael Dorncmann, head of the entertainment division, "If you have a decentralized corporate approach and have too many divisions, it becomes difficult to handle because there are so many overlapping strategic ideas." They now have four clearly differentiated divisions. The move has been enormously successful for them.[14]

Geographic Organization. Salespeople assume responsibility for selling the entire product line within a defined geographical region. This type of organization is probably the most common. If the product line is extensive, this method of organization hampers the salesperson's ability to gain enough detailed product knowledge. If the territory is large, the number of customers and the amount of travel required may cut the amount of service the salesperson can give to each account. The risk exists that such salespeople will choose to concentrate only on the products or services with the highest demand or that are easiest for them to sell.

Customer Organization. Organization on the basis of customer type assigns salespeople to serve a specific type of customer. Some call on industrial accounts, and others call on retail accounts. This method allows salespeople to become knowledgeable about the needs of a given industry or customer type. It also gives the salespeople time to employ personalized sales strategies.

Determining the Size of the Sales Team

The importance of determining how many salespeople to employ can hardly be overemphasized. An understaffed sales force produces sales levels that are too low; over-staffing, however, creates excessive costs and cuts profits. Although simple in theory, determining the appropriate number of people to hire may prove relatively difficult. The problem lies in estimating the impact on the marketplace of adding salespeople.

One frequently used method for determining how many salespeople to hire is called the *workload approach*. This method is based upon determining the total amount of sales work needed, estimating how much one salesperson can do, and then dividing. This method follows a four-step process:

1. Determine the *number of calls* needed. Companies may classify their customers into categories. Often these categories are based on the level of actual sales or potential sales to each customer. Not all accounts may get called on with equal frequency.

2. Determine the *average time necessary per call* and multiply this amount of time by the number of calls to be made to find the total working time needed.

3. Figure how much *actual selling time* (total hours per year) is available for each salesperson (allowing time for travel between appointments and other sales-related activities).

4. Divide the *total working time by the working time per salesperson* to find the number of salespeople needed.

The following formula—based on the four-step process listed above—provides an estimate for the number of salespeople needed:

Sales Force Size = Total Number of Customers and Prospects x Call Frequency x Call Time Required ÷ Selling Time Available for One Sales Person

For example:

Customers	150
Prospects	+600
Total	750

- Call frequency = call on each customer once a month (or 12 times/year)
- Average call time per visit = 45 minutes
- Actual selling time available per year = 4 hours/day x 250 days a year = 1,000 hours

$$\text{Sales force size} = \frac{750 \times 12 \times .75}{1,000} = \frac{6,750}{1,000} = 7 \text{ salespeople}$$

The more realistic the estimate for each factor, the more accurate the final determination will be. In addition to accurate estimates of these factors, other considerations include the quality of the people recruited: Level of selling skill, personal motivation, experience and product knowledge, initiative, and work habits. All of these factors play a part in whether the estimated levels of sales activity and the estimated results will be reached.[15] The sales manager's ability to determine how many people are needed improves with experience and with knowledge of the people already in the work unit.

Recruiting and Selecting a Sales Force

Building a winning sales force depends in large measure upon the sales manager's effectiveness in recruiting and selecting the best salespeople. The process, like every other selling activity, requires planning and preparation, careful tracking, and efficient carrying out of plans. At least four phases are included in the total process:

Phase I: Determine Requirements for the Position

Finding the right person to fill a sales position is a major concern for every sales organization regardless of size or type. Finding the right person is impossible before you know what qualities are necessary. Develop a profile of the candidates who will stand the best chance of succeeding. Make this profile realistic, not idealistic. Planning begins with development of a job description that sets out in written form all of the requirements for a given sales position. The process of writing a job description forces the sales manager to be explicit about what the job requires.

Once the activities are listed, the sales manager can more easily decide exactly what skills and experience a prospective salesperson must have to be considered as a viable applicant. All salespeople are not suited to all sales jobs. Some do an excellent job selling products with low unit value but are unable to close a sale on a big-ticket item. Others do well selling tangible products but have difficulty selling intangibles like insurance or mutual funds. A job description helps to avoid a mismatch between the job and the salesperson. In defining the qualifications for the job, the sales manager should consider four factors:

Educational Requirements. A basic requirement (high school or college degree) and any special training (accounting, liberal arts, pharmacy, computer science, etc.) should be defined.

Experience. Both the length and type of experience required or preferred must be identified. Must experience be in a particular line? What substitutes are acceptable? Will experience with a competitor be considered? Dartnell's Survey of Sales Force Compensation of more than 800 companies in 30 industries reported that companies are increasingly preferring senior and experienced salespeople over entry-level recruits. According to Christen Heide, "They realize they are not in the training business and don't mind paying more for what they need."[16]

Job Conditions. List any special conditions that affect the job: Seasonal or cyclical demand for the product, low ratio of sales to calls, long absences from home. Make sure the prospective salesperson is able to deal with these conditions both physically and emotionally.

Type of Customers. Determine whether the type of customers to be called on has any bearing on what type of salesperson is needed.

Thorough planning is as important in recruiting a sales force as in any other portion of the selling process. Too often, salespeople are hired for the wrong reasons. They are hired based on a résumé instead of whether or not they have the right values, attitudes, and motivations for a particular company. They're hired based on a "gut feeling" to the exclusion of critical objective evaluation data. They're hired based on a poorly thought-out set of criteria that doesn't address what the company really needs. Because of these failings, too much time can be spent rehiring, reorienting and retraining new people, instead of turning good hires into great, loyal, long-term sales stars.[17] Without planning, the people you hire may fail to fit into the job you offer them. You not only need good people—you need people who are good for a particular job.

Phase 2: Sources for Recruiting

Each sales manager learns through experience the best sources for finding recruits for specific types of sales jobs. Here are six possible sources:

Within the Organization. Occasionally an employee in the production or service portion of the business qualifies for a sales job. Students often take part-time jobs on the maintenance crew or in the office and are eager to enter sales when their education is complete.

Competitors. A competing company is a possible source, but caution should be exercised as ethical problems may be involved. Be sure that the salesperson has a legitimate reason for wanting to leave present employment. Take care to evaluate the person's stability, work habits, experience, and attitude toward selling.

The Internet. Companies are using the Internet to locate potential candidates for various sales positions. More and more Web sites are being established for this explicit purpose. For example, Monster.com is one of the sites most of us are familiar with.

Trade and Other Media Advertising. A well-written classified ad in the newspaper produces good prospects. A blind ad asking for a written application to be sent to a post office box number saves time by letting you weed out obviously unqualified applicants without taking time for a personal interview.

Schools. Technical schools and night schools, colleges, and universities are potential sources of prospects. Use the placement service in the school for screening.

Employment Agencies. The state employment agency in many cities is valuable. Private agencies are also in the business to find prospects. When using any type of agency, be sure to make the job requirements clear and perhaps set them a little higher than actually required. Get to know the service representative in the agency and you will get better prospects referred to you.

Tips for Effective Hiring

Skip the Learning Curve. Hire someone with experience in the areas specific to your needs.

Choose Marketing Skills Over Sales Skills. Some sales experience is beneficial, but marketing requires different abilities and approaches than does sales.

Hire Charismatic Types. Look for someone with leadership abilities and strong communication skills.

Raid the Big Guns. Some of the best training grounds are in companies such as Procter & Gamble. So try to entice their best.

Phase 3: Interview and Selection

The interview between the sales manager and the prospective salesperson accomplishes three primary objectives: To give information, to receive information, and to establish a friendly relationship. This applies whether the prospect qualifies for the position or not. The interview process may involve completion of an application form, check of references, personal interview(s), testing, physical examination, and the final decision to hire. Here are some aspects to consider when selecting potential sales team members:

Check References. One effective question that may be asked of former employers is, "Would you consider this person for further employment?" A similar question to put to other references is, "Why do you feel this person   would be good in sales?" Some sales managers use the telephone exclusively for checking references. They feel that information may be given on the phone that might never be put into writing in a letter.

The All-Important Interview. A personal interview can be designed to help the sales manager determine whether a prospect is right for the job. The interview process may require several meetings. One may be used to complete the application form and review it briefly; a second may be a more in-depth interview several days later when the sales manager has had time to check references. Depending on the organization of the company itself, several people other than the sales manager may also interview the applicant. Robert Head, president of Strategic Sales Services Inc., says, "Good hiring procedures for salespeople require a minimum of two interviews, preferably three."[18]

Asking the Right Questions. The session should be used to discover answers to these types of questions:

1. Is the individual actually qualified for the position?

2. How badly does the person want this sales position with our company?

3. Can the candidate demonstrate an understanding of our company's business?

4. Is this individual a problem-solver? Can this person think quickly on his feet?

"Most interviews are a waste of time because the candidate isn't prepared," says Mick Corcodilos, author of *Ask the Headhunter*. He suggests that sales managers ask the job candidates on the phone to come to the interview with solutions to two problems that their company is facing. This challenge stops most of the job seekers dead in their tracks. There is just too much work involved. What a way to reduce the pool of candidates and, at the same time, force those who do accept the challenge to demonstrate an understanding of the job's requirements.

Phase 4: Orientation

All the time and expense of the selection procedure are lost if the new salesperson is not properly integrated into the organization. Of course, the size of the organization affects what is done and how, but in every case a definite program should bring each new salesperson into the company as part of the team and establish for that person a feeling of belonging. The process should include items such as these:

- Introduction to fellow workers
- Office practices
- Company policies
- Vertical communication
- Company-sponsored recreation activities
- Expense account procedures

Determining Compensation

Compensation plans are usually straight commission, straight salary, or a combination of the two.

Straight Commission

A commission is usually figured as a percentage of sales volume. The plan might call for a simple percentage of total gross sales, or it could be based on a percentage of the sales less variable costs. The benefit of the latter plan is that it offers the salesperson concrete incentives for helping to keep selling costs low and therefore emphasizes profit instead of mere volume. The main benefit of a commission plan is the motivation it offers to salespeople for productivity. The disadvantage is that some salespeople are tempted to neglect activities that do not bring in short-term dollars, including service after the sale, helping with installation, and completing needed reports and related paperwork. The straight-commission plan is the plan of choice when aggressive selling is desired.

Straight Salary

At the other extreme is a plan based on a fixed amount regardless of volume. About 15 percent of companies use straight salary as their sole means of compensation.[19] A straight-salary plan gives management the greatest ability to control the activities of salespeople. If the company has an unusual need for post-sale activities, developing new territories, or continuing technical training, salespeople do not feel that they are cutting their own income by giving time to that work. However, a salary plan offers less motivation for intense sales effort than the commission plan. Therefore, a salary plan is the plan of choice when management needs to control salespeople's activities and when aggressive sales activity is not necessary.

Combination Plans

One method to exercise control over sales activities yet retain the incentive value of a commission is a combination of a base salary and a commission or bonus paid on sales above a set level. Another type of combination plan makes use of a commission plus a draw against future commissions earned. This plan protects salespeople in slow seasons or when some outside circumstance lowers productivity temporarily. The company sets a base amount that the salesperson is guaranteed to receive. If commissions earned fall below that figure, a draw is paid to bring income up to the base level. If the salesperson earns commissions above the base next month, the excess is used to repay the draw. Exhibit 16.6 shows how the draw operates.

Δ **Exhibit 16.6**

Sample Combination Compensation Plan ·

Month	Commissions Earned	Commissions Paid	Draw* Paid (Repaid)	Total Income
January	$1500	$1500	$0	$1500
February	900	900	300	1200
March	1400	1400	(200)	1200
April	1500	1500	(100)	1400
May	1700	1700	0	1700
June	1200	1200	0	1200
Total	**$8200**	**$8200**	**$0**	**$8200**

*Assumes company guarantees a base amount of $1200 per month. Some companies do not require an actual payback as shown in this example. They use the draw as a yardstick for performance.

There aren't many other topics that a professional salesperson or a sales manager is more eager to talk to someone about than sales compensation. With all of the requirements and devices used, compensation plans can be quite complex. They can also bring about unethical behavior. And in many cases they can be very difficult to administer. Turnover forecasts indicate that more salespeople are "job hopping" for a little more money or a change of pace. That explains why companies increasingly entice people with incentives like stock options. A number of companies, particularly those in the technology and telecommunications industries, have recently added stock options to salespeople's pay packages. The reason? Salespeople are demanding them.[20]

Exhibit 16.7 points out how much easier it is becoming for sales reps to keep track of the commissions they earn the moment a deal is closed, and the commissions they could earn on any deals that are pending.[21] The special challenge companies have is to keep themselves from cluttering up their incentive plan with everybody's favorite program "du jour." In the past, companies have failed because they end up with a sales plan where there are bonuses or a contest on just about every one of the products being sold.

△ Exhibit 16.7

. . . . **Computers' Impact on Compensation Plans**

A new software tool makes it possible for companies to go way beyond the minimum in communicating their compensation plans to their field sales forces. SalesOnline is a software product developed by Oracle that allows companies to manage and control their compensation plans. "It handles the whole sales compensation cycle, from designing the model to aligning it with your strategic objectives to getting approvals before executing it, then implementing it," says Juliette Sultan, vice president of CRM Product Strategy at Oracle. One powerful advantage of SalesOnline is its clarity. Sales reps can see what's going on each time a transaction comes in, and exactly what commission they will be paid. This is all about visibility and tracking progress. It enables them to understand the commission structure and increases their satisfaction.

SalesOnline also features an Income Planner that reinforces company incentives for long-term selling efforts. It will calculate future commissions for sales that are pending. A salesperson can see that when he closes a deal, here is what he will make. If sales reps are working on multiple deals, it motivates them to devote the right amount of time to each to work toward maximizing their company's profit. This feature will become even more significant as companies develop compensation plans with many variables: revenue and activity, current and historical, and single and multi-channel sales. The software tool is quite flexible and enables the compensation plan to be as complex as a company wants it to be.

High Price to Pay for Inadequate Plans. Although undercompensating salespeople may seem like an attractive cost-cutting strategy for companies in the short run, over time businesses pay the price for underpaying employees in the form of turnover and a general lack of loyalty. Many companies have yet to realize the importance of a solid, well-constructed compensation plan. According to a *Sales and Marketing Management* compensation survey, 64 percent of the sales executives rated their current pay plans as only "somewhat successful." Only 15 percent of sales managers give their compensation plans high marks, and the rest, a staggering 21 percent, say their plans are terrible. But company compensation plans don't have to be doomed. Executives at FedEx Corp realized they needed a new compensation plan for their sales organization because of the volume of complaints coming from field salespeople and sales managers about how confusing and unpredictable the pay program was. In a little more than a year with a new clearly laid-out incentive pay program, there was a dramatic shift in the sales force at FedEx and consequently, much happier salespeople.[22] Exhibit 16.8 shows how the automobile industry suffers from the use of inadequate compensation plans.[23]

Δ Exhibit 16.8

High Turnover Rates in the Automotive Industry

The negative perception that the public has of automobile salespeople can be traced to the compensation system in the industry. This compensation system has also contributed to the high turnover rates of salespeople in dealerships. High turnover rates are costing the dealerships in the form of lost sales and higher training expenses. Dealerships realize that they have to start changing how they compensate their sales force. Replacing the at-risk pay with salary and bonus will greatly improve salespeople's selling attitude and will also reduce turnover rates. It will also give novices a chance to enter the industry with more confidence without the unknown of commission-only salaries. Financial hardships during the training period has been the main deterrent for newcomers in entering the industry. Other non-cash incentives, such as profit sharing and pension plans will help sales force retention.

A TQM-Based Compensation Package

According to Dartnell's *Survey of Sales Force Compensation*, the importance of profitability is increasing in sales compensation plans. Companies should reward salespeople not only for making sales, but also for achieving corporate sales objectives. Sales managers who do not carefully consider specific marketing and sales objectives almost by default choose dollar sales volume as the incentive criterion. A compensation plan based only on numbers can be detrimental. Rather than satisfy the customer, salespeople are tempted to spend their time focused on exceeding their numbers to maximize their own personal income. A reasonable base salary shows commitment to your sales force.

If the compensation plan is salary-based, it can be structured to reward company loyalty and longevity. Turnover is expensive to a company through training costs and lost sales. It takes a salesperson time to learn the company, its products, policies, and customers. A company with a lot of turnover causes clients to question its stability and may result in business lost to the competition.

Today's sales professionals should be listeners, information gatherers, educators, relationship builders, counselors, and the primary sources of customer input to the company. Cultivate a longer-term focus on adding customer value and integrating sales with all other people in the company who impact customers and products. Their pay needs to reflect these expectations. Some of the newer approaches involve paying differentiated awards based on strategies concerning customers and products.[24] A Total Quality Management (TQM) based compensation plan includes:

Customer Retention Bonus. Reward the salesperson for maintaining long-term relationships. Retention is a good indication that customers are being satisfied. Hewlett Packard has instituted customer satisfaction into their sales force compensation as they move toward Total Quality Management. According to a survey of 300 top American companies by Handy HRM Corporation of New York, 54 percent of those surveyed tie pay directly to quality standards, including customer satisfaction.[25]

Penetration of Target Accounts Bonus. New, targeted accounts take longer to develop and often do not offer the immediate financial return of established customers. Some salespeople also fear the added rejection that invariably accompanies calling on new prospects. However, gaining the business of target accounts indicates a salesperson's ability better than traditional methods that focus only on volume. A bonus paid for securing the business of targeted individuals or companies will keep salespeople motivated to continue building their customer base and providing their company with expanded growth opportunities.

Company-Wide Performance Bonus. The success of the salesperson is tied to the overall performance of the company. Therefore, the bonus is based on company-wide goals. A national survey reported that 39 percent of companies have annual bonuses for salaried employees tied to company performance.[26] Marshall Industries has introduced a corporate-wide compensation system that pays everyone, including all 600 salespeople, on the same plan. Exhibit 16.9 discusses how a quality initiative inspired the plan and the positive results achieved.[27]

Δ **Exhibit 16.9**

Trends in Compensation Plans: No Commission

Could this non-commission form of compensation be a trend for salespeople in the future? Marshall Industries, an industrial electronics company based in El Monte, California, is evidence that a sales organization can work without commissions and incentives and that a company can grow without volume-based rewards.

Marshall has introduced a corporate-wide compensation system that pays everyone—from secretaries to the president—on the same plan, a salary plus a bonus based on the company's quarterly profits. Marshall's 600 inside and outside salespeople are included in the plan.

Robert Rodin, Marshall's president and chief operating officer, says that the change was not a compensation issue, but a quality issue aimed at "aligning our compensation to support customer service." Under the previous commission arrangement, salespeople were "too concerned with their own performance, rather than listening to the customer. Compensation had become an obstacle to world-class quality."

In the past, pay was determined by how much a salesperson had shipped the last quarter, and now it is a base salary and profit-based bonus. Base salaries are set on the basis of the internal value of a position to the company and external salary surveys, and factors like seniority, training, and education.

To those who argue that you can't motivate salespeople without commissions, or some form of incentive program, Rodin responds, "You can get people to do anything by offering a reward, but can you get them to sustain it? Can you get them to look at both sides of the sale?"

And does it produce results? The company reports that salespeople are earning, on average, more than they made under the commission plan, and turnover among salespeople is down by 80 percent.

Other Key Roles of a Manager

Sales Training

Every authority agrees that ongoing sales training is necessary, but measuring the benefits of sales training is a difficult process. In addition, what sales training should accomplish is also not clear, although almost everyone agrees that training is needed in product knowledge and in selling skills.[28] Companies are interested in sales training because they want to increase sales productivity. The emphasis is largely on results. The chairman and chief executive officer of U.S. Steel expressed it this way:[29]

> *We support training and development activities to get results.... We're interested in the specific things that provide greater rewards to the employee, increased return to the stockholder, and enable reinvestment of sales revenue to meet the growing needs of the business. In other words, [we're interested in] those things, which affect the "bottom line."*

Sales managers usually agree that company training programs should address the purpose of developing in salespeople the characteristics of success. These characteristics, though generally listed in a somewhat vague manner, usually include traits such as these:

1. Listening skills

2. Enthusiasm

3. Empathy

4. Planning skills

5. Personal organization

6. Problem-solving ability

7. Time and territory management

Designing and implementing the sales training program is the sales manager's responsibility. An effective program includes these basic elements:

Field Training and Observation. It is a good idea to have both an experienced salesperson and a manager assist in training new sales reps. Traveling with a senior sales rep to observe selling skills, personality, and work habits is very revealing for novice sales reps. It is also a good idea to have the new reps accompany different sales managers to pick out the strengths and weaknesses of each manager, and eventually create their own style. Both managers and senior sales reps can impart more wisdom on a newcomer than many training courses might offer.

Unfortunately, sales managers often let sales reports drive their coaching conversations. In sales, performance improvement occurs only through observations—preludes to behavioral coaching. Two important areas of observation are making joint calls and inspecting telephone appointment conversations.[30] One key reason for lackluster sales performance continues to be the lack of coaching as part of the cultural DNA, but effective observation will form the cornerstone of any performance environment.

Group Sessions. Sales training sessions that focus on a single topic (such as prospecting, closing, or product knowledge) are valuable in sharpening skills for all members of the sales group. The group training session provides valuable interaction between salespeople and allows individuals to learn from one another.

A common form of training within group sessions is *role-playing*: One trainee assumes the role of salesperson and another trainee or the sales manager plays the role of a prospect. A third person may act as observer to critique the performance. They go through the various steps of the sales process to gain experience in using the sales aids, giving the presentation, asking questions, and handling objections. A session may cover the entire selling process or concentrate on one specific step in the process. Some role- playing sessions are either audio taped or videotaped for later review.

One-on-One Sessions. The sales manager must be willing to spend time with individual salespeople to give specific feedback and encourage continuing development. One-on-one time can be used to pinpoint individual problems and help the salesperson to develop a program of personal growth to correct any problems discovered.

Interactive Training. The rate of learning from an interactive electronic medium is 35 percent higher than from traditional classroom approaches. Interactive multimedia sales training has arrived. With the interactive format you get the benefits of sound, videos, slide shows, and self-tests, and the capability to determine what you want to learn, when you want to learn it. Salespeople using this new interactive format will have higher rates of retention, take less time to train, have easier access to information, and have a higher comfort level. Sales managers now have the opportunity to work with one, or one hundred, salespeople in front of a computer to watch and learn new techniques or practice what they do best.[31]

Feedback. The sales training program must provide for feedback on performance. When a skill is noticed in a training session, a method for tracking field improvement shows whether the training has been effective. When salespeople see that the training has made a direct impact on their performance and their incomes, they are eager to receive more training and give their best efforts to learning.

The amount of time spent in sales training for recruits and for experienced salespeople varies from industry to industry and also from company to company. Time for training is affected by the complexity of the industry, the commitment of the company to training, and the company's experience with past training programs. The exact procedure also varies as a result of the same factors. Some companies conduct concentrated training for new recruits before they are allowed to go into the field. Others use a mix of training and field experience to help recruits learn by doing. A few still hand the recruit a sales kit and follow the sink-or-swim method. On the whole, the training period for recruits tends to be shorter for manufacturers of consumer products than for manufacturers of industrial products. Service companies including insurance, banking, public utilities, and transportation companies, generally have longer training programs than manufacturers.

Supervision and Motivation

A sales manager must see that salespeople call on their accounts with sufficient frequency, prospect for new business, keep up to date on new developments in the general market, and receive continuous training in new product technology or advanced sales techniques. Guiding salespeople in setting realistic goals, offering appropriate incentives to trigger achievement of those goals, and rewarding them for success are the sales manager's responsibility.

Motivation is at the heart of supervision. The sales manager's involvement in motivation is designed to provide an environment within which salespeople can develop the ability to motivate themselves. A sales manager is much like a professional sports coach. John Madden, legendary NFL coach, explained to a reporter his philosophy about motivating football players like this: "I don't motivate them. I find motivated men and teach them how to play football."

The principle is clear: If the basic functions of recruiting and selection are successfully performed, training and motivation of the sales force become less of a problem and more of a *solution* to making more sales—and in turn, profit.

SUMMARY

- The functions of the sales manager differ considerably from those of salespeople although organizations often promote leading salespeople to positions in sales management.

- The sales manager must be both a skillful salesperson and an efficient manager. The sales manager stands between field salespeople and company management.

- The sales manager performs the usual managerial functions of translating the goals of the company into strategies and tactics that the members of the sales department can address through daily activities and seeing that those activities result in the achievement of the department's responsibilities to the company.

- In addition, the sales manager is concerned with helping salespeople develop personally and professionally so that they can make the greatest possible contribution to achievement of the organization's goals.

- Specific tasks of the sales manager include:

    1. Organizing the sales force

    2. Determining personnel needs

    3. Recruiting and selecting salespeople

    4. Designing a compensation plan that motivates salespeople and assures that sales activities will achieve desired goals

    5. Training salespeople to sell the company's product or service effectively

    6. Supervising and motivating salespeople.

REVIEW QUESTIONS

1. List the advantages and disadvantages for choosing a sales manager in each of the following ways:

    a. Promoting the top-producing salesperson in the organization

    b. Lateral transfer of an effective manager from another department (such as finance, advertising, manufacturing)

    c. Hiring someone from outside the organization

2. Are top salespeople automatically likely to be good sales managers? Why or why not?

3. What are the six key functions of a sales manager?

4. How can a sales manager determine how large a sales force should be?

5. What are the most common components of sales training?

6. What does the sales manager need to learn through interviewing a prospective salesperson?

7. What do you consider the most important incentives for salesperson productivity that a sales manager could provide?

8. If a company wants to exercise a great deal of control over the time and activities of its salespeople and does not especially need aggressive selling, what kind of compensation package is most appropriate?

9. If the organization's goal is high-volume sales and management is willing to have salespeople structure their own time and activities, what type of compensation plan is most likely to result in achievement of that goal?

10. What are some of the most easily accessible sources of recruits for positions as salespeople? What are the advantages and the disadvantages of each of these sources?

ROLE-PLAY EXERCISES

The following role-play exercises help build teams, improve communication, and emphasize the "real-world" side of selling. They are meant to be challenging, to learn how to deal with problems that have no single "right" answer and to use a variety of skills beyond those employed in a typical review question. Read and complete each activity. Then in the next class, discuss and compare answers with other classmates. Have some students take the role of the salesperson, and see how they would react. Remember, *"You learn more about a person in an hour of play than in a lifetime of conversation."* — Plato

1. Check the Sunday paper classified advertisements for sales positions. Cut out three ads that include job descriptions and bring them to class.

2. Look in the employment section of The Wall Street Journal. Find several ads for sales management positions. What qualifications are listed and what compensation is offered for each?

3. Interview a sales manager in a local company. Ask about the sales manager's job responsibilities, what percentage of time is spent on each, and what is the biggest job frustration.

CASE STUDY

Case 16.1 —The Freewheeler

Jesse Schavey had been appointed branch manager for the Lyantic Electrical Switch Company in its Mideast region just three weeks ago and already he had to deal with a problem salesperson.

A week ago, Clarence Brewster, the hotshot salesperson, had demanded that the branch service engineer ignore scheduled calls and rush out to one of his good accounts and leave the office clerk to make excuses to the bypassed customers.

This morning, another problem came up. The credit manager from the home office phoned: "Your man Brewster is trying to pull another fast one. He says that the Myard Company is temporarily strapped for cash and he wants us to extend their discount date for another fifteen days."

"As you know," Jesse said, "I'm new in this territory. How good a customer is this Myard outfit?"

"I'd say they're about medium size. Of course, Brewster claims that if we do relax our rules, it'll put him in line for a huge order. It seems that Myard is coming out with a new product that will be using solid-state switches. They seem to think that the market for their product is virtually unlimited."

"This sounds like a pie-in-the-sky deal to me," Jesse said, "but you know your business better than I do; so if you do sometimes grant extensions, this might be a chance to find out if Brewster's just talking through his hat."

The credit manager agreed to go along with the experiment. As he said, "If the order does turn out to be a good one, we won't mind waiting a few days for payment. If it turns out to be a dud, we haven't lost much and we'll have a good argument for sticking to our regular discount schedule."

Jesse told the office clerk to keep an eye out for an order from Myard. A few days later, one came through that was actually smaller than usual. This incident prompted Jesse to do some investigating. First, he dug out Clarence's call report files; no reports had been received for the past two weeks. Each salesperson was required to leave a weekly call schedule in the office, so Jesse tried to reach Clarence by telephone. However, the three customers on Clarence's call list hadn't seen him.

That Jesse has a maverick on his hands was becoming clear. Clarence is obviously a nonconformist who ignores the usual business practices as he sees fit. He's developed and follows his own pattern of work, even though company policy, office routine, and sales methods fall by the wayside. Before he took any action or made any judgments, however, Jesse decided that fairness required looking at the results. What sort of business was he producing with his do-it-yourself methods?

The year's records showed him second in branch standing. He kept the orders rolling in; he ranked highest in new accounts; he was resourceful in developing new uses for the product, which increased business with present customers.

In talking with the rest of the staff, Jesse learned that Clarence had a close identification with the company, obvious pride in its products, and respect for the selling profession.

Despite Clarence's record and pride in the company and its products, Jesse thought that all concerned would benefit if Clarence were brought into line, as long as he did not lose his enthusiasm for selling.

1. Is Jesse attaching too much importance to Clarence's style? As long as he produces, should Jesse care about Clarence's little idiosyncrasies?

2. If Jesse is justified in thinking he has a problem, how should he approach Clarence to gain his cooperation and yet not dampen his enthusiasm for the company and his job?

"Leadership: The art of getting someone else to do something you want done because he wants to do it."

-Dwight D. Eisenhower

ENDNOTES

Chapter 1

1. Quote from the Conference Board: Found in *The Selling Advantage* (May 28, 1992), 2. A publication of *Progressive Business Publications*.

2. Dean M Brenner, "Task-oriented selling," *Advisor Today*. Vol. 98, Is. 12, (December 2003), 62.

3. Susan Hodges,"Recommissioning your sales," *ELT*, Vol.15, Is. 2 (February 2003), 22-28.

4. Anonymous, "B2BTechnology Sales and Lead Generation, Inside Sales Compensation Survey Q4 of 2005," *Inside Sales Professional;* (Tuesday, June 27, 2006), http://insidesalesprofessional. wordpress.com/2006/06/.

5. Christine Galea, "3rd Annual Compensation Survey," *Sales and Marketing Management*, Vol. 155, Is. 5 (May 2003), 32-35.

6. Anonymous, "Investment in Training Yields Profit," *Graphic Arts Monthly*, (November 2003), S9.

7. Bob O'Connor, "Business Sense: Training Yourself and Your Staff to Win," *Motor*; (Feb 2007).

8. Riotto, Starkie and Thompson, "Comment: Relationship Managers: The Private Bank's 'Brand'", *American Banker*, Vol. 167, Is. 81 (April 29, 2002), 6.

9. "Do Commissions Equal High Turnover?" *Sales & Marketing Management* (January 1994), 40.

10. Charles W. Stephens, "Why is Training so Important?" *Industrial Distribution*, Vol. 89, No. 2 (February 2000), 4.

11. See the following sources: D.L. Thompson, "Stereotype of the Salesperson," *Harvard Business Review*, Vol. 50, No. 1, (January/February 1972), 20-29; Robert W. Cook and Timothy Hartman, "Female College Student Interest in a Sales Career: A Comparison," *Journal of Personal Selling & Sales Management*, Vol. 6, (May 1986), 29-34; Michael Swenson, William Swinyard, Frederick Langrehr, and Scott Smith, "The Appeal of Personal Selling as a Career: A Decade Later," *The Journal of Personal Selling & Sales Management*, Vol. 13, No. 1 (Winter 1993), 51; "Sales Strikes Out on Campus," *Sales & Marketing Management* (November 1997), 13; "Selling Sales to Students," *Sales & Marketing Management* (January 1998), 15; Harry Harmon, "An Examination of Students' Perceptions of a Situationally Described Career in Personal Selling," *Journal of Professional Services Marketing*, Vol. 19, No. 1 (Fall 1999), 119-136; Susan DelVecchio, "An Investigation of African-American Perceptions of Sales Careers," *The Journal of Personal Selling & Sales Management*, Vol. 29, No. 1 (Winter 2000), 43-52.

12. Audrey Bottjen, "The Benefits of College Recruiting," *Sales & Marketing Management* (April 2001), 12.

13. Laura Mazur, "UK banks must refocus on the personal touch," *Marketing*, (March 4, 2004), 16.

14. Anonymous, "Power of self-image psychology," *The American Salesman*, Vol. 48, Is. 5, (May 2003), 21.

15. Interview, Josh Hinds, September 28, 2006, Can be accessed online at: http://common-ground.typepad.com/common_ground/2006/09/if_its_advice_a.html.

16. Mark Haering, "From the Recruiter," *Sales and Marketing Management*, Vol. 155, Is. 5, (May 2003), 55.

17. Roy Chitwood, "Best salesperson in the company should be the CEO," *Max Sacks International*, http://www.maxsacks.com/articles/article0706.html, accessed August 19, 2007.

18. Abraham H. Maslow, *Motivation and Personality*, 2nd ed. (New York: Harper & Row Publishing, 1970).

19. Andy Cohen, "The Best Route to CEO," *Sales & Marketing Management* (May 2001), 14.

20. Julia Angwin, "America Online CEO Makes Strides with Low-Key Style," *Wall Street Journal*. (Eastern edition), (September 2, 2003), B.1.

21. Sherry Siegel, "Selling Your Way to the Top," *Success*, (January/February 1987), Vol. 34, No. 1, 44.

22. Derek Newton, *Sales Force Performance and Turnover* (Cambridge, MA: Marketing Science Institute, 1973), 3; Derek Newton, "Get the Most Out of Your Sales Force," *Harvard Business Review* (September/October 1969), 130-143.

23. For those not familiar with network marketing I encourage

you to read: Richard Eisenberg, "The Mess Called Multilevel Marketing," *Money* (May 1987), 136-160; "Melaleuca: A Future to Bank On," *Inc.* (December 1991), 6-7; Mark Yarnell, "A Venture Expert's Advice," *Success* (July 1994), 26.

24. Maria Puente, "Direct selling brings it all home; Americans make a party of shopping," *USA TODAY*, (October 28, 2003), D.06.

25. These traits were gleaned from the following sources: David McClelland, "Hiring Top Performers," *Success* (May 1994), Vol. 41, No. 4, 34; Brian Azar, "Are You a Master Salesperson," *Personal Selling Power* (April 1992), Vol. 12, No. 3, 27; and "Qualities to Look for When You're Hiring," *Sales and Marketing Management*, (August 13, 1995), 84-87.

26. Ralph Waldo Emerson, "Circles," in *Essays: First Series* (1841).

27. Stan Moss, "What Sales Executives Look For in New Salespeople," *Sales & Marketing Management*, Vol. 120, No. 4 (March 1978), 47.

28. Howard Feiertag, "Listening skills, enthusiasm top list of salespeople's best traits," *Hotel and Motel Management*, Vol. 217, Is. 13, (July 15, 2002), 20.

29. Herb Greenberg, "Producers lack key personality traits of successful sales people," *National Underwriter*, (Property & casualty/risk & benefits management ed.), Vol. 107, Is. 47, (November 24, 2003), 11.

30. Joseph Jones, "Ten Sales Fundamentals," *Personal Selling Power*, Vol. 15, No. 2 (March 1995), 52.

31. Tanis Cornell, Phone Interview, October 20, 2007.

32. Betsy Cummings, "Increasing Face Time," *Sales and Marketing Management*, (January 2004), Vol. 156, Is. 1, 12.

33. Betsy Cummings, "Retire? No Thanks," *Sales & Marketing Management* (December 2000), 29.

34. Victor M Parachin, "Seven secrets for self-motivation," *The American Salesman*, Vol. 48, Is. 1, (January 2003), 16-21.

35. Geoffrey Brewer, "What Makes Great Salespeople?" *Sales and Marketing Management* (May 1994), 85.

Chapter 2

1. Scott Krugman and Ellen Tolley, "Online Retail Sales," Accessed February 12, 2007: www.shop.org.

2. Amy Gahran, "Yahoo's Big Deal with Papers: What About Local Ads?" Posted April 16, 2007, accessed Aug 24, 2007, http://www.poynter.org/dg.lts/id.31/aid.121538/column.htm.

3. Betsy Cummings, "Listen Don't Talk," *Sales and Marketing Management* (March 2001), 65; Judy Corwin, "Taking Sales Education Global," *Baylor Business Review* (Fall 1997), 16-17.

4. Debbie Howell, "Selling trust, expertise hits home with customers," *DSN Retailing Today*, March 27, 2006.

5. Joan Leotta, "How to Become a Business Asset to Your Customers," *Selling Power* (January/February 2000), 44.

6. Figure 2.1 created from ideas from the following: Nancy Arnott, "It's a Woman's World," *Sales and Marketing Management* (March 1995), 56; Larry Chambers, "Don't Let Fear Kill Your Sale," *Personal Selling Power*, Vol. 12, No. 6, (September 1992), 36; "Top Sales Reps Prove Their Worth," *Purchasing* (March 22, 1990), 27; and Tony Alessandra, Phil Wexler, and Rick Barerra, *Non-Manipulative Selling*, 2nd Ed. (1987).

7. Barbara Geraghty, *Visionary Selling* (New York: Simon and Schuster, 1998), 240.

8. Robert McGarvey and Babs S. Harrison, "How Tech Hip are You?" *Selling Power* (March 2001), 77.

9. Lois A. Mohr and Mary Jo Bittner, "The Role of Employee Effort in Service Satisfaction with Service Transactions," *Journal of Business Research*, Vol. 3, No. 3, (March 1995), 239-40.

10. George Pitcher, "Poor after-sales service will drive customers away," *Marketing Week*, London: (September 26, 2002), 29.

11. Manus Rungtusanatham, Jeffrey A Ogden, Bin Wu, "Advancing theory development in total quality management: A 'Deming management method' perspective," *International Journal of Operations & Production Management*, Bradford: (2003), Vol. 23, Is. 7/8, 918.

12. Ron Zemke, "TQM: Fatally Flawed or Simply Unfocused?" *Training*, (October 1992), 8; Paul Mears, "How to Stop Talking About and Begin the Process Toward TQM," *Business Horizons* (May/June 1993), 11-14.

13. Quint Studer, "How to achieve and sustain excellence: there are seven ways to hardwire excel-

lent outcomes. Do you know what they are?" *Healthcare Financial Management*; (June, 2007).

14. Jude P. Morte, "Special Feature: Best Employers in the Philippines," *BusinessWorld*, Manila: (May 29, 2003), 1.

15. Rose Knotts, "Rambo Doesn't Work Here Anymore," *Business Horizons*, (January February 1992), 44-46.

16. W. Edwards Deming, *Out of the Crisis* (Cambridge, MA: MIT, 1986).

17. John Tschohl, "Benefits of Customer Service," *The Selling Advantage*, Vol. 4, Iss. 82, (June 12, 1992), 3.

18. Tom Peters, "Meeting the Dangers and Opportunities of Chaos," *Personal Selling Power*, Vol. 10, No. 6, (September 1990), 49.

19. Adapted from a manuscript by Dr. James C. Cotham, Belmont University, Nashville, TN. First used on March 23, 1995. Actual Date Unknown, "Principles and Concepts of TQM, Competing in the Marketing Wars of the 1990s: Get Better or Get Beaten.

20. Anonymous, "TQM: A snapshot of the experts," *Measuring Business Excellence*, Bradford: (2002), Vol. 6, Is. 3, 54-57.

21. Louise Anderson, "The Bundling Advantage: How Team-based Approach Can Heat Up Sales," *Performance Management*; (January 2006).

22. This section on Team Selling was modified from the following sources: Andy Ferguson, "Sales Departments Claim Marketers Could do Better," *Marketing Week* (September 11, 1997), 28-29; Mark McCormack," Doubles Anyone," *Sales & Marketing Management* (December 1993) 35-36; Tom Murray, "Team Selling: What's the Incentive?" *Sales & Marketing Management* (June 1991), 90; Jack Falvey, "Team Selling: What It Is and Isn't," *Sales & Marketing Management* (June 1990), 8-10; "Team Selling: A Team Approach to Increasing Sales," *Small Business Report*, April 1985), 23-25; and "Calling in the Team," *Professional Selling*, (June 10, 1984), 1-3.

23. Don Green, "Count on strong relationships," *Paperboard Packaging*. Cleveland: (November 2001), Vol. 86, Is. 11, 8.

24. Malcolm Campbell, "How To Become a Top Performer," *Selling Power* (January/February 2000), 61.

25. Anonymous, "Team Marketing: A Simple Approach to Put a Plan Together," *Law Office Management & Administration Report*, New York: (January 2004), Vol. 04, Is. 1, 5.

26. Betsy Cummings, "Done Deal," *Sales and Marketing Management*, New York: (January 2004), Vol. 156, Is. 1, 16.

27. Malcolm Fleschner, "Anatomy of a Sale," *Selling Power* (May 1998), 94-96.

28. Henry Canaday, "Flyaway Sales," *Selling Power* (October 2000), 110.

Chapter 3

1. Lawrence Aragon "Eugene's Legacy." *Venture Capital Journal*. Wellesley Hills (January 1, 2004),

2. "Say it with pride: I am a salesman!" *Businessline*. Chennai (April 29, 2004), 1.

3. Murray Weidenbaum. "Business ethics: Everybody's favorite oxymoron." *Executive Speeches*. Dayton (April/May 2003), Vol.17, Is. 5, 15.

4. Stephen Koepp, "Having It All, Then Throwing It All Away," *Time* (May 25, 1987), 22.

5. Tom Black, *The Boxcar Millionaire: Tom Black's Proven System of Sales Success*, Tom Black Center for Selling, Inc, Nashville; 2007.

6. Clarence Walton, ed., *The Ethics of Corporate Conduct* (Englewood Cliffs, NJ: Prentice-Hall, 1977), 10.

7. Thomas R. Wotruba, "A Framework for Teaching Ethical Decision-Making in Marketing," *Marketing Education Review*, Vol. 3, No. 2 (Summer 1994), 4.

9. Allan Bloom, *The Closing of the American Mind* (New York: Simon and Schuster, 1987), 61.

10. Ari Galper, "Sales Ethics: When Did It Become Okay to Lie?" Accessed Aug 23, 2007http://www.unlockthegame.com/SalesEthics/. 8. Charles Schwepker and Thomas Ingram, "Improving Sales Performance Through Ethics: The Relationship Between Salesperson Moral Judgement and Job Performance," *Journal of Business Ethics* (November 1996), 3.

11. United Professional Sales Association, "The UPSA Professional Selling Ethics Framework," Washington D.C. Version 1, www.upsa-intl.org, http://www.upsa-intl.org/docs/UPSA_Professional_Selling_Ethics_

Framework.pdf, accessed Aug 21, 2007.

12. Sean Valentine, Tim Barnett. "Ethics Code Awareness, Perceived Ethical Values, and Organizational Commitment." *The Journal of Personal Selling & Sales Management.* New York (Fall 2003), Vol.23, Is. 4, 359.

13. Carlo Patetta Rotta, "Rules of behavior: the adoption of a code of conduct is a step toward improving the ethical culture in today's business world," *Internal Auditor* (June, 2007).

14. "Nice Guys Finish First," *Business Ethics*, Vol. 7, No. 3 (May/June 1993), 10.

15. Arthur Bragg, "Ethics in Selling, Honest," *Sales & Marketing Management*, Vol. 138, No. 7 (May 1987), 44.

16. Michele Marchetti, "Whatever it Takes," *Sales & Marketing Management.* (December 1997, 29-36.

17. Isabelle Maignan, O C Ferrell. "Corporate Social Responsibility and Marketing: An Integrative Framework." *Academy of Marketing Science Journal.* Greenvale (Winter 2004), Vol.32, Is. 1, 3.

18. Andy Cohen, "Slowdown Effect: Lack of Ethics," *Sales & Marketing Management* (June 2001), 13.

19. Charles Schwepker, O.C. Ferrell and Thomas Ingram, "The Influence of Ethical Climate and Ethical Conflict on Role Stress in the Sales Force," *Academy of Marketing Science Journal* (Spring 1997), 2-3.

20. Edmund G Seebauer. "Whistle-blowing: Is it Always Obligatory?" *Chemical Engineering Progress.* New York (June 2004), Vol. 100, Is. 6, 23.

21. Saul W. Gellerman, "Why 'Good' Managers Make Bad Ethical Choices," *Harvard Business Review*, Vol. 64 (July/August 1986), 89.

22. Karen Trent, "The Dangers of Groupthink," *Teamwork* (June 4, 1990), 1.

23. Erin Strout, "Doctoring Sales," *Sales & Marketing Management* (May 2001), 59.

24. "The Drummers of Groupthink; [Letter 1]" *New York Times.* Late Edition (East Coast). New York, (July 18, 2004), 4.12.

25. Jasmin Perrone, Margaret H. Vickers. "Emotions as Strategic Game in a Hostile Workplace: An Exemplar Case," *Employee Responsibilities and Rights Journal.* New York (September 2004), Vol.16, Is. 3, 167.

26. Patrick Willard, *The Nashville Tennessean* (November 24, 1987), 1A.

27. Dale Buss, "Ways to Curtail Employee Theft," *Nation's Business* (April 1993), 36.

28. Randy Schwantz. "Honesty Turns Out To Be The Best Policy" *National Underwriter.* (Property & casualty/risk & benefits management ed.). Erlanger, (February 2, 2004), Vol.108, Is. 4, 33.

29. Terence A. Hockenhull. "Weekender Marketing." *BusinessWorld.* Manila: (August 20, 2004), 1.

30. Kathleen O'Neill, "Firms Say Thank You with Business Gifts," *Public Relations Journal* (September 1991), 28.

31. "Ethical Eating," *U.S. News and World Report* (August 5, 1991), 11.

32. Lizabeth England, "Whistle-blowing English," Electronic Journal: *Language and Civil Society*, http://exchanges.state.gov/forum/journal/bus4background.htm, accessed March 24, 2007.

33. Nancy R. Hauserman, "Whistle-Blowing: Individual Morality in a Society," *Business Horizons*, Vol. 29 (March/April 1986), 4.

34. Janet Bamford, "When Do You Blow the Whistle?" *Forbes* (October 21, 1985), 168.

35. Glenn T. Wilson, "Ethics, Your Company or Your Conscience," *Working Woman* (June 1984), 67.

36. Robert Tucker, "Values: The Key To Winning in the New Millennium," *Sales Doctors.com* (November 22, 1999), 1.

37. Melinda Ligos, "Clicks and Misses," *Sales & Marketing Management* (June 2000), 74.

38. "Sexual Harassment: Injured at Work." [Online] Available http://www.lawguru.com/sexhara.html (April 22, 1998).

39. Claude Solnik, "Attorneys advise employers to prevent sexual harassment through policies, training, and procedures," *Long Island Business News* (Friday, September 15 2006).

40. Herff Moore and Don Bradley III, "Sexual Harassment in Manufacturing: Seven Strategics Successful Companies Use to Curb it," *Industrial Management* (Nov/Dec 1997), 14-18.

41. Betsy Cummings, "Falling Stars," *Sales & Marketing Management* (December 2000), 62.

42. Abby Brown, "Is Ethics Good Business?" *Personnel Administrator*, Vol. 32 (February 1987), 67.

43. David J. Lill, "Issue of Ethics Often Faces Professional Salespeople," *Nashville Business Journal* (April 22-26, 1991), 5.

44. Betsy Cummings. "Ethical Breach." *Sales and Marketing* code of conduct is a step toward improving the ethical culture in today's business world," *Internal Auditor* (June, 2007).

Chapter 4

1. Chester R. Wasson, *Consumer Behavior: A Managerial Viewpoint* (Austin, TX: Austin Press, 1975), 9.

2. Scott Young, "Measuring Success: Using Consumer Research to Document the Value of Package Design," *Design Management Review*, (Spring 2006).

3. George M Zinkhan, Karin Braunsberger. "The complexity of consumers' cognitive structures and its relevance to consumer behavior." *Journal of Business Research*. New York: (June 2004). Vol.57, Is. 6, 575.

4. For an expanded description of the model, see James F. Engel, Roger D. Blackwell, and Paul W. Miniard, *Consumer Behavior* (Hinsdale, IL: Dryden Press, 1990).

5. Niraj Dawar. "What Are Brands Good For?" *MIT Sloan Management Review*. Cambridge: (Fall 2004). Vol. 46, Is. 1, 31.

6. Interview with Paul O'Brian, "CEA Forum: HP Direct and Online Consumer Behavior Audio," Posted by Catherine Girardeau, October 19th, 2006.

7. There are 40 squares in the figure.

8. Craig Stimmel, "Building Customer Relations In 2006," *Office World News*, (Nov/Dec 2006).

9. Aron O'Cass. "Fashion clothing consumption: Antecedents and consequences of fashion clothing involvement." *European Journal of Marketing*. Bradford: (2004). Vol.38, Is. 7, 869.

10. Himadri Roy and Sitanath Majumdar, "Of Diamonds and Desires: Understanding Conspicuous Consumption from a Contemporary Marketing Perspective," *Academy of Marketing Science Review*, (2006).

11. Tim Connor, *The Soft Sell* (Crofton, MD: TR Training Associates, 1981), 16.

12. Nittin Esso and Sally Dibb." Religious Influences on Shopping Behavior: An Exploratory Study." *Journal of Marketing Management*. Helensburg: (September 2004). Vol.20, Is. 7, 683.

13. Betsy Cummings, "Selling Around the World,*" Sales & Marketing Management* (May 2001), 70.

14. Leonard Lynn and Hal Salzman, "Collaborative Advantage Issues," *Science and Technology*, (Winter 2006).

15. Jeffrey Gitomer. "Where's the Sales Beef? It's Client's Buying Motive." *Boulder County Business Report*. Boulder: (July 23-August 5, 2004). Vol. 23, Is. 16, 6A.

16. For an expanded analysis on the roles played see, Francy Blackwood, "Nowhere to Go But Up," *Selling* (April 1994), 16-19; William G. Zikmund and Michael d'Amico, *Effective Marketing* (St. Paul, MN: West Publishing Company, 2001), 165; and Frederick E. Webster, Jr. and Yoran Wind, "A General Model For Understanding Organizational Buying Behavior," *Journal of Marketing*, Vol. 36, No. 2 (April 1972).

17. Geok Theng Lau, Mohammed A Razzaque, Angeline Ong. "Gatekeeping in Organizational Purchasing: An Empirical Investigation." *The Journal of Business & Industrial Marketing*. Santa Barbara: (2003). Vol.18, Is. 1, 82.

18. Tim Connor, "Effective Sales Communication Skills," Salesdoctor.com (September 20, 1999), 1-5.

19. Anthony J. Alessandra and Philip S. Wexler, *Non-Manipulative Selling* (Reston, VA: Reston Publishing Company, 1979), 43-45.

20. William F. Schoell and Joseph P. Guiltinan, *Marketing*, 6th. ed. (Englewood Cliffs, NJ: Prentice Hall, 1995), 441-447.

21. Albert Mehrabian, *Silent Messages* (Belmont, CA: 1971).

22. Deb Varallo, *A Dress for Success Seminar*, Belmont University, Nashville, TN, (November, 2006).

23. Bob Ayrer and Ray Considine, "I Said, "Are You Listening To Me?" *Agency Sales Magazine* (January 2000), 58.

24. "Fine-Tuning Your Negotiating Skills," *Professional Selling*, Vol. 22, No. 4 (February 25, 1984), 2.

25. "The Perils of Miscommunication" *Professional Selling*, Vol.

27, No. 20 (October 25, 1989), 2.

26. Alessandra and Wexler, *Non-Manipulative Selling*, 48-51.

27. This section on the voice was adapted from: Jeffrey Jacobi, "Voice Power," *Selling Power* (October 2000), 66; Robert A. Peterson, Michael P. Cannito and Steven P. Brown, "An Exploratory Investigation of Voice Characteristics," *The Journal of Personal Selling & Sales Management* (Winter 1995), 1-16; John H. Melchinger, "Communication-One Key to Unlock Your Sales, " *Personal Selling Power*, Vol. 10, No. 3 (April 1990), 51.

28. Anne E Beall. "Body Language Speaks." *Communication World.* San Francisco: (March/April 2004). Vol. 21, Is. 2, 18.

29. This section was inspired by Alessandra and Wexler, *Non-Manipulative Selling*, 95-113; Gerhard Gschwandtner, *Non Verbal Selling Power* (Englewood Cliffs, NJ: Prentice-Hall, 1985), 3-80; and John T. Molloy, *Live for Success* (New York: Perigord Press, 1981).

30. T.R. Baron, "Using Gestures to Listen," *Personal Selling Power*, Vol. 3, No. 4 (May/June 1993), 45.

31. Kevin Daley, "See the Sale," *Selling Power* (May 1998), 42-44.

32. Julia Chang. "Selling in Action." *Sales and Marketing Management.* New York: (May 2004). Vol. 156, Is. 5, 22.

33. David J. Lill, James C. Cotham, and Jennie Carter Thomas, "Listen Up," Optometric Economics, Vol. 1, No. 4 (April 1991), 27. Contributed by Laurie

Bergman, PEP Strategies Editor, *Optometric Economics.*

34. Tom Metcalf, "Communicating Your Message: The Hidden Dimension," *Life Association News* (April 1997), 18-21.

Chapter 5

1. David Newton. "Sell to the Psyche." *Kitchen & Bath Business.* New York: (April 2004), Vol.51, Is. 4, 41.

2. Carl G. Jung, *Psychological Types* (New York: Harcourt Brace and Co., 1924).

3. I am indebted to these individuals and their companies for sharing this valuable information with me. For more detail, see David W. Merrill and Roger H. Reid, *Personal Styles and Effective Performance*, (Radnor, PA: Chilton Book Company, 1981); Paul Mok, *Communicating Styles Technology* (Dallas, TX: Training Associates Press, 1982); Larry Wilson, *Social Styles Sales Strategies* (Eden Prairie, MN: Wilson Learning Corporation, 2000); Tony Alessandra, Phil Wexler, and Rick Barrera, *Non-Manipulative Selling* (Englewood Cliffs, NJ: Prentice-Hall, 1987).

4. John R. Graham, "Four Basic Categories of Prospects," *Personal Selling Power*, Vol. 13, No. 8 (November/December 1993), 56.

5. John L. Bledsoe, "How to Improve Your Relationships with Clients- and Your Staff, Too," *The Practical Accountant* (Institute for Continuing Professional Development, 1984).

6. Michael E Rega, Lisa M Clayton. "Recognizing behavioral buying patterns," *Agency Sales.*

Irvine: (November 2003). Vol.33, Is. 11, 34.

7. Interpretation Manual for Communicating Styles Technology developed by Dr. Paul Mok, President of Training Associates Press of Richardson, Texas (Dallas: T A Press 1975), 5.

8. Robert F. Kantin and Mark W. Hardwick, *Quality Selling Through Quality Proposals* (Danvers, MA: Boyd and Fraser Publishing 1994), 28.

9. Chet Robie, "Effects of Perceived Selection Ratio on Personality Test Faking," *Social Behavior and Personality*, 2006.

10. Merrill and Reid, *Personal Styles*, 88-117.

11. Todd Duncan, "Your Sales Style," *Incentive* (December 1999), 64-66.

12. Hugh J. Ingrasci, "How to Reach Buyers in their Psychological 'Comfort Zones,'" *Industrial Marketing* (July 1981), 64; Merrill and Reid, *Personal Styles*, 88-117.

13. Seth Godin, "The Dating Game," *Sales & Marketing Management* (May 2001), 34.

14. David Newton. "Sell to the Psyche." *Kitchen & Bath Business.* New York: (April 2004), Vol.51, Is. 4, 41.

15. Tom Hoek, guest lecture at Belmont University, Nashville, TN, March 23, 2006. Mr. Hoek is president of Insurance Systems of Tennessee.

16. Wilson Learning Library, *Versatile Selling: Adapting Your Style so Customers Say Yes!* Nova Vista Publishing: Belgium, 2006.

17. Tony Alessandra, Phil Wexler, and Rick Barrera, *Non-Manipu-*

lative Selling (New York: Prentice Hall, 1987), 112.

18. Rod Nichols, "How to Sell to Different Personality Types," *Personal Selling Power*, Vol. 12, No. 8 (November/December 1992), 46; and Malcolm Fleschner, "The Microsoft Way," *Selling Power* (January/February 1998),86.

19. Jeff Thull. "Recognition Smarts," *Incentive*. New York: (September 2004), Vol.178, Is. 9, 120.

20. Bruce Seidman, "The Psychology of the Sale, Part 1," Salesdoctors.com (February 14, 2000),2.

21. Patrick Schul and Brent Wren, "The Emerging Role of Women in Industrial Selling: A Decade of Change," *Journal of Marketing*, 56 (July 1992), 38.

22. Henry Cole. "Marketing Real Estate Services: Smart Work versus Hard Work in Personal Selling." *Services Marketing Quarterly*. Binghamton: (2004). Vol. 25, Is. 2, 43.

23. John P Dugan, "Explorations Using the Social Change Model: Leadership Development among College Men and Women," *Journal of College Student Development*, (Mar/Apr 2006).

24. Fredrick A. Russ and Kevin A. McNeilly, "Links Among Satisfaction, Commitment, and Performance," *Journal of Business Research*, 34, 1 (September 1995), 57-61.

25. Judy A. Siguaw and Earl Honeycutt, Jr. "An Examination of Gender Differences in Selling Behaviors and Job Attitudes," *Industrial Marketing Management*, 24 (1995), 46; Robert

Sharoff, "She Said, He Said," *Selling* (May 1994), 54-58.

26. New England Cable News (NECN), "Education and Pay Differences by Gender," Online video clip, Accessed 7/11/07 http://www.boston.com/partners/worldnow/necn/landingpage.html?clipId=1578884&topVideoCatNo=83464.

27. Paula Zmudzinski, "Gender Mutters," *Selling Power* (March 2000), 8.

28. Gary Bachelor, "Selling Beyond Gender," *Selling Power* (January/February 1996), 66-67.

29. Personal Communication with Roger H. Reid (July 21, 2001).

30. Vincent Alonzo, "Role Call: Defining Your Reps' Personality Types Can Open a Window to Motivate," *Sales & Marketing Management* (June 2001), 34-35; Helen Berman,"Selling to Different Personalities," *Folio: The Magazine for Magazine Management* (June 1999), 34-35.

31. Richard Jensen and Roy Spungin, "Analyze Your Prospects to a tee," *Selling Power* (July/August 1997), 80-81.

32. Zenith Training and Development, "The Psychology of Selling Excellence," Accessed August 18, 2007. http://www.zenithtraining.ie/sales-training/.

33. Fran Abrams. "Learning? It's all in the mind." *The Times Educational Supplement*. London: (May 21, 2004), Is. 4584, F8.

34. Flo Conway and Jim Siegelman, "The Awesome Power of the Mind-Probers," *Science Digest* (September 1983), 72-73.

35. Ed Rigsbee, "Explore the Benefits of Partnership Selling,"

Personal Selling Power, Vol. 12, No. 7 (October 1992), 46.

36. Conway, *The Awesome*," 91.

37. William G. Nickels, Robert F. Everett, and Robert Klein, "Rapport Building for Salespeople: A Neuro-linguistic Approach," *Journal of Personal Selling & Sales Management* (November 1983), 2.

38. Ibid 1.

Chapter 6

1. Renee Houston Zemanski, "The Green Team," *Selling Power* (September 2000), 166.

2. Les Kiaschbaum, "How the Terms of Sale Can Impact Profits," *Personal Selling Power* (March 1990), 28.

3. James Mullen, "In (Name Here) We Trust," *Selling* (October 1995), 79.

4. George H Walper Jr. and Catherine S. McBreen, "Clients' Knowledge is Power" *On Wall Street*, Feb 2007.

5. Craig J Coffey. "Differentiating Yourself With Exemplary Service." *National Underwriter. Life & Health.* (August 23- August 30, 2004). Vol. 108, Is. 32, 18.

6. Tate Williams. "The Age-Old Face-Off." *Sales and Marketing Management*. New York: (April 2004). Vol. 156, Is. 4, 64.

7. George W. Colombo, "Need Info? Pick Up a Pen," *Selling* (May 1994), 24-26; and Malcolm K. Fleschner, "How to Automate Your Sales Force," *Personal Selling Power* (September 1991), 42.

8. Marshall Lager, "The Alignment: CRM capabilities and business processes enable tech-

nology to shine," *CRM Magazine*, July 2007.

9. Paul and Lauren Gibbons, "Cost Effective IT Training," *Network World*, March 7, 2007.

10. Malcolm Fleschner, "Easy Does It," *Selling Power* (March 2001), 120.

11. Anonymous, "WebEx Training Center Wins Three eLearning Guild Member's Choice Awards", *PR Newswire*, June 29, 2007.

12. "LDMI Connects With ePath Learning to Enhance Sales Training & Bolster Growth." *PR Newswire*. New York: (August 30, 2004), 1.

13. From a telephone interview with Paul Goldner on May 16, 2001; and adapted from Erika Rasmussan, "Training Goes Virtual," *Sales & Marketing Management* (September 2000), 108.

14. Adapted and modified from the following sources: James Kickie, "Lessons From An SFA Pioneer," *Sales & Field Automation* (March 1998), 31; and George Colombo, *Sales Force Automation: Using the Latest Technology to Make Your Sales Force More Competitive* (New York: McGraw-Hill, 1994).

15. Nelson King, "Contact Managers: Keep Your Sales Force in Touch," *Sales & Field Force Automation* (March 1998), 84.

16. Malcolm Fleschner, "Ooh, That Smarts!" *Selling Power* (January/February 2001), 30.

17. Anne Stanton. "The "Why" Behind CRM Software." *Infotech Update*. New York: (March /April 2004), Vol.13, Is. 2, 5.

18. "Acumentum Increases Sales Revenues Using Siebel CRM OnDemand." B*usiness Wire*. New York: (October 27, 2004), 1.

19. Adapted and modified from an article by Chad Kaydo, "A Position of Power, *Sales & Marketing Management* (June 2000), 105-112.

20. "Avon Rings Millions of New Bells," *Sales & Marketing Management* (October 1992), 25.

21. Don E. Schultz, "Objectives Drive Tactics in Integrated Marketing Communication Approach," *Marketing News* (May 9, 1994), 14; and Junu B. Kim, "Databases Open Doors For Retailers," *Advertising Age* (February 15, 1993).

22. Douglas B Holt, John A Quelch, Earl L Taylor. "How Global Brands Compete." *Harvard Business Review*. Boston: (September 2004), Vol.82, Is. 9, 68.

23. Michael E. Cavanagh, "In Search of Motivation," *Personnel Journal*, Vol.63, No.3 (March 1984), 76.

24. Robert McGarvey and Babs S. Harrison,"Easy as Pie," *Selling Power* (March 2000), 116.

25. The sections of this chapter dealing with motivation and goal setting were taken largely from Paul J. Meyer's *Dynamics of Personal Goal Setting, Dynamics of Personal Leadership, and Dynamics of Personal Motivation* (Waco, TX: Success Motivation, 1991, 1992, and 1993, respectively).

26. Chris Glass, "Getting to Know You," *Sales & Marketing Management* (December 1997), 24-25.

27. Harvey Mackay, "Life is a matter of perspective: It all depends on how you choose to see it," JustSell.com (May 1, 2000), 1.

28. Geoffrey Brewer, "Mind Reading," *Sales & Marketing Management* (May 1994), 85.

29. Edwin Bobrow, "Goal-Oriented Selling," *The American Salesman* (January 2000), 14.

30. Gary Bachelor, "Map Your Goals," *Personal Selling Power*, Vol. 14, No. 1 (January/February 1994), 58.

31. Jack Cullen and Len D'Innocenzo, "How to Set and Communicate Goals," *Personal Selling Power*, Vol. 13, No. 8 (November/December 1993), 69.

32. Paul J. Meyer, Dynamics of Personal Goal Setting, Lesson 5 (Waco, TX: Success Motivation, Inc., 1984), 2.

Chapter 7

1. Barry Farber, "Get On Track." *Entrepreneur* (February 2000), 138.

2. Anonymous, "Why Sales Leads Fall Through The Cracks, And How SFA Can Make The Difference" *Customer Interaction Solutions*, Jul 2006.

3. Renee Zemanski, "Developing New Leads*," Selling Power* (March 2000), 34.

4. Dirk Beveridge, "Qualifying Your Prospects," *The American Salesman*, Vol. 36, No. 6 (June 1991), 6-9.

5. Paul J. Meyer, Sales Training Material for Distributors of SMI International, Inc. (Waco, TX).

6. "Fewer Than 10 Percent of Decision-Makers Contacted by Salespeople One-Month Period," *The American Salesman*,

Vol. 33, No. 3 (March, 1988), 13-14.

7. Bill Cates, "Referrals 101," *Selling Power* (October 2000), 56.

8. Cliff Zalz, "Building Relationships," *Business Marketing* (August 1992), 34.

9. Michael Twining, "Million To Win," *Selling Power* (March 2000), 50.

10. Richard F. Libin, "Bring Back This Lost Art Form", *Ward's Dealer Business*, Feb 1, 2007.

11. Irby F. Stewart, "Golden Opportunities," in power tips section of *Selling Power* (March 2001), 62.

12. Andrea J. Moses, "Taking the Stress Out of Cold Calling," *The Selling Advantage*, Vol. 4, Issue 1 (May 28, 1992), 1-2.

13. "The Medium and the Message," *Direct Marketing*, Vol. 56, No. 9 (January 1994), 27.

14. Behram J. Hansotia, "List Segmentation: How to Find Your Best Direct Marketing Prospects," *Business Marketing*, Vol. 71, No. 6 (August 1986), 64.

15. Richard Pluntron, "On The Web With," *Sales & Marketing Management* (September 2000), 19.

16. Jeffrey Gitomer, "Networking Not Working? Try Smart-working," *Dallas Business Journal* (January 14, 2000), 43.

17. Tony Lee, "Networking; Only Connect," *Folio: the Magazine for Magazine Management*, Vol. 23, No. 2 (February 1, 1994), 33.

18. John Greenwald, "Sorry, Right Number," *Time*, Vol. 142, No. 11 (September 13, 1993), 66.

19. Michelle Amodio, "Are There Suitable/Affordable/Adequate Technologies For Small To Medium-Sized Call Centers?" *Customer Inter@ction Solutions*, Nov 2006.

20. Karen Starr, "If the Shoe Fits, Make it Personal," *Selling Power* (January/February 2001), 26.

21. Eduardo Javier Canto, "Survey Says: Where the Sales Are," *Sales & Marketing Management* (June 2001), 18.

22. Anonymous, "Marketing Software Optimizes Online Search Engine Management," *Product News Network*, July 16, 2007.

23. Gregory Jordan. "Online, Used Car Lots That Cover the Nation." *New York Times*. (Late Edition). New York, (October 22, 2003), G.13.

24. Teri Kelsh, "Converting virtual leads into actual sales: most dealerships that have Web sites don't have one sales rep dedicated to answering e-mail queries, survey finds." *Powersports Business*, April, 2007.

25. Robert McGarvey and Babs S. Harrison, "How Tech Are You," *Selling Power* (March 2001), 74; "The Sales Software Solution," *Personal Selling Power* (April 1990), 46-47.

26. Betsy Cummings. "In Their Shoes." *Sales and Marketing Management*. New York (October 2004), Vol. 156, Is. 10, 36.

Chapter 8

1. http://www-rohan.sdsu.edu/~renglish/377/notes/chapt08/. Accessed November 6, 2004.

2. Dave Dolak. "A Crash Course in Marketing." http://www.davedolak.com/c-mktg5.htm. Page 5. Accessed November 6, 2004.

3. Sharon Parker, "Stand and Deliver," *Sales & Marketing Management*, (January/ February 2001), 18; Bryan Hysdu, "Surviving the Cold Call without Freezing," *The Journal of Commercial Bank Lending* (November 1986), 49.

4. Long Island Business News Staff, "When it comes to sales, preparation is key," *Daily Record and the Kansas City Daily News-Press*, Jan 7, 2006.

5. Linda Richardson, "Winning Strategies for Meeting Prospects," *Selling Power* (September 2000), 44.

6. Chad Kaydo, "Lights! Camera! Sales!," *Sales & Marketing Management* (February 1998), 111.

7. Rich Wilkins, "Visualize Your Success," *Professional Selling Power*, Vol. 13, No. 1 (January/ February 1993), 69.

8. Robert E. Hite and Joseph A. Bellizzi, "Differences in the Importance of Selling Techniques between Consumer and Industrial Salespeople," *Journal of Personal Selling and Sales Management* (November 1985), 23.

9. Renee Zemanski, "Developing New Leads," *Selling Power* (March 2000), 34.

10. G. Berton Latamore, "Perfect Match," *Selling Power* (September 2000), 150-155.

11. Marcia A. Reed-Woodard, "What you look like online," *Black Enterprise*, Jan 2007.

12. John J. McCarthy, *Secrets of Super Selling* (Boardroom Books: New York, 1982), 91.

13. George N. Kahn, "Without Ammunition," *The Smooth Selling*

Series (New York: George N. Kahn Co., 1976) 3.

14. Graham Roberts-Phelps, "How to Add Value to Every Sales Call," *Personal Selling Power*, Vol. 14, No. 1 (January/February 1994), 47.

15. Adapted from John J. Franco, "Ring Up More Telephone Sales with Well-Trained Personnel," *Business Marketing*, Vol. 71, No. 8 (August 1986), 84; and "Telephone Closes Are Up," *Personal Selling Power*, Vol. 14, No. 4 (May/June 1994), 20.

16. Susan Greco, "The Need for Speed," *Inc.*, April, 2007.

17. "Getting Past the Gatekeeper," *Selling Power* (July/August 2000), 56; Jan Gelman, "Gatekeeper," *Selling*, Vol. 2, No. 1 (July/August 1994), 54-56; and Nanci McCann, "Protocol," *Selling*, Vol. 1, No. 9 (May 1994), 79.

18. http://saturn.ksi.edu/people/students/charliechen/charthesis/char02.html. Alex Tsai. Accessed November 7, 2004.

19. Wendy Weiss, "Top Ten Tips for Terminating Telephone Terror," *The American Salesman* (December 2000), 15-17.

20. June Johnson, "You Make a First Impression Only Once," *Selling Power* (June 2000), 42.

21. "Voice Concerns," *Personal Selling Power,* Vol. 13, No. 7 (October 1993), 44.

22. http://www.onlinewbc.gov/docs/market/mk_appear_phone.html. United States Small Business Administration, Accessed November 8, 2004.

23. "Making a Telephone Investment," *Professional Selling,* Vol. 22, No. 5 (March 10, 1984), 1-2.

24. Jeffrey Jacobi, "Voice Power," *Selling Power* (October 2000), 66.

25. Anonymous, "Contact Management Software synchs with wireless devices," *Product News Network*, March 27, 2006.

26. David Lill, "From phone to face-to-face," *Selling Power* (January/ February 1998), 46-47.

27. Barry Z. Masser and William M. Leeds, *Power-Selling by Telephone* (West Nyack, NY: Parker Publishing Company, 1982), 56.

28. Shafiroff and Shook, *Successful Telephone Selling*, 36-37.

29. Paul O'Neil, "Selling Services: Using the Phone to Secure Face-to-Face Appointments," *Salesdoctors Magazine* (October 25, 1999), 3; "Five Steps to Effective Telephone Sales," *Professional Selling*, Vol. 22, No. 13 (July 10, 1984), 2.

30. "Sixteen Ways to Improve Your Telemarketing Effort," *Personal Selling Power*, Vol. 12, No. 7 (October 1992), 42.

Chapter 9

1. Dave Dolak, "Sales and Personal Selling," http://www.davedolak.com/c-mktg5.htm, Accessed November 9, 2004.

2. Jenni Laidman, "Make it Count," *The Tennessean* (June 21, 2001), section D of the Nashville newspaper, 1-2; George N. Kahn, "The Impression You Make," *Smooth Selling*, Vol. 62 (1967), 2.

3. Anonymous, "Home staging assists sellers," *USA Today* (in Collaboration with the Society for the Advancement of Education), April, 2007.

4. Vithyaa L.R. "Importance of customer service," *Business Times*. Kuala Lumpur: (October 19, 2004), 1.

5. Isabel Lee. "Art of selling one's skills crucial in clinching job," *South China Morning Post*. Hong Kong: July 17, 2004. pg. 5.

6. Joan Leotta, "Dressed to Sell," *Selling Power* (October 2000), 89.

7. Anthony J. Alessandra and Phillip Wexler, *Non-manipulative Selling* (Reston, VA: Reston Publishing, Inc., 1979), 87-93.

8. Jerry Hayes, "Do You Look Like a Doctor?" *Optometric Management*, Jul 2006.

9. Maria Puente, "How NOT to dress for work," *USA TODAY*, Business, 11/30/2006.

10. Modified and adapted from the following sources: Melinda Ligos, "Does Image Matter," *Sales & Marketing Management* (March 2001), 53-56; Leo Green, "Ask an Expert: Five Do's and Don'ts for Dressing Down," *CA Magazine* (January/February 2001), 11; Geoffrey Brewer and Chad Kaydo, "Dressing for Success," *Sales & Marketing Management* (August 2000), 104.

11. Pat Shemek, "Super Duper Difference," *Selling Power* (July/August 2000), 56.

12. Claude Solnik, "Immaculate receptions: The art of greeting clients to your firm," *Long Island Business News*, Jul 21, 2006.

13. Melinda Ligos, "Does Image Matter?" *Sales & Marketing Management* (March 2001), 12.

14. Emily Huling, "Leading from the Front Line," *Rough Notes,* Mar 2007.

15. Lydia Ramsey, "Seal the Deal Sales Technique," http://sbinformation.about.com/ od/sales/ a/ucsaletechnique_2.htm. Accessed November 9, 2004.

16. Dorothea Johnson, director of The Protocol School of Washington, "Five Tips for International Handshaking," *Sales & Marketing Management* (July 1997), 90.

17. Henry Porter, "Opening for Every Occasion," *Sales Management*, Vol. 109, No. 9 (October 30,1972), 6-8.

18. Karl Witsman, "No More What's His Name Again," *The American Salesman*, Vol. 32, No. 2 (February 1987), 25.

19. Adapted from "Here's an Easy Way to Remember Your Customers' Names," *Master Salesmanship* (Concordville, PA: Clement Communications, Inc., 1979) 3; and Nanci McCann, "When You Forget a Prospect's Name," *Selling* (March 1994), 101.

20. Phillip Proctor, "A Well-Bread Sale," *Selling Power* (September 2000), 20.

21. Paul P. Mok, "CST Influencing Model" from *CST: Communicating Styles Technology* (Dallas: T.A. Press, Inc., 1982), 13.

22. Adapted from Kevin Maney, "Take the Internet with you in a phone, watch or shoe," USA TODAY (March 18, 1998), 2B; George W. Colombo, "Need Info? Pick Up a Pen," *Selling* (May 1994), 24-26; Ginger

Trumpio, "On-Line at the Prudential," *Sales & Marketing Management* (June 1994), 42-44.

23. "Personal Touch Perks up Sales," In a special section entitled: Make Promotional Products Work For You, *Sales & Marketing Management* (October 1997), 7.

Chapter 10

1. Jim Scheer, "Asking Good Questions," *Office World News*, Jan/Feb 2006.

2. Ginger Trumfio, "Underlying Motivation," *Sales & Marketing Management* (June 1994), 71.

3. Kristen des Chatelets. "Asking the Right Questions." *Dealerscope*. Philadelphia (June 2004). Vol.46, Is. 6, 26.

4. Terrence A. Hockenhull. "Weekender: Marketing." *BusinessWorld*. Manila (January 9, 2004), 1.

5. George Ludwig. "Earn Your 'Doctor of Selling' Degree." *National Underwriter. Life & Health*. Erlanger (August 23-August 30, 2004).Vol.108, Is. 32, 50.

6. Art Sobczak, "Proposal Worthy," *Selling Power* (June 1997), 56; and Tim Connor, *The Soft Sell* (Crofton, MD: TR Training Associates Int'l., 1981), 64.

7. James Lorenzen, "Needs Analysis Replacing Product Presentation," *Marketing News,* Vol. 20, No. 9 (April 25, 1986), 180.

8. John O'Toole, "The Want Makes the Sale," *Selling* (June 1994), 43.

9. Camille P. Schuster and Jeffrey E. Davis, "Asking Questions: Some Characteristics of

Successful Sales Encounters," *Journal of Personal Selling and Sales Management*, Vol. 6, No. 1 (May 1986), 17.

10. Anonymous, "Probing Skills Course Aims to Educate the Learner about the Role of Questions in Various Situations and the Importance of Asking the Right Question at the Right Time," *Business Wire,* Jan 17, 2006.

11. Anthony J. Alessandra and Phillip S. Wexler, *Non-Manipulative Selling* (Reston, VA.: Reston Publishing Co., 1979), adapted from 54-57.

12. Tim Connor, *The Soft Sell* (Crofton, MD: TR Training Associates Intl., 1981), 67.

13. The Sales Hunter Video Podcast, "Repeat the Key Question, Selling is all about asking better." PyroTV.com, July 12, 2007.

14. Neil Rackham, *SPIN Selling* (New York: McGraw-Hill), 1988.

15. Interview with Paula Wilson, District Manager for TSI in Nashville, TN, September 24, 2007.

16. Rackham, Ibid, 89.

17. Todd Youngblood, "Let Customers Sell Themselves," *Selling Power* (March 2001), 52.

18. William Kendy, "Probing For Real Customer Needs," *Selling Power* (January/ February 2001), 26.

19. Steve Atlas, "When and How to Use Your Favorite Close Effectively," *Selling Power* (September 2000), 48.

20. Jim Scheer, "Closing sales," *Office World News*, May/Jun 2006.

21. Warren Greshes, "Prospecting Skills III," *Warren Greshes Video*, Brightcove.com; Accessed 8/6/07.

22. Doug Krumrei, "Poor Listeners—Disappointed Customers," Bakery Production and Marketing (March 15, 1998), 9; Max Messmer, "Improving Your Listening Skills," *Management Accounting* (March 1998), 14; and Marjorie Brody, "How To Listen To What's Really Being Said," *Personal Selling Power*, Vol. 14, No. 4 (May/June 1994), 65.

23. Murray Raphel, "Listening Correctly Can Increase Your Sales," *Direct Marketing*, Vol. 41, No. 11 (November 1982), 113.

24. Bill Brooks. "Active Listening." *Advisor Today*. Washington, (June 2003). Vol.98, Is. 6, 82.

25. Barry Elms, "Effective Listening is the Key to Identifying Buying Signals," *Selling Power* (March 2000), 40.

26. Rick Phillips, "Listen for More Sales," *Selling Power* (June 1996), 58-59; and Robert C. Immel, "Listen to What the Prospect is Telling You," *Sales & Marketing Executive Report IX*, Vol. 20 (October 1, 1986), 4-5.

27. George W. Colombo, "Need Info? Pick up a Pen," *Selling* (May 1994), 24-25.

28. Sarah Mahoney, "Hear Between the Lines," *Home Office Computing* (October 1997), 126-128; and Ken Thoreson, "Communicate to Sell," *Personal Selling Power*, Vol. 14, No. 1 (January/February 1993), 62.

Chapter 11

1. Bill Brooks, "What is the Difference Between What Customers Need and What They Really Want," *The American Salesman* (January 2001), 3-5.

2. This section culled from a book written by Dr. James Canton entitled, *Technofutures: How Leading Edge Technology Will Transform Business in the 21st Century* (Hay House, 1999).

3. "Presentations That Sell," *Sales & Marketing Management*. As adapted from Diane DiResta, *Knockout Presentations*, Chandler House Press, 1998.

4. Bill Engler, *Marketing Magic Inspired by P.T. Barnum*, Accessed May 23, 2006, http://www.marketingprofs.com/6/engler1.asp?sp=1#split.

5. Bill Wilson, "Quick Tip: Preparation Time," Accessed September 1, 2007 at http://www.presentation-pointers.com/showarticle/articleid/195/.

6. Tali Arbel, "Proceed with Caution: Presentation Roadblocks, Even the most seasoned salespeople know it: Presentations cause anxiety," *Sales and Marketing Management*, Accessed online January 02, 2007, http://www.presentations.com/msg/content_display/sales/e3i778b0e5af917c8c6b92ad42115694838#.

7. Mack Hannan, "The Three C's of Selling: A Sure Cure for the Salesman's Curse," *Sales & Marketing Management*, Vol. 10, No. 7 (May 10, 1976), 93.

8. "Features and Benefits," Women's Business Center, www.onlinewbc.gov, Accessed November 23, 2004.

9. Ginger Trumfio, "Underlying Motivation," *Sales & Marketing Management* (June 1994), 71.

10. Robert F. Taylor, *Back to Basic Selling* (Englewood Cliffs, NJ: Prentice-Hall, 1985), 75.

11. Anonymous, "Ensemble's Key Features & Benefits," Accessed September 3, 2007http://www.intersystems.com/ensemble/fb-chart.html.

12. Modified and adapted from: U.S. Census Bureau, *Current Population Reports*, 1993.

13. George N. Kahn, "You're on Stage," *Smooth Selling* (1975), 2.

14. Staff of the National Sales Development Institute, 10 Steps to Greatness in Selling (Waterford, CT: The National Sales Development Institute, 1980), 10-12.

15. Taken from an interview with Greg Wright of AmSouth Bank in Nashville, TN, July 10, 2007.

16. Larry Tracy, "Preparing A Presentation, The Tell 'Em and 3-1-2 Method," Accessed August 23, 2007, http://www.presentation-pointers.com/showarticle/articleid/216/.

17. Ronald B. Marks, "Dramatize Your Presentation or Lose the Sale," www.advancedsselling.com, Accesses November 20, 2004.

18. Paul Piscitelli, "How to Wow an Audience," *Sales & Marketing Management* (June 1997), 63-69.

19. Adapted from Martha W. Holcombe and Judith K. Stein, "How to Deliver Dynamic Presentations: Use Visuals for Impact," *Business Marketing*, Vol. 71, No. 6 (June 1986), 163-164; and Richard Kern, "Mak-

ing Visual Aids Work for You," *Sales & Marketing Management* (February 1989), 46-49.

20. Adapted from these articles: "Multi-Faceted Laser Disk Player," *Business Marketing* (June 1992), 36.; George W. Columbo, "Presenting: A New Tool," *Selling*, Vol. 1, No. 10 (June 1994), 29.

21. Karen Starr, "Plug and Play!" *Selling Power* (October 2000), 32-34.

22. Ibid, 118.

23. For more information on Mimio and other Virtual Ink products, check them, out at www.mimio.com, Accessed November 2004.

24. Bob Alexander, "How Laptops Put You in the Driver's Seat," *Personal Selling Power*, Vol. 10, No. 2 (March 1990), 53.

Chapter 12

1. John Boe. "Overcome objections and close the sale," *Agency Sales*, (September 2003), Vol. 33, Is. 9, 27.

2. Roger M. Pell, "The Road to Success is Paved with Objections," *Bank Marketing*, Vol. 22 (February 1990), 16.

3. Howard Feiertag, "Finding out reasons for objections is key to overcoming them," *Hotel and Motel Management*, (October 21, 2002) Vol. 217, Is. 18, 14.

4. John Boe. "Overcome objections and close the sale," *Agency Sales*, (September 2003), Vol. 33, Is. 9, 27.

5. Thomas M Redmond Jr., "Prospect objections can be overcome'" *National Underwriter*. (June 24, 2002), Vol. 106, Is. 25, 19-20.

6. Robert Kaiser, "A couple of ideas for overcoming hidden objections," *National Underwriter*, (May 6, 2002), Vol. 106, Is. 18, 30-31.

7. Ted Pollock, "How good a closer are you?" *The American Salesman*, (June 2003), Vol. 48, Is. 6, 18.

8. "How do you address Objections? Here's a few ideas," *Life Association News* (November 1996), 16-18.

9. Customer Objections: Do You Have the Answers?" *Professional Selling*, Vol. 22, No. 5 (March 10, 1984), 3.

10. Steve Atlas, "Listening for Hidden Objections," *Selling Power* (June 2000), 36.

11. Brad Huisken, "Busting the sales busters, Part II," *JCK*, (March 2003), Vol. 174, Is. 3, 66-67.

12. D. Forbes Ley, "The Stall-A Decision Not to Make a Decision," *The Selling Advantage* (May 14, 1991), 1-2.

13. Brad Huisken, "Busting the sales busters, Part II," *JCK*, (March 2003), Vol. 174, Is. 3, 66-67.

14. Wilma G Anderson, "Nine mistakes to avoid when marketing to seniors," *National Underwriter* (May 19, 2003), Vol. 107, Is. 20, 22.

15. Graham Roberts-Phelps, "Objections Are Opportunities to Sell," *Personal Selling Power*, Vol. 12, No. 8 (November/December 1992), 34.

16. Bill Brooks, "Are you responsive enough for your prospects and customers?" *The American Salesman*, (February 2003), Vol. 48, Is. 2, 21-23.

17. Jim Kasper, "Objections: Questions in Disguise" Accessed Fri Sept 10, 2007 online at salesvantage.com. http://www.salesvantage.com/article/view.php?w=1110&Objections_Questions_in_Disguise/.

18. Bill Brooks, "Time, budgets and excuses...how do you overcome them?" *The American Salesman,* (January 2002), Vol. 47, Is. 1, 13-15.

19. John R Graham, "How to sell more when others are selling less," *The American Salesman,* (February 2003), Vol. 48, Is. 2, 15-20.

20. Robert D Ramsey, "How to pitch a new idea," *SuperVision*, (March 2004), Vol. 65, Iss. 3, 8-9.

21. Online video training, "How To Control Your Sales Appointment, How salespeople can get and keep the power all throughout their selling interaction," Accessed July 17, 2007, http://www.5min.com/Video/How-To-Control-Your-Sales-Appointment-1185.

22. Josh Gordon, *Tough Calls: Selling Strategies to Win Over Your Most Difficult Customers* (Amacom Publishing, 1997), 120.

23. David Farneti, "Opening Doors And Establishing Winning Sales Relationships," *Agency Sales*. (February 2004), Vol. 34, Is. 2, 28-30.

24. Todd B. Natenberg, "Overcoming Objections," Accessed September 1, 2007, http://www.selfgrowth.com/articles/Natenberg4.html.

25. Frederic A. Russell, Frank H. Beach, and Richard H. Buskirk, *Selling: Principles and Practices* (New York: McGraw-Hill,

1982), 321; and Erika Rasmusson, "The Pitfalls of Price-Cutting," *Sales & Marketing Management* (May 1997), 17.

26. T. Scott Gross, "The Service Factor," *Selling Power* (October 2000), 45.

27. Wendy Weiss, "The Price Is Right? How to handle a customer's objections to price of an item," *American Salesman*, (January 2001) Vol. 46, Is. 1, 6.

28. John J. McCarthy, *Secrets of Super Selling* (New York: Boardroom Books, 1982), 324.

29. Radhika Chadha, "Sellers of stuff: Salespeople should be trained to meet the demands of the ever-changing marketplace to stay abreast of competition. How do you distinguish your brand from the competition?" *Businessline*, (January 22, 2004), 1.

30. William F. Kendy, "Handling the Price Objection," *Selling Power* (September 2000), 41.

Chapter 13

1. "The Ingredients and Timing of the Perfect Close," *Sales Management*, Vol. 106, No. 12 (June 1971), 3.

2. Gerhard Gschwandtner, "On Closing the Sale," *Personal Selling Power*, Vol. 17, No. 5 (July/August 1987), 6.

3. Anonymous, "Closing the sale can be tough, but guidelines can ease the way," *San Fransisco Chronicle*, Wednesday, December 28, 2005; Page C-4.

4. Paul H. Green, "Closing A Sale," (Web site - www.multiplex.com/Greensheet), July 9, 2001; and Gregg Berlie, "Anatomy of a Closing," *The American Salesman* (January 1986), 6.

5. Jeffrey Gitomer, "A funny thing happened to me on the way to closing a sale," (Web site - www.insiderbiz.com), July 15, 2001. Jeffrey Gitomer is author of *The Sales Bible* and *Customer Satisfaction is Worthless, Customer Loyalty is Priceless.*

6. "Eight Ways to Become More Trump-Like in Your Career," sellingpower.com, November 22, 2004.

7. "Sales Persistence: Pushing without Being Pushy," *Professional Selling*, Vol. 22, No. 6 (March 25, 1984), 2.

8. Tim Rudlaff, "The Power of Persistence," *Teamwork* (May 21, 1990), 1.

9. Selling Power Editors, "Persistence Leads to Success: Just Ask Gerhard Gschwandtner and Joe Sugarman," *Selling Power*, sellingpower.com, (January 5, 2004).

10. Graham Roberts-Phelps, "Make Persistence Pay," *Personal Selling Power*, Vol. 14, No. 4 (May/June 1994), 68.

11. Vincent Alonzo, "Addicted to Failure," *Sales & Marketing Management* (November 1997), 28.

12. William Kendy, "Handling Rejection," *Selling Power* (July/August 2000), 44; and Jack Falvey, "Adventures in No-Man's Land," *Selling* (April 1996), 83,

13. Adapted and modified from "Sometimes I Say No," Selling Power.com (November 24, 2004), Pam Lontos, "Rejection Conditioning," *Selling Power* (June 1997), 78; and Tom Reilly, "Salespeople: Develop the Means to Handle Rejection,"

Personal Selling Power, Vol. 7, No. 5 (July/August 1987), 15.

14. Stephen Robinett, "The Final Step," *Success* (November 1986), 18.

15. Napolean Hill, "When Is the Psychological Moment to Close a Sale?," *Personal Selling Power*, Vol. 1, No. 3 (April 1991), 34. This article was originally written in the 1930's and reprinted in this issue.

16. Tom Reilly, "When You Ask for Commitment," *The Selling Advantage*, Vol. 4 (June 26, 1992), 1.

17. Cameron McPherson, "Remember: Ask for the Order," *Successful Closing Techniques* (Dartnell Corporation, 1986), 1.

18. Steve Atlas, "Listening For Buying Signals," *Selling Power* (March 2000), 38.

19. Keith Rosen, "How to Avoid a Prolonged Close," http://www.allbusiness.com/sales/selling-techniques-closing-sales/4001385-1.html, Accessed July 23, 2007.

20. Adapted and modified from "Read the (closing) signs," *Selling Power* (September 1997), In the SELLING IDEAS section of the magazine, 108; and Adapted from William J. Tobin, "Watch for the Right Signal," *Telephony*, Vol. 197, No. 15 (October 8, 1979), 114-115.

21. William Kendy, "Body of Knowledge," *Selling Power* (March 2001), 68.

22. Jeanne Pritt, "Fifteen Secrets to Closing A Sale," *The Profit Zone Newsletter* (July 1998). From "The Profit Zone" at www.profitzone.com.

23. James J. Morrisey, "How to Use the Power of Silence," *Personal Selling Power*, Vol. 14, No. 55 (March 1994).

24. http://changingminds.org/disciplines/sales/closing/ownership_close.htm. Accessed June 24, 2007.

25. Andy Cohen, "Are Your Reps Afraid to Close?" *Sales & Marketing Management* (March 1996), 43.

26. James O'Hara, "The Silent Barriers to Closing the Sale," *Selling* (May 1997), 9.

27. http://changingminds.org/disciplines/sales/closing/never_best_time_close.htm. Accessed June 26, 2007

28. http://changingminds.org/disciplines/sales/closing/123_close.htm Accessed June 28, 2007

29. "Closing Tips," *Selling Power*, sellingpower.com, November 2004.

30. Susan DelVecchio, James Zemanek, Roger McIntyre, Reid Claxton. "Updating the Adaptive Selling Behaviours: Tactics to Keep and Tactics to Discard," *Journal of Marketing Management*. (September 2004), Vol.20, Is. 7, 8, 859.

Chapter 14

1. Brian Tracy, "Customer Retention Driving Profits Through Giving Customers Lots of Reasons to Stay," http://www.1000advices.com/guru/customer_retaining_4life_bt.html, Accessed September 1, 2007.

2. Kim Kinter, "No. 1 In Customer Satisfaction," Selling (April 1994), 98-100; and Daniel V. Byrne, "Delivering on a Guarantee: Perfect Service, No

Exceptions," *Nation's Business* (August 1991), 6.

3. Ginger Trumfio, "Anything for a Client," *Sales & Marketing Management* (June 1994), 102; and Kate Bertrand, "In Service, Perception Counts," *Business Marketing* (April 1989), 44.

4. Anonymous, "Do the Right Thing," *Professional Builder*, Newton: (December 2003), Vol. 68, Is. 12, 76.

5. Boone, Elisabeth "From Better to Best: The Power of Benchmarking," *Rough Notes*. May 2007. FindArticles.com. 04 Sep. 2007. http://findarticles.com/p/articles/mi_qa3615/is_200705/ai_n19431629.

6. Paul R. Timm, *Customer Service: Career Success Through Customer Satisfaction* (New Jersey: Prentice-Hall, 1988), 45.

7. Julie Monahan, "Small Businesses Want Products, Advice, More," *American Banker*, New York: (May 18, 2004), Vol. 169, Is. 95, 3.A.

8. John Tschohl, "Exceptional Service-The Secret Weapon," *The Selling Advantage* (July 29, 1991), 2.

9. Steven Brown, "Service Recovery Through IT," *Marketing Management* (Fall 1997), 25-27;and Jan Carlzon, *Moments of Truth* (New York: Ballinger, 1987).

10. Anonymous, "VIRTUATel: Charity begins at the call centre; VIRTUATel's customer satisfaction surveys generate charitable donations for The Beacon Appeal," *M2 Presswire*, Coventry: (May 6, 2004), 1.

11. Jim Jewett, *Discovering Fast Track Success* (Columbus, OH: ESRL Press, 1988), 53.

12. Anonymous, "Catuity Launches Ameribanc Gift Card Program". *Market Wire*. January 2007. FindArticles.com. 04 Sep. 2007. http://findarticles.com/p/articles/mi_pwwi/is_200701/ai_n17144361.

13. Kevin Freiberg and Jackie Freiberg, "Nuts! Southwest Airlines' Crazy Recipe for Business and Personal Success," 1996. Adapted an insert in *Selling Power* (September 1997), 103

14. Daniel Yee, "Chick-fil-A cooks up recipe of customer loyalty," *Deseret News* (Salt Lake City), Sep 18, 2006.

15. "Get More From Current Customers," in the Selling Ideas section of *Selling Power* (October 2000), 62.

16. William Kendy, "How to Move the Customer to a Higher Purchasing Level," *Selling Power* (June 2000), 33-34.

17. Kathleen Cholewka, "CRM: Calling All Customers," *Sales & Marketing Management* (May 2001), 25-26.

18. Todd Beck and Anne Smith, "Four Keys to Customer Loyalty," *The Catalyst*, Spring 2006.

19. Marc Hochstein, "A Subprime Servicer Aiming for Friendly," *American Banker*, New York: (June 4, 2004), Vol. 169, Is. 107, 1.

20. Steve Atlas, "Focus on Solutions," *Selling Power* (March 2001), 40.

21. Angi Semler, "Cranking up Customer Service," *Automotive Body Repair News*, Cleveland: (June 2004), Vol. 43, Is. 6, 30-35.

22. Ray Dreyfack, "Good Complaints," in the Selling Ideas

section of *Selling Power* (March 2000), 54.

23. Karl Albrecht and Ron Zemke, *Service America! Doing Business in the New Economy* (Homewood: Richard D. Irwin, 1985), 7-8.

24. Frederick H. Reichheld, "Learning from Customer Defections," *Harvard Business Review* (March/April 1996), 56-59; and Glenn DeSouza, "Designing a Customer Retention Plan," *The Journal of Business Strategy* (March/April 1992), 26.

25. Karen Krebsbach, "Targeted Marketing: Redrawing Clients' Financial Picture," *Bank Technology News*, New York: (July 2003), Vol. 16, Is. 7, 1.

26. Geoffrey Brewer, "Winning Back Angry Customers," *Sales & Marketing Management* (October 1997), 131; and John R. Graham, "Why Customers Leave (and the reason they don't bother telling us why)," *The Selling Advantage* (June 12, 1992), Vol. 4, 2.

27. "Turn Conflict with a Customer Into a Selling Opportunity," *Personal Selling Power,* Vol. 12, No. 8 (September 1992), 73.

28. Dr. Ken Blanchard, "Mistake Proof," *Selling Power* (January/February 1998), 42; and ''Do You Deliver on Your Promises?" *Professional Selling*, Vol. 22, No. 10 (May 25, 1984), 4.

29. Terence A. Hockenhull, "Weekender: Marketing," *BusinessWorld*, Manila: (June 13, 2003), 1.

30. Anthony Urbaniak, "After the sale - what really happens to customer service," *The Ameri-*

can Salesman (February 2000), 14-17.

31. Steve Atlas, "Telephone Selling," in the Skills Workshop section of *Selling Power* (July/August 2000), 50.

32. Geoffrey Brewer, "How to Stay in Touch," *Sales & Marketing Management* (February 1998), 109.

33. Julie Puckett, "A Quick Thank-You," in the Reader To Reader Hot Tips section of *Selling Power* (September 2000), 60.

Chapter 15

1. Amy Feldman, "We'll Make You Scary," *Forbes* (February, 14, 1994), 96.

2. Jim Summers, "Delegation and monkeys: who's in charge? Are you working harder and falling farther behind? Maybe you have too many monkeys". *Healthcare Financial Management*. June 2006. FindArticles.com. 06 Sep. 2007. http://findarticles.com/p/articles/mi_m3257/is_6_60/ai_n16497914.

3. William L More, "Protecting Your Resources," *Advisor Today*, Washington: (April 2004), Vol. 99, Is. 4, 48.

4. Joseph Block, "Just a Habit," *Personal Selling Power*, Vol. 14, No. 6 (September 1994), 90.

5. Gail Garfinkel Weiss, "Don't Have Time? Read This," *Medical Economics*, Oradell: (March 7, 2003), Vol. 80, Is. 5, 72.

6. "Success is in her Makeup," *Selling Power* (November/December 1997), 96. A Tip from Mary Kay, Founder of Mary Kay Cosmetics.

7. L.B. Gschwandtner, "A Terrible Waste of Time," *Personal Sell-*

ing Power* (July/August 1994), 52.

8. Steven Berglas," Chronic Time Abuse," *Harvard Business Review*, Boston: (June 2004), Vol. 82, Is. 6, 90.

9. Roger Leslie, "Time Management," *Listen*, Hagerstown: (May 2004), Vol. 57, Is. 9, 20-21.

10. Anonymous, "Will the Piles Ever Go Away?" *USA Today,* New York: (March 2004) Vol. 132, Is. 2706, 8

11. Loretta D. Foxman and Walter L. Polsky, "Five Steps to Get- and Stay-Organized," *Personnel Journal*, Vol. 63, No. 9 (August 1984), 18.

12. Anonymous, "Get on Top of Your Time Management," *Pulse*, Tonbridge: (April 5, 2004), 38.

13. Thayer C. Taylor, "Giving Sales Leads a Leading Edge," *Sales and Marketing Management*, Vol. 127, No. 4 (September 14, 1991), 35.

14. Cary Cooper, "Ignore your Inbox for your In-tray," *Accountancy Age*, London: (April 15, 2004), 20.

15. Rick Davis, "All systems go: a systemized approach to selling can lead to organizational success". *Prosales*. Jan 2006. FindArticles.com. 06 Sep. 2007. http://findarticles.com/p/articles/mi_m0NTC/is_1_18/ai_n16005254.

16. Carl Clayton, How to Manage Your Time and Territory for Better Sales Results," *Personal Selling Power*, Vol. 10, No. 2 (March 1990), 46.

17. Brian Jeffrey, "Make a List and Check It Twice," *Selling Power*

(January/February 2000), 39; and Ed Brown, "Stephen Covey's New One-Day Seminar," *Fortune* (January 1999), 138.

18. "Goal Setting Basics," *Professional Selling*, Bureau of Business Practice, Vol. 127, No. 20 (October 25, 1989), 5.

19. Robert Tardiff, "Control Your Time," *Personal Selling Power* (May/June 1995), 72.

20. Foxman and Polsky, "Five Steps," 18.

21. Melinda Ligos, "Cutting Meetings Down to Size," *New York Times*, (Late Edition, East Coast). New York: (January 11, 2004), 3.10.

22. Anonymous, "The Secrets of Time Management," *Agency Sales*, Irvine: (May 2004), Vol. 34, Is. 5, 40-41.

23. Stephen Rush, "From Baseball to Business," *Nation's Business* (October 1996), 50.

24. Taken from an article by David Lill, "Time to Spare," *Selling Power*, (May 1997), 72-73.

25. Renee Zemanski, "Using your time on the road effectively," *Selling Power* (January/February 2000), 34.

26. Steve Atlas, "When the Customer Isn't Right," *Selling Power* (January/February 2001), 32.

27. For a more thorough discussion on "How to Run Your Territory Like a Business," See the booklet *Territory Management*, Bureau of Business Practice, Inc. (1989), 6-16.

28. Karen Starr, "Have PDA, Will Travel," *Selling Power* (March 2001), 28.

29. Melanie Berger, "Take a Right At the Light And..." *Sales &*

Marketing Management (September 1997), 91-94.

30. Dan Gutman, "The Road More Traveled," *Success* (May 1996), 56.

31. Rich Bohn, "Territory Management Better Sales," *Sales & Field Force Automation* (April 1998), 76.

32. See these sources for more information on computer mapping systems: Niklas Von Daehne, "The Technology Edge," *Success* (May 1994), 53-54; Charles Lee Browne, "On the Road Again," *Personal Selling Power* (March 1994), 36; George W. Colombo, "Putting Sales on the Map," *Selling* (July/August 1994), 27-29; Thayer C. Taylor, "Mapping Out a Strategy," *Sales & Marketing Management* (February 1994), 51-52.

Chapter 16

1. Gerhard Gschwandtner, "World Class Sales," *Selling Power* (January/February 1998), 75.

2. John Sullivan, "Cost Factors and Business Impacts of Turnover," *Chicago Job Resources*, chicagojobresource.com, Accessed November 12, 2006.

3. Dr. Ken Blanchard, "Coaches, Facilitators and Cheerleaders," *Personal Selling Power*, Vol. 14, No. 1 (January/February 1994), 54-55.

4. Erika Rasmusson, "Setting Your Sights on Videoconferencing," *Sales & Marketing Management* (September 1997), 106.

5. Mary Boone, "The E-Vangelist: Face Time," *Sales & Marketing Management* (June 2001), 29.

6. Kathleen Cholewka, "Seven Signs You're Failing as a Manager and How to Avoid Them,"

Sales & Marketing Management (March 2001), 42.

7. Boone, Elisabeth, "Sales Management: Choices and Challenges," *Rough Notes*. Dec 2006. FindArticles.com. 09 Sep. 2007. http://findarticles.com/p/articles/mi_qa3615/is_200612/ai_n17193461.

8. Audrey Bottjen and Eduardo Canto, "Pep Talks That Inspire Reps," *Sales & Marketing Management* (June 2001), 66.

9. "Streetwise Tips on Motivation", *Streetwise Managing People*, www.businesstown.com, Accessed November 15, 2004.

10. Quint Studer, "How to achieve and sustain excellence: there are seven ways to hardwire excellent outcomes. Do you know what they are?" *Healthcare Financial Management*. June 2007. FindArticles.com. 09 Sep. 2007. http://findarticles.com/p/articles/mi_m3257/is_6_61/ai_n19311760.

11. Melissa Campbell, "'What Price Sales Force Satisfaction?," Sales & Marketing Management (July 1994), 37.

12. John E. Baer, "The cost of inadequate leadership: ineffective management carries a hefty price tag for the typical 120-bed nursing home". *Nursing Homes*. Sept 2006. FindArticles.com. 09 Sep. 2007. http://findarticles.com/p/articles/mi_m3830/is_9_55/ai_n19041583,

13. Julie Strugeon, "Wanted Successful Sales Manager," *Selling Power* (September 2000), 114.

14. Malcolm Fleschner, "Perfect Pitch," *Selling Power* (November/December 1997), 25.

15. For a more detailed example and discussion of this useful approach, see Gilbert A. Churchill, Jr., Neil M. Ford, and Orville C. Walker, Jr., *Sales Force Management*, 4th ed. (Homewood, IL: Richard D. Irwin, Inc., 1993), 231-237.

16. Christen Heide, Dartnell's 29th "Survey of Sales Force Compensation, 1997-1998," reported in *Selling Power* (April 1998), 73.

17. Gary Duncan, "Poor Hiring Often Leads to Astronomical Turnover Costs," *Denver Business Journal,* (March 12, 2004).

18. Robert G. Head, "Select Salespeople Systematically," *Personal Selling Power*, Vol. 13, No. 4 (May/June 1993), 68-69; and Geoffrey Brewer, "Mind Reading: What Drives Top Salespeople to Greatness?" *Sales & Marketing Management* (May 1994), 86.

19. "Twenty-Sixth Survey of Sales Force Compensation," (Chicago, IL: 1990: The Dartnell Corporation). Reported in *Inc magazine* (August 1991), 82; and Dick Vink, "Can You Explain Your Comp Plan in 10 Minutes or Less?," *Sales & Marketing Management* (September 1992), 119; Jim M. Graber, Roger E. Breisch, and Walter E. Breisch, "Performance Appraisals and Deming: A Misunderstanding?," *Quality Progress* (June 1992), 59-62.

20. Michele Marchetti, "What a sales call costs," *Sales and Marketing Management.* New York: (September 2003), Vol. 152, Is. 9, 80.

21. Henry Canaday, "What Are You Worth," *Selling Power* (January/February 2001), 83.

22. Andy Cohen, Jennifer Gilbert, Melinda Ligos."Extreme Makeovers." *Sales and Marketing Management.* New York: (May 2004), Vol.156, Is. 9, 36.

23. Edwin Joetan, Brian H Kleiner. "Incentive Practices in the US Automobile Industry", *Management Research News.* Patrington: 2004. Vol.27, Is. 7, 49

24. Patricia Zingheim, "Are your salespeople out of line*?" Selling Power* (July/August 2000), 81; Robert Head, "Restoring Balance to Sales compensation," *Sales & Marketing Management* (August 1992), 39-44; and James F. Carey, *The Complete Guide to Sales Force Compensation* (Business One Irwin, 1991).

25. Susan Greco, "The Customer Driven Bonus Plan," *Inc magazine* (September 1995), 89; Kerry Rottenberger and Richard Kern, "'The Upside-Down Deming Principle," *Sales & Marketing Management* (June 1992), 39-44

26. Todd Nelson, "Employee Compensation Likely to Change," *The Tennessean*, Section E (October 1, 1992), 4.

27. "Selling Without Commissions," *Sales & Marketing Management* (June 1994), 97.

28. Churchill, Ford, Walker, *Sales Force Management*, 486.

29. Edgar Speer, "The Role of Training at United States Steel," *Training and Development Journal*, Vol. 30, No. 6 (June 1976), 18-21.

30. Jack Hubbard, "Making coaching part of the performance culture's DNA: Part 1". *The RMA Journal*, Sept 2006. FindArticles.com. 09 Sep. 2007. http://findarticles.com/p/articles/mi_m0ITW/is_1_89/ai_n18617434.

31. Lawrence J. Tuttle, "A Training Revolution," *Personal Selling Power*, Vol. 14, No. 4 (May/June 1994), 32-33.

CREDITS

Written permission to use the following materials has been obtained from the appropriate rights holders:

Sales & Marketing Management
Categories of Salespeople, VNU Business Publications USA, formerly Bill Communications, Inc.

Journal of Personal Selling & Sales Management
Rapport Building for Salespeople: A Neurolinguistic Approach, Nickels, William G, Robert F Everett and Robert Klein; Dr. Ron Michaels, Dept. of Marketing

How Important it is to Listen – pamphlet cartoon, Unisys Corporation

Andy Capp cartoon, North America Syndicate

Adobe Image Library, *The Creative Professional's Catalog*, Volume 5/98. Adobe Systems Incorporated

iStock Photos—All photos in the text were purchased through this company and used with permission.

A special thanks and acknowledgement to Barbara Grieninger, Permissions Manager, and to Michael Reaggs and Lisa Abelson, former Reprint Managers, for *Sales & Marketing Management* magazine for giving me permission to modify and adapt exhibits, charts, articles, and pictures from issues of the magazine. The pages listed here have items used from various issues of *Sales & Marketing Management* magazine:16, 25, 61, 75, 128, 131, 152, 195, 197, 203, 246, 305, 355

INDEX